CASUAL
AFFAIRS

CASUAL AFFAIRS

The Life and Fiction of Sally Benson

Maryellen V. Keefe

For Sue,
With fond memories
and admiration!
Love,
Maryellen Keefe, osu

excelsior editions

State University of New York Press
Albany, New York

Photograph of Sally Benson courtesy of the Barbara Benson Golseth estate.

Published by State University of New York Press, Albany

© 2014 State University of New York

Excelsior Editions is an imprint of State University of New York Press

For information, contact State University of New York Press, Albany, NY
www.sunypress.edu

Production by Ryan Morris
Marketing by Kate McDonnell

Library of Congress Cataloging-in-Publication Data

Keefe, Maryellen V.
    Casual affairs : the life and fiction of Sally Benson / Maryellen V. Keefe.
        pages cm. — (Excelsior editions)
    Includes bibliographical references and index.
    ISBN 978-1-4384-5089-6 (pbk. : alk. paper)
    1. Benson, Sally, 1900–1972.   2. Authors, American—20th century—Biography.
3. Women screenwriters—United States—Biography.   I. Title.

PS3503.E5625Z46 2014
813'.52—dc23
[B]   2013025961

10 9 8 7 6 5 4 3 2 1

This biography of Sally Benson is dedicated to
my dear friend Sr. Madeline Welch, OSU, J.D., J.C.L.,
for her unending encouragement and support.
May she rest in peace.
Soli Deo Gloria!

CONTENTS

PART III

ILLUSTRATIONS

All images from the Benson estate are used with permission.

ACKNOWLEDGMENTS

My profound thanks to the family of Sally Benson: to Barbara Benson Golseth (of happy memory), who generously shared memories of her mother as well as ample files of Benson's correspondence and memorabilia, but most importantly, for introducing me to her children—Alexis (Dusty) Doster, Sara Wohl, Robert (Booter) Campbell, and Susan Ramsey—Sally Benson's grandchildren. In turn, I thank Susan Ramsey and her husband Jo-Ben for their gracious hospitality at their Tucson, Arizona home while I conducted my research. (Susie even assisted in scanning documents and photos.) I also thank my friend Mary Dehn van Dessel for driving me from her Sun City West home all the way to Tucson for my first interview with Barbara Benson Golseth in May of 2001.

I extend heartfelt gratitude to my friend and colleague Dr. Susan Goodman, who directed my research during my doctoral studies at the University of Delaware and who has remained a supportive and helpful guide in creating this biography. In this vein I need to recognize Dr. Elaine Safer and Professor Ben Yagoda, also of the University of Delaware, for providing me with the inspiration to pursue Sally Benson as my subject.

That said, I need to express thanks to the staff of the Special Collections division of the New York Public Library on 42nd Street—home of *The New Yorker* archives. I thank Christopher Shay, *New Yorker* librarian, for providing records of Benson's *New Yorker* short stories.

I thank Dorothy Lobrano Guth, daughter of Gus—one of Sally's editors—for sharing letters from Sally to her father and sharing memories of Sally's presence in the Lobrano home.

I thank the staff of Iona College's Ryan Library and C.E.L.T.I.C., especially Diana Breen and Theresa Alifante for their ever generous readiness to help either with printing chapters in the initial stages of this project or providing access to materials needed.

Most of all, I wish to express deep gratitude to friend and colleague Dr. Barbara Solomon for her encouragement along the way and for her tireless reading and rereading of each chapter with invaluable annotations, suggestions, and corrections.

I thank the staff of Maritime College, notably Shafeek Fazal and David Dhanpat, for assistance with photo scanning, and my colleagues in the Humanities Department—especially my chair, Dr. Karen Markoe, and colleague, Dr. John Rocco—for their support and encouragement. I am also grateful to Maritime for awarding me a course release to do my final research in the spring of 2012. I wish to thank Terry Eppridge, OSU, and TE Graphics for scanning all the images for this book, and Anne T. Dillen, OSU, for her original sketch of the Smith home in St. Louis.

Finally, I thank my siblings—John J. Keefe and Veronica T. Kiernan—for their endless support.

INTRODUCTION

In November of 1940 on the tenth floor of 25 West 43rd Street, a woman sat at a Royal typewriter. The tiny *New Yorker* office she occupied, its carpeting dull, its walls drab, its furnishings spare, provided dramatic contrast to the fiery redhead feverishly typing. A photographer from Random House caught Sally Benson unaware, a semi-pleased, half-questioning expression on her upturned face. Curly bangs frame Benson's high forehead and a navy blue hat of velvet bows matches her navy blue dress, its stark simplicity accented by gold bracelet, brooch, and earrings. This photo of the writer at work would be used to advertise *Junior Miss*, Benson's third collection of short fiction.

Within months of its release, *Junior Miss* would become a best-seller, then a weekly radio program broadcast nationally, and finally, a long-running Broadway show that traveled to other urban stages before becoming a television movie. Sally Benson's success with *Junior Miss* led her to publish a fourth short story collection, *Meet Me in St Louis*. Originally titled "5135 Kensington," Benson's twelve pieces had appeared in *The New Yorker* from June of 1941 to May of 1942. As *Meet Me in St Louis* they inspired a Hollywood film that won four Academy Award nominations. Benson's career continued with three more Broadway shows, several award-winning short stories, and fifteen Hollywood screenplays. A similar record of accomplishment today would make her a celebrity, as it did in the 1930s when Sally Benson was a household name among *New Yorker* readers. Most significantly, Benson's published collections—*People Are Fascinating, Emily, Junior Miss, Meet Me in St. Louis*, and *Women and Children First*—won recognition in America, Canada, and England before being translated into other languages.

Three quarters of a century after Benson's first story appeared in *The New Yorker*, the editors of *Fierce Pajamas*—a 2001 anthology of humorous

New Yorker fiction—honor Sally Benson's achievement by explaining her absence from their collection (Remnick and Finder xix), and a 2005 anthology—*Christmas at the New Yorker: Stories, Poems, Humor, and Art*—contains three Benson pieces. Yet, most contemporary readers have never heard of Sally Benson. Her 164 stories are virtually unread and movie viewers, despite enjoying films based on Benson's screenplays, remember the films without recalling her name. Who she was, how she blossomed into a successful and popular writer but later fell into relative obscurity is a story that needs to be told.

Benson's life and work reveal a complex character and gifted writer who made the short story her own. Observing people in varied venues from turn-of-the-century St. Louis, Jazz-Age and post–Depression era New York, to pre- and postwar suburbia, Benson created "casuals"—brief, humorous, character sketches. Benson's "snatches," as the reviewer in *Punch* phrased it, resulted from her pouncing on the "dominating wish, thought, or whim in a person's mind" and creating from it a complete picture as a clever doctor might diagnose a patient's condition from symptoms unconsciously betrayed. Despite occasional cynicism in portraying human foibles, Benson, on the whole, prompts kindly laughter rather than contempt. Her method is to present character and situation immediately, develop both, and build to an epiphany/ending that leaves the reader laughing or wondering. Blended with Benson's satiric realism is a note of humor as characters, unaware of the reality implied in their words, reveal themselves to readers and readers to themselves. At other times, Benson shocks readers into awareness of social issues, implicitly inviting a reappraisal of their thinking.

Though *Meet Me in St. Louis*, Benson's most memorable fiction, presents a nostalgic vision of peace-time, childhood innocence, and the quirky behavior of adolescence, the bulk of her oeuvre deals with serious issues of concern to readers past and present. These issues include: divorce, suicide, aging, poverty, alcoholism, financial insecurity, loneliness, and boredom, particularly as experienced by women. Her pieces often critique the pretentiousness and snobbery indicative of empty lives based on conformity to social protocol. Without didacticism, she challenges middle-class values while portraying her characters with a mixture of irony and compassion. This approach sets her apart from such contemporaries as Dorothy Parker and John O'Hara, known best for their mordant wit and harsh stance toward life.

Drawn from her experience of combining career with motherhood, Benson's later fiction comments on the emptiness encountered by women whose lived experience belied the fulfillment promised by the traditional wife/mother role. To fill the void created by sudden postwar leisure and prosperity, many women turned to rounds of bridge playing or charitable and cultural events—to no avail. Benson vividly illustrates the plight of such women in pieces like "War with Connecticut." After detailing the fictional Mrs. Champlin's effort to reduce accidents by having the road outside her suburban home straightened, the proactive citizen realizes she will have to sacrifice her prized lilac hedge. Defeated—especially at the thought that a new hedge will take twenty years to grow—she glimpses herself in the car's mirror only to see herself: "an aging woman in a worn felt hat, wisps of gray hair blowing across her cheeks, her eyes faded and filled with tears."

Benson's fictional subjects—chiefly women—may seem to lead trivial lives; yet, Benson did not trivialize these women. Far ahead of her time, she anticipated elements of feminism that would emerge years later. Decades before Betty Friedan and the women's movement of the 1960s, Benson's work raised such questions as: "Is this the way women should live? Is there nothing more satisfying available to them?" Describing the loneliness, desperation, or duplicity of her female characters, Benson holds before the reader an unkind mirror, perhaps. However, her purpose is to shock the reader into awareness of the extremes to which women were driven by loneliness or inner emptiness.

Benson's best fiction arose from her experience and observations of people remembered from childhood days in St. Louis, teenage years in Manhattan, working at *The New Yorker*, and vacationing in suburban Connecticut or rural Vermont. A successful writer in a predominantly male world—an accomplishment foreign to most women of the 1940s—she forsook Manhattan, financial and cultural center of America, for Los Angeles, California, heart of the burgeoning film industry. Yet, for all her richness of experience and relative affluence, Benson remained a down-to-earth citizen who scorned putting on airs. All her life, she exhibited the same hardworking spirit she had demonstrated as a young woman and never lost her sense of humor, even when confined in a rehabilitation center for alcohol abuse.

Unfortunately, Benson suffered from the special blend of hubris and insecurity that wreaked havoc at times in the lives of those she loved and about whom she wrote. She could be mean on occasion and regularly suffered bouts of depression that led to binge drinking. She genuinely loved life and people—including her husband and daughter—but being temperamental and needing time for herself or freedom from routine responsibilities, she could sometimes do the unexpected—abandon her family for a solo European jaunt or become caught up in casual love affairs. Finally, like many storytellers, Sally Benson was an inveterate liar.

Always alert to capitalize on her surroundings and turn her experiences into fiction, Benson could hear a story told by a luncheon companion at Delmonico's and return to her office where her typewriter would spring into action as she transformed the luncheon conversation into a publishable *New Yorker* piece that same day. She recreated teenage daughter Barbara as *Junior Miss* and mined older sister Rose's 1903 diary for *Meet Me in St. Louis*. Whether driven by an actual need for money as was often the case, or the desire to re-create an absorbing human encounter, Sally Benson, it seemed, had to write. Who she was, where she originated, how she attained remarkable success first on the *New Yorker* staff—when women were barely represented in the workforce—and later in Hollywood, is the subject of this book.

PART I

Figure 1. Sketch of the Smith family home in St. Louis

1

THE WRITER'S ORIGINS

ST. LOUIS, MISSOURI—
THE SMITH FAMILY ALBUM—1909

"Tootie's too smart for her own good."

—*Meet Me in St. Louis*

Moviegoers of the mid-1940s found themselves captivated by *Meet Me in St. Louis* with its Midwestern Smith family living amid their city's preparations to host the 1903 World's Fair. The melodies of "Meet Me in St. Louis," the "Trolley Song," and "Have Yourself a Merry Little Christmas" were catchy and easy to sing. The lyrics, made memorable by Judy Garland's voice, were enchanting. A welcome diversion from daily newspaper headlines' grim reports of U.S. casualties on the European front, the film reminded audiences of their own childhood and evoked laughter at the shenanigans of Agnes and little Tootie (as young Sara Smith was known to her family). They applauded Rose's and Esther's efforts to win the hearts of local suitors; they shared the family's reluctance to embrace Pa's news that a move to New York was imminent; they sighed in relief along with the onscreen Smiths when Pa, acknowledging its impact, reversed his decision to accept his New York promotion. Such audiences left the theaters happily satisfied and returned to their ordinary lives somewhat refreshed. In actuality, however, they had been deceived. The Smiths' story, though partially true, ended quite differently.

Sara Mahala Redway Smith, the future Sally Benson, was born on September 3, 1897, in St. Louis, Missouri. Less elegant than its Hollywood counterpart, her family home—a modest, red brick dwelling—stood on a rise above a lawn sloping down to Kensington Avenue. Like its neighbors, close together—separated by about twenty feet—the Smith house sat five feet above the street. Purchased in 1891 by Sara's father, Alonzo Smith, the house had a tiny front yard and an eight-stepped stoop leading to the front door. The first of its three floors was for living—kitchen, dining room, living room, and reception hall; the second and third, for sleeping. With its gabled roof, dormer windows, two chimneys, and large, arched window adjoining the front porch and main entrance, the Smith residence was striking in its day and served as the family home for eighteen years. Then, in the spring of 1909, unlike the fictional Alonzo Smith of *Meet Me in St. Louis*, Sara's father decided to start his own business in New York City. Just eleven at the time, Sara could hardly imagine the life awaiting her in Manhattan.

Youngest of the five children of Anna Cora Prophater and Alonzo Redway Smith, Sara was a precocious and perky child. Full of life and

Figure 2. John Sidney Prophater, grandfather of Sally Benson, in his Civil War uniform, 1863

gifted with imagination, she readily made up stories from an early age. She had many friends—both girls and boys—and she was especially close to Agnes, her sibling nearest in age and spirit. Older siblings Alonzo Jr., Rose, and Esther completed the family picture until, when Tootie was six, their maternal grandfather retired from his position as steward on the Anchor Line and moved into the Smith home.

Benson loved and admired her grandfather, but she recorded in *Meet Me in St. Louis* little of his Civil War career beyond a poignant passage alluding to his brother James's death. Her *New Yorker* piece, "January 1904," situates Grandpa Prophater at a window. The leaden sky outside, the commonplace, ugly houses, their white porches stained with rust and soot, take his mind back to the day

> when he had heard by rumor, for he was in Andersonville Prison Camp at the time, that his brother Jim had been killed, and of how he thought Jim was better off dead than sleeping on the cold hard ground without a blanket to keep him warm. (179)

Writing in December 1941, as the United States entered World War II, Benson highlighted not Prophater's prowess and courage but his suffering and melancholy, implying her negative critique of the then pro-war stance's gaining popular support.[1]

But where and how did Sally Benson's writing career begin? The answer lies among her familial roots and is traceable to childhood days in St. Louis. The earliest extant sample of Benson's writing is a letter mailed from Manitowoc, Wisconsin on August 27, 1903 to reach St. Louis for her father's fifty-first birthday. In penciled, back-slanted handwriting—the same that Sally Benson maintained all her life—the almost six-year-old Sara wrote: "Dear Papa, We are going to play dolls and we got a playroom by ourselfs [*sic*] and have a lot of fun in it. I wish you many happy returns of the day. Sara."[2] Though young Tootie had not yet started school, her strong interest and high motivation to learn had inspired Agnes to teach her how to read and write. By the time she was ready for kindergarten, Tootie could already read all of Agnes's primary grade books. For this reason, Anna Cora refused to send her to kindergarten. The adult Benson proudly reflected this intellectual prowess in a passage of *Meet Me in St. Louis*. Tootie, her fictional alter ego, after only half a day, dismisses kindergarten as beneath her—"The children in that kindergarten couldn't even read." Unwittingly, the child occasions a major argument between her parents.

The fictional Alonzo, reproaching his wife for "carrying on about her being the baby," states defiantly: "Tootie should have been in school this year" (246). The fictional Anna Cora, however, defends keeping their daughter at home, arguing that even Alonzo thought it "foolish to have her running around pretending to be a squirrel. . . . Tootie's too smart for that" (246). Alonzo's angry retort—"Tootie's too smart for her own good. . . . She needs to have someone over her who'll put his foot down" (247)—reflects the real Alonzo's viewpoint and suggests that similar disagreements occurred between Benson's parents. If Alonzo's analysis of Tootie were correct, however, he did little to discipline her—largely because of his lengthy absences from the family—some necessitated by business, others for questionable motives—as shall be seen.

A brown-eyed, golden-haired child,[3] Benson had shown signs of her complex personality at an early age. A natural daredevil, she enjoyed taking risks like skating down Union Hill in St. Louis just in time to slide under the noses of an oncoming team of horses. Well into adulthood, Benson exhibited the traits of her fictional "Tootie"—part tomboy, part rebel—ever ready to seek adventure. Dorothy Lobrano Guth, daughter of Gus Lobrano, one of Benson's *New Yorker* editors, remembers Benson's visiting the Lobrano home in Chappaqua, New York. "My brother and I had spent an entire afternoon creating a steep and slippery sled run," she relates. At twilight, Sally Benson, after a few drinks, "insisted on going for a sled ride. She had no boots and would have killed herself if she hadn't dragged her high-heeled shoes all the way—ruining our afternoon's work."[4]

Benson's love of challenges found an outlet also in reading adventure stories and mysteries—two genres that accompanied her into adulthood as did her gift for storytelling. As Benson's grandson, Alexis Doster, explains, Alonzo Smith, though he "didn't interact much," was particularly fond of Charles Dickens and frequently read aloud to his children from Dickens's novels. In fact, Dickens was such a favorite that the Smiths named their third daughter Agnes Wickfield for the *David Copperfield* character. Hearing Dickens read by her father engendered in Sally a similar love for Dickens that continued into adolescence.[5]

As her father's love of reading had taken root in Sally, so, too, had her mother's habit of storytelling. Anna Cora's fertile imagination and sense of timing enlivened family gatherings. Her dinner table in St. Louis provided a natural setting for the storytelling trait shared by Sally and her sisters. The pattern continued years later at Anna Cora's home in Connecticut, where, during family visits, young Barbara Benson and cousins Albert and Bobbie Thompson, Toby Wherry, and Tony Smith sat around the dining-room table absolutely in awe as their mothers (Rose, Esther, Agnes, and Sally) and grandmother talked.[6]

Besides being gifted storytellers, Benson's sisters were also talented writers. When Rose lived in Madison, Connecticut, she was a columnist for the *Shore Line Times*. Esther was an advertising copyeditor at Franklin Simon's Department Store in New York City and Agnes, after graduating from the Horace Mann School in 1912, had a regular column—"In Passing"—in the *New York Telegraph*. She was also an editor for the *New York Sun*, wrote twenty-four articles and reviews for *Photoplay*, and then became managing editor at *Motion Picture* magazine. Eventually, Agnes married another writer—Frederick James Smith, editor of *Screenplay* magazine—and moved with him to Hollywood to write for silent movies.[7] (Barbara, Benson's daughter, would also have a career in journalism as editor of the women's section of the *Arizona Sun* in her later years, and her son, Alexis Doster, would become editor of the *Smithsonian* magazine. Esther's son also had a career in publishing.)

Whether Benson's talent for writing stories was innate or acquired, she once attributed her gift for "the brilliantly malicious phrase" to her mother: "She seems all Irish to me. She never gives anybody a compliment. She used to say, 'Go on to your party, you look terrible, but maybe somebody will dance with you' " (Block 69). While many Irish parents encourage humility in their children by giving them scant praise, Benson had to be fabricating in this discussion of her mother's "Irishness." The numerous letters Anna Cora wrote to Benson over the years reveal her to be a caring and loving presence in Sally's and her siblings' lives. On August 18, 1910, for example, Anna Cora wrote to Sara, who was vacationing as she did every summer with Grandma Esther Smith in Manitowoc, Wisconsin. After giving family news, Anna Cora enclosed some money: "You are all but broke, I know, so here is a 'bone.' So, go while the going is good." She closed by giving Sally her "fondest love" and her "heart's best," then signed, "Lovingly, Mother."[8]

With the money Anna Cora sent, Benson hired a horse and buggy to drive out to Uncle Jay's farm with Bunchie, a summer friend. More importantly, the gift occasioned a second extant letter—this time to her mother—and its contents reveal traits found throughout Benson's life—a flair for the dramatic, a love of challenges and horses, and a willingness to help the underdog:

Dear Darling Sweet Precious Mama,

I got your letter this morning when I was in bed at nine-thirty. Yesterday was my day to write to you, but I couldn't because Bunchie and I went to Jay's farm. Sunday I told Jay that we were coming out there Monday and for him to leave Susie so I could drive out there. He said he couldn't that I would have to walk. It's a mile and a half out there and it has been quite warm, so I told him I wasn't going to because it was too hot. He asked me what I was going to do then? And I told him to never mind. I knew. He laughed and bet a dollar I wouldn't be there. The next day Bunchie and I went over to a livery stable and priced a horse. We could get one for three-quarters-of-an-hour for fifty cents and so we took it. . . . The buggy came at twelve-thirty and we took off. We had a fine horse that wasn't afraid of anything and a pretty buggy. A man came along with us and sat in the box part in back. He told me the way so I drove there. Jay was so surprised to see us and he wouldn't believe that we rode out there. But he saw the horse and buggy coming up with us in it. We worked awfully hard. First we got up in the hayloft. I don't know how we ever did because it's so high. But it wouldn't have hurt us if we had fallen because we [would have] landed on a whole pile of hay. Then we rode out on a wagon to where they were going to get in the hay. We came home through the woods. We then got in with a bull. I think we came out faster than we went in.[9]

The letter is a window into Benson's early sense of humor, determination to reach a goal, willingness to work, and ability to write a narrative with strong dramatic interest. Undaunted by obstacles like the height of the hayloft, she engineered a system for helping Delmar Hansen, Jay's thirteen-year-old hired hand, to transfer hay from one loft to another. With insight into the ornery Jay and empathy for an injured horse, Benson describes the situation with humor. "Jay kept calling him to hurry up," she writes, "and he couldn't because Charlie [the horse] was lame so we pulled the rope back for him. I told him to holler up to Jay, 'Are you ready?'" Benson, a mere twelve-year-old, had taken charge of the situation as though she were an adult, yet her narrative voice is charming in its simplicity. Her advice to

Delmar made Jay "mad and he came down and kicked Charlie the horse twice in the stomach. I got mad at him. I just scolded him like everything. He got ashamed of himself." The conclusion to her story is striking: "Before I got threw [*sic*] Delmar had to go after the cows so we did it for him." Benson ends the letter without further comment, suggesting no heroism on her part. She had done merely what should be done: "We went home in a wagon. The colt followed us all over. Well, I must close. Lovingly, Sara. P.S. Thanks for *Desperate Desmond*. P.S. I got my herpicide."[10]

The situation of middle-class vacationers voluntarily helping a farm-hand is rare, but to Benson it was second nature to help when help was needed. Years later in *Meet Me in St. Louis*, she portrayed six-year-old Tootie walking into the kitchen through the back door to see if Katie the maid needed help with dinner. Tootie then chides her sisters: "If everybody helped with the work in this house, we'd be all right" (162).

Though the letter to Anna Cora and the aforementioned one to her father are the only examples of Benson's early writing, the Smiths' moving to New York in 1909 gave rise to regular correspondence between eleven-year-old Benson and her friends. Extant letters from Helen Yule, Emma Stuyvesant, Mary Johann, and Katherine Pierce indicate their recognition of Benson's giftedness in composing stories and her interest in attending the theater. Pierce, for example, misses "the funny way [Benson] used to say things."[11] Yule appreciates Benson's recommendation of a show: "I'll try to go see *The Arcadians*. I'd love to."[12] Yule also thanks Benson for sending her a copy of "The Moon," a newspaper they had written together. "I thought I'd die," said Yule, having reread the humorous pieces she had "absolutely forgotten all about." As early as her elementary school days, Benson had begun the habit of writing—a distinct foreshadowing of a career that lay ahead.

2

MANHATTAN DAZE

1909–1912

"To record your heart throbs, 1911–1912."

—Agnes Smith

Though Sara Smith did not realize it at the time, her father's decision to leave St. Louis for New York City would change her life significantly and impact the lives of the entire family. Alonzo Redway Smith, tired of serving as second vice president of the Ferguson-McKinney Dry Goods Co. on 1201 Washington Avenue in St. Louis, wanted to start his own business and have his son join him as partner. The new company, A. R. Smith & Co. / Dry Goods, would specialize, as Alonzo's business card indicated, in "Direct Mill Shipments" and be located at 350 Broadway. Though he expressed interest in his father's project, Lon—now twenty-four—chose to remain in St. Louis where he had been working for the Waters Pierce Oil Company since his graduation from Princeton in 1907. Rose had married, Esther was a junior at Smith College, and Agnes—a freshman at Mary Institute—begged to stay in St. Louis with Lon to finish the school year. So, at St. Louis's Union Station on an early March morning in 1909, she and Lon bade farewell to their parents and eleven-year-old Sara.

As the Chicago Limited headed for New York, Sara began to read "train letters" from her sixth-grade friends.[1] She would miss them but not as much as they—especially the boy whose pin she wore—would miss her. Most of all Sara would miss Agnes, who somehow won her parents' permission to stay at Mary Institute even longer—until May 1910—the end of her sophomore year. A popular student and an avid lover of theater, Agnes had tried out for and won the part of "Bottom" in Mary Institute's annual fall play—a production of Shakespeare's *Midsummer Night's Dream*—scheduled for November 13, 1909.

When Agnes was finally ready to join her family in New York, Anna Cora wrote to Sara in Manitowoc, Wisconsin:

My darling little girl,

I know I have been dilatory about writing to you, but you know how very much I have to do. Agnes will stay at camp until September 3rd. She is enjoying every minute of her time there and . . . doesn't think anything of walking fifteen miles a day and sleeping on the ground at night. She can swim almost a mile without resting. I'm not going to decide on a school for you until Agnes comes.

Though Alonzo was with her in New York, Anna Cora alone dealt with choosing a school for their daughters, and she was unusual in seeking their input. Both agreed on public schools near their home in Manhattan. In September of 1910, Agnes enrolled as a high school junior; Sara, as an eighth grader.

As for the rest of the family, Esther had graduated from Smith College in May and sailed to Europe for a year abroad. In Italy, she came close to marrying an Italian count but returned instead to New York because she had been "offered her first job as a copy writer in the advertising department of the John Wanamaker Store!"[2] Older brother Lon, while traveling through the Southwest on business, had met the love of his life—Josephine Belle Nicks, daughter of a wealthy Texan. On a subsequent business trip the couple became engaged, set their wedding date, and planned an elegant ceremony and reception for June 1, 1911, in Fort Worth. Both the Smith and the Nicks families were excited for the young couple, but problems inevitably arose concerning where they would live—St. Louis or Fort Worth, Texas. Alonzo persuaded his son that a compromise might be the solution—the time had come for Lon to join his father as a business partner in New York, and Josephine agreed. With his growing income and the newlyweds' coming to New York, Alonzo decided to move the family to a luxury tenth-floor apartment large enough to accommodate Lon and Jo while they looked for a suitable place of their own. In September 1911, after two-and-a-half years of renting on fashionable Central Park West, the

Smiths were finally settled at 29 Claremont Avenue—or so it seemed.[3] Tall and luxurious even to the present day, the twelve-story apartment buildings lining Claremont Avenue's west side had been designed by Gaetano Ajello and erected in 1909. The Smith's new apartment boasted windows six-feet tall, fireplaces in the common rooms, an elevator, doorman, and concierge. Facing west, the Smiths enjoyed unobstructed views of the Hudson River, Riverside Drive, and the park. To the east, they surveyed Broadway and the campuses of Columbia University and Barnard College.[4]

After much unpacking and rearranging of furniture, shopping for school clothes and supplies, it was time to register the girls at their new private school. On September 19th, Anna Cora accompanied her two youngest daughters to the exclusive Horace Mann School on 120th Street and Broadway.[5] An imposing, freestanding structure, the school's secular Gothic style matched its neighboring buildings, their sandstone bases topped with red brick "enlivened with a diaper pattern of darker burned bricks above." (If Sally or Agnes noticed "on the entrance pavilion in the center of the Broadway frontage . . . [a] steep gabled roof capped by a cupola . . . crowned with a weather vane in the form of a quill pen" [Dolkart 234], they might have considered it an omen of their future lives as writers.) Nearby stood Thompson Hall, Horace Mann's architectural twin—primarily the gymnasium for Teachers College—but also the site of Horace Mann's class parties.[6]

Inside Horace Mann, the Smiths encountered a majestic statue of Athena standing proudly in the front hallway. Classical bas-relief lined both the entrance and the stairways. Suffusing all was state-of-the-art lighting. In sum, the building epitomized the school's spirit, expressing the "same combination of classical solidity and innovation that characterized the curriculum" (Bauld 13). Sara's appearance contrasted markedly with Athena's. A record card from the school nurse's office indicates that Sara Smith weighed a mere seventy pounds and stood just slightly more than four-feet-ten-inches tall as she joined the "Second Years"—the class of 1915—while Agnes registered as a fifth-year student—the class of 1912.[7] Three days of orientation followed, giving new and transfer students a chance to meet one another. Bill Stayton, a transferring senior like Agnes, became a lifelong friend, especially to Sara—soon to be called Sally—and Agnes who now became "Smithie."[8]

Initially a working laboratory for educational experimentation and teacher training—a demonstration school where Columbia University's Teachers College students could learn by observing superior teachers and classroom managers—Horace Mann had become by 1911 "an exclusive private school" with a deliberately selective admissions policy designed to "keep the social tone . . . above that of the public schools of New York City." It showcased the best educational facilities and methods of the time. Correspondingly, tuition during Sally's time there increased gradually from $250 in first form to $300 for fifth and sixth forms.[9] Though the majority of Horace Mann's student population—the Smith girls included—clearly came from the ranks of upper- and upper-middle-class New Yorkers,[10] the student body of 1,320 was different in composition and size from that of their previous schools.

Before long Sally and Agnes had made several friends and become involved in extracurricular activities. At Christmas Sally received a new diary from Agnes. Gilt-edged and bound in black leather, the slim volume became Sally's confidant, and her faithful daily entries provide a glimpse of her activities during the second semester of freshman year. Inscribed on the title page in Agnes's handwriting are the words: "to record your heart throbs / 1911–12 / Christmas 1911 / Sara R. Smith, from Agnes." In those first months Agnes had recognized Sally's need to record her "heart throbs"—many of them seniors—like Jack Molthan, Agnes's classmate.[11] The diary's pages witness Sally's efforts to attract and maintain friendships with several boys; her close relationship with Lon and his wife, Jo; her circle of female friends; the books she read; the plays, vaudeville shows, and silent films she saw. Most significantly, the diary tracks the beginnings of Sally's friendship with Columbia University freshman Reynolds "Babe" Benson, her future husband.

Sally's diary reveals a typical teenager devoted to friends and family, seeking and finding adventure in many forms, and most notably, intensely interested in older boys, romance, and dating. On school days she used her time between classes to monitor a current boyfriend's behavior or to fan the flames of jealousy. "Went up to 411 and [hung] around. Saw Jack in the hall and didn't speak to him." Room 411 was one of several upper-level classrooms on the fourth floor. Sally and her friends, despite being lower-level freshmen, frequently visited the fourth floor to attend mandatory study hall when their classes ended before 2 p.m.—the hour when they had to leave the building unless they had written parental permission to remain.[12] If they failed to win the attention of the senior boys in study hall, the girls would amble down to Broadway and 112th Street for a "cool, comforting, delicious ice cream soda."[13]

Friedgen's offered the "Best Sodas in New York City" and, as Sally and her cohort sipped away, their eyes focused occasionally on Friedgen's famous stuffed goat—a "relic of the days when the path to school from the 125th Street [subway] station was fraught with the minor dangers of glaring goats and lunging geese" (Bauld 15). Friedgen's boasted long, high counters with barstools. Silver glass-holders, ready to receive a freshly made ice cream soda, lined the counter in anticipation of customer orders. The counterman, formally dressed in white shirt and bow tie, stood ready and waiting to serve, while behind him, as behind the bar in Monet's painting, a wall-sized mirror reflected the scene. Light gleamed from sparkling syrup containers and a tall samovar. Framing all was a backdrop of rich mahogany woodwork and a decorative tin ceiling hung with chandeliers.[14]

Lively, pretty, and vivacious, Sally attracted Jack Molthan and other seniors, but the attention they paid her did not keep her from her other love, reading. Whether Miriam Michelson's *Michael Thwaites's Wife* or Charles Dickens's *Hard Times*, she found novels "awfully interesting." Ignored by Jack, she escaped to the library and started Nathaniel Hawthorne's *The House of the Seven Gables*. By Saturday February 4th, she had finished Dickens's *Dombey and Son*. "It was great!" was her appraisal. In addition to the reading required of all Horace Mann students, Benson read an astounding number of books on her own. She could spend a Friday afternoon after school seeing a music teacher about starting piano lessons, then visit Lon and Jo, return to school for a game, talk to Jack "a long time," yet sit up at night reading *David Copperfield* (Diary, February 10, 1912). Little did she know that the number and quality of the books she devoured throughout the school year and during vacations were preparing her for her future—reading and reviewing a book a night for *The New Yorker*.[15]

As for writing, her other love, Sally often spent Saturday afternoons with Emily Hume writing stories: "Went to Emeline's. We wrote a story. Hum! After I got home I wrote another story" (Diary, March 30, 1912). The next day, Sally wrote yet another, and on April 1st, she and a friend named Kate "came home and read our stories [and] . . . made them into a book" (Diary, April 1, 1912). None of these early examples of Benson's writing is extant, but the pattern of composing with friends indicates that she enjoyed writing and found friends who, like those left behind in St. Louis, shared that interest and enjoyed working with her.

Besides writing and dating, Sally devoted time to one club—the Girls' League—which further developed her devotion to social justice.

Of all the clubs Horace Mann offered, this one combined recreational activities, charitable work, and lectures on social issues. For several years, members had been contributing five cents a week to support "a nurse down in the slums."[16] A typical December meeting involved planning the annual fundraising fair, a visit to the Florence Crittenton Mission shortly after Christmas, and a discussion about how to provide for the "families the League . . . offered to help this year."[17] A March 27th league meeting introduced the International Institute's Miss Donnee Pannayotova to speak of her work among immigrant girls newly arrived from Ellis Island. As a follow-up to her lecture, the Horace Mann Girls' League visited Ellis Island with Miss Pannayotova.[18] That evening, Sally recorded in her diary: "Emeline, Margaret, and I volunteered to go see this girl on the Eastside. Her name is Grace O'Hara."[19] On the appointed day they "all went in Natalie's machine to the Riverside Mission on Laurence Street and arranged to meet Grace on Tuesday."[20]

Occasionally, more formal social activities claimed Benson's time. Such an event was Margaret Sommerville's party on January 19, 1912. Jack would be Sally's escort, and Hump, Margaret's.[21] The girls had several planning teas. Margaret usually served "lemon tarts and chocolate éclairs" to accompany conversations about Jack and Hump. When the boys arrived to drive Sally home in their machine, they motored up Riverside Drive. Views of the Hudson below stretched for miles on their left while the right offered architectural gems. That night, in cramped handwriting because she had so much to tell, Benson wrote an entry that, retrospectively, epitomizes her lifelong pattern of relating to men:

> Going down on the subway we had lots of fun. When we got to Margaret's, Bill took my arm and said he wanted to marry me. So we were married and went strolling off arm in arm. Jack was with Annette! Then I rode on the Irish Mail with Bill.[22] Finally, Jack came up and took Margaret's and Edna's arm and my hands. We were married. Then John Benore sat on the sofa with me and we held hands. I fed Bill and Jack fed me almonds. Then Jack sat on the sofa with me and showed me card tricks. . . . All the way home Agnes and Bill acted mildly. I had my hands in Jack's pockets and he held them there. I'm awfully crazy about him. Bill was nice too. I am engaged to Jack. But in a joke of course.[23]

The diary continues in this vein, recounting Sally's flirtation with Jack Molthan. Some days she snubs him by taking a girlfriend's arm and deliberately turning away from him. Yet, she faithfully attends his basketball games, recording the team's scores and Jack's baskets. Though she misses Jack on days when she doesn't see him, she spends Saturdays with Charles ("we went for a walk up to 145th," January 21) or has long talks with John ("He is a peach!").[24] At a school party, she admits to not having the nerve to ask anybody to dance but accepts when Dick Lester and Jim Parnell invite her. Occasionally, she meets Boyd or David Van Alstyne, Hump or Bill Stayton, but from January to late April, her consistent interest is in Jack Molthan.[25]

William Henry Stayton Jr. had met both Smiths at orientation and soon became their good friend. Though new to Horace Mann, he was elected business manager of *The Mannikin*—the Horace Mann yearbook— and won a part in the senior play. Before long he became enamored of Sally and continued to call and write her throughout his first year at Harvard.[26] The truth of his *Mannikin* senior blurb made Sally laugh: "When I go out a walking / I look so nice, they say, / I have to take a dog along / To keep the girls away."[27]

As a high school freshman, Sally socialized with a crowd of wealthy, upper-level peers and enjoyed a freedom regarding dating, behavior, and curfews unusual for the time. When, for example, Grandma Esther Smith died, Alonzo and Anna Cora left for Manitowoc on May 17th to attend the funeral. With her mother away, Sally enjoyed even more freedom than usual.

> Lon and Jo's for dinner. Then to Edna's. Margaret and I played with Jack at first. Then James and I read this book. After that we went up on the roof and Fred teased me so then Jack took me around and we spooned perfectly awfully, all but kissed me. He is a wonder. Fred and Jack picked me up and carried me. Jack's very spoony. He and I had a fight but we made up. Edna is a pill. (Diary, May 19, 1912)

Edna, four years Sally's senior and her hostess, had acted responsibly in trying to make her guests behave properly—much to Sally's annoyance.

Two days later Bill Stayton called to announce that he was going to have another dinner party and it would be at Delmonico's—a "notable entertainment palace"—located at Fifth Avenue and 44th Street.[28] Jack invited Sally and Agnes to accompany him and "met us at the steps and took me in," Sally wrote. "Jack was slightly off," she continued, so "John took me home. He talked about Babe all the time. Babe is coming over tomorrow." Sally's first mention of Babe Benson coincides with her virtually last reference to Jack.[29]

A graduate of Horace Mann's class of 1911, Sally's future husband was finishing his freshman year at nearby Columbia University. An impressive high school athlete, he had been captain and right forward of the Horace Mann basketball team in an unbeaten season and a member of the track, swimming, baseball, and tennis teams. Nicknamed "Babe" because his older brother Claus had also attended Horace Mann, Benson was student council president in his senior year and served as class treasurer and secretary of the Horace Mann General Association—a group that managed all athletic and social activities.

Figure 3. Reynolds "Babe" Benson, captain of Horace Mann's varsity basketball team, 1910–1911

When Babe telephoned the next day, he invited Sally to a boat ride on May 30—a date she listed among her "Star Days":

Babe came and we went down to the 96th Street dock and waited for the tug to come. . . . Babe and I sat on the back of the boat and then we went to the front and talked. Then it rained and Babe held my hand during the storm. When we got to West Point they wouldn't let us land without a permit so we actually went up farther. We walked around. Coming home we got on top of the [illegible] . . . when it got dark. Babe held both [my hands] and we didn't say much. It was awfully exciting. Jack didn't give Maude a very good time.

It is striking that Babe, four years her senior and now a Columbia rising sophomore, should have been so captivated by the much younger Sally. It is also interesting that though Jack has replaced her with Maude, a senior classmate, Sally is keeping track of his behavior.

The following day, May 31st, the Smiths attended Agnes's graduation and the reception afterward. Sally knew many of the graduates and "congratulated everybody" but secretly hoped for another meeting with Babe. As soon as she spotted him coming over to her, she separated from the family, happy to be with him. After saying goodbye to Mr. Nagle, their Latin teacher, she and Babe walked home. "It was so thrilling," she wrote. "He said he thought he'd come over tomorrow." But when Babe telephoned, it was to cancel—he was going to Alaska. Sally wrote in her fickle way, "I am mad. Jack is sweet," unconsciously foreshadowing how she would deal with future marital difficulties and begin the pattern of "casual little affairs" that would start in the twenties. However, more than awe at having captivated someone so much older characterized Sally's attraction to Babe: she was in love for the first time.

3

SUMMER OF DISCONTENT

1912

"I wish to God I knew something exactly would happen. . . . Summer in New York is *hell*."

—Diary, July 13, 1912

After a mere three years in New York, Sally had grown beyond the preteen boundaries that had shaped her life in St. Louis. No longer surrounded by girls who called themselves "Sarasick" at her departure, Benson approached her fifteenth birthday well initiated into the New York lifestyle that became her fictional stock-in-trade. Her diary entry for the week of June 18th is particularly characteristic of this chapter in her life and shows that she enjoyed a social freedom not common for the average fourteen-year-old in 1912. In one day she had phone calls and invitations from six friends, all popular, involved, upper-level students or alumni of Horace Mann: Annette Burr, Edna Colding, Natalie Norris, John Benore, Bill Stayton, and Boyd Sommerville. Natalie asked Sally to Coney Island, but she went with Jane instead to see *Zasic* at the West End Theater. Then, in the evening she "went to Coney with Boyd. War with John all the time I was there," she wrote. "I came home with Bill and Boyd."

The next day she had lunch at Natalie's before visiting Marion Strauch with Annette. Bill Stayton and Gilby were there, and afterward, Sally and Jane went down to Wanamaker's Department Store. That evening Betty Wilds came over for dinner. On the 20th Sally telephoned Margaret and made plans to meet at 101st Street and go to the athletic field to discuss Hump, Babe, and Jack. The next day she "went over to Maude's and talked till one." A typical adolescent, Benson was vulnerable to her changing moods, which depended increasingly on Babe and caused her both real and imagined slights.[1]

On Thursday, July 4th, Sally and Babe

> went to Yonkers and took a ferry to the Palisades, then climbed miles up them until we really found a place to sit. Babe and I sat on the rocks all afternoon. We had supper. It sure did taste good. Had to walk miles in a dash . . . and then missed our train. Took a machine to some town and then a trolley to the Palisades and home.

The next day Sally told Margaret "all about Babe [and] L. Le C. (an apparent rival).[2] She blamed it on me. Then she wrote a note that I was to give him. Haven't heard a thing from him." Sally concluded her day as she often did by reading—in this case *The Four Degree Ball*.

To compensate for whatever difficulties she was experiencing with Babe, Sally spent the next day down at the field playing tennis with Annette and Agnes. They met Esther, had some ginger ale, ate candy, and abandoned themselves to childhood pleasures like riding on the merry-go-round and Ferris wheel (July 6). However, when Margaret received a twelve-page letter from Hump and read it to Sally, she became depressed. Presumably, its contents revealed more of Babe's involvement with L. Le C. By July 9th, all Sally could write was: "I'm awfully mad at Babe."

With anger and boredom clouding her spirit, Benson turned to *The Circular Staircase*, but it did not lighten her mood: "I wish to God I knew something exactly would happen" (July 13). What she wanted was word of a definite breakup between Babe and L. Le C. Until that happened, Benson fended off loneliness and disappointment by reading mysteries[3] or watching silent movies—remote preparation for the book and film reviews she would write for magazines and newspapers in the twenties. She attended several matinees—including *In the Bishop's Carriage* and *The Winsome Widow*—and some silent movies: *Paid in Full*, *The White Sister*, *The Woman in the Case*, *The Girl of the Golden West*, and *Officer 000*. Among other diversions helping to keep her mind off Babe were Bill Stayton's invitations to games at the Polo Grounds, shopping trips with Agnes to Stern's or Wanamaker's, and lunches at the Tally-Ho—"Awfully cute. Like a stable or Child's" (July 26).[4]

At her lowest points, Sally complained to her diary in successive entries: "Any more days like this and I'll die of ennui"; "Rain and drizzle doesn't improve my temper"; "Sundays *are* stupid." After seeing *Paid in Full*, however, she wrote immediately to Babe to share the "very exciting" show. What the diary makes clearer as her summer evolves is Benson's growing dependency on Babe, her intense hatred of inactivity, and her concomitant need for stimulation. She had no idea what lay ahead, nor could she foresee that within a few months the boring summer of 1912, viewed retrospectively, would seem paradisal.

Toward the end of July, Sally confided to her diary: "That Babe person still maintains a frosty silence" (July 24). Finally, on July 30th, the mail brought the long-awaited letter from Babe plus a dinner invitation from Bill. Her spirits picked up immediately. The next day she felt like shopping but had no money. Undeterred, she took the Sixth Avenue "El" down to Esther's apartment at 116 Waverly Place to ask for some cash. Esther gladly obliged, and Sally went to "look for a hat"—the first of many hat-shopping excursions. Finding "no nice ones," she decided to design and trim one herself. A "sweet bathing suit, cap, garters, etc." completed her purchases.[5]

Although shopping, theater, films, teas or luncheons with friends usually alleviated Sally's ennui and diverted her attention from Babe's absence, a problem much worse than boredom loomed. Arriving home from her shopping expedition, Sally was surprised to find that Lon had come over for supper. He seemed tense and unhappy. As the Smiths finished eating, everyone learned the purpose of Lon's visit. He had unwelcome and shocking news: he, Jo, and their son would be moving to Texas. Even more shocking to Sally was that she and her mother would also be moving. Only Agnes would remain behind, but rather than going off to college, she would need to find a job and share Esther's Greenwich Village apartment. Alonzo's business had failed and, in desperation, he had fled to the West Coast where he hoped to find employment with one of his brothers.[6] At this point, Alonzo Jr.—his son and partner—decided to pursue business opportunities in Texas with Fred Parker, a Princeton classmate.

After living in fairly affluent style, Anna Cora and Sally would now be dependent on Lon and his future success in Texas. Though not so surprising to the older Smiths, this new and unexpected turn of fortune completely overwhelmed Sally. She had not lived long enough to observe her father's behavioral patterns. Whether the cause of this most recent family crisis lay in Alonzo's alcoholism or his habitual wanderlust, Anna Cora had grown accustomed to such behavior from the early days of her marriage. Barbara Golseth explained: "Though he had come from a wealthy and prominent family, Alonzo Redway Smith was not very ambitious. He was also an alcoholic." Anna Cora, having met Alonzo at twenty-one while working as a chambermaid in Hurst's Hotel in St. Louis, had married him two years later. She had no career to return to so she had to agree to the move. Devastated, Sally later wrote, "I never felt so badly in my life."

Despite the immediate upset to the Smiths, the effects of Alonzo's choices had both negative and positive results. For Sally, the move was an unwelcome disruption to her burgeoning social life at Horace Mann. To Agnes, it meant a reluctant relinquishing of any plans to follow Esther's collegiate path. To Esther and Anna Cora, it offered one more revelation of an all-important truth: Foolish are the women who depend for sustenance on men. Wise are those who pursue the means to be self-supporting. Eventually, Agnes and Sally would also embrace that truth as they too welcomed opportunities to become financially independent.

Preparations for the move began in earnest. Harriet came over on the tenth and sewed with Sally for most of the morning.[7] That night Sally "read and pinned all evening. Some seamstress!" she exclaimed. Strangely, she expressed nothing about the forthcoming relocation beyond a reference to Emeline's letter: "She [Emeline] is sorry I am going away." The diary is surprisingly silent on whether she told Babe of the move or how he reacted. As summer waned, however, a growing nostalgia impelled her to glance through the pages of *The Mannikin* until, becoming angry, she simply "gave up . . . so homesick, St. Louis sick and everything else." This is the closest Benson came to verbalizing her feelings. Characteristically, she dealt with emotional pain by avoidance—through distractions like movies or reading.

On the other hand, Sally approached physical pain directly. Mid-August presented health challenges—a dreaded series of visits to the dentist. On the 13th she wrote: "Dentist. Ugh! Dr. Walker gently but quietly informed me that two of my teeth were on the brink. Cheerful!" was her sarcastic comment.[8] Later, she met Esther for an ice cream at the Belview. At home, meanwhile, Agnes had developed a high fever, and the next morning, Anna Cora awakened Sally early and sent her to buy meat for a beef broth, her traditional panacea. That afternoon, Sally gave in to a rare admission of loneliness. "New York is lonesome without anyone. To be sure there's Harriet, but . . . Margaret hasn't written. Must be sick. . . . For heaven's sakes! If only something or somebody like Emeline could come to town." Again on the 15th, Sally was sent to the store for Agnes's medicine. The rest of the morning she straightened her room, ran errands all afternoon, and "got myself a book, *The Forsaken Inn*. Sure is exciting. Dentist tomorrow. Ugh!!!" The next day, after that visit to Dr. Walker, she wrote miserably: "It is better left unsaid. I go again Monday." She read "every available thing including *The Smart Set* until tea time,"[9] perking up only when "Mr. Lord came to take Esther out."

On August 19th, after yet another visit to the dentist—"an event that sure does put me on the brink"—Sally started Charlotte Brontë's *Jane Eyre*. "Awfully good!" was her response, but even Brontë could not alleviate Sally's boredom: "Summer in New York is *hell!* Believe me! Oh, for the sight of Emeline!" Her depression worsened over the next few days, despite a welcome letter from Margaret and a movie with Agnes (August 20). On August 22nd, brooding on Babe's neglect, Sally observed angrily: "Positively nothing doing in this old town! . . . I hate Babe," and two days later: "New York is about as stupid as they come. But just the same I'll hate to leave it. . . . If only something would happen!" (August 24).

Finally, on September 2nd, she confided to her diary: "I *wish* we weren't going to Texas. Nothing doing. It's not worthwhile to write." The next day was her birthday, but she makes no mention of a celebration beyond going to see *Seven Days* at the West End Theater with Agnes and Jane. The play, at least, made her laugh, but she spent the whole evening reading. Three days later, Sally wrote: "We sure are going to Texas"—as though previously in denial or, by hoping against hope, she might prevent the move. On the 10th, missing Babe's attention, she wrote bitterly: "Babe doesn't care about me. Darn Jack! He said he'd be over Friday, but I never take his word." Two blank diary pages follow—the first ever—speaking silently but eloquently to Sally's busyness and sadness. On the 19th she went to Margaret's in the morning, and in the evening, "Babe came over. No time to write these days," was her brief entry. On the 20th, her final full day in New York, Sally's agenda was packed. After going to Margaret's to get her middy and "request a *pleurant*," she went to Harriet's and then to school where she talked to Gilby.[10] Bare facts are stated simply with no reflection or expression of feeling. On the 21st Sally wrote: "Last day in New York. Sailed at 1 p.m. *S.S. Brazor*. Margaret, Elise, Natalie, Annette, and Marion came to see us. Met Clyde Everett."

Once aboard the *S.S. Brazor*, a Southern Pacific steamship, she wrote even less: "Nothing doing. Life is dull." But during the five-day sailing, she struck up a friendship with Peterson, the wireless operator, and on September 26, she spent the whole morning in the wireless room with him. Excitement crept back into the diary on the 27th: "All excited on landing. I talked to Mr. Peterson. We landed at 2 p.m. I was disappointed in Galveston. Awful place. Came up on train with Mr. Grimes. Stopping at Hotel Bender, Houston. Houston a nice place."[11]

4

HOUSTON

1912–1913

"I am a raving fiend. No heart left to write in a diary where I've written such good times. . . . Life is one damn thing after another."

—Diary, December 12, 1912

After living in the heart of Manhattan, Sally's labeling Houston a "nice place" was a very positive statement. A bayou-based city, Houston had become the "chief rail center of Texas" and was enjoying a period of "explosive growth" (Johnston 98, 111). Its wealth derived from cotton, oil, and lumber plus a coalescence of sea and rail access to other United States cities and Mexico. It had six department stores, nine hotels, eight office buildings, nine banks, and four theaters (McComb XX). It also boasted a library built in Renaissance style—a gift from Andrew Carnegie—streetcars, telephones, telegraphs, plus social and cultural advantages: "an embryo country club," a Museum of Fine Arts housed in a Greek Revival–style building, and a "remarkable array of musicians" (Johnston 129, 184). In 1912, Congress finally approved funding for dredging a new channel to replace the one leading to Galveston, where cargo was transferred to ocean-going vessels. A "Direct Navigation Company" could now send its own steel barges from the new port of Houston. Lon, already experienced in cotton trading, anticipated a lucrative future. His office was in the sixteen-story Cotton Exchange Building—an impressive structure of "red tapestry brick" and "Algonite white stone"—that had cost $1,500,000 (McComb XX).

As the first decade of the twentieth century ended, many Houstonians fled the city's congestion and noise for the quieter suburbs—Westmoreland, Courtlandt Place, and Houston Heights—which promised electricity, paved roads, water, gas, sewerage, and telephones plus streetcar access to town. Lon also explored these neighborhoods before choosing less-upscale Fairview, and on September 28th, the day after Anna Cora's and Sally's arrival, he took them to see "our house. I suppose it's all right," Sally wrote. "The yard is swell." Passing signs for the Magnolia Brewery, the Eureka Ice Company, and Jim Abercrombie's Dairy, Benson recalled St. Louis days and hoped she might be happy in Houston despite its not being New York. What she did not know was that her stay in Texas would be over by late spring.

At noon, the customary dinnertime in Houston, the Smiths dined at the Bristol, a ten-story hotel with a roof garden and a superb chef (Johnston 143). Refreshed by the rooftop breezes and lunch, the Smiths then "went down to Lon's office," Sally wrote, to check on the mail. She continued happily, "I got a letter from Margaret and Lester. Then we went into my future school run by a Professor Welch . . ." Welch's schoolhouse on Caroline and Hadley streets was a simple, two-story, white frame house, but the "schooling was outstanding."[3] For Sally, accustomed to Horace Mann's size and grandeur, the appearance of Welch's academy, with its clapboard frame and open porches, evoked the negative: "I didn't like it much."

One day at Welch's School was all she could bear. She hated it so much that Anna Cora enrolled her in the Waldo School where Sally's reaction was similar: she "didn't like it at all"—she was "too advanced." Worse, it was an all-girls school.[4] Next day Sally began at a third school—Mrs. Gray's Group—and seemed satisfied at first:

> I like it rather. Mrs. Gray seems a peach. One of the girls walked over to the car [streetcar] with me. She sure is pretty. Her name is Jewel. Gladys Brice met me downtown. We went to the movies and then for my books. We got a soda too. I hate Houston. (Diary, October 9)

As her diary shows, however, Mrs. Gray's proved far less challenging than Horace Mann. Within two weeks Sally wrote: "School was rather interrupted as too many people called Dr. Gray. But after having to write 'I must not talk without permission,' fifty times, we at last got leave to go." A likely initiator of the ruckus, Sally was undeterred. Her November 19th entry offers proof: "School—nothing doing—except that we act up a lot." She coped with the boredom of unchallenging, unproductive school days by correspondence with Horace Mann friends, especially Elise and Emeline, and was delighted to have an unexpected holiday because of "the doings at Rice Institute."[5]

Sally's October diary entries became increasingly sporadic and brief as she confides her loneliness and her yearning to be back home: "Nothing to do. Not even ink to write. . . . Nothing to write. Simply wacky. Played victrola all day. Hot. Nothing doing." The contrast between the eloquent silence of the diary's many blank pages and the full entries of the previous spring is remarkable. Three separate pages—their pithiness speaking volumes—consist of just one word: "Rain." Other than the comfort of reading, Sally found little inner vitality to compensate for her negative feelings. One exception was attending Sarah Bernhardt's performance in *La Force* at Pillot's Opera House. Sally wrote that evening to Babe, and his response on the 19th made her ecstatic.

Sally's spirits continued to soar on October 23rd: "Mama's birthday. She and Papa celebrated their 29th anniversary." That Alonzo had returned or how and with whom they celebrated were too unimportant to mention. More important was Sally's meeting a nice but "ugly" boy at Gladys's. With nothing to do, she read *The Gilded Age* and later wrote miserably: "I wish I were back in New York at Horace Mann. This is the stupidest place I've ever known. . . . So little to write that I hate to use up space writing it." When she did write, her focus was on meeting boys, alternately liking and despising Gladys Brice, or finding Lauren and Gladys Hudson sweet. As her fickleness became a constant, her academic motivation waned: "School! I never know a thing. Can't say that I did a darn thing all day." Other dismal entries followed: November 10, "Impossible! School! Brrr. How I hate it!"

On the positive side, November 5th was Election Day, and Sally rejoiced that Wilson had won. She watched the Labor Day parade on the 16th with Jo and thought it was "fine." Jo also took her to see two movies at the new Majestic Theater. Sally particularly enjoyed one—*Oliver Twist*—and the next day she was amused to read in the *Chronicle* that some moviegoers felt the theater should enforce "separation of the sexes" or have "policewomen patrol the dark aisles" (Johnston 146). She wondered what Babe or Bill Stayton would think if such regulations were enforced in Manhattan movie houses.

Reading the *Saturday Evening Post* occupied her one evening but she wrote nothing for nine days. In fact, November's entries show increasing frustration and hint at depression. The many blank pages eerily foreshadow the blankness of the blackouts that would later characterize Benson's periods of binge drinking. December's entries are a series of stark, staccato sentences: "I certainly do wish I were back home" (December 1); "School is stupid" (December 3); "Oh! I simply despise every last girl in that darned old school, most of all Wilma and Gladys! Ugh!" (December 4). December 5th was a bit better: "Mother and I went downtown and I bought Emeline and Harriet a present. Went to a movie. Letter from Babe and I answered it." On the 11th, Sally entered: "Nothing doing except rain. No mail. . . . Fred came over this evening. He is going to New York. I wish I were him [*sic*]." On the 12th Sally desperately wrote: "Rain !!!!!!!!!! No mail. Positively nothing doing. I am a raving fiend. No heart left to write in a diary where I've written such good times."

The following day she reminisced: "Six months ago Babe and Bill were over. Oh! Nothing much doing, but instead of history we had Mrs. Gray which did us ten times more good. . . . a woman [is] better than a man." On December 22: "Sunday and rain . . . one combination to make one faint. Simply dying of ennui. Cold." Then, as Christmas approaches, she is more spirited:

> December 23: Downtown with Mother. Got some things. Went to "Isis." Pretty good show. Read *A Connecticut Yankee in King Arthur's Court.*

> December 24: Downtown for candy and flowers. We trimmed the tree and fixed things generally. Quite a difference from last Christmas.

On the day itself there is no mention of attending church:

> December 25: Opened presents after breakfast. I got a fountain pen, some Teddy Bears, gloves, suit, hat, shoes, chain, powder . . . sandalwood scarab, kimono, pair of silk stockings.

The next day Lon's gift—books by O. Henry and Kipling—came, she attended a "picture show" with Elise, and read "The Trimmed Lamp" by O. Henry. "Very, very good," she commented. On December 28 she read *Scribner's* all evening and observed: "Old diary has almost ended. Some changes in one year! New York to Texas." On the 29th she admitted: "I sound like a Weather report but there is nothing else to write about."

It is striking that for her psychological survival Sally depended heavily on amusement, the company of friends, and reading. Inactivity seemed like death. The diary's final entry on New Year's Eve delivers a powerful summary of the year as she bemoans her unplanned removal to Texas in a series of striking contrasts:

> Believe me, a lot of things can happen in 365 days. Texas and New York. Horace Mann with 1,000 pupils, Mrs. Gray's with twelve. One block from Broadway on the tenth floor, to a frame house in Fairview. Maillard's to Anderson's Drug Store. Mary Elizabeth's for this palace. J. Sweets and A #1 plays to "The Bloody Boot." Life is one damn thing after another.

Sally had grown accustomed to the good life in Manhattan. Her recollection of Maillard's noted ambience made the nondescript reality of Anderson's suffer by comparison, as nostalgia for her absent, familiar world reinforced feelings of loss and exile. She had loved popping into Maillard's with friends for tea. Its décor evoked the "grandly scaled dining room . . . [of] the great houses and clubs of the city's upper crust" (Stern et al. 275). Like Schrafft's, Maillard's afforded a nostalgic space that appealed to Sally's romantic nature. It also sold the chocolates and baked goods she relished.[6] What was she doing in Anderson's drab, plainly furnished drugstore? Years later she honored Maillard's by including it in her first *New Yorker* short story.[7]

Always socially active, Sally had continued to make friends easily, but they were no substitute for her popular, older New York crowd. She particularly missed Babe. As 1913 dawned, Christmas vacation ended, and the second semester in Mrs. Gray's School continued much like the first. The weeks dragged on. However, much to Sally's surprise and delight, she learned toward the end of spring that her Texas exile was almost at an end. She and Anna Cora would move back to New York in the summer, and Sally could return to Horace Mann for her junior year. She was overjoyed. The longest, most desolate year of her life would soon be all but forgotten.

5

RISING SPIRITS

HOME AGAIN—1913–1915

So "full of a careless, healthy, radiant happiness . . . [she] was almost breath-taking."

—Bill Stayton

Sally Smith's joyful return to New York came about largely through the generosity of her sisters. Independent and financially successful women—without any reliance on men, including their father—Esther and Agnes rescued their mother and sister. An advertising copy writer for John Wanamaker, Esther earned enough to support herself and help her mother. A writer for both *The Morning Telegraph* and *Puck* and a regular columnist for *Moving Picture World*, Agnes would pay Sally's tuition at Horace Mann. Rose would provide housing.

During Anna Cora's and Sally's Texas sojourn, Guy Thompson had earned a promotion and been assigned to his company's New York office. At first he and Rose lived in an East Village townhouse (at 950 Second Street), but in 1913, with an increase in Guy's salary and hopes for another child, he and Rose rented two floors of a more fashionable building at 14 Fifth Avenue, near Washington Square and the Waverly Place apartment shared by Esther and Agnes.[1] Having so much space, Rose persuaded Guy to allow her mother and Sally to live with them for a time, and Anna Cora gratefully accepted the Thompsons' hospitality.

The idea of returning to New York City thrilled Sally. She couldn't wait to reconnect with her Horace Mann friends, especially Bill Stayton and Boyd Sommerville, who were equally happy to hear of her return. First, however, she would spend a short vacation with Agnes at the Old

Lyme Inn in Old Lyme, Connecticut. On Monday, June 30th, Bill Stayton wrote that he, Boyd Sommerville, and Gilby had met at Times Square and, unaware that she was away, had tried to call Sally at her house. "Don't let Agnes get to acting like Leo Tolstoy," Bill cautioned, "or she's apt to lose her job. Let me know when you are coming down," he urged, adding: "I was thinking of coming up Sunday. For the love of Mike, hurry back to town. Gilby hasn't seen a regular girl for over a month and will go crazy pretty soon. We need you to cheer things up in this gloomy and very hot town."[2]

Smitten by Sally since their first meeting at Horace Mann's orientation in 1911, Bill explained years later: "She was so full of a careless, healthy, radiant happiness . . . that [she] was almost breath-taking."[3] On July 4th, Bill Stayton wrote a second time, begging Sally to return to the city. The Old Lyme Inn, as Bill saw it, was "a colony of artists and a giddy place to spend a vacation but not like Rector's ('the supreme shrine of the cult of pleasure') or Bustanoby's"—noted for impeccable cuisine, Broadway beauties, and soft music—where the smart set gathered and feminine beauty was showcased.[4] Old Lyme, though lacking the excitement of the Great White Way, was a distinct improvement over Houston and allowed Sally a necessary transition between her Texas experience and what lay ahead. Enjoying vacation with Agnes and her writer friends, Sally could wait another few days to join Bill and resume her social life in New York.

Not yet sixteen—although attractive to college men like Bill and accustomed to socializing with him at trendy places like Bustanoby's—Sally remained an adolescent at heart. A good example is Lon's June 9th telegram to "Miss Sara Smith, c/o Mrs. G. V. Thompson" to report news of "Pussentater," their cat: "Abie Marcel and Mandy Pussentater arrived this morning." The next day, Lon sent Sally a lengthy, updated account, including the arrival of a third kitten.[5] Addressed to "Dearest Toots," Lon's letter elaborates on the kittens' names and appearance. Having named the parent cat together with Sally, Lon knew she would appreciate his humorous pedigree for each of the offspring.[6]

Living near Washington Square meant Sally would commute to Horace Mann by crosstown trolley and Interborough Rapid Transit, one of four elevated lines. Wearing high button shoes, ankle-length dark skirt and white middy blouse—standard garb for women of that era—Sally set out on September 29th to resume her high school career. Academically, she struggled to catch up as her 1913–1914 report card indicates. Socially, on the other hand, she fared very well, adjusting easily to the whirl of activity she loved. However, rumors and gossip were circulating about plans to establish a separate boys' school, effective the following September. Sally couldn't imagine Horace Mann without its male component, but already, the football and baseball teams were practicing at the new Van Cortlandt Park field.[7]

Commuting by train, though a new experience for Sally, did not daunt her. Rather, she sat in the IRT car each morning and afternoon observing fellow riders "so varied in type as to form a perfect 'New York' ensemble."[8] From the homeless vagrant reclining nearest the door to the "fat, fair, and forty lady" annoyed by her unsteady neighbor on the right and trying hard to keep "her august person from contact with his unaugust one," Sally did not miss a thing. A particularly funny scene occurred one morning when an elderly gentleman with long, white whiskers sat beside a woman holding a curious child. "With a benevolent air," he opened wide his newspaper and settled himself "somewhere off at the front."[9] Suddenly, the child slipped its hand behind the newspaper causing the gentleman to jump and swear. When the passengers regained their composure, the child chuckled and attacked again, thrusting its hand "somewhere behind Wilson's latest message." After the third such attack, the gentleman finally saw the humor of the situation, "burst into a mighty roar," and made friends with the child, giving fellow riders a chuckle. Sally was amazed at the number of women passengers who *must* talk "even if they know nothing to say or nobody to say it to." One such woman, "sharply boned, sharply featured," inquired in a "sharp voice" of a male seatmate lost in thought: "Could you please tell me what is the next station?" He answered "more hurriedly than politely," noted Sally, and resumed his train of thought. The woman next tried a male to her left who gave an incredulous stare and an "Er-er, beg pardon?"

Next to catch Sally's attention was a young man of about twenty-two whose chief aim in life, she decided, was to "get there" un-mussed. In one hand, he gingerly clasped three gardenias wrapped in waxed paper, gazed at them intermittently, and blushed to the roots of his hair. With the other yellow-gloved hand he extracted, at intervals of about sixty seconds, a large gold watch and glanced at it hurriedly and often. When the train neared the young swain's stop, his nervousness increased and his blush deepened. As he departed, Sally suddenly realized she was three stops beyond her own and rushed from the car "in a manner more speedy than dignified." Such subway travels provided Sally with a window on city-dwellers of all classes, and her eye never tired of feasting on details of individual behavior, whether ordinary or quirky. As she wrote these experiences into articles for the *Record*, she was also storing up the vivid images that would appear later in her *New Yorker* fiction.

The writing Sally had begun in her first year at Horace Mann now intensified. Blaine Webb and Phil Kerby, classmates of Agnes, were collaborating on a writing project and needed Sally's help.[10] After telling her about their project, Blaine wrote:

> Did you tell Esther about our intrigue? What did she say? Is she game to help us out? I was thinking about the great work I dictated needlessly last night—nay—futilely for you failed to take down what I said, and decided we should start something like this: "My God, the water main has busted" said he, waking from a busy day at the office. You see, that would give the reader something to think about from the very start. But I gotta get to woik. Tomorrow afternoon at three-thirty. I shall be miserable until then.[11]

Besides helping with projects such as Blaine Webb's, Sally had several short stories published in *Literary Quarterly*, the Horace Mann literary magazine.[12]

During her junior year Sally started another scrapbook. Pasted in front—as if to suggest her desire for privacy—is one of the cardboard signs used by faculty members if they wished not to be disturbed by students, teachers, or parents: "This room is not open to visitors today." Sally's penciled signature, "Sara Smith," lends authority to the message. Several postcards of Horace Mann are next, introduced by Sally's caption: "On the Hills above the Hudson."[13]

The scrapbook also contains Sally's 1913–1914 report card:

Horace Mann High School Report of: Smith, Sara				Class IV Section 405		
1913–1914	English	Cicero	French	Plane Geometry	Latin Prose	English History
December 1	E	F	B	C	F	C
February 1	D	drop	B	C		B
April 1	C		D	C		C
May 29	B		C			C

This junior year record of Sally's academic achievement indicates the difficulty she found in catching up with New York classmates. A diary entry for January 7th in her freshman year had referred to difficulty with math: "I can't do my algebra at all." However, by February 7th she had improved and wrote happily: "Got report. A_in algebra!" If, as a freshman, Sally mastered so quickly a subject she initially struggled with, she must have been highly motivated and willing to work hard despite maintaining her active social life.[14] An entry for March 31, 1912 reflects Sally's satisfaction: "Got all B's on my report card." As a junior who realized she was not going to college because of financial circumstances, Sally characteristically decided not to bother herself—especially with subjects she did not enjoy. Rather, she invested some energy and effort in what she loved—writing and drama—and eventually pulled up her English grade. Sally's junior English classes met only twice a week because stress was placed on "drill in English composition with only enough supplementary reading to illustrate the types of composition practiced." A long theme, due each week, could be based on "a subject studied in history" (Course of Study 16).

Although Sally had never considered herself a good student and her junior year report card lends credence to her belief, she did exercise leadership at Horace Mann especially in her senior year. Sally's class of 1915 was the first to function as a separate unit from the Boys' School, which had relocated to its new country setting in the Riverdale section of the Bronx. Already an active member of the Senior Dramatic Society committee, Sally now took on additional roles: *Bulletin* editor of *The Horace Mann Record*, the school's newspaper, and yearbook editor-in-chief of the first *Mannikin* published by the Horace Mann School for Girls. While geographic removal of the male component of the class allowed the female segment to assume leadership roles formerly denied them, it also presented challenges—one being the girls' need to overcome habitual reliance on male classmates to be the leaders and decision-makers.

Sally's becoming the *Bulletin* editor was no small feat. Applicants for the position had to submit several editorials, a list of "good editorial subjects," and a paper on the policy of the *Record*.[15] Sally's editorials during her tenure exhibited her usual frank and direct approach to situations, whether local, national, or international. In the Girls' School's inaugural issue of the *Record*, for example, Sally addressed the fears many girls harbored regarding the boys' absence:

Figure 4. Sara Smith as member of Horace Mann Dramatic Society, 1914–1915

Everything seems different; but "different" does not necessarily mean unpleasant. . . . rumors regarding the division of Horace Mann . . . [suggested it] would kill all social activities and end the splendid free spirit which Horace Mann, as the best co-educational school, has been noted for. Now that the division is accomplished, it is surprising to see what an enterprising spirit abounds and what progressive ideas are advanced. . . . This year will be a great adjusting year. Other years will follow the path we take, but now it is up to us to start things.[16]

This readiness to take charge had always been part of Sally. It would serve her well in her new leadership roles and develop further in the years ahead—especially as she embarked on a writing career and began to manage her own financial affairs.

In an article titled "To the Memory of the Dear Departed" published in the same inaugural issue, Sally's satiric voice can be heard. "Sympathy from a mourning body" (the Girls' division) is directed to "friends in dire distress." First are the "beloved teachers" who suffer the "country stillness" bereft of "the delightful music of the city streets" while study hall silence is disrupted "by the occasional roar of a lion and the lonely howl of wolves." Male students, without their old school's "perfect ventilation system" have become "long-suffering heroes trudging up the icy and steep hill" to the new seat of learning, while in the "Girl-Horace Seminary" students come to school with "red eyes and somber mien." The *Record*, therefore, "extends its sincerest sympathy, mingled with hopes for a cheerful outcome."[17] This humorous, pseudo-sympathetic tone would emerge more fully developed in her later work.

Under Sally's leadership, the *Bi-weekly Bulletin of the Horace Mann Record* changed to *The Weekly Bulletin of the Horace Mann School for Girls*. Its second issue, replacing the prior year's total sports coverage, brought dramatics to prominence with a first-page, center column: "All the World's a Stage." As editor, Sally instructs readers that while this year's senior play will not be exactly the same, not enough thought has been given to the "possibilities of plays acted by girls alone." With encouragement, she writes:

Do not get the idea that girls cannot successfully portray male characters. We admit that the modern man with his uncompromising masculinity would be very difficult for a girl to act; but what about . . . the time of doublet and hose, of powdered wig and knee breeches?

Sally next addresses the "principal trouble in school dramatics"—the time wasted in "changing the cast, neglecting to learn lines well, and rehearsing carelessly." Her remedy is the college model: "semi-impromptu plays . . . acted with great vigor and snap . . . costumes hurriedly gotten up . . . only those lines learned that are absolutely necessary."[18] A free spirit herself, she could easily adjust to untraditional methods.

One area where Sally particularly felt the boys' absence was the *Record*'s content. Decisively, Sally alerted readers to their need to subscribe to avoid their paper's "going to the dickens" by becoming filled with ads.

With "fewer persons here to subscribe," it was all the more imperative for the girls to show their interest and support by "subscribing right away."[19] Sally's editorial, "Alms for the Love of Allah!" was not the issue's lone voice. In a column titled "Horace Mannerisms," little blurbs reinforce her message: "We just received a letter from the Boys' School wishing us success with the *Record*." Then, "Augusta Wales . . . has got more subscriptions than any other room agent." And, "What's the matter with the school anyway? Why don't you subscribe to the *Record*? You know perfectly well it's the best one that has ever been published." In a final comment she admits: "Yes, the *Record* Board is certainly conceited."

By the third issue, the *Record's* first page contained nothing on sports. An effect of Sally's prioritizing, the cover page was devoted to just three articles: one on *The Mannikin*, one on the South's imminent financial ruin because the war prevented cotton sales, and one on the senior show. Of the three, the *Mannikin* article reflected Sally's chief concern. Threatened by the possible amalgamation of the 1915 yearbook into one volume for the two schools, Sally argued wisely that in prior years the schools had shared the same interests but now their interests were "widely different." It would be very difficult to arrange meetings of *The Mannikin's* two boards because the boys and girls were now on different schedules. In a voice unmistakably Sally's, the reader is persuaded:

> Nineteen-fifteen is the first class to graduate under the new plan. Upon us, then, lies the responsibility of making over the old customs, and why not begin with the *Mannikin*? As classes graduate, all connections between the schools are bound to be severed, and even if we did not originate the plan of having separate yearbooks, future classes would change from the old way.

In the same October 16th issue, Sally's influence appears in a new column, titled simply, "Book Review." In it, Sally's coeditor, Maxime Harrison, critiques a short story by Victor François from the collection *Introductory French Prose Composition*, but the next issue carried Sally's review of David Saville Muzzey's *American History*, a subject she found fascinating. Her critique, prescriptive of Sally's future fiction, cites Muzzey's "naturalness and directness" and his "easy, fluent, but perfectly clear" style. "He wastes no time in needless descriptions but records the facts as closely as possible . . . [after] close study and careful observation."[20] Benson's critique, like her style, was spare and concise, clear and precise. Like Muzzey, she would observe carefully and waste no words—habits she maintained consistently.

Sally's October 30th editorial, "A Sweet Disorder in the Dress," exhibits her characteristic humor.[21] Though relaxed rules now allow wearing inconspicuous jewelry, Sally argues that Horace Mann needs dress regulation:

> The great essential of being well-dressed is being *suitably* dressed. Some of the clothes being worn at Horace Mann are about as suitable for school as a negligee would be for the street. A school dress should be simple, neat, and of conservative color. If a skirt and waist are worn, each should be of some inconspicuous shade, and *not* joined by a loud and shrieking girdle.

The post–World War I era would usher in an entirely new approach to fashion. Short skirts and bright colors would be the order of the day, but in 1914, even Sally adhered to conservative dress standards for women.

The *Record*'s December 11th issue confronted readers with an unusual "most important article." The right-hand column pleaded: "Help Wanted." The first part begs readers for letters to the editor and accuses them of being "singularly lacking in ideas and ideals." Though the *Record* board is more than willing to print "knocks," Sally challenges readers to find something good to say about the school. "Is it all bad? Think it over and when you decide, write . . . the *Record* about it," Sally implores. "Somebody ought to write us just for the sake of argument." The article's second half pleads for *The Mannikin*. Staff is needed, but more importantly, the help of the whole class is required. The glory of the senior play is very tempting, she acknowledges, but "soon gone." If "your name is in the *Mannikin*," however, "you will achieve everlasting literary and artistic fame," she promises. A final point—the boys will be asking for subscribers to their *Mannikin*, and "if we subscribe to theirs, they'll subscribe to ours," she cajoles. Recognizing that the $1.50 cost is a "great deal to ask before Christmas,"[22] she reminds them that the extra fifty cents will bring them a "handsome picture of your favorite Senior sent on request."

For the December 23rd issue, Sally decided to focus her editorial on the history of Christmas and the various rituals that accompanied its celebration around the world. She described the feast's origins "as an institution . . . attributed to Pope Telesphorus who died in 138" and the origin of celebrating Christ's birth on December 25th as deriving from the

fourth century. Details from the medieval period—the mystery and moral-
ity plays—carol singing to replace Latin for the common people—"feasts of
fools and asses when everything serious was burlesqued . . . and disgraceful
orgies were held"—precede a description of German Protestants' "children's
festival" (yew bough/Christmas tree and giving of gifts). The Yule log in
England, decorating homes with holly and mistletoe, appointing the "lord
of misrule"—all were far better, Sally concluded, than the Christmas spirit
of today "when people give presents because they think they must, and
when gifts are measured by their monetary value." Such sentiments about
gift-giving would take concrete form in 1922 when Sally urged her sisters
to simplify their gift-giving.[23]

Though much of her middle-school writing had involved humor and
parody, Benson's early concern for the underdog and the disadvantaged
surfaced in her editorials for the *Record* and in her short stories for the
Literary Quarterly. Not surprisingly, these concerns continued to color her
later writing for *The New Yorker.* Benson often punished oppressors, allowing their victims to triumph in some small but pointed way. One example
is "The Raffle," a cautionary tale in which a young, female protagonist,
Millie Osborne, turns the tables on her condescending, penny-pinching
cousin, Margaret Reade, by donating her newly won blankets—a prize
Cousin Margaret coveted—to the local charity. Such retribution compensated Millie for her class-conscious cousin's prior coldness and superior airs.
Benson's ending invites readers to share Millie's triumphal satisfaction in
punishing Margaret's snobbish, patronizing behavior. "Cousin Margaret's
eyes were opaque and cold. Millie smiled softly. 'It will help a lot, dear
Cousin . . . and it's for charity, you know.' " Besides showing her penchant
for siding with the oppressed, "The Raffle" reveals Benson's satiric humor
and poetic justice at its best.[24]

Sally Benson's youthful ability to transcend class lines—riding with
the ice man, sharing the work of a farmhand, helping Katie in the kitch-
en—characterized her approach to people throughout her life and fiction.
Neighbors and friends, strangers and colleagues, family members and chance
acquaintances—all supplied Benson with raw material. In writing "Junior
Miss," for example, Benson claimed inspiration from an experience on a
New York City double-decker bus. She observed the interaction between an
embarrassed mother and her clumsy, preteen daughter who had missed the
fare box, spilling coins everywhere. Benson capitalized on the embarrassing
moment by creating the character of Judy Graves.

Through Judy Graves and her family, Benson portrayed class differences and favored characters who did not have class prejudice. For example, the preteen Judy of "The Paragon" causes consternation by asking to spend a day helping her friend's family paint furniture. At Judy's friend's apartment, the family shares household chores, mother washing dishes and children drying, because they, unlike the Graves, have no maid. Benson conveys contrasting attitudes toward class and illustrates differences between lower- and upper-class lifestyles through Judy's observations to her class-conscious mother. Later that day, befriending an old man selling peanuts in the park because he is "very poor," Judy promises to "start a campaign and raise money so he can have his teeth fixed. . . . I'm going to put down the names of everyone we know, and how much they should give."[25] Hearing this, even the uppity Mrs. Graves is touched and becomes the first to support her daughter by contributing a quarter. Benson at twelve, helping Delmar Hansen on Uncle Jay's farm—and Judy Graves pitching in to paint her friend's family's furniture or raise funds for a poor stranger—these are kindred spirits.

Sally's January 22nd *Bulletin* editorial echoes the social justice principles that had already taken root in her. She opposed child labor and analyzed some states' policies on the issue. "It is almost impossible to check this great social evil by state laws," she explained, because "state laws are not uniform." The Palmer-Owen bill must pass, she argued, because it would prohibit the interstate transporting of products mined or manufactured by children under fourteen years of age or by children laboring more than eight hours a day for six days a week, after 7 p.m. or before 7 a.m. The bill must be passed before Congress recesses on March 4th for two reasons. The work would have to be done all over again—clearly a waste of valuable time and a violation of Sally's work ethic—and more importantly, "after the war is over, there will be many immigrants to this country, poor and broken in spirit, and ready to let their children work under any conditions." Anticipating her readers' reaction—"What does this have to do with me?", at a time when women still did not have the right to vote—Sally answers: "You must do your part to push this bill through. Get your father and cousins and uncles to write to their Congressmen and Senators urging them to support it. Write yourself," she urges. "They represent you, even if you don't vote for them. This is what the National Child Labor Brigade asks of you." As an alternative, she recommends joining the "telegraph brigade. Promise to telegraph any Congressman who is reported to you as standing in the way of passage of the bill." Waxing eloquent as she approaches her favorite theme, Sally challenges: "Don't leave it all to other people. Do your share, small though it may be. And, remember, you must hurry!"[26]

The 1915 *Mannikin* featured a "Review of the Year" summarizing the *Record*'s staff's accomplishment in producing the paper unaided by any male classmates. The page glows with pride in having met the challenge: "Notwithstanding the gloomy predictions to the contrary, the *Record* pulled through this year without the boys." Sally elaborates:

> Everyone predicted that the combination of Maxime Harris[27] and Sara Smith would prove a worse one than orange and cerise. However, they were sadly disappointed. Speak of the lion and the lamb lying down peacefully side by side! Added to the social embarrassments of "dear friends" being on the Board, and lack of news, due to "poor school spirit," were numerous financial embarrassments and a printer. Every time the Board endeavored to become a little humorous so as to lighten the dreary monotony of the *Bulletin*, it was promptly and effectually sat upon by the vigilant Faculty (though we never suspected that they read the *Record*).

Benson humorously compares the editors' "inexperience . . . and lack of news" to a child's "losing its front teeth . . . [the] spaces . . . occasionally filled in by startling announcements, shrieking that millions of people were dying in some language, or that 'the *Record* needs your help.' " Irony takes over as she recalls that the board, adopting the "gentle art of 'stretching,' [produced] a six-column write-up of an elementary school play" or three columns containing only six alumnae notes. The page concludes, however, on a kindly note: "Yet, who are we to condemn? [The members of the board] did their humble best and suffered with the rest of the School." Summing up, Sally concludes: "If asked concerning the success of the *Record* this year, we should quote that old saying, 'Faith, Hope, and Charity, these three, but the greatest of these is Charity' " (41). Though signed "Those Who Know" followed by two sets of initials—M.H. and S.R.S.—the article echoes the sentiments of Sally Redway Smith. The page significantly epitomizes the spirit that later enlivened Sally's *New Yorker* pieces—a spirit of perceptive irony seasoned with gentle compassion.

Another *Mannikin* page lists senior awards. Sally received two of the eighteen awards—one for "Wittiest," the other for "Noisiest." Of eighteen quotable quotes selected for a page titled "The Hobby-horses Great Ones Ride," the 1915 *Mannikin* credits Sally's: "Bob Chambers I just cannot stand, / But I think Johnson's simply grand!"—an unsurprising quote to those who knew her (70). Another page—"Horace Mann Bookshelf"—listing favorite books of both faculty and seniors—has two recommended by Sally: *The Desired Woman* and *A Woman's Will*. Each title, in retrospect, becomes an ironic commentary, given Sally's social life during her Horace Mann days and beyond. As she had in freshman year, Sally once again demonstrated leadership in the Girls' League, which sponsored two annual events: a fair to raise money for the Red Cross and home charities such as the French Day Nursery, the Manhattanville Nursery, and the National Child Labor Committee and a play. In Sally's senior year, at her initiative, the fair changed venue to Thompson Gym, an "audacious move," since some feared it was too large. However, "the place was literally packed" and the profit was $450—"more than was ever raised before." Sally proudly appraised its success: "Everyone did her part and helped to make this the most successful Girls' League Fair in the School's history" (38). As for the play, Sally's editorial voice explains that the money made by the play had been used in former years to send Horace Mann delegates to an annual summer conference at Silver Bay.[28] "This year, however, in view of the terrible distress among our poor, on account of the war in Europe . . . it [the money] was given for the benefit of specific home charities." Sally concludes:

> Taken all in all, this year has been one of the most, if not the most, successful years in the history of the League, and its success has been largely due to the support of the girls. The last wish of this year's executive committee is that next year's committee will keep up the good work and make the year of 1916 even more successful than was this year. (38)

The same generous spirit would later motivate Benson to donate to the British Ambulance Corps all the royalties from the fiction she published in England during World War II.

Sally did not find it easy to work with staff members who were slackers. In "How to Run the *Mannikin*" her sarcasm abounds:

The associate editor must not attend meetings and the business managers must interfere constantly with the rest of the book. It is 'the thing' for the editor-in-chief to desert her post in a crisis to go motoring, while the athletic editor must ask the whole class to help her with her work. . . . All contributions written in pencil and on miscellaneous paper will be gladly accepted. In fact, that is the only 'chic' way of writing for the *Mannikin*.

Considering that in later years Benson's stories were sent to her publisher just as they came from her typewriter with rarely a correction or cross-out, one suspects that her high standards and penchant for perfection caused her to be too hard on her peers.

Sally's exasperation multiplied as the responsibilities demanded by her roles—editor of the weekly bulletin of the *Record*, member of the senior play committee—conflicted. The implied complaints that follow are laced with ironic humor:

First of all, always elect a temporary board some time along in December. It is the duty of this board to have ideas, collect money, hunt up photographers, cheap estimates and printing presses. The *Mannikin* is then forgotten about until sometime in January, when Miss Baker finds a rare collection of old *Mannikin*s in her cupboard, which reminds one that they, too must edit a yearbook. The final board is then chosen but never by any chance is a member of the temporary board on it. For a while nothing is done until the Senior Play cast is chosen. Then the editor-in-chief, who is elected because of her irresponsibility and general incompetence, decides to call a meeting on a day when no one can possibly attend.

In the meetings the following disorder should be strictly observed: it is quite unnecessary for anyone to be on time. The editor-in-chief should be shown her place at once. She has no power to interfere, suggest or offer any ideas which would conflict with those of the rest of the board. The girl who gets the floor first keeps it for the rest of the meeting. It is a fine place to argue about the 1914 *Mannikin*, the cost of the senior play scenery, why the *Record* never had enough news, and whether we ought to give up our Saturday afternoons to the *Mannikin*.

> The Senior Play rehearsals must . . . fall on the same day
> as the *Mannikin* meetings. In fact, on the last week of the Senior
> Play the *Mannikin* must not concern the girls.

The second page continues in this vein but addresses the injustice she sees related to money collecting. Seniors, although they have tried to make the junior high school subscribe, are last-minute purchasers of the yearbook and have not helped to sell ads but expect the elementary school and freshmen to "help willingly." Seniors have violated a principle dear to Sally: "Doing one's part," a principle that marked her work effort throughout her life. In 1955 Marshall Jamison, director of *The Young and the Beautiful*, worked closely with Benson in producing the show's Broadway run. He appreciated her for "doing the job the best way she knew how."

Characteristically, Sally put great effort into activities she enjoyed and drama was one. As a Horace Mann senior, she contributed as writer, director, and producer of the Senior Dramatic Society plays, acting the part of Mrs. Campbell in *The Likely Story*. Her senior scrapbook contains pictures of the senior play, *Aucassin and Nicolette*, whose production occasioned Sally's introduction to playwright John Lawson.[29] Working with Lawson and being immersed in drama developed her skill in handling dialogue and capturing character concisely through word and gesture, qualities that distinguish her later fiction.[30]

As her classmates prepared for graduation, they welcomed the 1915 *Mannikin*'s arrival. The blurb below Sara Redway Smith's name reads: "She had a head to contrive, a tongue to persuade, and a hand to create any mischief" (20). Whoever wrote those words could not have known how prophetic they were. In her senior portrait Sally stares straight at the camera full face, her head tilted slightly to the right. Her expression is open and thoughtful with just a hint of sadness and a touch of defiance. She wears a v-necked white blouse and a simple chain with small pendant. Close-cropped dark hair and curly bangs frame a face that seems to say: "I am ready for any challenge."

Sally's father, still in California, did not attend her graduation on Friday, May 28th but wrote to her from Los Angeles:

My dear Sally,

I send congratulations on your graduation day. Done with school—Don't be afraid of the world—it is not so big or so

Figure 5. Sara Redway (Sally) Smith in her Horace Mann yearbook, *The Man-nikin,* class of 1915

bad but what you can make it better by your good life. Follow the noble example of your dear mother and good sisters, and all will be well with you wherever you may be.

Always with my best love—
Papa[31]

Though interesting that Alonzo recognizes his wife's "noble example," it is sad that he makes no pretext of having given his daughter anything comparable. Worse, predisposition to alcoholism—now known to be inter-generational—would prove to be part of Alonzo's legacy to Sally.

The Horace Mann chapel, filled with friends and family members of the graduating class of 1915, heard the strains of "unusually good music" that began promptly at 3 p.m. on May 28. Wearing white and carrying bouquets of daisies, Sally and her fellow seniors marched slowly down the aisle, led by Ruth Murray, president of the junior class. All heads were bowed while Chaplain Knox of Columbia University gave the blessing. After singing the commencement hymn, the graduates and their guests listened as Professor Beard of Columbia spoke on the "changes in opportunities open to women since the early times in England." The *Record* for October 1, 1915 observed that Beard "cleverly kept his audience from guessing whether he was for or against Woman's Suffrage"—a hotly debated issue at the time. The Glee Club sang two selections. Then, Mr. Pearson awarded diplomas, each graduate receiving "volumes of applause" as she reached the platform banked with daisies. Highest honors were bestowed on Maxime Harrison, Sally's future sister-in-law. Dean Russell gave a few parting remarks, the closing hymn was sung, and the class of 1915 filed out into the Thompson Gym. At their reception, Sally's and her classmates' voices "rang out clear and strong in their farewell song to the school." Arms filled with flowers, surrounded by an admiring circle of family, Babe, and other friends, a smiling Sally Smith walked away from Horace Mann prepared to meet the challenge of her absent father's letter.

6

A WORLD AT WAR

ARMS AND THE MEN—PRELUDE TO A MARRIAGE—1915–1918

"I became engaged to all the men I was dating in those war years [as they were] leaving for overseas . . . in the morbid belief that they would all be killed. . . . To my embarrassment, they all came back."

—Sally Benson

The dominant personality and aggressive approach to life discernible in Sally's senior portrait served her well when she sought employment in August of 1915. Just before her eighteenth birthday, Sally walked confidently into National City Bank, asked to see the president, and successfully negotiated a job as "one of the paying tellers."[1] Two years later, as the United States entered the Great War, Sally advanced to the Foreign Exchange Department, while Agnes joined Louella Parsons's writing staff at the *New York Morning Telegraph* before moving on to write movie reviews and articles for *Photoplay* and *The New Yorker.*

Like the confession magazines that shortly followed them, movie magazines such as *Screenplay* and *Photoplay* attracted the same class of readers—consumers of mass culture—and the same advertisers. Both types of magazine "offered escape by giving the reader a glimpse into someone else's most intimate affairs." Fans devoured articles on what the stars were really like, how they spent their money and free time, how they stayed handsome or glamorous, or what they looked for in a mate. Growing in popularity in tandem with the movie industry's star system, *Screenplay* and its ilk mirrored the real life of Hollywood and its movie stars—a picture as "synthetic as the world that the movies themselves portrayed" (Peterson 305)—but typical readers reveled in the pseudo-reality of their favorite stars' lives.

Because of Agnes's connections, Sally also began writing movie reviews and articles for *Screenplay*, *Picture-Play*, *Motion Picture Classic*, and Brewster Publications. Rather than use "Sara Smith" for her byline, she experimented with several noms de plume—"Mahala Redway," "Sara Redway," "Carol White"—and later, as a regular feature writer for "The Screen in Review," her married name, "Sally Benson." In a few months, she followed Agnes into the pages of the *New York Sun* and *The New Yorker*.

Along with her budding writing career, Sally maintained an active social life in dating Babe and several other men.[2] Actively involved in Columbia as an undergraduate, Babe had added a fifth year of study to obtain a master's degree in metallurgical engineering. When he graduated in 1916 from Columbia's School of Applied Science, Sally attended the ceremony and the family celebration afterward at 155 West 101st Street. A four-story brownstone close to Riverside Drive, the Benson home was set back from the sidewalk and boasted a patio adorned with flowering shrubs. A three-stepped, walled stoop led to the front door. Above the entrance was a double-hung window with wrought iron balcony, and above that, a wider bay window. A crenellated roof and four-foot frieze enhanced the home's elegant appearance, as did its most unique architectural feature—the two thick-framed oval windows, one on the second and one on the fourth floors, in a narrow, further recessed section. Today, except for a coat of lavender paint, the building looks much as it did in 1916.

By November, having broken up with Babe once again, Sally turned her attention to Peter Milne whom she had dated earlier. She invited him to play bridge, and he responded:

Dear Miss Smith,

I have just recovered from the shock of receiving your letter. I thought I was never to hear from you again. But now, as they say in the movies, "I'm the happiest person in the world."

I told you once you know that I couldn't play bridge— that's my misfortune. But, if you say so, I'll come down Tuesday night anyway and tackle poker or hearts.

Figure 6. Reynolds "Babe" Benson, student at Columbia University, member of basketball team, 1914–1915

Suppose you aren't coming to the Screen Club ball tonight. And now wouldn't it be dreadful if you had something else for Tuesday.

Very sincerely yours,
Peter Milne[3]

Sally maintained her interest in Peter into December and persuaded Margaret Sommerville to invite him to her party. Milne subsequently replied:

Dear Sal(ly),

(I refuse to go through the formality of writing out "Miss"). I
got Miss Sommerville's card and accepted. Thanks ever so much.
So I'll see you there then, won't I? Not before, I suppose.

You know you so staggered me the other evening by running off at least thirty-four of the gallant swains you were inviting that I didn't have the nerve to offer my base and menial
services as an escort. I do now, though, knowing it's too late.

Merry Christmas and all that.
Peter Milne[4]

Typically, Sally had enumerated the "gallant swains" to impress Peter. In
one of her early *New Yorker* stories, "The Girl Who Went Everywhere,"
Benson reflects a similar pride in numbers by creating a female protagonist
who mentors another girl at a party. "I can't tell you who you will like
here, but I can tell you who to steer clear of," Ellen Hastings volunteered.
She then delivered an account of four "swains," detailing each one's dating
style and warning Miss Smith to avoid "Allen Drummond [who] makes
love to every girl he sees."[5] Though Sally gave her surname to the fictional
ingénue, her alter ego is Ellen Hastings, the character who freely shares
her insider knowledge of multiple men with a stranger.

Before long, Sally's dating patterns grew more complicated as the
German bombing of American merchant ships convinced Woodrow Wilson
it was time to "save the world for democracy." When the United States
officially entered the World War on April 6, 1917, Peter Milne, like many
of Sally's acquaintances and friends, enlisted. So also did Babe, motivated
by the importance of his family's mercantile interests and zeal to destroy
the "Krauts."[6] Ironically, though his mother was of German descent, Babe
claimed his roots were Alsatian and rejected any ties either to Germany or
to his father's English ancestors.

Sally had always admired Woodrow Wilson's peace efforts as had her
friend, Tracy [H.], who had landed a job as correspondent for the president.[7] Using the casual slang and offhand phrases characteristic of the age,
Tracy wrote to Sally offering to use "pull" to have Babe and two other
friends assigned to an inland post:

War! I have been compelled to get "war" into the first paragraph so often that I can't get out of the habit of it even when I am writing a letter. . . . Tell Peter they won't need any American troops at London—the Germans haven't gotten there yet, but I'll use my pull with the Navy Department to get him, Reynolds, and John a job inland if he wishes.[8]

Tracy also appeared to be on intimate terms with Woodrow Wilson:

I've got to stop now and go and call the president. I give him a jingle about two o'clock every morning. He says it gives him a homey feeling to know I'm around and thinking of him, dear old chap, Woodrow. Fond of me too in his diffident, scholarly way. It was only the other day that . . . he tapped me on the shoulder and said, "Trace, old pal," (he calls me Tracc when others are not around) "Trace, old pal, only you know how shy I am at heart." . . . "Yes Woody, I know." . . . I tore my eyes off the coal fire and said abruptly, "Woody, I gotta go." Will I ever forget his heart-racking sob as the White House door banged behind me. Tracy

Tracy's tone—that of the brash flapper—reflects the culture of liberated youth already rejecting outdated ideals as the postwar years would demonstrate even more fully. So too would Benson's later fiction.[9] Her Connecticut stories, based on her teenage daughter—"After the Ball" and "Summer Evening"—satirize the male pursuit of the liberated flapper, defining women's true liberation as freedom from dependence on men, something Sally had promoted in the *Bulletin* during her senior year at Horace Mann.

When Sally mentioned Tracy's offer to Babe, he politely declined. Instead, he enlisted in the Aviation Section of the Signal Corps and served as a pilot with the French army at Verdun, St. Mihiel, and the Argonne, earning the rank of captain in the U.S. Army Air Corps (now the U.S. Air Force) and receiving the prestigious Croix de Guerre.

Given Sally's admiration for Babe, their five-year friendship, and probable engagement, it is difficult to understand why Sally became engaged to nine other male friends in turn as they went off to serve in the Great War. Several of these fiancés—Peter Milne, Jack Johnston, John Lawson, George

Figure 7. Reynolds "Babe" Benson, circa 1917

Ely, and Frank Brady—corresponded regularly with Sally from overseas. How, one is forced to wonder, did Sally convincingly respond to their letters? Only a practiced, inveterate liar or a gifted, imaginative storyteller could manage such a feat. (In this she ironically resembles the "Josephine" of F. Scott Fitzgerald's short stories published in the *Saturday Evening Post*. A kindred spirit, Sally Benson would later transform the Josephine stories into a play, *The Young and the Beautiful*).[10] At home on furlough, George William Ely II wrote to Sally on August 23rd, 1917, asking her to find a date for his friend, Rathbone, so that they might spend Tuesday afternoon together "bus-riding or something. I want to see you again," he urged, "so you fix it as you please, if you please."[11]

As Benson's habitual lying eroded her integrity, her capacity for risk-taking waxed inversely strong and, swept away by the romantic patriotism of the age, she convinced herself that she was in love with each "fiancé" as he went off to war. A similar interpretation lies in Harrison Kinney's appraisal of such behavior on the part of James Thurber's friends, Elliott Nugent and Minnette Fritts. Referring to an engagement that "didn't make sense," Nugent commented in his memoirs that with the men going into the service, "everybody was getting engaged or married" (Kinney 178). As for Minnette Fritts, "she may have been playing the patriotic role with all the romantic fervor that that uncertain period stimulated. She would have done her best not to cause any young man heading overseas in wartime to feel rejected." Kinney refers to Benson's engagements in support of his analysis of Fritts. The argument could easily be reversed to make Benson appear less culpable of hypocrisy. However, Benson's pattern of entertaining multiple relationships predated and followed the Great War. It seems justifiable to regard her several engagements as ethically, if not morally, objectionable.

No matter how many boys she had known and dated during the war, when World War I ended on November 11, 1918, Sally and Babe were reunited and, forsaking the others, Sally honored her engagement to Babe, who began working as an engineer for the Baltimore Steamship Company.[12] One is hard-pressed to know how Sally broke the news to each of her other "fiancés." George Ely, obviously heartbroken, wrote a polite note on the occasion of Sally's wedding, offering congratulations and assuring her a lifetime of happiness. Reflecting on this period of her life, Sally Benson explained in a 1939 interview:

> All the men I was dating in those war years were leaving for overseas. They all asked me to marry them. I became engaged to every one of them in the *morbid belief that they would all be killed*.[13] I was also playing the odds that at least one might survive and come back to me in the midst of what I supposed would be a man shortage. To my embarrassment, they all came back. I married Babe Benson because, as a decorated hero and flyer, he had probably come closer to *getting killed* than the others. If that doesn't make sense, very little in those days did. (Kinney 185, emphasis mine)

When Harrison Kinney interviewed Benson in 1949 while researching his biography of James Thurber, Sally elaborated on her choice of Babe. Besides admiring him as an ace pilot in World War I, she was attracted to him, she said, because he was "strong, silent, and handsome." She read the "most unimaginable wisdom into his silences," she confided. In their friends' eyes, Babe appeared to be a highly desirable "catch" for Sally. Indeed, Sally knew it was a great coup to have snared Babe Benson. His family had plenty of money and he was respected and well liked by all of their friends. However, for Babe's mother, Clausine Doscher Benson, Sally's flighty nature was problematic, if not a distinct obstacle to her son's future happiness.

Characteristically, Sally did nothing to change the behavior that offended her future mother-in-law. Already considered socially inferior to Babe, she made no effort to redeem herself, forging ahead with her marriage plans undaunted. When summoned by an ailing Mrs. Benson to her hospital room, Sally continued making flip responses, causing the ill woman to feel victimized as she lay dying of cancer. As Barbara Benson Golseth explained: "For [Sally's] generation sarcastic humor was everything. It was the in thing in that age. But Mrs. Benson didn't appreciate it. Her family were rather serious German types."[14]

7

WEDDING BELLS

1919–1922

"A girl of her high standards and gay and vivacious temperament will make an ideal wife and companion."

—Katherine Louise Leonard

Shortly after announcing their engagement, Sally and Babe set their wedding date. The ceremony would take place on January 25, 1919 at Sally's home—14 Fifth Avenue—where the newlyweds would live until they found a suitable place of their own. Formal wedding invitations went out to all the family and to some friends. Lon and Jo, living at a distance, had to send regrets: travel from Houston with their three sons was prohibitive. Sally's father also sent regrets from Los Angeles, California. On "Cooper, Coate, and Casey, Dry Goods Co." letterhead, he wrote on January 9th: "Here is $100—for a little spending money. Remember me to Bensonhurst and love to you both. Papa."

On Sally's wedding night, the third and fourth floor windows were unusually festive and bright, spilling light onto the street below as music filled the evening air. The Benson wedding guests entered the building as present-day residents still do, by descending a set of five steps leading to a central door that opens into a small vestibule. Casement windows, six feet tall, flank this door at ground level and repeat in each of the four stories above.

Anna Cora, proud mother of the bride, was happy that Esther (Mrs. Henry Probasco Wherry since the preceding March) was Sally's matron of honor. Agnes and her fiancé, Frederick James Smith, editor of *Motion Picture Classic*, stood next to Rose, Guy, and their boys. On the groom's

Figure 8. Formal portrait of Sara Smith, circa 1919

side were: Edwin J. Benson, Babe's father and a widower since the previous May; Babe's brother and best man, Claus Doscher Benson; and Claus's wife, the former Maxime Harrison-Berlitz, Sally's classmate.[1] A few close friends completed the small circle of guests gathered to witness Sally and Babe's exchanging of vows. Reverend Charles H. Ricker, curate of St. George's Episcopal Church, presided and distributed to all a booklet bound in white leatherette with gold-embossed title: "Marriage Service, Solemnization of Marriage as contained in the *Book of Common Prayer.*" After a brief but solemn ceremony, Mr. and Mrs. Reynolds Benson were proud and happy to celebrate with their guests. In the ample space of parlor, dining room, and library, friends and family mingled. Brown-eyed Sally gazed with mischief into Babe's blue eyes as they danced to "Love's Old Sweet Song" with its haunting first line, "Just a kiss at twilight, when the lights are low." As partners they were well-matched in height—Sally, five-feet-two inches and Babe, despite all his basketball success, just a few inches taller.

Letters of regret had arrived from some of the invited. In one that Anna Cora received from her old friend, Katherine Louise Leonard, a glowing picture of Sally emerges:

Dearest Mrs. Smith—

Most wonderful of mothers that you are! Two weddings in less than a year is going some! It is very sweet of you to ask me to be present at little Sally's marriage next Saturday evening. How I wish it were possible. My thoughts will be with you all. Do give Sally my love and best wishes for great happiness. She must be on the heights indeed to have her Reynolds back again after having passed through these perilous times!

Captain Benson is certainly to be congratulated in being the choice of such a girl as Sally. A girl of her high standards and gay and vivacious temperament will make an ideal wife and companion.[2]

Even those of Sally's friends not invited to her wedding sent congratulations. Ruth, for example, had merely heard about the forthcoming wedding and "not from direct authority."[3] In a January 20th letter from Northampton, Massachusetts, she wrote: "There's a splendid match feeling" surrounding "yours and Babe's step into the realms of matrimony. What a wonder he is! I know you'll be so happy etc." The letter continues:

But, old dear, if you remember in the dark ages I said that Babe was my favorite out of that real crowd, and well, you know what I thought of yourself. You two make me very envious because there really is nothing more ideal, is there, than having the big thing come off. To someone with whom you have so much in common too. I can just see you two having a time. Please call if you're not too busy after the honeymoon. Write and tell us where you're going to live etc. and all about the wedding because even if I haven't seen you all in ages I am still terribly interested. And next year I expect to make myself a nuisance by just visiting all old friends. I wish you both all the happiness which I know you will surely have. . . . please, Sara, occasionally let your old friend Ruth hear from you.

Such letters show that Sally was admired and remembered by many, even those Horace Mann classmates who were not her close friends.

On Thursday, January 23, 1919, two days before the wedding, Sally was surprised by a warm, congratulatory letter from Emma Lenore MacAlarney, one of her English teachers at Horace Mann.[4] On leave during Sally's senior year, Miss MacAlarney had not been in touch with Sally for five years and had known her only as a freshman and junior. It is evident from her comments about Babe, however, that she not only maintained a connection with him but also held him in high regard. From her office at 521 West 121st Street she wrote:

> My dear Sara,
>
> I wonder if you'll have a single minute in your busy tomorrow to read this note of greeting, affection, and congratulations.
>
> Reynolds is such a dear, as you know, and I am so very happy that he is so happy as he deserves. Do you realize the real compliment hidden in that? My very best wishes for your happiness. May the future merely look back in suffering and hardship buried with other hideous things in Germany's downfall. It will be, I know, a future filled with worthwhile things.
>
> Have you discovered, my dear, that the war has made Reynolds expressive?
>
> My warmest regards,
> Emma L. MacAlarney[5]

Emma MacAlarney's remarks about the war and the future seem unnecessarily gloomy in a letter intended to express joy. Possibly, she sensed that Sally couldn't fully appreciate Babe. Or, since she knew Babe's German roots and his family's business ties to several German accounts, she hoped her words might sweeten somewhat the bitter flow of anti-German sentiment still permeating postwar America. During the war and in its wake, such was the American patriotic spirit that the German language and music had been banned.[6]

After a brief honeymoon, Sally and Babe returned to their jobs—Babe to his Baltimore Steamship Company office on lower Broadway and Sally to her First National Bank branch. She spent most of February helping Rose and their mother prepare a first anniversary party for Esther and Henry Wherry. On March 23rd, hosted by the Thompsons, the dinner party concluded with Anna Cora's special cake and a glass or two of wine. Shortly afterward, Sally began to feel squeamish. She suspected she was pregnant, though she had not planned to become a mother so soon. However, watching Rose's pleasure in her newborn, Bobbin, and remembering the fun she used to have babysitting nephew Albert made Sally eager for a child of her own. Wanting to be sure, Sally waited until April to tell Babe and she hoped the news would make him happy. On weekends, when Babe wasn't playing basketball with friends, he and Sally took leisurely walks through the neighborhood or spent long afternoons on the shaded lawns of Washington Square Park. One particularly beautiful Saturday, Sally pointed to a pram and announced to Babe that she wanted one just like it. The secret she had been keeping for weeks was finally out and Babe greeted her news with genuine joy, giving Sally a giant hug. As Sally had hoped, Babe was ecstatic at the thought of becoming a father. He immediately began making plans to find their own apartment, but that would have to wait until Clausine Benson's will was probated.

Anna Cora and Rose were delighted at the news of Sally's pregnancy, and Esther and Agnes hoped they would finally have a niece. During coffee breaks Esther began visiting the infants' department at Franklin Simon to get ideas about outfitting Sally's baby, and Agnes was full of suggestions for decorating Sally's nursery. More interested in reading the latest literature on pregnancy, nutrition, and children's books, Sally took her sisters' enthusiasm in stride. When summer arrived, the Bensons decided it was time for Sally to resign from the bank and they sailed to Asbury Park, New Jersey for their last vacation as a couple. In September they moved into their own apartment on West 101st Street, close to Central Park.

As autumn approached, Sally planned a small party for Thursday, September 23rd, Babe's twenty-sixth birthday. Esther, Agnes, and Rose were willing collaborators, but Sally insisted on making the cake. However, for the November 13th party to celebrate Claus Benson's thirtieth, Sally sent Maxime regrets—her due date was fast approaching. Then, early in the morning on Wednesday, November 26, Sally went into labor. She awakened Babe, who dressed quickly and called a taxi for the ride to St. Vincent's Hospital on 11th Street. After a seemingly endless day, at 10 p.m. on Thanksgiving eve, Sally gave birth to seven-pound-twelve-ounce Barbara Clausine Benson. Telegrams poured in on Thanksgiving Day—from Claus in Washington, D.C., from cousin Champlin (Lon's son) in Houston, Texas: "All kinds of love to our first little girl cousin from Dick and I, Mother, Daddy, and Uncle Hiram." The Baltimore Steamship Company sent theirs the following day, and by Saturday, even Alonzo had cabled from

San Francisco, "My best love to the new baby and surely all of the old babies also, especially the dear little mother, my own Sally baby. Hope to see you all in January." Despite past differences with her father, Sally was touched. She noted, however, that his message was two days late.

Returning from the hospital, Sally was overwhelmed by gifts: flowers from the Madison Floral Company sent by Aunt Ess for "Miss Barbara Benson," a wicker crib and baby cap from Aunt Rose, a silk quilt and two blankets from Anna Cora, a baby jacket and two bath towels from Aunt Jo, two dresses from Aunt Agnes. More gifts arrived from her Horace Mann friends: Ruth Seggerman, Helen O'Connor and her father, Margaret Sommerville, Annette Burr, Alice Tatnall, Harriet van Dusen, Annie Uhink. Eventually, in between Barbara's feedings, Sally wrote each one a clever thank-you note, and before she knew it, Christmas had arrived.

Recalling the festivities later, Sally creatively captured her memories in Barbara's baby book. Though only a month old, Barbara was "not at all put out by the Santa Claus talk and cried as usual on Christmas eve." Her presents were: a set of comb, brush, powder box, and soap dish with forget-me-nots from her father; a spool rattle for her carriage from her mother; a rattle from Ess; a doll from Agnes; this book from Grandma; a set of gold baby pins from Uncle Claus; a pair of pink canvas slippers from Mrs. Parsons (possibly Rachel, Rose's maid), a pair of silk stockings from Helen O'Connor. "Barbara noticed the candles on her tree," Sally added, and on Christmas Eve, when told "Santy Claus wouldn't come if she didn't stop crying," though she "didn't sleep any sooner, she did sleep eight hours to make up for being bad."[7]

How long after Barbara's birth Sally Benson would play the traditional role of stay-at-home mother was uncertain. At first, Benson was so captivated by Barbara's beauty that she spent hours just staring at her in awe.[8] However, such wonder began to fade as the reality of breast-feeding, diaper-changing, and doing laundry encroached on Sally's time. On Tuesday, January 20th, "Barbara's first outing," Sally bundled the baby in "all her coats, sweaters, bonnets, and quilts" and took a taxi to Bachrach's studio on Fifth Avenue and 42nd Street to have Barbara's picture taken. Though it was snowing and sleeting, the ever-reckless Sally kept their appointment, determined that Babe would have his first anniversary gift—Barbara's framed portrait—by Sunday the 25th.

That afternoon Sally confided to Agnes that she was growing bored with motherhood and impatient to return to work of some sort. Not surprisingly, by February 19th when "Bobsie" was only three months old, Sally had already obtained a letter of introduction from Theodora Bean, editor of the *New York Sun*, requesting an interview at the *Morning Telegraph*. Addressed to "Keedick Lecture Bureau, 50th Street and Eighth Avenue," Bean's letter read: "Gentlemen: I shall appreciate very much any assistance you may give the bearer of this, Mrs. Sally R. Benson, to obtain an interview with Sir Oliver Lodge." Since Agnes had previously worked at the *Telegraph* and knew Bean, the interview was easily arranged and Sally's considerable experience, confidence, and energy won her a place at the *Telegraph*—her first paid writing job. When Anna Cora agreed to take care of Barbara, Sally happily wrote in the baby book: "Barbara was put on a bottle on the 26th of February." Sally began her new job the following Monday.

Not until the first warm Saturday in March did Benson get to take Barbara out in her "dark blue English carriage." For the occasion, Barbara wore "a pale pink-and-white sweater, a white bonnet (gift from Aunt Rose), and a white coat embroidered and scalloped." Sally focused on such details of dress often. A further example is her description of the doll Aunt Agnes gave Barbara on her first Christmas. It was "soft and squishy with embroidered features, blue eyes and brown worsted hair, a blue knit jacket and cap, blue shoes and a white dress," Sally noted, adding: "When Barbara first saw the doll sitting under the Christmas tree, she showed that she was a modern woman by turning away and yawning."

As they sipped their Christmas eggnog, Sally invited her sisters and Babe to write their descriptions of the doll on the same page. Agnes observed that the doll's name was Tillie, it "had no hair, beautiful limpid eyes, and feet smaller than Barbara's." Esther's entry was more humorous and personal: "At birth silly Tilly weighed one ounce, eight milligrams and so far has cried much less than her mother. Aunt Ess and Uncle Henry prefer her as an inmate of their house because she is more quiet." Babe's description is the funniest: "Tilly looks slightly cross-eyed but then she's pretty young and her control should improve. She's exempt from baths, hair oil, and therefore misses all the little attentions of Barbara's Ma." One senses that Babe has some experience in bathing Barbara, an effect, no doubt, of a strategy adopted by modern mother Sally to involve modern father in his fair share of domestic duties. Like the doll, however, Babe, too, began missing some "attentions of Barbara's Ma" now that she had joined the workforce.

As Sally and Babe adjusted to their roles as parents, Sally met her new challenges with saving humor. On the subject of bathing Barbara, for example, she wrote:

> This is to certify that Barbara Benson is naturally and instinctively a slovenly child. When she was first bathed, she cried when the water touched her and didn't stop until she was entirely dry. We are happy to report, however, a marked improvement. In fact, it might almost be said that she enjoys her bath. Whether this is due to more advanced civilization or whether she realizes that she is powerless in our hands, we do not know. We only hope that with time and patience we will someday be able to place her dry-eyed in the tub.

Though initially adept at balancing her parenting and writing roles, Sally soon tired of the routine tasks demanded by motherhood. Years later, writing to Katharine S. White at *The New Yorker*, Benson complained, "I never realized what it would be like or I might have drowned her when she was a handy size to get rid of."[9]

Spring brought the discovery of Barbara's first tooth on Thursday, May 13th. "She was eating a little sugar on a spoon and it clicked against her tiny little tooth. Her Aunt Esther felt it first and so was placed under obligations for a present which will be recorded here when received," Sally wrote. On May 18th, pretending that motherhood was like child's play, Benson described dressing her daughter in terms reminiscent of playing with Margaretha and Maude Rockefeller:[10] "Today Barbara is wearing her first short clothes with white silk socks and pink and white booties. She has round, fat little knees and she tries to pull her booties off. She called on her Grandma and startled Washington Square by a dazzling display of limb."

As Benson's writing commitments began to demand more of her time, she and Babe hired a "black woman brought up by nuns" to care for Barbara. Her name was Florence Stewart, and though only twenty-five—just two years older than Sally—she was "old before her time."[11] As Sally had grown up with the Smiths' Irish maid, Katie, so Barbara would have two mothers in a sense, each of a different social class. Sally expected to have household help since the Bensons could afford it, but the most important reason for hiring Florence was that Benson hated being a housewife. For a while, at least, Sally had made efforts at domesticity, unlike Dorothy Parker, who purportedly could not boil an egg and ate all her meals in restaurants (Meade 46).

On October 28, when "Bobsie" was almost a year old, Anna Cora spent several months with Rose at the Thompsons' summer cottage in Madison, Connecticut. Sally wrote often:

Dearest Mother,

Here we are in bed again, I writing and Babe reading *Stories of the Great War*. I haven't anything much to write to you this time since we painted for two days and cleaned up the third and the kitchen is really beautiful.

I am having a Halloween party maybe. Emily and Phil[13] called up to say they couldn't make it. . . . Mrs. Many is away so she has nobody to leave the baby with. Little Bobs is fine now. She got her postal today and she was too cute with it. I told her the mousie went "Squeak, squeak" and the Pumpkinhead went "Booh" and she would point her little fat finger at them. She wants to stand at the window all day by herself—only she gets excited and beats on the pane and pushes herself over backwards. She's about as big as a minute—and smells flowers now.

I bought a fireless cooker at a sale at McCreery's. It hasn't come yet but I am a wreck over it. Ess wanted one too but was afraid Julia couldn't work it. Aggie and I have been getting together on movie scenarios and she's coming to my party.

It's almost one and I'm sleepy—besides this pencil is horrible. We are glad you are coming along so well, poor darling, but hurry home.

Lots of love from, Sally, Babe, and Barbara

The "fireless cooker" Sally mentioned was her new electric stove, a purchase occasioned by an injury Sally incurred by accidentally dropping a stove lid on her foot. When news of her injury reached Alonzo, he wrote from San Francisco:

My dear Sally,

I am sorry to learn from Mama's recent letter of your encounter with the stove lid. If little Barbara herself had dropped a stove lid on her sweet little big toe, I couldn't feel "badder" about it. I am sorry, too, that you are alone although you have Reynolds to keep you and the baby company—at the same time it seems strange that you should be alone. I imagine it seems odd for Ma and Raggie too.

Mama wrote that little Barbara is the best baby in the world—that is saying a good deal. I am sure as we had some pretty good babies ourselves—and Mama should be a very good judge of babies. I hope you will take good care of yourself—don't break any more toes. Give my love to all. Kiss Barbara.

Be a good, dear girl. Papa[13]

Sally was very surprised to hear from her father, who had never visited since 1913 when he had departed for California, causing her and Anna Cora's move to Texas.

Within two years after moving into their own place, Sally and Babe were hunting for another place to live. They had spent the summer of 1921 with Anna Cora in Madison but returned to Manhattan in September. On Wednesday, October 6, 1921, Sally wrote to Anna Cora in apparent distress:

Dearest Wongus,[14]

We have been in such turmoil that I haven't been able to lay a finger on a peice [sic] of paper—toilet or writing—for nearly a week now. Babe found an apartment for us for two months at 2542 Creston Ave. near Emily Many's. It's kind of a chaste looking place belonging to a Professor and his wife and child. Their diplomas from the University of Indiana are hung above the bed and a paper saying that the Professor is a recipient of the Foster prize on his essay on "Conditions Arising in the Pre-Spanish War Period" hangs where the first rays of the morning sun hit it. There is practically no furniture but there is an over-flow of books—the Harvard Classics and what not. In fact, the atmosphere has affected Bobsie to such a degree that she

brought me "Foreign Financial Control in China" the other day
and said, "Mamma, I want to read a book." She plays with all
the other little girl's toys and they willed us a very nice "Goky"
(Russian for Go-cart). The pictures are grand—so tasty—as is
the whole place—dark blue curtains, an Aeolian Vocalion (the
main spring is broken) and two good chairs.[15] Babe took it for
the bathroom which is enormous and has eight towel racks in
it. We are only paying $110 a month for it . . . the main point.

(The professor referred to was most likely employed either at New York
University's Bronx campus or at nearby Fordham University.) The letter's
tone indicates that the Bensons had to move in a hurry, and their intention
to rent for only two months suggests that the turmoil Sally mentions has
arisen from Babe's plan to visit Outer Mongolia and open a trading post
with the fortune left to him by his mother.

In 1921, this north Bronx area was a newly developed, middle-class
enclave bordering the Grand Concourse (today, a broad, heavily traf-
ficked boulevard lined with tall apartment houses). Designed to resemble
the Champs-Élysées in Paris, this main north-south boulevard linked the
Bronx—Borough of Parks and Universities—with Manhattan to the south
and Westchester County to the north. One block west, Creston Avenue
parallels the Concourse, and 2542, the Bensons' new address and the site
of Barbara's second birthday celebration, is just north of Fordham Road,
a major east-west thoroughfare south of 191st Street. One of several five-
story adjoining structures, 2542 was a cream-colored brick building facing
St. James Park, an extensive green area surrounding St. James Episcopal
Church. Today the park extends from 190th to 194th Street, but in 1921
it extended southward, balancing the present parkland to its north. This
beautiful setting provided a fine environment for Bobsie and excellent subway access to Babe's office. The rent—$110 per month—shows that the
Bensons were far from poor.[16] Meanwhile, Anna Cora continued to play
an important role in Sally's life and lavished Barbara with gifts. One was
the coat Sally describes as she deplores her mother's extravagance:

Mother,

Bobsie's coat is beautiful, but it was much too large. When I
took it back, the woman told me it was a two-to-three-year

size. They didn't have one like it in tan her size, so I got one in a kind of gray-green. That sounds awful, but it's lovely with a beaver collar. I also got a green hat trimmed with beaver and made to match the coat. Rose and Ess were along and they were wild with joy. You were a terrible booby hatch to get her such a nice one—for after all is said and done, she's only a skink.

It is interesting that Sally has no ostentatious pride in displaying Bobsie. She is "only a skink."

With amusing detail, Sally wrote Anna Cora to share a scene typical of new mothers unwittingly expecting to shop despite having toddlers in tow. The letter is remarkable because it shows Sally preoccupied with selecting hats to the neglect of Bobsie. Indeed, both Sally and Rose appear unconcerned about their own benign forgetfulness as well as their children's undisciplined behavior:

> We had Bobbin and Barbara downtown yesterday and had lunch with Ess. They were awfully good at lunch but in Best's they let loose.[17] Bobsie had a little chair that the aisle man gave her and Bobbin kept knocking it over—which caused Bobsie to scream every time, and then Bobbin stuck his finger in her eye in a fit of morbid curiosity—so that her eye was red and bloodshot all the time we tried on hats. Then, to retaliate she hit him on the head with a little red wagon. They both ran away and got lost in the Lilliputian Bazaar—and you could hear them shouting "Mama, Mama" in the distance. When we tried on her hat she got in a frenzy and snatched all the hats and clapped them on her head and wouldn't stop—so then every woman in the place wanted to try their hats on her. "She makes such a lovely little model—and she's just my little girl's size"—so finally Barbara was carried screaming from the store with frantic women jamming hats on her head as she went out.

Though unembarrassed by the children's rambunctiousness in the aisles of Best's, Sally was mortified by Bobbin's conversation after lunch in the Vanity Fair tea room: "After lunch I took her in to the toilet and Bobbin waited with Rose across the room on a bench, and when she emerged from the toilet he shouted, 'Babie, did you pee-pee, Babie?' and

she answered gravely, 'I pee-pee'—all this in the Vanity Fair Tea Room."
Talking over the day's adventure later with Babe, Sally could laugh at
the incident, but Babe was amused that the children's conversation about
"pee-pee" had embarrassed her more than their disorderly conduct. Experiences of child-rearing like this shopping expedition inspired later Benson
fiction, notably "No More Cradles," a story that treats of sibling rivalry
in a Christmas setting and implies a mother's wish to have no more
children.[18]

In living through her first years of motherhood, Benson was—like
many of her peers—struggling against the time-honored tradition that
predicated the stay-at-home mother as the ideal role for married women.
The more daring took on careers as did Sally. However, as late as the forties and through the fifties, women's magazines like *Ladies' Home Journal*
continued to publish articles protesting such career choices as destructive
of marriage, detrimental to the children, and productive of discontented
husbands. A married woman's "fundamental job [was that] of being the
heart of the household, with the responsibilities of emotion and imagination which belong to a wife and mother." The drive to achieve success outside the home was deemed "suicidal" by those who believed "the modern,
happy wife and mother in her forties is apt to look like a better-adjusted
and younger woman than her successful professional contemporary in a
thirty-dollar hat."[19]

Sally had always been close to each of her sisters and they were
mutually fortunate that living nearby allowed them to get together often
for shopping expeditions and lunches. Of one such occasion, she wrote to
her mother then visiting Agnes in California:

> I had lunch with Rose today and we went to Wahnie's[20] to look
> for some English golf suits for Rose—but they were awful—I got
> a darling Poiret twill dress and a black felt hat with a black quill.
>
> Rose and Ess are coming up Friday. . . . Did Aggie ever
> get my letters?
>
> Poor Wongus, we didn't give you a single gift and all the
> rest of the house busted their mazzards—but you stick to me
> kid, and you'll wear diamonds. Give old Rags [Agnes] my love,
> and I imagine we'll see you soon. Lots and lots of love to every-
> body from xxxxx Sally and Bobsie.

On December 4, 1921, eight days after Bobsie's second birthday, the Bensons left the Bronx for the West Coast. Shortly, Babe would depart for Outer Mongolia to establish a trading post, leaving Sally and Bobsie with Agnes—now married to Fred—and writing for silent films. During Babe's absence, Sally spent her days writing, planning a vacation in Europe, and taking Bobsie horseback riding. After several months, Babe realized the futility of his trading-post scheme and sailed from Mongolia for California. "He paid the wrong warlord," explained Golseth, "and barely escaped with his life. His partner was killed. Upon returning, he invested unwisely in several projects, among them, the Knickerbocker Ice Co. which went into bankruptcy."[21]

Sally was delighted to be reunited with Babe in July after seven months of separation, the first since their marriage. They spent a few days like tourists, exploring the California missions, Beverly Hills, and Hollywood studios while Agnes took care of Bobsie. On the return train ride to New York, they regaled each other with anecdotes, Babe recounting his experiences in China and Sally reporting on Bobsie's progress and escapades.

At Chicago, the Bensons had to change trains before proceeding to New York. When Ess met them at Grand Central Station, "she was a wreck with excitement" and so was Sally. After many affectionate hugs, kisses, and exclamations, they settled Barbara in the Wherrys' home at 9 East 96th Street in Manhattan while Babe and Sally went to "see about [Sally's] passport." When they returned, Ess had already given her niece a bath and "a beautiful lunch—[she was] perfectly at home." In no time, Bobsie "adored Ess and cried when she left."[22] That afternoon, Sally took Bobsie to Madison, Connecticut, where Rose and Bobbin met them at the train station. Once again, excited greetings and hugs were exchanged, while at the Thompson home, awaiting their arrival, was the lobster salad Rose had fixed earlier. "Bobsie has a dear room," Sally wrote. "She had a hunch I was going to leave her and followed me everywhere. I think she'll be lonesome for a few days," she added, but predicted Bobsie would love staying in Rose's "dear cottage."[23]

Sally's frequent correspondence with her mother during these early years of marriage demonstrates her evolution into a mature woman and devoted daughter. Her feelings toward her father, however, remained hostile. In the summer of 1922, for example, while the Bensons were preparing for their first trip abroad, Sally wanted Anna Cora to join them, but her mother could not. She had gone to Alonzo's home in Santee, California in an attempt to nurse him back to health. On Thursday, July 21st, while Bobsie napped, Sally settled into her room at the Commodore Hotel in Manhattan and wrote a reflective letter:

Dearest Mother,

This is the first moment I have had from the time the train pulled out of the station until now. The trip through the desert was terribly hot, but Barbara was a little angel—played, took her nap, slept until 8:30 every morning (I kept her up later to keep cool at night) and ate like a lamb. I gave her things like cold soups, chicken, and things of that sort and she didn't seem to feel the heat at all.

Reflecting on their train experience, she confided:

Bobsie is awfully funny about you. When I took off her dress on the train, she said, "My Grandma doesn't want my dress off." In the morning she said, "My Grandma wants me to put on my good shoes" or "My Grandma doesn't want you to do that." She says: "My Grandma says I can have candy." You've become a sort of sop to her conscience.

This letter is significant first because it indicates one effect of Sally's working. At two-and-a-half, Bobsie had already established a strong bond with Anna Cora who had babysat both in New York and then California during Sally's stay with Agnes. Secondly, it contains the first overt indication of Sally's hostility toward her father. Before this, she never mentioned Alonzo, though she always asked for Agnes and inquired specifically how Rose and Anna Cora were. Now Sally's concern—whether Anna Cora's car has been repaired—is followed by the warning, "Don't kill yourself in it" and a heartfelt wish that Anna Cora could be going with her and Babe to Europe. "Hurry and come home," Sally urges, concluding, "Kick Pa where he needs it most. Love and kisses, Sally." Both Sally and Babe, coincidentally, were estranged from their fathers. Babe had been so close to his mother that he could not accept his father's remarrying just months after her death. Consequently, Babe never visited the family home and never spoke to his father again.[24]

While in New York, Babe and Sally crowded their days with cultural activities and catching up with friends. On Wednesday the 20th, they saw *The Cat and the Canary*. On Thursday, Ess treated Sally to lunch and a shopping spree at Franklin Simon's where Sally bought a "pretty blue tweed" suit. In the evening, the Bensons treated the Wherrys to "dinner and a debauch," and on Friday they rode to Brooklyn to visit the Vogts.[25] They swam in the ocean and enjoyed dinner before settling into third-row seats at the *Follies*. On Saturday they rose early, finished packing, and bade farewell to Ess and Harry who had arranged a *bon voyage* party aboard the *Rotterdam*. At 11 a.m. sharp, the gangplanks were hoisted up, the departure horn sounded, and the Bensons were on their way to Europe.

8

SECOND HONEYMOON

1922

"Anything to declare?" "Ein puppchen . . ."

—Sally Benson

On August 12 Sally wrote to Anna Cora from the Hotel Ritz on Place Vendome in Paris. "It's one o'clock," Sally confides with pleasure, having just consumed a breakfast of "chocolate and rolls, melon, and a lamb chop wrapped in bacon—ain't we got fun?" She was also ecstatic about their room and savored its details for a future piece of fiction. It was the

> loveliest—gray and rose—with a beautiful, marble mantel and an open fireplace, a huge heavenly dressing table—and a rose and pale green chaise longue with pillows with real lace covers and pink silk ribbons. The beds are covered with rose silk and drawn linen spreads with real lace medallions. Off our room is a good-sized hall for our trunks and a bath.

Both Sally and Babe were "delighted to be out of Germany." Never one to disguise antipathy, she declared: "The only inclination I had there was to kick one and all in the pants. We were three days in Berlin. We stayed at the Adlon—a really excellent hotel—but God how I hated the 'Bittes'—when you step into the elevator the boy gets out and says 'Bitteschoen'; when you get out he says 'Bitteschoen.'" Then, with a mixture of the still brewing anti-German sentiment and a touch of meanness, Sally added: "When you kick him in the face, he says 'Bitteschoen'—It's all they say." Clearly, she had no love for Germany and little awareness that the Germans may have shared a similar dislike of her American speech patterns.[1]

While in Germany, Babe had attended to some business. With a letter of introduction from a Mr. Cooper, Babe visited a firm Cooper recommended. Its manager, Mr. Sachs, had lived for seven years in America, so Sally found him to be "very nice." When Babe had finished with Mr. Sachs, the Bensons rented a car for about ten dollars and drove to Potsdam to see Kaiser Wilhelm's "gorgeous palace with some of the most stupendous rooms. The walls are hung with the loveliest paintings—some beautiful Watteaus." In the mocking tone that colors her fiction, she added: "and over the mantel in the hall, a large picture of old Bill himself." One room particularly impressed Sally. It was "enormous and entirely made up of precious and semi-precious stones and metals—walls, ceilings, and floors—a dazzling spectacle. He had a lovely theatre there, and there were movie cameras and lights in it for some historical picture they are going to make." Little did Sally realize then that twenty years later, in the wake of *Meet Me in St. Louis*, she, too, would be involved in movie-making.

The Bensons next visited Sans Souci, a castle "built for the wild, wild women of the reigning Emperor." Sally marveled at its "millions of stairs leading from one beautiful garden to another. A lot of the rooms were designed for Voltaire who was a *great friend* of Frederick the Great who built the palace. His particular room was designed with monkeys and foxes because that's what Frederick claimed he was," she explained. At the tomb of the "present or erstwhile Kaiser's" parents the Bensons found lifelike figures of the emperor and his wife (Queen Victoria's daughter) lying "on marble couches over the graves. The Prince of Wales is the living image of this Emperor," she added. The Bensons had to bribe the attendant to admit them into the "tomb of Joachim, the Kaiser's son, who killed himself." Echoes of Benson's continual fascination with death pervade her description: "It was really very sad. His sword and plumed hat lay on the tomb, withered wreaths, and the most pathetic message from the Kaiser and his wife—you see he was in exile in Holland and wasn't allowed to come to the funeral."

Sally's mood improved over "tea at some darling palace overlooking the lakes." That evening she enjoyed dinner at

> a restaurant at Luna Park—a regular Coney Island. It was lots of fun—a jazzy orchestra—Americans—and champagne for dinner—you ought to see one of the jazzy Berlin boys—the son

of one of the largest bankers there—with a belted-in coat and shaking a nasty hoof—doing steps at the side like Bert Williams—tell Aggie.

The day ended with Mrs. Sachs joining them for dinner at the Barberina, a "lovely place full of Ambassadors and whatnot. The American-Austrian ambassador sat at the next table to us," Sally noted proudly. Her initial antipathy toward Germans diminished as she began to move among the German upper class.

Not surprisingly, on her last day in Berlin, Sally shopped for hats. She "broke up the place" as everyone watched her trying them on, "with loud cries on my beauty. And they wanted my picture in all the hats." But in spite of all the flattery, Sally purchased only one—a dark red toque. "There was a beautiful hat with egrets for $22—about 19,000 marks—but I didn't want to pine away in jail all my life," she explained. Since graduating from Horace Mann in 1915, Benson had literally tried on many hats—a fitting symbol of the changing identity in process as she experimented with shifting roles—career girl, wife, freelance writer/mother, and finally, fiction writer. When they left Berlin for Paris, Mr. Sachs saw them off and gave Sally "some lovely red roses—the nearest thing he could get to American beauties."

The train to Paris took about twenty-four hours, and Sally knew that about 2 a.m. they would cross the Belgian frontier and be subject to examination by German authorities. "They are very strict about taking things out of Germany," she wrote, "and I was lousy with things." In keeping with her mendacious and manipulative nature, Sally solved the potential problem by putting all her contraband "in bed with me—trusting that my youth and beauty would save me." She fixed her hair before retiring, but "didn't wash off all the powder or lipstick." It was 3 a.m. (the train was late) when "a handsome German officer burst into the room shouting, 'Anything to declare?' and I sat up so innocent and said, 'Ein puppchen' (a doll—it was in my suitcase being too bulky to take into bed with me). 'Oh! Ein puppie' (like saying a dollie) and he smiled tolerantly." The Bensons demanded that he look at it—which he did very much amused—and then left. Sally had co-opted Babe into her deception without any difficulty and the border crisis passed to her satisfaction.

French customs officials were also strict, Sally had been warned, and they hated German goods per se because they were "made so much cheaper than French." Sally had bought Rose a beaded bag because "she's never had one and has missed out on a lot of foolishness like that." At about ten in the morning, Sally put the beaded bag and "several other things in [her] bloomers and sat still." A bearded customs officer knocked to ask what they had to declare. Again, Sally's answer, "A doll," evoked a laugh and the officer quietly moved on. However, "another bird followed" and searched the room "for loot—but mine wasn't in the room. Believe me, dearie, if you've ever slept and sat on a bead bag, and other whatnots, you'd know I suffered. I have designs on me yet," she boasted.

In Paris, because they knew the search would be thorough, the Bensons—with one exception—"declared everything they had in their trunks." In one of her riding boots, Sally had a "funny Dutch doll" and tricked the inspector. "When the officer felt the paper, he thought he had trapped me smuggling jewels across the border and then he hauled out this silly Dutch doll—it's a rag doll and cross-eyed. He got the raspberry from one and all and we came in scot [sic] free—although I have some lovely linen centerpieces, gloves, bags, and toys." The deceptive Sally had surfaced once again. By now, Anna Cora was beyond being shocked by her daughter's dishonesty.

Benson found Paris "Heavenly" compared to Germany, which had seemed "sunk in gloom . . . a very disagreeable atmosphere pervades the place. They hate the French as the French are demanding every cent of the indemnity—and I'm darned glad they are," she gloated. Especially upsetting to Sally was the "vile" German food—"questionable meat cooked in vile oleomargarine." As though needing support, she assured Anna Cora, "You would thoroughly dislike the German people. They are heavy and stupid"—a word used with adolescent abandon in her 1912 diary. In France, by contrast, "everything was different" and Sally's mood lifted dramatically:

The little French towns are pictures and everyone is working like a beaver, building new things. We passed through St. Quentin, Liege, and all the places whose names are so familiar—and the darling little old houses and churches are flat as a pancake—and there isn't a roof on a single house—big shell holes in everything—but in spite of it all—little new houses have sprung up—little shingle houses—and they have put red and green stripes in boards around the windows and doors with darling window boxes—and everything so sweet—although the old stone places with the red roofs are knocked [down] for a row of stoves.

They are building new stations all along the line (with German money) and I'm darned glad of it. The Germans chopped every tree down all along their line of march—but they [the French] have planted new ones and cleared away all the barbed wire for their little gardens.

Experiencing the effects of war was traumatic for Sally no matter how much she admired the energetic French and their recovery efforts. For Babe, revisiting lands he had flown over and bombed was bittersweet. Along with the ruins and ravaged landscape, he could see firsthand what his military service had meant to the French. Sally shared his feelings and thought of how Grandpa Prophater had witnessed similar destruction in his Civil War experience.

Ever conscious of her sweet tooth, Sally suggested a stop at Rumplemeyer's for a chocolate ice cream soda that afternoon. In the evening she and Babe dined at Ciro's. Sally raved about the service and the "marvelous dinner—hors d'oeuvres—chicken Americaine—roasted little young ones with fried tomatoes, heavenly fresh peas, artichokes, pear tarts, and champagne." From the restaurant, they proceeded to the Folies Bergère, which Sally critiqued as:

> very punk—just like a third-rate burlesque show. The girls have nothing on above the waist, but as Ziegfeld is doing that also this year, I suppose it's all right. We went in a little side show and saw some hootchy-kootchy dancers—pretty rough—but then, you don't have to look—as there is a naked lady out in front leading you to expect the worst. However, they aren't naked, so Babe felt he had been gypped.

The next day, Sally loved seeing "all the beautiful things" as the Bensons toured the palace of Versailles. She wished Aggie could have seen "the room where Louis XV's eleven babies were born—three belonging to Madame de la Valliere—four to his wife (a total loss if her picture tells the story. She was Anne of Austria)—and three to another Jane." She explored the apartments of Du Barry and pronounced the "little dressing rooms of Marie Antoinette—very darling," explaining to Anna Cora that Pompadour wouldn't stay in the same house with the Queen so they built her a separate place." Babe wanted to see the Buc aviation fields so they drove there next and "peered around." Obviously, the fields held no interest for Sally. Dinner at Annenville was more to her liking, and she could not help exclaiming: "I *wish* you were here—you'd love it—it's the heavenliest place." She also wished Anna Cora would be in New York when they returned, but acknowledged,

> there is no such luck. Goodbye for the present, angel-face. I'll write again soon. Tell Agnes they sell statues of naked ladies that are made of rubber and wiggle—a large admiring crowd was looking at them—and I wanted to look too, but Babe pulled me away—but I saw for sure that they wiggled.

> Love and kisses, Sally.

A second letter sent from Paris contains a poppy that Sally "picked off the battlefield. The fields are scarlet with them, where the grass has grown up again," she writes. Repeating once again, "You never saw such beautiful country," Sally attaches the sad disclaimer: "But miles and miles of it is utterly devastated . . . the farmers have cleared away the barbed wire and plowed and planted. Yet, in other places it is barren and what trees aren't broken off completely by shells, have been killed by the gas." Though Sally never directly addresses the war's effects, she poignantly hints at the plight of people she has met—working like beavers to reconstruct simple dwellings, reclaiming their land's beauty and fruitfulness. Fields of poppies (in French, *coqueslicots*), though now a magnificent scarlet blanketing the area, had only recently borne the darker red of killing fields.

The next day, Sally and Babe caught their two-hour flight to London. They would sail from Liverpool aboard the *S.S. Cedric* on Saturday, the 26th of August. The seas were rough, and on Tuesday, the 29th, Sally wrote to Anna Cora:

Dearest Mother,

> I can't tell how long this letter will be, or when I may suddenly have to dash away to my bed of pain—for the painful truth is that I've been seasick for three days now. I stagger forth at intervals only to give a low moan and dash back. Food is stranger to me—although olives and ginger ale aren't so repulsive to me.

We sailed Saturday from Liverpool and the boat immediately began to roll about and it hasn't stopped since. Babe says the dining room is quite empty of an evening. I'm all right flat on my back so that I have some minutes of peace.

Despite being seasick, Sally managed to write a rather long, entertaining letter. She and Babe had had a lovely time in London "not so much sight-seeing—but just bumming around." They had seen Westminster Abbey, of course,

> full of tombs—a most impressive spot—guides, tourists, horrible statues—for instance, an enormous statue of James Watt, the "choo-choo King," amid tombs of Queens and Dukes—lots of funny smells—and horrible vestry men conducting parties of sightseers through the place, hurrying them and talking out of the sides of their mouths.[2]

Benson's juxtaposition of "choo-choo king"—notice that she mentions Queens rather than Kings—and royal figures, smells, and vestry men—provides an excellent commentary on the ironic spectacle: the dead lay silent in their royal catafalques, while commoners—the pompous vestry men—disturb the ambience by noisily commandeering tourist gaggles of every social class. Benson's sarcasm emerged full-blown in her next comment: "Also, the Tower of London, where they waste time by telling you to note the thickness of the walls, which is obvious." Expecting the tower to be dark and damp, Sally was surprised to find "it is now used as a museum and troops are quartered there."

Suddenly seized again, Sally abandoned writing until the following day when the ocean was calmer. Sitting in a deck chair and leaning on a small book, she continued her letter in pencil. She started with "small talk"—the *Cedric* was not so clean as the *Rotterdam* but she enjoyed her table mates—two Australians and their mother.[3] Returning to her sightseeing theme, Sally described her "regular Cook's tour of London: saw all the Crown jewels, all Queen Victoria's court dresses, and what not." The rest of the time, she complained, "wasn't put to very good use. We went to teas mostly—and Babe picked me out a chenille hat . . ."

While Sally read or wrote letters, Babe was also busily reading one war book after another—*1914, The Dover Patrol* (2 volumes) and *The Grand*

Fleet, 1914–1916. He had become a "tool in the hands of the [ship's library's] steward," Sally wrote. Ever a shopper, Benson next reported her European acquisitions to Anna Cora: the beaded bag for Rose, a black suede bag for Esther, a pin "painted in China—very cute" for Agnes, a dress for Bobsie, monogrammed handkerchiefs for Guy, a "whatnot" for Anna Cora, some silly things for Bobbin and Barbara, a tiny beaded necklace and a "bottle of perfume on a long green cord to carry in a bag—vile perfume" for Rachel.[4] Sally would have purchased even more in Germany because "the things were beautiful there. Dolls as tall as Barb, beautifully dressed—with eyes that moved from side to side and shut too—for about ten or fifteen dollars."

Benson's interest in dolls and her comparing them to Barbara is noteworthy because it echoes the repeated doll burials in Manitowoc and reappears in her later fiction. "Margaretha," for example, besides being the only doll Tootie Smith did not bury, reappears in "Nouveautes de Paris," a piece rejected by the *New Yorker* but published by *Scribner's* in 1936. In the story an older woman, Miss Hildegarde Ross, sets out to purchase a doll as a Christmas gift for "little Marie Louise Thornton." Benson writes:

> She remembered with pardonable sentiment her own doll, a gorgeous blonde named Margaretha, who had finally rolled down the terrace in her carriage and had been *smashed to bits. Her elaborate funeral had more than compensated Miss Ross for her taking off.* . . . All the way downtown on the bus she turned over tender memories of Margaretha in her mind and by the time she reached Thirty-fourth Street, she was in a pleasant state of anticipation. She wanted a big doll with long yellow curls; a jointed doll with large blue eyes that opened and closed. (57)

As "Nouveautes de Paris" continues, Miss Ross finds the toy department's "corner reserved for dolls." Decorated in blue and white enamel, it "looked for all the world like a modern hospital." A young woman dressed in a nurse's uniform approached, offered assistance, and reached into a crib for "what seemed to be a real baby." This is "our sleepy-time Baby. She looks like a real baby, doesn't she?" asked the sales lady. Miss Ross assented "a little grimly. . . . Yes, she does." The nurse/saleslady continued: "The sleepy-time Baby was designed in wax from a six-weeks old baby . . . That . . . gives the child who owns one a feeling of possession and responsibility." Miss Ross replies: "I can see it might, but haven't you a doll that is more advanced in years?" While the saleslady searches the stock room, Miss Ross examines the showcases and is startled to discover "a complete set of doll's jewelry . . . just such a set as Margaretha had owned." The box contained "a pink and white pearl necklace, a tiny watch that pinned on, a bracelet, a gilt mesh bag, a painted scent bottle and a pair of earrings made for pierced ears. On the card in elaborate gold lettering was printed '*Nouveautes de Paris. Pour la Poupee.*'"

Miss Ross settles for a doll other than the one she envisioned. Its hair is "painted on . . . in the latest bob . . . [its] eyes permanently mischievous and . . . cheeks . . . too fat, giving her a squirrel-like appearance" somewhat like a Kewpie doll. However, when she tries to purchase the jewelry, the saleslady protests, "But that doesn't go with the Debsie Doll," earning Miss Ross's cryptic response: "No . . . I'm sure it doesn't." She has obtained a gift for little Mary Louise but failed to achieve her fantasy wish. She cannot bring back the past. Nothing remains but the "Margaretha" jewelry, a Parisian novelty. Like many Benson stories, this one's ending allows readers to draw their own conclusion.

9

BACK TO REALITY

1922–1926

". . . with your clever pen, you turned out a most enjoyable interview, quite the best I have ever had printed."

—W. C. Fields

The months after their return from Europe saw the Bensons searching for a new apartment. By October, they were settled in their new townhouse, a five-story brick building at 102 North Waverly Place, east of Sixth Avenue and near the Washington Square Hotel. (Built in 1898 as the Hotel Earle, it became the setting for "Apartment Hotel"—Benson's first published piece in *The New Yorker*.)[1] Their Greenwich Village neighborhood comprised several diagonally patterned streets intersecting at various angles, a quaint, haphazard arrangement dating from New York's earliest days. Socially, it constituted a "borderland between the Irish and Italian middle-and-working-class West Village" and the more upscale residential area where Rose and Guy Thompson lived. Four- and five-story townhouses lined both sides of the street, most having exterior steps flanked by wrought-iron banisters leading up to the first floor entrance. Close to Sixth Avenue, Sally and Babe now had to adjust to the regular rattling of the Sixth Avenue elevated train.

Though its deafening rumble often hindered conversation,[2] the Bensons nonetheless entertained friends and family and often paid reciprocal visits to Maxime and Claus, Esther and Henry, or Rose and Guy. They dined occasionally at Delmonico's or Paglieri's, the local Italian restaurant on 11th Street where they sometimes stayed for the dances sponsored by Paul Paglieri. (After diners had finished eating and waiters cleared tables and chairs, the music would begin [McFarland 186].) At other times, Sally and Babe caught a movie at the little cinema on Eighth Street—later the Eighth Street Playhouse.[3] For Sally, such an evening was an important part of her job as movie reviewer.

Interwoven with her writing career was Benson's other occupation: motherhood. On Saturday, November 11th, 1922, cousin Bobbin's third birthday, Sally took Barbara to his party. Outside Rose's house, marching up Fifth Avenue from Washington Square was the annual parade celebrating the Armistice, and the children watched the marchers from Rose's third-floor windows. Two weeks later, as Sally prepared for Bobsie's third birthday on November 26th, she faced an unexpected problem—how to explain why there would be no parade. "Bobbin had a parade for his birthday. Why can't I?" whimpered Barbara. Unable to explain, Sally turned her daughter's attention to packages that the mailman had brought.

Always close to her sister Agnes, Sally and "Raggie" (as Agnes was known in the family) became even better friends as young adults, and Sally regularly kept their mother informed of Agnes's doings. "She looks fine and is going to Rose's for Thanksgiving. I wanted her here because we had a beau for her, but Rose beat me to it." On Bobsie's birthday Agnes visited twice, first to see the party and present "a darling basket of pink and yellow flowers for the table" and later for dinner with a "big bottle of 4711."[4] During the months they had shared in California, when she wasn't writing or taking care of Bobsie, Sally would join "Rags" for lunch and Agnes would regularly invite her to special events like "a festive meeting at the woman's [illegible] club." On one occasion, Agnes took a booth at the "newspaper woman's bazaar" and wanted Sally to help her. By the same token, Sally felt free to invite Agnes to babysit and spend the night so the Bensons could attend the theater or enjoy such events as a "six-day bicycle race with their friends, Danny Meehan and his wife."[5]

A few days after Bobsie's party, on November 30, 1922, Sally wrote to thank her mother for sending two gift books: "She loves her animal book and was awfully impressed with the morals of Robert Louis Stevenson." Then, concerned once again lest her mother dote on Barbara and overspend, Benson chided: "Why did you buy her two, you poor Goof, one would have been plenty." After apologizing for delaying the thank-you note, citing busyness as her excuse, Sally described Bobsie's birthday celebration in great detail. For someone who hated housewifery, Sally had made gargantuan efforts:

Barbara had a party Friday—a luncheon party. There were nine children, including Barbara and Bobbin. The table looked very pretty. I had a wild rose pattern paper table cloth and napkins with blue and pink baskets filled with hard candies, blue and pink poppers, and lolly pops tied with blue and pink ribbon (all ten-cent store things). They played games afterward and every guest won a prize. They had a beautiful time. I had lamb chops, frenched and with the panties on, peas, mashed potatoes, ice cream and a beautiful cake contributed by Mrs. Steinhardt—a pink one with a large "B" on it and three tiny candles.

Benson explained that Mrs. Steinhardt (a neighbor) was "always sending soup over to Bobsie for her supper." Then Benson added with a mixture of pride: "Everyone makes a great fuss over the little fiend. She is so polite and full of manners that she enchants everyone. On her own hook she will say, 'Tell Mrs. Steinhardt, thank you very much.'"

Benson's letter continues with a collection of descriptive statements about her daughter. The first shows Bobsie's growing appreciation for Anna Cora: "My Grandma sent me two books. You can look at one, Mom." The second, "My Grandma lives under the kitchen table," surprised Benson as did Bobsie's insistence on it. Then, Sally cryptically added: "I bet it's nearly the truth." It is difficult to interpret this comment. Barbara could have been indulging in imaginary companionship as an antidote to loneliness—as children commonly invent imaginary playmates. Or, since Benson's choice of a writing career over tending house and raising her daughter potentially distanced Bobsie from her mother, she compensated by attaching herself instead to her grandmother. Yet, Benson clearly loved Barbara. One of her letters to Anna Cora ends: "Barbara is a darling. She knows so much it terrifies me."[6]

As Christmas drew near, Sally joined Rose and Ess in a shopping expedition. All three had agreed with Rags to send "only one box to Lon and Jo" and one large gift to Anna Cora "from the crowd." They established "a real two dollar limit and very modest presents." Correspondingly, Sally warned her mother: "Don't you dare send anything." Seemingly a caution against unnecessary spending, the admonition became an attack on Benson's father: "How can you possibly do anything like that with that old drawback at your heels?" This is the second directly negative reference to Alonzo contained in Benson's letters. Her contempt worsens: "Ess thought me very hard-hearted when I said he could freeze his tail before he got anything from me, but I mean it. I can't see this ten-cent sentimentality of giving things on Christmas to people that you cuss out the rest of the year."[7]

Again on December 8, 1922, as though to remind her mother that all the girls had agreed to send one gift, Benson wrote:

> Dearest Wongus,
>
> Babe is wrapping up the final layer of your Christmas box. There is no special gift from any one person—each gift is from one and all. Aggie couldn't get a hand in tonight to write a card and sent regrets. Rose and I did some this afternoon, and Harry and Ess dropped in for a few minutes this evening. The gifts aren't much. In fact, they are pretty cockeyed.

Snow earlier that day did not deter Rose, Bobbin, and Ess from coming for lunch. Benson served a "grand mess of creamed chicken" and was gratified that a "swell time was had." On December 28, 1922, Anna Cora wrote to Sally from Dallas, describing her trip from California with Alonzo:

> . . . As you know, we arrived here Wednesday the twentieth at 7:10. Lon met us . . . and Josephine was at the station with a wheel chair for Daddy. She is very kind and thoughtful. The trip was hot and dusty—the drawing room in a Pullman is a lonely, stupid place but Daddy was not able to sit up, of course, so I had to take one with an electric fan working overtime. We were sweltering and you, Agnes, know it takes the whole day and more to cross the desert—fortunately we did not change cars, our sleeper came straight through to Dallas. This is a nice bright town, but it's like a country village compared to Los Angeles, but one can see at a glance it's a hustler and Lon seems happy here—poor dear works very hard.

As her mother's letter continues, one notes a striking resemblance between Benson's and Anna Cora's diction.

> I forgot to mention before that we had no idea of leaving L.A. until some time in January—but Daddy was quite bad, and I

felt I could not stay alone any longer. It was getting horribly on my nerves, and when he was feeling a little better, I feared he was annoying Mr. Cooper going in every day. He may not have, but I think when one is a bit off they are as companionable as a jellyfish. I had applied for reservations to leave Wednesday but the boobs disposed of it and we were forced to go earlier or wait until after Christmas.

One can see that in some respects Sally had acquired some of her mother's temperament. "The boobs disposed of it" is something Sally might have said in a moment of pique. She also shares to some degree her mother's interest in material things, while simultaneously recognizing the absurdity of excess. Interestingly, Rose is the only one who sent her father a Christmas card.[8]

Benson could not have known that Christmas of 1922 was to be Alonzo's last. He died the following May at St. Paul's Sanitarium in Dallas, Texas, from a cerebral hemorrhage. Anna Cora had been with him during his last year, giving him "constant care and watching," first in Santee, California, while Sally was in Europe, then accompanying him to Texas for his last months. Sally, if she had her way, would have kept her mother from journeying to Alonzo's bedside. Neither Esther (particularly bitter about her father's absence) nor Sally—lacking any compassion toward her father—attended Alonzo's funeral. Yet, friends who comforted Anna Cora considered Alonzo "one who was loved by all who met him." They also praised Anna Cora's devotion to Alonzo despite its taking so heartbreaking a toll on her.

Concern for her mother's finances continued to echo in Benson's letters to Anna Cora. After Christmas, she added this postscript: "You poor Goof, how much was the freight on our stuff you sent—if you don't tell me, I'll send ten dollars anyway, so you'd better come across." Though she was not extravagant, Benson always enjoyed shopping trips. "Yesterday," she wrote, "I got a lovely dress . . . long and dashing." She drew a picture for her mother, explaining the embroidered designs in red and gray and blue, the circular skirt long at the sides, and the dark blue dimity (or something) fabric. She confided the price—forty-five dollars—and asked: "That isn't bad, is it?" (Ironically, later on Sally would become a spend-thrift—buying anything she saw and turning to alcohol when she could not face the bills.)

During these early years of her marriage, Sally continued to publish regular movie reviews in *Screenplay*, *Photoplay*, and *Moviegoer's Guide*. Her feature, "The Screen in Review," for *Picture-Play* in 1925 was often two and three pages long. Her cynical, offhand tone and diction in these reviews echo her letters and diary. Using first person, she expresses likes and dislikes with equal emotion. Take for example: "*Chickie* is the type of picture I dislike on literal principle, but it is bound to be popular. Any story showing the struggles of a poor working girl is bound to find an audience, and a pretty large audience, too." As for the actress, Dorothy Mackaill, "she manages to make the role appealing in spite of the fact that she gives the impression of walking in her sleep." Overall, the movie struck Benson as "a lot of false, silly, distorted nonsense," in a word, "bunk." She concluded, "I would like to have the money that this picture is bound to make. I am sure that it will be considered a thoroughly moral story. It isn't." Though her critical terms are unsophisticated, her critical judgment is perceptive and provides a clue to the fiction Benson would later write—moral, but serious—and laced with humor and wit.

Benson sprinkled her reviews of several silent films with her characteristic humor. Her appraisal of *The Talker*, for example, was: "Someone looking in the old trunk in the attic must have come across the story of *The Talker*. The moths had eaten a good bit of it, which is just as well, and I bet it made them ill." Waxing positive about the *Crowded Hour*, Benson praised its female star: "Bebe Daniels is *fine* [Benson's favorite word for something she really likes]. She has a tremendous lot of vitality, and her acting is never dull." As for Theda Bara's return in *The Unchastened Woman*, Benson found most of the film "vulgar, badly directed, badly acted, and in every way perfectly hopeless." With a surprising twist, however, she ended: "I enjoyed it."

Benson's feature articles—"Maxims of the Super-Flapper of the Films" and "Normalcy and Miss Gish"—appeared in *Motion Picture Classic* in August and September of 1925, respectively, both under her Sara Redway pseudonym. Subsequent issues contained articles titled: "W. C. Fields Pleads for Rough Humor," "Not a Dry Martini Story," "D. W. Griffith: The Man Who Kept to Himself." In October 1925, "A Jazz Interview with Harrison Ford" appeared in *Picture-Play*, and in February 1926, *Motion Picture Classic* published "Just the Victim of Publicity" (Sally's article on Gloria Swanson) under her Carol White pseudonym. Benson also wrote articles on Belle Bennett, Adolph Zukor, John Roche, and Richard Dix for *Motion Picture Classic*. She received positive fan mail from readers and sometimes from her celebrity subjects. One glowing note, for example, came from W. C. Fields:

Astor Hotel,
New York City,
August 22, 1925.
Miss Sara Redway,
Brewster Publications Inc.,
175 Duffield Street
Brooklyn, N.Y.

Dear Miss Redway:

Many thanks for the Wonderful and interesting interview you wrote concerning myself in the September *Motion Picture Classic*. I was afraid that with the meager [*sic*] and uninteresting details I gave you, there would be little material with which to work; however with your clever pen, you turned out a most enjoyable interview, quite the best I have ever had printed.

> With many, many thanks.
> Believe me sincerely,
> [signed] W. C. Fields

Recounting the story of her writing career years later in an interview on May 18, 1941, Benson told Robert van Gelder that she started writing as an interviewer on the *Morning Telegraph* and "did a piece each week. . . . Saw authors, actors, actresses, all kinds . . ." She particularly remembered "a mass interview when a whole flock of girls went to work on Sinclair Lewis." Benson, seated next to him, was appalled by the kinds of questions he was asked. One, for example, was "how he thought English women compared to American women." She claimed that she liked Lewis, that he held her hand, and that when he asked her what she would like to know, she replied that she "hadn't any questions at all." She added the disclaimer, "That was the interview. But I guess I got some space out of it." It is difficult to determine whether Benson is once again lying, exaggerating, or actually telling the truth. In any event, she moved on to a "pulp paper house" where she wrote reviews of movies—about thirty-two a month—and earned a monthly salary of $75, supplementing it "by doing more interviews" (Van Gelder 182–83).

Marsha McCreadie's study, *The Women Who Write the Movies*, provides more precise information on Benson's start at the *Telegraph*. Not only does

McCreadie's account differ from Benson's version, but it also shows Benson being deliberately deceptive in her effort to gain employment at the paper. As she had talked her way into her first job at National City Bank, now she maneuvered herself into a writing job. At a performance of *Queen Victoria* in 1923, Benson was impressed by Ulrich Haupt in the role of Prince Albert. Determined to meet him, she "went backstage . . . introduced herself as a reporter . . . and asked for an interview." Having subsequent qualms on the "deception she had practiced," she wrote a story about him and sent it to the *Morning Telegraph*. The editors not only accepted it—they also "asked her to write special features for their Sunday editions" (128). McCreadie also notes Benson's writing for several "fanzines," particularly *Photoplay* (where Agnes's husband Fred Smith was editor).

When Agnes Smith began to experience difficulties in her marriage, she moved back to New York and stayed temporarily with Rose and Guy. Needing a job, she made an appointment with Harold Ross, editor of *Judge*—an American humor magazine—to explore her chances of filling a position as movie reviewer.[9] Ross was known to both Anna Cora and Agnes through his wife, Jane Grant, and after the interview, Agnes reported to Anna Cora in Texas:

> Darling Mother,
>
> . . . You remember Harold Ross, don't you? He is Jane Grant's ugly husband. Anyway, he thinks he might want someone to do the movie reviews but it is rather unsettled yet, so for the present he just wants contributions. Frank Adams and Bob Benchley recommended me, which was very sweet of them.

Before starting at *Judge*, Agnes spent several afternoons and evenings with Sally. She described how despite Sally's aversion to housework, she met culinary challenges such as inviting Agnes and her friend Alison Russell for dinner and managing to serve "roast pork, Irish and sweets [potatoes], apple sauce, string beans and a fruit salad"—though she arrived from work "at nearly five-thirty" without having done one thing for dinner—except the Spanish cream she made that morning. On another occasion Agnes described for her mother, "Yesterday, Fred, Woody Cowan, and I had dinner with her. Fred and Woody are on diets and couldn't eat a thing but everything in sight. However, they couldn't drink anything so after dinner

Woody took some pills for rheumatism and got quite bummed so we sat around and sang until late." At Rose's, Rachel got Agnes's breakfast every morning, but Agnes "straightened up [her] room and the bed looks all roughed up like a fever chart." Fred, she reports, is the "same old fool . . . and very wearying. I'd scrap with him and tell him where to go only I don't want to pay for my own meals. I think he knows he has me in his power while you are away." Like Sally, Agnes urged her mother, "Hurry up and come back. Don't let them kid you into staying."

When Bobsie was a little older, the Bensons moved once again, this time to their own Greenwich Village townhouse at 243 West 11th Street. One of two attached four-story, red brick buildings, its front yard boasted an ivy bed bordered by flagstone sidewalks, urns of red geraniums, and an eight-step exterior staircase with wrought-iron balustrades leading to the main entrance. Wrought-iron guard rails and balconies adorned casement windows and French doors, respectively, while crenellated woodwork and chimney pots framed the roof. Directly across the street was a church.

As Benson became more involved in her writing, Barbara grew up virtually alone and complained of having nothing to do and no friends to play with. Working mothers were a rarity in the early twenties, and it took several years for Barbara to understand how much her mother had needed her writing career. "My mother's idea of hell was 'to be a house-wife.' She was very defensive on the subject of home-making."[10] While Sally's independent personality and aversion to domesticity caused Barbara occasional distress and feelings of rejection, her mother also suffered. The tension she experienced from combining the roles of stay-at-home mother with professional writer eventually surfaced in the paradoxically titled "One Fine Day." Rejected by *The New Yorker*, the piece was published in Scribner's and included in Benson's *People Are Fascinating*, "One Fine Day" portrays a young mother wallowing in depression and striking her child for an apparently trivial reason. The reader is clearly aware of the woman's sense of entrapment in a room "small and dark and ugly" with dingy, cream-colored walls. "She hated the room and its small neatness and the sight of the two dull green plants on the window sill," which the florist said would grow anywhere (285). But these didn't grow, nor did they die. Like Benson, feeling doubly trapped within her roles as mother and wife, they merely sat on the windowsill collecting dust and soot. Yearning to be outdoors in the bright sunshine, she pulls a chair close to the window to prepare her daughter's lunch.

Shelling peas—ironically freeing them from their containing pods while she remains trapped in the pod of her own life—the woman suddenly longs to be "a little girl again, hurrying through small chores so that she could be free to run, hot and excited, down the road to the sound of children's voices playing." Nostalgic for her childhood freedom Benson wrote: "She could see herself running on thin legs, scratched and bruised, pounding down the path, . . . hair blowing back from her face." Such memories of her twelve-year-old self make this woman's apartment "grow very small" and give her the "dreadful feeling of being shut in" among cheap furnishings and things that evoked "meanness . . . bordering on poverty. . . . She saw the mediocrity of herself and Sam, and Agatha and of their life together" (287). Depressed, she overwhelmingly desires "some stroke of good luck or sudden tragedy" to "quicken the beat of the day." One is reminded of Benson's diary entries during her Texas exile: "If only something would happen."

When the daughter refuses to eat lunch from the bare, white porcelain-topped kitchen table and stubbornly insists on her customary setting in the living room, irrational anger prompts the mother to strike her several times "sharply across the face." Ordering her to get out, she blurts: "I'm sick of the sight of your face. . . . get out, before I give you the worst whipping you ever had in your life" (291). The sniffling, terrified child runs out of the apartment, and the piece ends with the mother face-down on her bed, sobbing in despair. Benson avoids sentimentality with a surprise touch: "But even in her despair, the noise of her sobs in the dull little room somehow sounded good to her" (291). Given Sally's antipathy toward being a housewife, it was fortunate for Barbara that the *Morning Telegraph* and the various pulp magazines had decided to employ her mother.

Barbara's complaints of boredom and loneliness as she grew up in Greenwich Village are reminiscent of Al Hirschfeld's drawing "A Greenwich Village Childhood" (Bell 56). It portrays a girl of eight or so, leaning on a windowsill and forlornly gazing at the street below. The interior of the apartment is sketched in some detail—draperies frame the large window, a chandelier hangs overhead, a large planter containing an amaryllis stands to the right just below a German beer stein. To the left is the dining room table with tufted chair. Decorative plates line the wall above. Centering the scene is the foreshortened backside of a pigtailed child, one leg crossed over the other, elbows leaning on the sill. Across the way are three townhouses that match her own. What she views in the street below is matter for speculation: women wearing short skirts and bobbed hair, now more widely acceptable in 1926 than in prewar years; a horse-drawn carriage or two with passengers; or a fruit-and-vegetable wagon stopped curbside, its old horse feeding from a bag of oats strapped around its neck while the driver-turned-vendor bargains with customers; a street cleaner with large-bristled broom, ensuring the street's tidy appearance; but, no children. At about the same time, Babe brought home a wire-haired terrier, but when Bobsie asked what its name was, her father answered, "Call him 'Temporary' because he's not staying very long." (Tempy was a great companion for Bobsie after school and she managed to keep him until he died of old age when she was sixteen.)

Wanting a reprieve from parenting, in the summer of 1926, Sally and Babe sent their six-year-old daughter off to Cathedral Pines, a camp for girls on a lovely lake two miles from Winthrop, Maine. Whether real or exaggerated, Sally reasoned, Barbara's loneliness might abate somewhat if she spent a few weeks at camp. However, as it turned out, Barbara was one of the youngest campers, and worse, there were no other six-year-olds. She cried all the time because she was so homesick.[11] Finally, in early July Sally and Babe drove to Maine to visit her. On Saturday morning, July 17th, Sally wrote to Anna Cora from St. John, New Brunswick, Canada, describing their trip. The letter reveals a more poetic, even contemplative side to Benson and an appreciation of natural beauty that rarely surfaces in her fiction:

> There isn't one other soul on the lake but the children. Their tents are ten feet from the water in amongst beautiful tall pines and the ground is simply a carpet of pine needles. She sleeps in the tent with Mrs. Schloemer and two little children her own age. The tents have elevated wood floors and wood cots. Bobsie had her rabbit elaborately pinned in a bath towel and the other little girls had towels around seedy looking dolls.

The contrast between Bobsie's carefully wrapped rabbit and the other children's "towels around seedy looking dolls" hints indirectly at Benson's pride in providing her daughter's apparently new toy as though to compensate for the time and attention Bobsie lacked. Yet, in her later fiction, Benson often ridiculed materialistic women for attaching importance to possessions—an effect of wisdom gained through experience.[12]

The letter continues:

> They were on a nature walk when we got there, and the first thing we heard was Bobsie saying, "That wasn't a nature walk. That was a poison ivy walk." The riding teacher says that she is the best pupil in camp and rides far better than the older girls, and they were all full of praise for her. Mrs. Schloemer said she was less trouble and more capable of taking care of herself than any of the others.

Naturally, having grown accustomed to entertaining herself, Bobsie had acquired independence by default. It is no wonder that the child appeared to love camp. Benson wrote:

> I asked her if she wanted to leave and she said she was afraid New York would be too hot. They are in the water twice a day and on the fourth of July they had a masquerade. They dressed Bobsie in her mosquito netting as a fairy. She is painting pine cones and told me that what we call "snake spit" wasn't that at all but was grasshopper eggs.

Though proud of Bobsie's accomplishments—riding, learning, participating in camp activities—Benson fails to communicate her appreciation to Barbara.

> We stayed for supper—every night the supper committee picks a different spot to eat and this time we ate on a high rock overlooking the lake. Big wicker baskets of sandwiches, home-made ginger bread and fruit, and an icy cold 3 gallon can of milk from the morning's milking are carried to the spot—and the girls certainly do clean up on everything. There are thirty-two girls. Bobsie doesn't turn her hand—the girls hold her on their laps and wait on her. They call her "Goofer" and told me a long string of her bon mots. You don't need to worry about the attention she's getting. I am afraid there is too much of it. They laugh at every-thing she says. . . . Mrs. Doust's son who goes to Columbia is there and Bobsie adores him. He carried her around most of the time.

The latter detail sheds light on the general sadness coloring Benson's relationship with Bobsie. Any child who hadn't seen her parents in weeks would have been clinging to them with delight when they visited. But, Bobsie, as if ignoring her parents, clings to her favorite camp councilor and lets him carry her around. Was she trying to make her mother jealous? Ironically, Sally added: "She was a little sick on the boat and so were the others as it was a little rough. She asked after Toby and you and Ess." Nowhere in the letter does she mention that Barbara was happy to see her or Babe, for that matter. When Bobsie chooses to remain at camp, the Bensons depart as they had arrived—without much display of emotion. Benson's letter continues: "Mother, you have no idea of the beauty of these woods. They are not filled with underbrush but are clean and heavenly." Though Barbara remembers being miserable, her mother makes no mention of her daughter's camp experience to Anna Cora. Yet the evidence is clear in a letter to Sally from the camp director, Mrs. Doust:

> I am extremely sorry for any anxiety you have had concerning her, and can understand your not being satisfied with the philosophy that "no news is good news" especially with such a little fellow. She's a darling child and is gaining splendidly now with good color. Everybody is fond of her but as I told you before, nothing spoils her. She just takes the world as a great big friend. It's lovely to have her with us. I know you are lonesome for her, but please don't worry about her as she is well, happy, and beloved.[13]

Obviously, Sally had been very concerned when she visited Bobsie at Cathedral Pines and had spoken with Mrs. Doust to complain of Bobsie's weight loss and pallid appearance. She never betrayed such thoughts to Anna Cora to spare her any worry or, more likely, she was unwilling to intimate even to her mother that sending a six-year-old to camp for an entire summer had been a poor and unwise decision.[14]

Traveling together unhampered by having to entertain a child, the Bensons proceeded from Winthrop to Augusta and spent the night in a typical small town hotel "where the Senators stay." The following day, they headed for Bangor, "branch[ing] off the main roads . . . on the airline route . . . a wood road over the tops of the mountains, just wide enough for one car to pass." It was absolutely deserted, and when they finally met one old fellow driving a wagon, they asked, "Where is the town of Beddington?" Sally had never heard the native, Maine woods accent and couldn't believe her ears when the man took his pipe out of his mouth and said: "Wall, I guess you're about in the heart of the city now." Driving further, they passed through sections of

> deserted houses or poor, poor, inhabited ones. And as far as you could see not a soul or a village, only lovely lakes and mountain streams. And the wild flowers! Lupin [sic], iris, waxy white flowers, big orange ones—all perfectly beautiful—and out of the wilderness you come to Calais, the last town in Maine, called "Callous" by the natives.[15]

In this section of the letter, Benson's love of nature is palpable—a far cry from the cynicism many critics ascribe to her public, fictional persona. Freed of her confining, New York world, Benson blossoms when surrounded by natural beauty.

As the letter continues, Sally recounts their itinerary as many vacationers might. Passing through customs, they encountered "horrible American officers" and "exquisitely polite and handsome Canadian ones." When they arrived at the Admiral Beatty Hotel in New Brunswick, Canada, they discovered they were in a dry area, but some drugstores, at least, were legal vendors of "hootch." After leaving New Brunswick, the Bensons came to what Sally considered "the sweetest town—St. Andrews." When she discovered "a real little English Inn with hunting prints and steel engravings all over the walls," she convinced Babe that this was the perfect place for dinner. They enjoyed a hearty meal and "a couple of bottles of ale." The next day Babe announced that he had to "pay a call on these old people named 'Odell'—Uncle and Aunt of Dr. Elliott of Columbia." (Professor Elliott was a member of Columbia's Department of Physical Education and Babe was his assistant.) Taking a "little town boy along" as guide, they found the Odells' place and what proved to be a very moving experience for Sally.

Her account of this visit presents a very different view of a woman so often labeled as cynical and mordantly witty. Filled with compassion, Sally exclaimed:

> And, oh! Mother, I wish I'd never gone. It was the most terrible thing I'd ever had happen to me. They live in a lovely big home

and they were sweet and old. They said they had expected us to stay a few days, and we sat and talked pleasantly for a while, and then I said: "This is the loveliest big house I ever saw." And the old lady said, "Yes, it is big for just two of us. We built it when things were different. When we had Percy, our boy who died." And she took me upstairs in this huge place followed by an old wheezy spaniel up to this boy's room where all his things were—just as he left them. He was a young man killed in the war and they showed us every picture of him. Taken like Lon in a little velvet suit with a white lace collar—taken in snow shoes—in every way—taken with the dog when the dog was a puppy—it was terrible. And the house was huge and neat and these distracted people living there. I can't tell you how sad it was. They begged us to stay and I wanted to, but Babe wouldn't. They literally clung to us. When we left I was a shattered wreck.

Sally's strong, compassionate reaction to the plight of the Odells had to have sprung from memories of the pain, loss, and sorrow surrounding her family's loss of John Perry—a loss Sally never consciously acknowledged but one that haunted her throughout life.

Also surprising is the capacity for deep feeling Benson reveals as well as her certainty that her mother would share her emotion. She senses not only the Odells' loneliness and sadness at losing their son but also how the size of the house magnified that loss, emphasizing Percy's absence.[16] The detailing of "all his things" left in his room and the contrast between the puppy of the photos and the "wheezy spaniel" that followed them upstairs, most likely sniffing familiar objects for the scent of his dead master, verges on the sentimental but allows an insight into Benson's capacity for empathy rarely found elsewhere. This is not the flip young woman who irritated her prospective mother-in-law or strode into First National Bank demanding a good job, nor the thoughtless twenty-year-old accepting engagement rings from several men. Indeed, Benson was a more complex woman than most people realized. Her compassion for the elderly couple was such that she was moved when they begged the Bensons to stay and "literally clung" to her and Babe. She wanted to comfort the Odells by extending the visit; Babe disagreed. One can only imagine their conversation, Sally pleading and Babe refusing. How, one wonders, did he deal with Sally's feeling like "a shattered wreck" as they left?

Having long practiced the art of putting her own feelings aside, she did so once again. Years later she evoked the powerlessness she felt at the Odells' loss in a *New Yorker* piece titled "Homecoming." In this case, the loss was not caused by a death but by the protagonist's son's marriage. Mrs. Scott chooses not to attend her son's wedding, preferring that she meet his wife in her "own little place" where she has not changed a thing in Richard's room. She offers to send him his things, and as she prepares to do so, experiences a powerful sense of loss similar to Benson's evocation of the Odells' loss.[17]

Sally and Babe next drove on to St. John, another eighty miles, making it three hundred for the day. Coming through a patch of woods, they thought they saw a horse cross in front of the car so they slowed up only to discover a "big cow moose and her child. Imagine, Mother, a moose!" Sally exclaimed. "It stood a minute and crashed into the woods again with her baby. I saw a hedgehog too," she added. Still enamored of the natural beauty surrounding her, she continued: "This is the loveliest town in the world and Canada is heavenly."[18] Sally ends with some homey details—no Americans are registered at the Admiral Beatty, fresh mackerel and hot muffins were served for breakfast—and most significant of all, a strong expression of feeling: "I never want to go home. No matter where you stop here it's clean and pretty—no gasoline pumps nor hot dog stands— just lovely villages smelling fishy and heavenly. We are going to cross the Bay of Fundy to Nova Scotia tomorrow." Just as she was finishing, Sally was nicely surprised: "I am just presented with a glass of ale by my husband—made in New Brunswick," and she splattered a few drops on the stationery for her mother to smell as "a souvenir from Babe. Love to Ess, Toby, and yourself—Sally."[19]

PART II

10

A WIDER WORLD BECKONS

THE FIRST CASUAL AFFAIR—1927

"We didn't bother divorcing; we just took up with other people."

—Sally Benson

When Bobsie returned from camp, Sally enrolled her in public school and began inviting Betty Knight, Bobsie's kindergarten friend, to spend weekends. (Betty was the daughter of Eric Knight, author of *Lassie, Come Home.*) While Bobsie was enjoying Betty's companionship or playing with Tempy, her mother was exploring greener pastures. In the spring of 1927, to Babe's consternation and Bobsie's dismay, Sally abruptly set off on a trip to France by herself "to have some fun." She boarded the *S.S. De Grasse*, leaving Babe and Florence Stewart, the Bensons' maid, in charge of Bobsie. A photograph shows Benson on the ship's top deck beside a flotation device labeled "De Grasse." She appears *très chic* in fashionable cloche, dark coat—its white lining contrasting with her flapper dress—and high-heeled, ankle strap pumps. Her pose is slightly "rakish"—one leg straight, the other, bent as she leans on the railing. One hand in coat pocket, the other holds an envelope purse. Though supposedly alone, Benson most likely had a companion—one of the many *beaux* with whom she began the first of her "casual little affairs."[1] His identity remains unknown, but several possible candidates exist, among them an unidentified "Jim" who wrote on December 5, 1927:

Sally,

I have tried several times to reach you in the last few days and am beginning to suspect like the fellow after he had been kicked downstairs for the third time, that I am not wanted. But I can't say "Goodbye"—if that's what all this means—without telling you how wretchedly and sincerely sorry I am if I have hurt or offended you in any way. I offer my most heartfelt apologies to you and would gladly do the same if the opportunity presented itself to any persons in whose eyes I have hurt you.

As Jim tries to analyze the reasons for Sally's apparent rejection, he provides a glimpse of her unconventional relationships:

I suppose you are angry because I did not immediately come over to your table at Jack Delaney's the other night. That is the only thing I can think of. Please take my word for it that I did that NOT in an unfriendly way or with the idea of putting on the indifference stuff in an attempt to put you in your place. I may be dumb but not that dumb. . . . You were there with friends, and one of those friends, unavoidably perhaps, had broken up or broken into three parties of mine with you. I decided I, at least, wouldn't break into any party of his. Of course, I can understand why I should take a back seat when Bill Stayton comes to town and I was taking it that night— not from pique or jealousy but because of rather foolish pride and a sincere belief that that was my rightful place. I am sure that if I took you into Jack's, I wouldn't want every fellow you knew to leap up and run to our table. And as far as Bill and his brother knew, I was just a fellow you knew. The reason I finally came over was because of what you said to me out in the hall. It hurt me dreadfully and I knew you were offended and I tried to make amends for what was an honest mistake on my part. If this is not the cause, then I am all at sea, for I know of no other.

That I should hurt you deliberately, Sally, is unthinkable. I would as soon strike you in the face. You mean far too much to me and have done far too much for me. I couldn't do it. If your idea is to punish me, then believe me that I have been punished enough already. . . . I've suffered beyond your fondest expectations. You may think you've been hurt and unhappy, but you're just an amateur. . . . If you'll believe me and not dislike me *too* violently in the future, then I'll have peace of mind, at least.

Before ending, Jim begs Sally to let him see her once more because "he'd like to explain and say 'goodbye' in person." He repeats his fear that Benson is "terribly angry" and claims certainty of it because, "Florence is such a clumsy prevaricator. Write 'Yes' or 'No' on a sheet of paper and send it to the *Times*," he implores. If Sally should refuse, he offers his "goodbye," adding: "You made me very, very happy, and the rest of it I won't go into here. I hoped that you would give me the things that have never been—for me. But—Sincerely, Jim." A postscript begs: "And please don't let a foolish mistake of mine break up our friendship. You know what it would mean to me never to see you again. You haven't got it in you to be that cruel, have you, Sally? Jim." The intensity of Jim's feelings for Sally and his expressing them so close to her European vacation point to him as a likely companion. How Sally received the letter and what her feelings were for Jim are matter for speculation.

Given Benson's lifelong pattern of attracting boys and men, one suspects she simply ignored Jim's plaintive missive, trampling on his feelings as she had done a decade earlier in dismissing her fiancés. Jim's adulation could have fed a certain arrogance in Benson as her imperious, disdainful mien in photographs from this period suggest. Or, did she hate men as daughter Barbara claimed? One thing is certain: she kept the letter. Whether to count it among her many conquests or to affirm her sense of identity when bouts of depression threatened, Sally valued the letter's sentiments, if not its scribe.

Jim's references to Sally's nights of partying place her solidly within the social context of the twenties and ring true to the persona revealed in her teenage diary. His letter also indicates that she returned from her European cruise in time for Christmas—evidence that Babe's ploy had worked. He had sent Sally an enlarged snapshot of Bobsie hoping it would prompt her mother's return from France. In the photo, eight-year-old Barbara, in plaid dress and drooping knee socks, sits in a slip-covered armchair, gazing forlornly at the floor and hugging Tempy. "My father had it taken to try to get her to come back," Golseth recalled.

A second possible companion for Sally's European venture is "Auden," who wrote on July 17, 1930 on Hotel Moliere letterhead:

Dear Sally,

I returned last week to Paris and will remain here for quite a long time. As you can see, I am again in Hotel Moliere, where *nothing has been changed and everything is full of memories* and that's why I'm writing you this letter which however may not receive a cordial welcome. *But Paris makes one remember* [italics mine]. I am sending you wishes of best of auguries.

　Sincerely yours, Auden

Sally was clearly part of the Parisian memories Auden cherished. Why he doubted her cordial response to his letter is unclear.

A third candidate for the mysterious partner/partners is John Lawson, the playwright who, while traveling all over the country and the world, had continually corresponded with Sally since 1917. Just three years her senior, Lawson found in Benson an appreciative audience for his ideas on theater in general and his accounts of his own productions, in particular. Writing to Benson on Tuesday, August 5, 1930, he informs her that he wouldn't be arriving in town until Monday, August 11th. "Please, oh please, leave word with Florence when I may see you," he pleads. "Any day after that [the 11th] will be alright [*sic*]—but this silence is breaking my heart. I'm glad you haven't come to the city because it's so frightfully hot," he adds, "but you might have left a message. Please [triply underlined] do. John."

The years from 1915 to 1927 had been eventful for Sally Benson. She had experienced a World War and had been initiated into the worlds of business, marriage, and motherhood. She had also moved into her own home but changed addresses several times. With a two-year-old in tow, she had traveled to Los Angeles and back after sampling life in Agnes's screenwriter's world. She had embarked solo on a European voyage and indulged in several casual affairs.[2] As a writer she had adopted several pen names—Mahala Redway, Sara Redway, Carol White—besides using her own, Sally Benson. At home she was "Ma" to Bobsie and "Goofer" to Babe. Sustaining her through the process of self-discovery was the abiding love of Anna Cora, Rose, Esther, Babe, and Bobsie. With their support, no matter how difficult her life became at times, Sally Benson would not trade places with anyone.

As for Sally's relationship with Babe, Golseth had this appraisal: "My parents were not at all compatible. My mother had not one athletic bone in her body and I have no idea why she married him."[3] Though Sally and Babe were opposites, the truth was they remained good friends throughout their lives.[4] Their correspondence—both in its regularity and content—illustrates their enduring good will and love for one another, their shared love of natural beauty, their humorous approach to life, and their concern for each other's well-being. Sally later explained: "I realized he really didn't have anything to say to me, so we went our separate ways. We didn't bother divorcing; we just took up with other people" (Kinney 513). Her recollection contains half-truths. Babe was reserved, but as James Thurber later commented after Babe dropped in on one of his parties: "Babe was boring everybody stiff; he couldn't talk about books or anything anybody else was interested in. He didn't leave until four or five a.m." (Kinney 610).[5]

In abandoning conventional attitudes toward marital fidelity, Sally and Babe were not alone. The twenties, in Gilman Ostrander's view, witnessed an American revolution against traditional morals in the wake of Darwin's and Freud's theories on evolution and sex. Postwar manifestations in the popular culture erupted notably among the young who were swept away by ragtime-inspired dances like the Charleston and the Fox Trot. The flapper image became the new norm for women who readily shed their mothers' ankle-length skirts for knee-length ones and their upswept hairdos for boyish bobs. Modesty thrown to the wind, women began smoking and frequenting speakeasies. Kissing, once the preserve of the engaged couple, now became common practice in any budding relationship and led to greater freedom regarding petting and extramarital sex. As women embraced this new sexual freedom, they also questioned their traditional role as housewives. Many sought employment outside the home—as factory workers, telephone operators, secretaries, teachers, or professional entertainers. Finally, some attained positions as writers—initially in publishing—and shortly in the growing music and film industries. Sally Benson would stake her claim to fame among the latter.

11

CLIMBING THE CAREER LADDER

BENSON AT *THE NEW YORKER*—1928–1929

"We consider this to be one of the best first pieces from someone who has never written for us."

—K. Angell

Sally Benson's prior experiences—interviewing celebrities of the publishing and theater worlds for the *Morning Telegraph*, writing movie reviews for pulp magazines—made her a successful candidate for similar work at *The New Yorker*. Her sister, Agnes Smith, already hired as staff member by the magazine's managing editor and founder, Harold Ross, once again steered Sally into a position tailored to her talent and interests. Benson would read each night a newly published mystery—a genre she loved—write her review the next day and send it to the magazine. At the same time she continued her feature, "The Screen in Review," for *Screenplay*. Then, in 1928, in response to a request for serious fiction from *New Yorker* editor Katharine Angell, Benson submitted "Apartment Hotel."[1] To Benson's great delight, the piece was accepted for publication and appeared in the magazine's January 12, 1929 issue.[2] Sally Benson's successful career as short fiction writer for *The New Yorker* had been launched.

Ironically, Benson partly owed this new development in her career path to the shifting nature of her relationship with Babe. When Sally Benson returned before Christmas from her extended stay in Paris, she and Babe reconciled but agreed to continue "taking up with other people" while remaining friends—an unconventional pattern but one not uncommon in the twenties. Whether cause or consequence of the Bensons' marital difficulties, in 1927—eight years into their marriage—Babe Benson had taken an apartment in the Hotel Earle at 32 Washington Square. Sally often visited. Besides maintaining their friendship, such visits also furnished Sally with the theme and material for "Apartment Hotel," a story that treats boredom as a problem facing both young and old.

The nine-story, red brick Earle had been built in 1902 as a residential hotel in a then-affluent section of Greenwich Village and named for its owner, Earl S. L'Amoureux. In 1908 an identical building was added to create one grand apartment hotel with reading rooms, a restaurant, and banquet facilities.[3] Here Sally Benson observed the hotel's upper-class residents, especially those who regularly dined in its restaurant. She rubbed shoulders with couples like the "Morrisons" and learned their daily routines:

> Although the dining room opened at seven and closed at nine, they made it a rule to breakfast at eight. Their table was in a corner by the window . . . distinguished from the others by a fern in an etched silver bowl. It was Mrs. Morrison's fern and Mrs. Morrison's bowl. Sometimes . . . she took the fern up to their sitting room . . . to give it a breath of fresh air. . . . The sitting room was full of personal touches. Even if Mrs. Morrison did live in an hotel she believed in trying to make it homelike. (*People Are Fascinating* 203)

Benson's story follows Mrs. Morrison through her typical day and focuses on her need for change from deadening routine activities—shopping, crocheting, entertaining friends by day and playing two-handed rummy in the evenings. While this pattern was not Benson's, she seems to have shared a strange kinship with characters like Mrs. Morrison and Agatha's mother in "One Fine Day." Both pieces reflect Benson's growing difficulties in accepting the roles of mother and wife—difficulties compounded by the Bensons' casual affairs. Written in 1928, in the wake of Benson's sojourn in France, "Apartment Hotel" ends on a note of mild disappointment and resignation. By contrast, "One Fine Day," written six years later and published, not by *The New Yorker* but by Scribner's, concludes in anger, violence, and rejection.[4]

Benson, like her female protagonists, felt trapped within her marriage. Like Mrs. Morrison, she hated routine.[5] She could easily imagine Mrs. Morrison on a bus, her ears perking up as a young couple converse about their previous night's drinking and clubbing. Her mind turns to strategies for persuading her husband to dine out—for a change—in the club mentioned. Neither she nor the agreeable Mr. Morrison realizes the place is a speakeasy, and ignorant of the password, they are denied admission. Returning just in time to order the "regular dinner" in their hotel's dining room, they fall back into familiar, inevitable routine. Benson concludes: "As Mrs. Morrison waited for her consommé vermicelli, she leaned over and picked a dead leaf from the fern in the etched silver bowl."[6] A magnificent touch, the dead leaf symbolically represents the death of Mrs. Morrison's hope for some excitement and variation in her life. It also conveys a suggestion of Benson's awareness of her own social isolation and the diminished vitality of her marriage.

Benson learned *The New Yorker* had accepted "Apartment Hotel" from Katharine S. Angell's letter, which arrived in the post-Christmas mail. Dated December 24, 1928, it read:

Dear Miss Benson:

We are delighted with your story on the old couple living in the apartment house and are very much pleased to use it in the *New Yorker*. Our check in payment is enclosed now. We are so glad you sent it to us because we feel sure that you should contribute regularly to the magazine and we consider this one of the best first pieces we have had from someone who has never written for us.

Years later Benson still savored the sweet taste of success that the piece represented. During a 1941 interview Benson claimed: "It ['Apartment Hotel'] was immediately accepted and the editors told me it was the best manuscript they had ever received from an unknown." During the same interview, Benson falsely stated that she "had only one story rejected" by *The New Yorker* and had "never written an unpublished story."[7] Clearly, besides forgetting her first story's publication date (she cited 1930), Benson exaggerated Angell's wording. "One of the best" had become "the best" in Benson's mind.

Angell's acceptance letter also noted what Benson omitted—that *The New Yorker* editorial staff had made "one slight cut" and were still "anxious for a title." If you have no ideas at all, Angell continued, "perhaps we can think of one, but I am sure your own will be better." Before concluding,

Angell encouraged Benson, "And do remember more manuscripts soon."[8] Benson later admitted to editor Wolcott Gibbs that she hated to "wrack [her] brain" for titles. She frequently submitted untitled pieces or merely suggested titles. In the case of "Apartment Hotel," Babe's move to 32 Washington Square had simplified Sally's choice. What specifically impressed Katharine Angell in Benson's "Apartment Hotel" was its "lack of elaborateness" and "plot," standards she subsequently advised Benson to maintain.[9] As the magazine's chief literary editor, Angell (soon to become Mrs. E. B. White) played a major formative role in Benson's budding career.

While publication of her first story gave Benson entrée into the world of *New Yorker* fiction writers and Benson rejoiced in her first payment, some bad luck followed. Just as the January 12th issue carrying Benson's piece went to press, Benson suffered a personal violation—her house was robbed—and she lost favorite pieces of jewelry and some cash. She immediately telephoned Ess, who wrote to their mother, then traveling in Italy with Rose and her son, Bobbin. (Rose had embarked with Anna Cora on a European retreat after Guy Thompson discovered Rose was having an affair with a Frenchman— Pierre Houpert—and filed for divorce. As a diversion from the pending ugliness surrounding the case and as an opportunity to meet someone else, Rose had taken her mother's suggestion and booked passage immediately.)[10]

Anna Cora wrote to Sally from Florence as soon as she could:

Sunday, January 27, 1929

Dearest Sally,

A letter from Esther a few days ago telling us of your heart- breaking experience with sneak thieves—I just cannot tell you how very sorry I feel for you—it is almost more than I can bear to dwell on for I know how keenly you feel, my dear little girl. Esther had two or three bitter experiences in that neighborhood.[11]

Anna Cora's affection for Benson, her youngest daughter and still her "dear little girl," is palpable in the salutation and in her hoping that Benson's thyroid is giving her less trouble.

She also complains—she would have frozen were it not for the "*Scaldi- nos*" that "fat old priests . . . put in [our] beds"—and praises Mrs. Godkins's hotel overlooking the Arno, where the food was plain but "wonderfully cooked" and plentifully served and the accommodations first class—"nice, warm drawing room, a base runner—unusual here—furnishing the heat and the stone floors covered by a heavy carpet."[12] The next day she visited a beautiful, old Carthusian monastery. Set "high upon the hills with magnificent terraced gardens and lovely orchards of edible chestnuts and olive trees," it afforded a perfect view of Florence and an opportunity to buy "fine liqueurs, soap, and chocolates, all made by the monks."

Benson's 1922 letters to her mother conveyed trust that Anna Cora would understand, if not condone, her deceptive ploys to evade French and German customs duties. By the same token, the content and tone of Anna Cora's letters to Sally imply Benson's appreciation for her mother's faith: "I went to Mass in the Cathedral this morning, the atmosphere all one could ask, the service not at all as devout and inspiring as in our country." Across from the cathedral, Anna Cora adds, is the famous baptistery where she met Rose and Bobbin:

> —we saw these dear little Italian babies baptized—from five days old to fifteen. Never have seen prettier little creatures—all so well dressed—and the priest handled them all so gently and so carefully dried their heads so they wouldn't take cold—and the old assistant did his bit by coming forward with a powder puff and dust[ing] the little damp heads. From there we went to the Cathedral museum, then to the Bargello . . . the Palace of the Podesta . . . where all the executions took place. It was a cold spot so we started for our Pensione [and] on the way came upon Dante's house.

Her mother's determination not to miss a thing was a quality Sally inherited. "This afternoon we go to Fiesole—five miles out of Florence by tramway—we must hustle a bit—we plan to leave here Thursday for Rome." Anna Cora's stamina, unflagging at sixty-seven, was another part of her mother's legacy. Amused by Anna Cora's comic touch—"We always dread heading for a new stop, with our piles of luggage which at every stop grows some heavier," Benson also noted the juxtaposed irony of Rose's securing a "very reasonably-priced Pensione." Shopping and budgetary restrictions rarely had conflicted in Benson's youth, and if such conflicts arose in adulthood, spending always won—even if Sally had to borrow money.

Anna Cora's letter also offers insight into her parenting. Glad that Rose had taken her suggestion to travel as a diversion from the Thompsons' imminent divorce proceedings, Anna Cora was also engineering Rose's future: "I think Rose will have a better time in Rome . . . socially, I mean. There are so few travelers . . . here . . . but in Rome we catch up with the Harold Lamb family and other people we met on the ship." Ever a practical woman, Anna Cora, like Jane Austen's Mrs. Bennett, had always been on the alert for an eligible match for her daughters. Her thoughts next turned to Westport, Connecticut, where Agnes and Fred Smith awaited their firstborn: "I think of dear Agnes. I'm glad for her sake the ordeal [Agnes's pregnancy] will soon be over. Do you see her often? Has she kept well?" Benson, always in close touch with Agnes by visits and telephone calls, was glad to share her prenatal expertise—a first—since Agnes until now, had been the older, wiser sister. The two bonded more deeply as they awaited the baby's birth.

Anna Cora's letter also reveals a major development in Benson's relationship to "things": "Darling, I won't bore you longer. Don't worry too much over things . . . bear it. You have always my fondest love, Sally dear, and in the loss of your precious rings and trinkets, my sympathy—it's heartbreaking. Affectionately, Mother." Sally essentially shared Anna Cora's spirit of detachment from perishable possessions. Both mother and daughter cherished what really matters—enduring love and compassion—and in some *New Yorker* pieces Benson satirizes characters who prize objects to the neglect of personal relationships and simple pleasures. In "The Perfect Hostess," for example, Benson critiques class-conscious snobs like Andrew Selby who, unlike his hostess, Mrs. Torrey, prides himself on never having set foot in Woolworth's. A "lover of the beautiful" and a collector of "Stiegel glass and pewter," Selby feels bound to be reticent about such interests "because people are so funny about anything of that sort nowadays."[13]

Inwardly appalled at Mrs. Torrey's custom of buying cheap earrings at Woolworth's, he merely pretends to like her costume jewelry. Mr. Torrey increases Selby's discomfort by mixing cocktails in a "bottle that had once contained tomato juice." Benson slices away at Selby's pretentiousness as his hostess, thinking to make him feel at home by inviting him to help prepare dinner, pins a bath towel around his waist unaware of his horror at the lint it deposits on his suit. Mrs. Torrey, in fact, has succeeded so well in making people feel at home that most of her "nice things, wedding presents and some china" of her husband's grandmother "had been broken." Selby may even throw his cigarette ashes on the floor, she assures him, because "That's what a home is for, isn't it?" The final sentence—"Mr. Selby . . . had never been so miserable in his life"—completes Benson's study in contrasts, leaving the reader disgusted at both Torrey's crassness and Selby's condescension, while appreciating the "perfect" hostess's unique, if misguided effort, to place her guests' comfort above her pride in possessions.[14]

Benson's stance vis-à-vis material goods was complicated. While she knew her readers' propensity for social climbing and the magazine's commitment to satisfy such readers (even courting advertisers whose ads might entice readers to buy both the magazine and its advertised items), Benson frequently articulated a different aesthetic. Though she liked fine things and avidly "consumed" hats in particular, her fiction often cautions against preoccupation with possessions despite *The New Yorker's* "upper echelon of middle-class readers' [reliance] upon consumption to establish status and distinguish themselves from others" (Corey 203). From childhood, Benson had demonstrated an egalitarian spirit, circulating with ease among poor farmhands like Delmar Hansen or the wealthy peers she knew at Horace Mann.[15] In adulthood, when money was no object, Benson spared no expense in her personal life but also gave charitably to the needy. She had known both deprivation and prosperity, and, though her family enjoyed upper-middle-class, privileged lives for the most part, Benson had also witnessed Anna Cora's cultivation of moderation and avoidance of unnecessary expense.[16]

While Anna Cora, Rose, and Bobbin continued their tour of Italy, another more serious event occurred: Benson's brother, Lon, died suddenly in Dallas, Texas, on February 25th. Funeral services were held on the 27th at Highland Park Methodist Church.[17] Reportedly caused by "an apoplexy," Lon's unexpected death at the age of forty-four resulted from alcohol abuse, a pattern—like his multiple job moves—learned from his father.[18]

When Lon's partnership in Houston with fellow Princeton classmate Fred Parker had dissolved in 1920, Lon returned to New York with Jo and the three boys to become a sales executive with Converse and Company at 88 Worth Street in Manhattan. For a year and a half, he was content to commute from his 33 Sanford Avenue home in Rye, New York, but, in 1922, responding to the "lure of the Southwest," Lon took a job with the Lamport Manufacturing Co. and moved the family back to Dallas. Their new home at 3824 Miramar Avenue was spacious enough to accommodate Lon's sickly father and Anna Cora when she decided she could no longer care for him alone in California. However, seven years later, Lon was "Dallas representative of Max Kaufman, a New York wholesale cotton cloth firm."[19] Nine at the time, Barbara Benson remembered that when he visited Esther during a business trip to New York, Uncle Lon was so ill with pneumonia that "Aunt Esther brought him to a doctor who sent him to a hospital. Not long after that we learned Uncle Lon had died."[20]

Benson had always liked Lon and found his death particularly difficult. Worse, with their mother and Rose in Europe and Agnes's baby due momentarily, only Esther or Sally could represent the family at the funeral in Dallas, but because of the distance involved, both decided to remain at home near to their children and Agnes. As she confronted the reality of Lon's death, Benson thought of John Perry's death long ago and wondered how her mother in Rome would handle the news being wired to her. Benson drew consolation from Babe's presence and she determined to preserve Lon's memory one day in her fiction. On a happier note, the family rejoiced five days later when, on March 2nd, Agnes and Fred Smith welcomed Frederick Anthony's birth.

12

PUBLIC SUCCESS AND PRIVATE SORROW

1930–1931

"I wouldn't write so much as a recipe for fifty dollars. . . . And I walked out."

—Sally Benson

Benson published nothing for the remainder of 1929, but when she resumed writing fiction in 1930 as the Depression worsened, she drew upon a rich base of experience. Like F. Scott Fitzgerald, Sally Benson was beginning to question her role in "a whole world going hedonistic."[1] With the confluence of Lon's death from excessive drinking and awareness of Babe's and her own binge-drinking weighing on her mind, Benson produced several pieces reflecting both nostalgia for her Midwestern roots and concern about alcohol. In "Summer Evening" (August 16, 1930), for example, lonely Miss Barrett muses over a solitary dinner at the Vagabond Tea Shoppe about how she will spend her evening. Options are: invite Ethel to spend a night of "cold-cream, manicure, and gossip"; wait on a call to play bridge with the Sayers; "take a book from Womrath's and read all evening"—as Benson frequently did.

En route to her New York apartment, Miss Barrett waxes nostalgic for home and "people . . . sitting out on their front porches smoking and talking in the dark." Barrett takes "three turns around the block" before she can face going in—a sentiment Benson understood. Once inside, Barrett's telephone rings. The caller, Dutch, announces, as John Lawson or Bill Stayton or any of Benson's other male friends often did, "Here I am in town [after two years] . . . with a big shaker of ice-cold cocktails. . . . I've been crazy to see you. You know I've been sorry I made such a fool of myself. Will you let me see you?" Directly echoing "Jim's" sentiments in a 1930 letter to Benson,[2] Dutch then lays out the evening's plans—dinner on "some roof," "some place cool . . . ride around a bit . . . and go someplace and dance . . . [maybe] Riverside Drive about One Hundred and Eightieth Street where it's just like the country." Having allowed Dutch to elaborate on his evening plans, Barrett finally admits: "This isn't Betty." After Dutch's awkward silence and apology, she responds, "That's quite all right . . . I had a perfectly lovely time." The reader smiles wryly (as Benson likely had when finishing the piece) at Dutch's embarrassment and Barrett's vicarious pleasure in her fantasy date.

"When Witches Ride," Benson's third *New Yorker* piece (October 25, 1930), sharpens the contrast between a remembered world of simple, Midwestern social patterns and the actual, sophisticated New York venue Benson shared with her protagonist. Mrs. Bixby stands wistfully looking out the window of a four-room Central Park West apartment and "feeling vaguely, after Saturday nights, that something was wrong with the world. On Sunday afternoons she looked back on her youth . . . in a Middle-Western town . . . the good times she used to have and the crazy things she used to do." Bixby confronts her nostalgia this time by deciding to have a "real old-fashioned Halloween party. With games and everything."

As she plans the event with her husband, he protests: "You can't give those folks just plain cider" and he laughs for the first time that day. As for the punch his wife next proposes, Mr. Bixby refuses to "feed that crowd any of my good rum. Nor any of my good Scotch. Do we ever get anything like that when we go to their houses? Do we? . . . Let them drink gin." (It is easy to imagine the Bensons having the same discussion, especially since Sally had planned a similar Halloween party when she and Babe were first married.)[3] As Mrs. Bixby acquiesces, the doorbell rings and a friend enters with a pint of rye. When they invite him to the Halloween party, their visitor, in turn, proposes taking all twelve Bixby guests to dinner at "Romeo's" on 53rd Street beforehand. "How about it?" he queries, looking at Mrs. Bixby expectantly and "anxious to please her." Mrs. Bixby returns: "That will be wonderful," the flatness and brevity of her response in stark contrast to her earlier, enthusiastic party-planning. Benson's abrupt ending underscores her protagonist's unwilling but expected compliance to the men's wishes while delivering an implicit three-pronged critique. First is the men's failure to understand Mrs. Bixby's desire for a simple party; second, their inability to break familiar, urbane, social patterns; and third, Mrs. Bixby's passive capitulation to their wishes.

In Mrs. Bixby, Benson reflects her experience of being surfeited with the sophisticated formality she observed about her. She participated actively in New York's social scene—partying in Greenwich Village with Wolcott Gibbs, James and Helen Thurber, John O'Hara, Aristide Mian—but Golseth pointed out that her mother "was not really one of the Roundtablers."[4] She was not "sure of herself and put on a big act. She was never relaxed with them."[5] Her true self rejoiced in the freedom from city noise, "gas pumps [and] hot dog stands" she experienced while driving "clean and pretty" Maine roads to Canada in 1926. For the same reason, she loved Connecticut's beautiful countryside and shoreline.[6]

Benson's "When Witches Ride" appealed to those readers who shared her love of nature and simple, family traditions.[7] It also spoke to Benson's editor, who sent an encouraging note along with Benson's check:

> Everyone thinks [it] is one of the best you've done for us. As we're using it right away—in the issue of October 25th . . . I took the liberty of putting a working title on it which you may or may not like. If you don't, will you give us another, of approximately the same length, as soon as you can. . . . Mrs. White wanted me to tell you to be sure to send us a lot more pieces.
>
> Sincerely yours, Wolcott Gibbs[8]

To *New Yorker* editor Wolcott Gibbs and his staff, bent on appealing to the magazine's audience of upper-middle-class "wannabes," Benson's Halloween piece satirized Mrs. Bixby's gauche, unsophisticated, Midwestern style of socializing. Readers, he assumed, would identify with native New Yorkers like Mr. Bixby and the visitor. In their view, neither Halloween nor the presence of fourteen guests should interrupt one's pattern of dining and drinking at expensive restaurants. Rather, Halloween constituted another good excuse to indulge in a night on the town. Benson could identify with such recipients of ostentatious splurging, having dined often as a guest of Bill Stayton (and others) in some of New York's finest dining clubs and restaurants. But, like Mrs. Bixby, she preferred simplicity. Gibbs and the magazine's staff, however, considered the real object of Benson's satire to be people like Mr. Bixby, normally a tightwad host, but a *bon vivant* when feasting at someone else's expense.

Gibbs wrote again with another check for an untitled Benson story he tentatively titled "Play School." Gibbs explained that two slight cuts had been necessary "entirely for length" but gave Benson the prerogative of suggesting others if she did not approve his excisions. He reiterated Katharine White's plea, "Most important, please send us a lot more pieces."[9] Once again, his "complimentary close" is the formal "Sincerely," but within a few months it would change to "Love, Wolcott." That simple change, achieved so quickly by Benson, is a tribute to her engaging personality and charm, for Gibbs "liked few people and had a bitter tongue" (Kinney 514). A New York "swell," he was the *New Yorker*'s drama critic and John O'Hara's intimate friend and drinking companion. Both met regularly after work at Bleeck's on West 40th Street next to the *New York Herald Tribune*'s back entrance.

Pronounced "Blakes" and known as the Artist and Writers' Club, Bleeck's speakeasy had become a watering hole for neighborhood journalists. Though "women were not encouraged to enter the premises until 1935," it is not inconceivable that the deceptive Sally Benson managed to slip in on occasion. If so, she would have found an unpretentious room with plain furniture and a low ceiling, its walls adorned with hunting scenes and Thurber drawings "depicting the match game whose losing players had to buy drinks for all the others" (McShane 39). Often Gibbs and fellow drinkers like St. Clair McKelway and William Maxwell moved on to dinner at Tony's and the theater, followed by more drinks afterward (McShane 42). Sometimes Sally Benson was included because—besides Benson's charming personality, her ease in male company, and her readiness to socialize—the quality of her fiction had endeared her to Gibbs. In this she distinguished herself from John O'Hara who, despite his close friendship with Gibbs, had his submissions to *The New Yorker* regularly rejected by its editors as "too obscure" for the magazine's "pretty dull" readers (Bruccoli 1975, 63).

Though elated by her career's upward spiral, Benson soon found sorrow and loss shadowing her success. One example was Babe's growing involvement with her good friend Helen Wismer, who had been dating sculptor Aristide Mian. Sally and Helen had shared common interests—writing, humor, drinking, and men, including Mian—and now, Babe. Superior to Babe intellectually but craving the entrée into Village life that he could

provide, Helen often invited Babe to visit her office at the Fawcett Building next to the Algonquin Hotel. Since Helen edited pulp magazines like
Daredevil Aces—a publication Babe read with avid interest—their friendship
naturally and easily developed.[10] Earlier, Sally had marveled at Helen Wismer's determination to "marry somebody on the *New Yorker*" since many
of Benson's male colleagues considered Helen unattractive. "Brown-eyed,
worrisomely thin, tall, lantern-jawed, flat-chested, knock-kneed . . . near-
sighted" was Harrison Kinney's appraisal of Wismer, though he conceded,
"there was an attractive cuteness about her" (513).

Like Dorothy Parker and other *New Yorker* staffers, both Babe and
Sally Benson indulged in the hard living and overdrinking common during
the twenties.[11] Helen Wismer remembered a typical party in 1929 hosted
by Ann Honeycutt. Wismer knew that Ann had a "semiserious intention
of announcing her engagement." Wismer recalled: "It was a very drunken
evening. God knows what we were drinking—raw alcohol, gin drops, and
grapefruit juice, probably. We all drank so much. We ended up in a base-
ment speakeasy, and Gibbs's head fell in the soup when the engagement
was announced" (Bernstein 215–216). Wismer met James Thurber that
night but did not get to know him until a year later "at the Bensons' New
Year's Eve party."[12]

A second example of the troubles stalking Benson revolved about
family. Even before Lon's unexpected death in 1929, the Smiths and Ben-
sons had encountered changes in fortune, some predictable, others not.
Rose's impending divorce had meant, among other things, giving up her
Fifth Avenue home to settle permanently in Madison, Connecticut, where
she and Guy had summered since 1921. This move necessitated, in turn,
Anna Cora's purchasing a small house in nearby East River, Connecticut.
After returning from Europe, Rose made several trips to Ohio while the
divorce was pending. During one such trip, she met an Ohioan—Herbert
Wright (Sam) Shuttleworth—who had inherited the estate of his wealthy
wife, Jessie King Tolese, after years of serving as her chauffeur. A scandal to
Ohio's upper class and to Tolese's children, Sam's crossing of class lines to
marry Jessie mattered not to Rose—a girl "in need of a fortune."[13] When
the Thompsons' divorce became final, Rose married Sam Shuttleworth and
brought him to Madison where they purchased "The Captain's House."[14]

Always outgoing and interested in people, Rose became actively
involved in Madison's social life and began writing articles for the *Shore
Line Times*. Later, she also served as president of the Madison Historical

Society and supported Principessa Constance Wilcox Pignatelli's project, the Jitney Players, even acting in their productions.[15] Anna Cora and Sally frequently attended performances and after-parties hosted by the principessa.

While summer provided moments of relaxation for Sally, Babe faced the unpleasant task of visiting his brother at Saranac Lake, New York, where Claus had relocated in the hope of recovering from tuberculosis. On July 28, 1930, after dropping Sally and Tempy at Grand Central Station to catch the train to Madison, Babe drove a friend to Haverstraw, New York and proceeded "up the west shore" and across the Hudson via the Bear Mountain Bridge before checking into the Marion House Hotel for the night. After a hearty meal, he "smilingly refused" both the hotel matron's invitation to play bridge or "meet some of the girls" and the manager's suggestion of a poker game. "I know these hotel slickers," he boasted in his customary next-day letter to Sally. He had taken "two cut-offs on dirt roads through some gorgeous country—much like Smuggler's Notch—with occasional park-like meadows opening out, a stream always nearby and the smell of the pines and hemlocks thrown in free." He arrived early enough to play eighteen holes of golf, leaving his legs "all done up in knots." The course, he complained, was "shorter than the one in Madison [but he] got a good workout and a swim" before the ten-mile drive to Saranac Lake[16] He found Claus

> very fat, but that's all it is, and there's not much to be cheerful about. Saranac is the most ghastly, pathetic place I have ever been in. Far worse than any hospital in the war—for there you either got better soon or croaked soon. Here they are just hanging on. I'm going over there in the morning and have dinner there and then I'm going to Vermont. I may stop off and bow to your ancestors at East Middlebury. I feel very funereal tonight. . . . If I should get to Madison (if you should still be there) about Friday would you like to ride toward Newport and then ferry over to Long Island and stop at Montauk for a day or so? If so, I can be reached at the Hanover Inn, Hanover, New Hampshire.
>
> Love, Babe.

Sally recognized Babe's need for company and agreed to join him.

A third unexpected twist in the Bensons' lives concerned Bobsie. Eleven years old in 1930, their daughter Barbara had witnessed the unpleasant effects of her mother's growing dependence on alcohol and asked to live with her grandmother. Disenchanted with life on 11th Street, Bobsie could no longer bear being driven to "Gadget's," the bootlegger on Eighth Street, and sent in to purchase booze while her mother waited in the car. Sally's alcoholic binges plus the hours she devoted to writing had left Bobsie feeling robbed of her mother's time and attention. Anna Cora's agreeing to care for Barbara relieved Babe of remaining with Sally on their daughter's account. By the end of the year, Sally and Babe agreed to separate, and Benson's career, initially a self-chosen option, became a necessity.[17] Reflecting on her childhood, Barbara Golseth recalled that Helen Wismer, of all the adults who frequented the Benson parties, "was the only one who was kind to me."

Three years later, Benson captured Bobsie's pain in the character of Elise—the "Hotel Child" in a *New Yorker* story titled "Mr. Martin and the Hotel Child" (December 23, 1933). Elise, trying to retrieve her frightened dog from hiding under the sofa—his usual manner of coping with party noise—is introduced by her mother to Mr. Martin, a guest from Minnesota. A non–New Yorker, he piques Elise's curiosity. It is a relief to "talk to someone who doesn't say the same old things over and over," she confides. She complains of having no home—she has grown up living in hotels—lonely and "looked after by chambermaids and bellhops." Then she queries, "Do you ever feel like just putting on your hat and coat and running way from everything sometimes? . . . Because you feel you can't stand it? I do. I just like to put on my hat and coat and run and run and run." Another instance of Benson's weaving life experience into fiction, the piece also reflects the feelings that had triggered Sally's abrupt departure for Paris three years earlier.

With Babe and Barbara living elsewhere, Sally became a productive writer and attracted the attention of other magazine editors. Of the eight Benson stories *The New Yorker* published in 1931, "The Girl Who Went Everywhere" had "enormously charmed" Margaret Case Morgan at *Vanity Fair*. Published in March, it prompted Morgan's letter of solicitation on April 10th: "Have you anything on hand that you would like to let me see for *Vanity Fair*? If not, I should be glad if you could drop in at my office one day next week and talk to me about the possibility of doing a short piece for us." Addressed to a narrow audience, the chic monthly had a small circulation and featured art, theater, literature, and a "wide span of subjects" (Peterson 270–271). Occasionally, however, *Vanity Fair* adopted the "zealous overtones of a social missionary" and tried, by promoting cheerfulness and good humor, to counter its puritanical, antipleasure stance. It focused on the "ravages of bad taste" rather than bad government, finance, or morals, but more importantly, *Vanity Fair* aimed to give women what no other American magazine had given them—"a chance to think" (Nourie and Nourie 547–548).

Impressed that *Vanity Fair* might want her fiction, Benson responded to Morgan's invitation. Afterward, she blamed her *Vanity Fair* interview with Clare Boothe Luce for turning her against magazine women of a certain type:

> There she [Luce] sat with her hat on, looking lovely. She told me how *Vanity Fair* had finally decided it might like to buy a story from me. So I said crassly, "How much?" And she said, "Fifty dollars." And I said, looking at her lovely clothes, because I don't go in for being smart, that I wouldn't write so much as a recipe for fifty dollars. And she smiled her beautiful smile and said so sweetly, "But think of the prestige for you, my dear." And I walked out.[18]

The unpretentious Sally Benson had come of age.

Six more Benson stories appeared in *The New Yorker* in 1932, followed by four in 1933,[19] ten in 1934, eight in 1935, seven in 1936, and two in 1937 for a total of thirty-seven—but unlike James Thurber, she never bragged about her productivity.[20] Thurber, by contrast, in referring to writing seventeen stories and articles between 1947 and 1948—over seventy-five thousand words in a little over a year—bragged about his accomplishment and paid a left-handed compliment to Benson: "I submit that not even Sally Benson, gifted as she is in fluency, has even come close to the mark." Actually, Benson had surpassed Thurber (Thurber and Weeks 61). While Sally's career escalated, Babe accepted an offer from Columbia University to serve as manager of athletics. He visited Madison whenever his schedule allowed and often sent tickets for Columbia Lions' games to Bobsie for her teachers. Occasionally, Sally also attended football games with Bobsie. Observing the stadium spectators furnished Sally with material for "Pour le Sport," a piece published in *The New Yorker* on November 14, 1931 and later anthologized in a Columbia University composition text. Benson's protagonist, likely a reflection of herself, is more interested in training her date's binoculars on a handsome player than in following the game. As Babe most likely had done when Sally and Barbara attended sporting events, the fictional date tolerates his girlfriend's behavior with polite patience but becomes exasperated when she asks to leave before the game has ended—to get some food.[21]

During the fall of 1931, both Babe and Sally interrupted their schedules to drive to Saranac Lake where Claus Benson now lay close to death. It was a difficult visit and they left knowing death was imminent. When Claus died on November 13th, Anna Cora, Rose and Sam, Esther and Harry, and Fred and Agnes attended the wake and funeral. Since Babe barely spoke to his father, tension contributed to the sadness of the memorial service and made the funeral particularly stressful for Sally. She did her best to comfort her sister-in-law, Maxime, Babe, their niece Rose Mary, and Babe's father, Edwin, before heading to Brooklyn's Greenwood Cemetery where Claus was buried next to his mother in the Benson family plot. The thirties had begun for Sally Benson with a mixture of success and sorrow. Both she and Babe would increasingly taste life's bittersweetness as the decade progressed.

13

THE WRITER MAKES STRIDES

1932–1933

"Sometimes I feel that my family has provided me with such a wealth of material . . . at other times it just annoys me."

—Sally Benson

Unlike James Thurber and despite periods of separation from Sally, Babe Benson continued to socialize with Sally and their Village friends. On one occasion they "produced" a play called *The King of Kings*. Largely a spoof, it was accompanied by printed playbills—party invitations—for the "world premiere" presented by "Plymouth Productions." Glossed in Sally's penciled handwriting, "Plymouth" derived from the name of "the gin we used to drink." The cast included:

JESUS H. CHRIST	Reynolds Benson
FOR CRYING OUT LOUD	Sally Benson
12 APOSTLES	William H. Stayton
PAUL POIRET	Aristide Mian
EDDIE FOY AND FAMILY	Agnes Smith
MAXIME, the Wonder Dog	By Herself[1]

Directed and photographed by Frederick James Smith (Agnes's husband), *The King of Kings* had a chorus of "Sports Writers and Re-write Men" with "Musical setting" by Harrison "Roxy" Dowd. The playbill advertised: "AFTER THE SHOW get your cool refreshing drinks at BABE'S PLACE."[2]

As the thirties unfolded, the repeal of the Eighteenth Amendment and the passing of the Twenty-first on December 5, 1933 ended Prohibition.

Partying continued at Sally and Babe's, and one evening Helen Wismer saw Sally throw John O'Hara's guitar out a window. "It caught in a tree and nobody could reach it," she recalled. After another Benson party, O'Hara went home without his overcoat. Not knowing whose it was, Sally eventually gave it to the janitor, who refused to give it up later when O'Hara tried to retrieve it.[3] As Helen Wismer recalled, "O'Hara was still poor at that time and couldn't afford another coat" (Kinney 514). Reflecting on those parties in 1934, Benson wrote "The Very Thing," a story whose male protagonist struck Wolcott Gibbs as suggestive of John O'Hara. Benson denied the connection, claiming:

> This story had nothing to do with John O'Hara. Boy, you can better belive [sic] I feel pretty cheap about *him*. At the time it seemed the easiest way out of a tight place. And such was my state of mind then, that now, in the clear light of day, I can't remember what I threw out. Whether it was the banjo, the overcoat, or John O'Hara. Knowing myself as I do, I hardly think I'd ever throw out anything in a pair of pants, so it must have been the banjo. Come to think of it, I wouldn't mind having a nice banjo this very minute.[4]

Meanwhile, Wismer's affair with Babe soon paralleled the one she had begun with Thurber, but both ended abruptly after Thurber learned that *New Yorker* editor St. Clair McKelway had become engaged to Ann Honeycutt. Long enamored of "Honey," Thurber was so overcome at losing her to McKelway that he compensated by quickly proposing to Helen, who readily accepted.[5]

Though Thurber's loss of "Honey" embittered him, he soon found Helen "adoring, witty, bright, supportive in all his difficulties, and a good listener." Besides, her frequent dates with Babe Benson had intrigued him and piqued his jealousy. Though he viewed her bony body as "put together like the insides of a tool kit," he soon discovered her to be his perfect soul mate. Best of all, she put his finances in order, and he was happy to "save face" by marrying Helen well before the McKelway/Honeycutt wedding occurred.

For Sally Benson, personal and family problems began to multiply. Though Rose was happily married to Sam Shuttleworth, Agnes's marriage was foundering and she confided to both Sally and Anna Cora that she was contemplating divorce—Fred had been having several affairs. Agnes cautioned, "you might get the impression I am more interested in holding my property than holding my husband." She then dismissed the issue of Fred-vs.-property with a casual comment: "Well, after all, a good cigar is a good cigar." Except for being angry about his using her name for his current mistress, Agnes explained,

> I am not at all cut up. Years ago I read some letters that this girl wrote and I swear Ring Lardner had a hand in them. Everything was in quotes and words not commonly used in tabloids were misspelled. The kind of gal who talks wistfully about dreams coming true . . . the sort that is always moving from a small town to a small town on the lam, and never gets more than three installments paid on a radio before the sweetie's wife gets wise, or the sweetie gets fed up on the expenses or before the current traveling man gets shifted to a new territory for the course of her wanderings. She must have deserted about a thousand cats because her way of starting things off on a cozy basis is to acquire a cat and to open a charge account at the nearest delicatessen. I suspect that at such times when she doesn't think she is pregnant, she is thinking of going on the stage or into the movies or something. Since Fred has an installment-plan mind and wavers between sloppy sentiment and shanty-Irish ill humor, I think that she is just the girl for him. And I told him so. And it was the only thing I ever said to him that nearly jarred him into his senses and it worried him.

Though Agnes blamed her marital problems on Fred's repeated philandering, she, like Sally, had been abusing alcohol and drugs. (Sally's use of Demerol was not discovered until much later.) Whether Fred's infidelity caused Agnes's substance abuse or whether her problem-drinking caused Fred's philandering is difficult to know. In any event, one of Fred's women, had particularly offended Agnes and, like Sally, Agnes considered turning this current mistress's bold exploits into fiction. She recounted for Sally how she discovered Fred's dalliance:

> One of the items she had ordered the bootlegger to fetch her— and be charged to Mrs. F. J. Smith—was two pints of rye, two

tickets to a movie, and a box of Kotex. I told Fred that under the circumstances she should have ordered gin. The coon rum runner who came over with all the funny documents thought that I was the Mrs. Frederick James that had stuck him for the bill and he was apologetic about it and acted as though I might call the Klan out on him. He was shocked when I laughed as it seemed to offend his sense of the proprieties.

I am thinking of using some of the letters and documents and the cat doctor episode for a sketch for the *New Yorker*. I have a swell title for it: "Jersey City du Barry."[6]

Agnes never produced the intended short story.

Immediately after New Year's in 1932, amid efforts to write and to help Agnes resolve her difficulties with Fred, Benson was rushed to the emergency room of New York's Madison Avenue Hospital with a high fever and great pain. Barbara wrote to her on Mickey Mouse stationery, a gift from Rose:

Dear Mama,

I am so sorry you are sick. Are you still in the hospital? I hope you will be well soon. I got my report card. . . . My marks were: Composition B+, Grammer [sic] A-, Spelling B-, Arithmetic B, History B-, Geography B+, Civics B-, Penmanship C+. I have improved in everything. . . . How are Daddy, Florence, and Tempy? . . . I wrote a crazy poem in school today. I will read it to you when you come up. Love, Bobs

Benson was pleased with Bobsie's language arts grades, curious to hear the poem, and happy that her daughter had enjoyed Mrs. Eastland's reading *David Copperfield* aloud. It stirred memories of Alonzo's reading to her and Agnes when they were young, and she admired Barbara's critical evaluation: "I think I like *The Tale of Two Cities* better though." After sharing news of "some swell sliding" with her friend Betty Knight who had spent Christmas vacation with her, Bobsie asked: "When you come up again will you bring your diary? I would like to read it." Now twelve, Barbara had developed great curiosity and interest in knowing her mother's experiences at the same age.[7] The diary's pages, full of Benson's youthful New York escapades, would seem exciting compared to Bobsie's quiet life in suburban Connecticut.

As Benson lay in the hospital, a letter from Anna Cora arrived:

Sally darling,

I'm so sorry you are ill. I am where I cannot run in to see you. . . . Reynolds says 'nothing to worry about' but I spent a most miserable night. Well, that is life and it takes a lot of courage to meet the blows it hands us. I shall be miserably uneasy until I have news of—good news—of you. . . . Barbara is well and her school report is good![8]

Daily letters followed, full of concern that Benson was "recovering well" despite the stubborn "infection menacing [her] health. If doctors cannot trace it, that's just too bad for the profession," Anna Cora commented. "It may be your appendix," she surmised, "so have it out. It is difficult to trace these little poisons." Apparently, Benson had been ailing for several months. "It isn't right that you should have your eyes, ears, and innards acting up at intervals," she complained, "so be good and firm and demand a thorough exam. You are like the rest of us, if you can smile, have spirit, stand on your own feet—the good doctors will say, as they did to Rose: 'Oh, you're all right, Mrs. T. Get out in the open and walk, walk." Along with concern for Sally, Anna Cora was working on "getting her home in order for closing." Having sold her house in East River because of the bad economy, she was about to move in with Rose and Sam.

For two weeks Sally remained in Room 1101 at the Madison Avenue Hospital on 76th Street before doctors confirmed what Anna Cora had already diagnosed: appendicitis. Babe visited frequently, as did Esther and Harry. The Shuttleworths paid Anna Cora's train fare to New York so she could visit—"that was their bouquet." When she entered Sally's hospital room, she discovered her daughter "overwhelmed with flowers and books" from personal friends and *New Yorker* colleagues. She urged Sally to ask the doctor when she could travel to Madison. "It will be so pleasant for you near the shore where, if the sun does shine, you will receive its full benefit." While in Manhattan, Anna Cora took the opportunity to visit son-in-law Frederick Smith at the Algonquin Hotel to see whether she could help resolve the problems he and Agnes were having. After learning that Fred wasn't there, Anna Cora left a message and Esther's number, then took a double-decker bus to the Wherrys' apartment on 96th Street just off Fifth Avenue. When Fred later telephoned, Anna Cora "went right down and had a short visit," never expecting to learn from him that Agnes had become addicted to alcohol and drugs. Fred then accompanied Anna Cora from the Algonquin to Grand Central Station to catch their respective trains for Westport and Madison.

Days later she confided to Sally: "I think my poor Raggie is in a pathetic state—so is he, poor lamb. He wrote me to go out with him, but I felt I could not endure another shock. I shall try to see the poor darling soon and may land on my neck. That's what mothers are for, I'm thinking." In the space of one decade, Anna Cora had lost her husband and her firstborn to alcohol and witnessed three of her daughters developing serious marital problems. Rose had divorced and remarried, Agnes was toying with divorce, Agnes and Sally were substance abusers, and Sally had almost died of a ruptured appendix. Only Esther, the "proper, judgmental daughter,"[9] was enjoying a stable marriage and successfully combining her role as mother of Toby with her career as advertising manager for Franklin Simon Stores.

As soon as Agnes learned of Sally's hospitalization, she wrote from her home on Red Coat Road in Westport:

Dear Sal,

Well, from your letters I see that you are belly-aching again, crabbing at people who are trying to help you, biting the hand that feeds you custards, and turning up your nose at the kindly bedpan.

Apologizing for using a pencil, Agnes explained, "Tony thinks he would like to typewrite. Mamma's darling is at my knee, bedeviling me, and in about one minute he is going to catch hell. I am sorry you are sick." Agnes sympathized but in a fit of self-pity complained: "I would like to have something very contagious so no one could come near me with requests for another ton of coal, and bag of flour, and a new grate for the stove, and a check for the laundry man, and five bucks to take an advertising man to luncheon." With characteristic sarcasm Agnes added: "If I were to break out with little red marks, everyone would flee from me in horror. And would I care? I would not. I bet lepers have nice dispositions." Promising to send books, Agnes concluded with get-well wishes and the observation: "It isn't funny to be sick and all cooped up when you'd rather be going places and doing things." Though Agnes attempted to disguise her pain with flip humor, her letter's tone is bitter, even caustic.

Living at home and caring for little Tony, Agnes admittedly missed her glamorous career and its attendant social life, but she assured Sally she intended to do "nothing quickly" about pursuing a divorce. Apparently, Sally had encouraged her sister to dress up and make herself more attractive, but Agnes had rejected the advice as unwise for the moment:

> My old man might think I was making a pass at him. He gets all his ideas from the movies, and in the movies, cheated wives always appear in the last reel with a permanent wave and a mass of sex appeal. But sex appeal at this moment would disturb the legal status, and by sitting here, paying off on the place and watching my own interests for months and maybe a couple of years, I can acquire what at the age of forty, will be greater than love. As for making dreams come true, Fred can bother about that because if one allows nature to take its course, one is seldom disappointed. Meanwhile, as long as he sticks around here, he'll eat bakery cakes in future—and like it.

> Your loving sister, Agnes.

Written in 1932 when Agnes was thirty-eight, the letter invites comparison with Sally. Both used the slang expressions popular at the time and both preferred to be "out and about" rather than stay-at-home mothers.

Agnes's attitude and her diction echo in the dialogue of Benson's fictional women, and her letter offers a glimpse of Benson's strategy for retaining Babe's interest: keep oneself attractive and dress well. Following her own advice had apparently been working for Sally. Despite their occasional affairs and periodic separations, Sally and Babe had remained devoted to one another. Alone in hotel rooms while traveling with the Columbia Lions, Babe often sent an account of his day's activities to Sally. On February 20th, 1932, for example, Babe wrote from the Hanover Inn at Dartmouth:

Darling Goofer,

My God, it's cold up here. We've gathered about the open fire
in the lobby trying to keep warm. Last night was a big one in
Greenfield. Mr. Meenan entertained until 6 a.m. However, a
good sleep and a hearty breakfast at noon put us back in the
pink.

How are you and Bobs? Write me a note when you're in
the mood.

Lots of love, Babe

By August of 1932, however, Babe's bouts of drinking caused his
return to the "Farm," a rehabilitation center near New Haven. Sally played
the supportive wife and Babe was grateful:

Darling Lambis:

Your two darling letters came and made me sad and happy
both. I miss you very, very much and time hangs heavy without
your cute visits. No one could have been more wonderful than
you have and don't think I don't know what you have been up
against.

No doubt you've been most busy in the big city, but not
having fun at all the jobs you have to look after, poor rabbit.
Never mind, we'll be mobilized soon in our own hutch so keep
your chin up.[10]

Babe reported on his treatments—shots in his arm—and Dr. Lyman's satisfaction that the therapy was progressing satisfactorily. He would see Dr.
Blake and have a fourth shot by Monday. "Will you be able to be back
there by then?" he asked. "Please let me know so I can plan accordingly."
He described his rehabilitation regimen:

thirty minutes exercise mornings now and Lyman said I could
probably have a half hour twice a day by the end of next week.
I hope it's not too hellish in New York, little Goofer, and that
you'll get in some amusement. Don't forget to get your hair

done, and write me when you will be coming back, cause I'll
be watching for you to drive up in the old Limozyne [sic].

I love you, Tiny—Babe.[11]

Babe's thank-you for Sally's birthday gift further demonstrated the
Bensons' continuing love and friendship. On September 24th, the day after
his 39th birthday, Babe wrote:

Darling,

Bright and early today I opened my present and found your cute
note. The whatever you call it . . . is nothing short of beautiful
and it fits perfectly. Your letter came today, too, so my birthday
was good as it could be without you too. I'm dying for you to
get back so we can be together, and a week from tomorrow, we
move to our new palace. . . . You have been the dearest person
that ever lived and don't think I don't know it. No other girl
could or would have crashed through the way you did—but
then, how could they. I know you must be having a lousy time
but try to get in a bit of unlaxing [sic] along with the moving.
    All the love in the world, my darling. Babe[12]

During 1932, besides moving to her own place in Madison, Connecticut, Benson managed to write six stories for *The New Yorker* between
March 5th and September 10th. By November, Thayer Hobson of William
Morrow and Co. was so impressed with her fiction that he sought out
Wolcott Gibbs at Bleeck's to discuss Benson and the "way [she] wrote and
what [she] wrote."[13] Hobson was particularly interested in whether Benson
planned to write anything of book length and after probing Gibbs for the
fourth time, Gibbs became "a little impatient" but volunteered that Benson
was planning a detective story. He didn't think she would ever finish it and
suggested Hobson write Benson directly. Hobson followed Gibbs's advice
and, after explaining the reason for and origin of his letter to Benson,
stated: "If you wrote a novel, you know, it would probably be good. This
letter calls for an answer." Benson not only replied but also stopped to see
Hobson during her next foray into New York for shopping and catching
up with colleagues at her *New Yorker* office.[14] On December 22nd, Hob-

son wrote to thank Benson, wishing her a "Merry Christmas" and urging, "Don't forget the novel—I am waiting for the first few chapters."[15]

By January 7th of 1933, Gibbs had also discussed Benson's detective story with Ogden Nash at Farrar & Rinehart. Nash immediately wrote Benson that her "stuff in the *New Yorker*" had given him "so much pleasure that [I] shall be most interested in seeing anything you write. If you are not irrevocably committed elsewhere, mightn't [I] see what you are doing and won't you stop in for a talk next time you are in town?" Nash sent a copy of his letter to both Benson's *New Yorker* office and her home in Madison "just to be sure." Benson responded with some thoughts on Barnaby Ross and Philo Vance,[16] which, though understandable to Nash, led to his objecting, "But, I would like to read a story about Connecticut. I have just finished reading one that strikes me as something pretty extra, James Cozzens [*sic*] THE LAST ADAM. Have you come across it yet?" Nash concluded: "I do wish you would write a good novel and make plenty of money for you and a little bit for us. Yours, Ogden Nash."[17] Benson acted on Nash's suggestion but not until the following July and not in the manner he wished. Instead, she proposed the idea for a Connecticut series to Harold Ross. In the interim, Benson kept Hobson tethered to her projected novel but did little more than promise to send him chapters. During the first half of 1933 she published only one *New Yorker* piece, "A Single Rose," in the March 18th issue—with good reason—as shall be seen.

Babe, meanwhile, had been traveling frequently in his role as Columbia University's athletic director and trying to abstain from booze after completing his drying out treatment the previous August. Shortly after the Christmas holidays, when he learned that Sally had contracted the flu, he wrote to her in Madison:

Dear little Rabbitt [*sic*],

Here I am in the heart of the world, but practically frozen withal [*sic*]. The trip down wasn't so bad, only my dogs were cold. I wore a heavy sweater and with the old fur coat and my Christmas fur-lined gloves [Sally's gift], the rest of me kept nice and warm. . . . While slightly large, they are just about right for cold weather driving. . . . We had our meeting . . . stayed at the club [Columbia Alumni] for dinner, and sat and chatted and philosophized until ten-thirty, after which I walked home, or rather here

[The Shelton Hotel, New York]. It's bitter cold out but the air felt good. Everyone commiserated with me as to no alcoholic beverages. The usual gang were at the bar, and countless people came over and said they were glad I was back and how well I looked and such fol de rol. Sam was genuinely pleased to see me, also Mike, though I shall no longer be one of his customers.

Babe also reported that Ralph, Dan, Lou and the "others who knew you were ill . . . asked very solicitously after you."[18] He hoped the bitter, cold weather had not marooned her and that:

Florence [the Bensons' maid] kept the fire roaring alright [sic]. . . . I hope you are feeling hotsy-totsy, Lamb. How are you liking getting up? Maybe not so well just at first, but you'll get to enjoy it after a bit. Be a good girl or you won't get any present. I'll phone you tomorrow (Fri.) and try to get through a message which will probably have a Jamaican-Hunnish tinge [a reference to his German ancestry and Florence's accent].

Babe planned to "come up" Sunday en route to Providence for a meeting at Brown University. He reiterated: "You be good, you hear, and mind the kind nurse and laugh at all her jokes or poke her in the jaw if you'd rather. I'll be seeing you, Tiny. Love and kisses and hugs. Babe."[19] The letter's caring, affectionate tone shows, as Golseth has observed, that her parents maintained a warm friendship despite, or perhaps because of, their frequent separations. Sally responded in kind but, unfortunately, her letters to Babe, like those to her close friends, are unavailable. Suffice it to say that her respondents repeatedly acclaimed her "wonderful letters."

The next communication from Babe was a brief note on Columbia letterhead:

Hello Baby,

I'm in the midst of heaps of papers, reports, folders and what not and am beginning to dig my way out. . . . I'll tell you more about it when I get time to write a bit. Be a good rabbit and get big and strong with all speed.

Love, Babe[20]

Later that evening, on letterhead from the Hotel Croydon on 86th Street—America's Pre-eminent Apartment Hotel—Babe explained that his special rate of two dollars a day meant the hotel would guard any luggage he wanted to leave and his accommodations included a "commissary, delicatessen, beauty parlor." He had a suite, rather than a room (because they had run out of rooms), and it was a good size though unattractive. His friend Andy, after his Holy Cross dinner, came home at ten and suggested a bridge game, but Babe was too tired and preferred to "climb in a hot tub and read."

Babe complained the next day of being unable to work beyond sorting stuff and moving it around. Before he knew it, it was eight o'clock, and, "When I walked over to the subway and waited for a train, it seemed as if I'd been doing the same thing for about a thousand years. Just to be on track, I went to Piroll's for dinner but didn't have much of an appetite. However," he stated proudly, "I steered clear of the club as the only people I know there are draped on the bar and there's not much kick in listening to a bunch of drunks hold forth. By the time I was finished it was nine o'clock and I thought I'd walk up Fifth Avenue a bit. It was quite cold but felt good and I wound up walking all the way up here." It is interesting that Babe was so open about his efforts to avoid situations where he might fall into drinking again. There is no available sharing of a similar kind from Sally other than indirect reflections of rehabilitation experiences in pieces such as "Retreat," published in *The New Yorker* in October of 1940.

The following day, a holiday (February 22nd), Babe would go to his office "and put in the morning and part of the afternoon. The charity basketball games are at the Garden tomorrow afternoon and evening," he explained, "and I shall probably see both sessions with Dave and Paul." He planned to come back (to Madison) Sunday afternoon "if nothing untoward happens to prevent it—I'll let you know." Providing an insight into how Sally spent her free hours, he teased: "I hope the animals have deviled the soul out of you and that jigsaw puzzles have driven you mad—I should like to be doing nothing better than to be cursing over one with you now—this is a big town when you are alone and not acclimated." Babe concluded: "Drop me a line and let me know how you are feeling and if you are getting any fatter, rabbit. You be good now, or I'll beat you when I catch you. Love and kisses, Babe."

On March 24th, Babe sent Sally a check for Bobs, explaining he had to stop off at his Columbia University office for "dough. Hope you got the bounder there without any murders," he adds—a comment on her driving. "If you want to, you can write to me at the Hanover Inn" (New Hampshire) where "I'll be . . . about Tuesday or Wednesday. Love and kisses, Babe." Sally continued writing in Madison for most of the spring. Then, in early May, she finally went into the city, spoke with Hobson in his William Morrow office at 386 Fourth Avenue, and assured him she would drop off at least half the manuscript. On May 12th, however, an exasperated Hobson wrote:

Dear Mrs. Benson:

If I have ever heard of a snide trick or a low character, you pulled it and are it. My disgust with you is unfathomable. (That's a good word). You may guess that this has to do with your sneaking back to Madison without leaving half the manuscript. There is only one possible way for you to return to the state of grace and that is to *finish* it on or before June 15. I am not chattering idly about a date. If the manuscript isn't here by the end of June, the curses that I'll call down upon your head will blight what might otherwise be a fairly happy life. I hope you are satisfied and pleased with yourself—nobody else is.

In a rather disappointed manner,
Thayer Hobson

Imagine Hobson's dismay could he have foreseen Benson's imminent dose of bad fortune, the worst to befall her yet.

On Saturday morning, June 17th, 1933, Agnes Wickfield Smith was found dead from self-administered rat and nicotine poison in her Westport, Connecticut, home.[21] Anna Cora had been staying with her and discovered her body before Fred or three-year-old Tony awakened. When she could find the strength, Anna Cora telephoned Rose, who, in turn, relayed the news to Esther and Sally. Each one was shocked. Though aware of Agnes's troubled relationship with Fred, no one, not even Sally, realized the extent of Agnes's depression or the degree to which drug and alcohol abuse had deepened it. Adding to Anna Cora's grief, besides the shame associated with such a death at the time, was her knowledge that, although baptized a Catholic, Agnes would be denied a Catholic burial. Canon law at that time considered suicide so grave a sin that the victim's body could neither be brought into church for funeral rites nor buried in the consecrated ground of a Catholic cemetery. When Anna Cora gathered her family to comfort Fred, Tony, and each other, they agreed that after a private funeral, Agnes's body would be interred in Ferndale, a nonsectarian cemetery in Old Saybrook, Connecticut.

On June 20th, unaware of Agnes's death, Babe wrote: "Dear Rabbit, I clean forgot today my installment on the Plymouth—it is past due—will you take care of it for me please? The bill is in the middle right hand drawer of the desk, clipped with others—there are two groups and I don't know which it is in but you can find it I'm sure—see you soon, Babe."[22] Babe had not been informed of Agnes's death, nor had he attended the funeral. Two days later, having learned of the tragedy, he wrote to explain that his busy schedule prevented him from

> get[ting] to the country 'til Sunday damn it to hell—there's a lousy mess in the football schedule and I shall have to go to Philadelphia to straighten it out and it will take them Thurs. till Sat. to get their end of it in shape so we can confer—the Navy is the cause of the whole ruction. . . . If there's any change in these plans I'll let you know but I don't see much hope. It's hot as hell here too—oh yeah, New York is a swell place. Be a good towser.
>
> Lots of love, Babe.[23]

He added a thoughtful postscript—"I'll ask Helen if she if she wants to go up Saturday if you like—let me know." Although it is inconceivable that he would place business before family obligation, that is apparently what occurred. Offering to ask Helen to go up on Saturday was one way he hoped would compensate for his absence.

In early July, Anna Cora wrote one letter to both Rose and Sally from Westport where she was staying until Fred could find a housekeeper for Tony. After apologizing to Rose for missing her birthday on June 3rd, she thanked both daughters for their telephone call—an "appreciated moment among so many lonely hours"—and congratulated Rose for winning "prize and praise" in the Madison Garden show. She also thanked them again for arranging "the adorable bouquet my Raggie held in her tired hands—Oh, you were so sweet to do that for me. Fred says you are coming up again soon, Sally. I'll love it, of course, but I don't want you to feel you must . . ." Fred, she reported, has been "talking to a woman about coming to work." Never one to mince words, Anna Cora continued: "She lives in Bridgeport, [is] fifty-two years old . . . she seems too doddering to me. I could not see that she would make Tony happy. I'm no spring chicken but I do give him a lot of my time and thought, poor little boy!"

Benson, after observing the housekeeper, fused both Anna Cora and the hired caretaker into one character for a new piece based on a jealous conflict between a second wife and a hired childcare helper. Titled "Home Atmosphere," it appeared in the March 12, 1938 issue of *The New Yorker*. Mattie is the hired caretaker of Billie and balks at preparing sandwiches for the stepmother, Mildred Kirk. Resentfully, Mattie refers to her as "That Woman" and hates being ordered to give up her favorite part of her job: giving Billie his bath, talking to him in the dark, and telling him stories. Kirk is concerned with the superficial: entertaining friends, providing a special lunch, enjoying the elegantly furnished house and fireplace. These she equates with a "real home." In sharp contrast to Mattie who has nurtured the child since birth, Kirk appears cold and disconnected from him—hence the title's irony.

Having been close to "Raggie" from childhood, Sally had been deeply affected by her senseless death. Occurring in the midst of a burgeoning fictional output, her sister's suicide disrupted Benson's writing schedule, but she maintained silence regarding her painful loss and made no mention of Agnes's death to any of her *New Yorker* colleagues.[24] Then, three weeks later, she accused her agent, Ben Wasson, of leaking the news of Agnes's suicide. On July 12th, Wasson hastened to set Benson straight:

Dear Sally:

Thanks so much, Honey, for your letter. I would like to correct you about one thing. Alison Smith is the one who told me about Agnes and she was terribly distressed. I called Charlie Towne at the paper and he didn't even hear about it and called me later to confirm it giving me your mother's telephone number. Alison asked me to convey her sympathies and we wanted to send flowers but your mother said it was too late. I also extended sympathies for Gibbs, with whom I had talked a few minutes

before. Gibbs is now away. I don't think he's been catching
fire recently.[25] I won't burn up unless you fail to send me your
manuscript of that novel. When you come to town, call me. I
want to see you. Love, Ben[26]

Harold Ross, writing two weeks after Wasson, made no reference to
Benson's loss of Agnes. Rather, he wrote in a businesslike but mock-serious
tone:

Dear Mrs. Benson:

Mr. Gibbs told me that you suggested doing some pieces about
your grandfather and family, and this is to urge you to get at
them and let us see them. We feel that both Day and Thurber
have only plumbed the depths, not scraped the surface, and you
know if you scrape the surface you scrape all. We are particularly
interested in the time your mother thought the Galveston flood
was merely the icebox overflowing and your aunt, who could
see, knew about it. Do send us three or four "samples" to start
with, preferably border-line pieces which are not quite up our
alley. If you have anything that is a bit too thin for us, please
send that too, or any longer pieces that fall from their own
weight. As you have probably noticed from skipping through
the magazine, we must begin rejecting things soon.

Yours, H. W. Ross[27]

Possibly, Ross omitted any reference to Agnes because he knew Benson's
wishes. More likely, he knew that prodding Benson to write would help
heal her pain.

Benson's inspiration for her proposed series arose from the confluence of Agnes's death and Rose's recent rediscovery of her 1903 diary
that Benson now read for the first time.[28] Her nostalgia for family and
St. Louis was timely—the stories she envisioned about the Smiths would
nicely parallel Clarence Day's "Life with Father" series recently published
in *The New Yorker*. However, although Benson presented the idea to Gibbs
and through him, to Ross, she did not begin her "5135 Kensington" series
until seven years later.

In replying to Ross's July 26th letter, Benson affects the naïve posture of a novice writer clutching at straws for story material. Yet, at the same time, she is confident enough in her relationship with Ross to adopt a playful, brash tone. Given Benson's propensity for lying, the reader might justifiably suspect that she is manipulating Ross, using her inexperience to enlist favorable, father-like encouragement:

Dear Mr. Ross,

It is nice of you to take an interest in my work. I hope you don't think for one minute that I would try to imitate Day or Thurber. Because I wouldn't for anything. Sometimes I feel that my family has provided me with such a wealth of material that I had better let sleeping dogs lie. At other times it just annoys me. As we lived in St. Louis quite near Fannie Hurst, I might even work her in a piece. It would sort of tie it up to something concrete, I think. If you like stories with children in them, I might do a few about my daughter. I could make out that she was my nephew and call her "Peter" so people wouldn't suspect. For instance, she wants to make a collection of dog licenses. This could be worked up some way. But let me know what you think. After all, you're the boss, aren't you?

Sincerely, Sally Benson[29]

Ross's response reveals openness to Benson's ideas and appreciation of her work:

Dear Miss Benson:

I am not the boss but I am sometimes very influential. I say try any ideas you have. It is always impossible to judge anything before it is written. You are a good writer and we nearly always like your things. I say go ahead on any ideas you have, either about your daughter or the older generations of your family, and see how they come out when you get them on paper.

Yours sincerely,
H. W. Ross[30]

"Fifty Years Young," Benson's most recent submission, was a study in contrast between youth and age. Set in Madison, Connecticut, it presents Dr. Hopkins, a Yale professor, who loves children and habitually dunks them after swimming out to the stationary raft off Island Avenue. One little girl, unwilling to be dunked again, darts at Hopkins's legs, knocking him into the Sound and almost drowning him. Emerging, the humiliated, winded Hopkins must accept a young boy's offer of a boat ride back to shore, where, stepping onto *terra firma*, he hears a young girl commenting to her laughing companion, "The old fool!" Hopkins turns to see the object of their scorn, "But there was no one there," concluded Benson. Gibbs considered the piece "good" and wrote two days later to request that Benson "fix" three items, one of them a *non sequitur*. More importantly, he bemoaned Benson's "lack of energy" because the magazine needed more pieces. "You better call Wasson when you come to town. I'd just take you to Schrafft's," Gibbs added.

After making only one of the three suggested changes, Benson returned her piece and *The New Yorker* published the story on August 19, 1933, just two months after Agnes's death. One wonders how Benson snapped back so quickly from grieving. Was she repressing her sorrow and pain or did plunging into writing provide an escape? From the tone of her next letter to Gibbs, one would not suspect that its writer was bereft:

Dear Wolcott,

I can tell you're in perfect health because you write longer letters. You are more painstaking. I fixed the story. You were right about the part where he falls off the raft. But when you are fifty and take a fall, you are still fifty no matter how you keep up. I ought to know. I like Schrafft's. I like their Luxuro chocolate cream cakes. They used to cost forty cents. You can take me there and think up funny things to tell the way you do. And, you know I always have a funny story or two. All we know up here is what we read in Winchell's column. Of course, if it weren't for Rinso, I'd be tied down even more than I am.

Love from, Sally[31]

As Benson temporarily abandoned her proposed series—"5135 Kensington"—life in America changed dramatically. Prohibition's demise led to the proliferation of nightclubs as speakeasies disappeared. As an institution, the speakeasy had lowered class barriers already blurred as a result of the war. The rise of the subway, allowing New Yorkers to mingle with diverse people they might never have met a decade earlier, further eradicated class distinctions. Upper-middle-class readers—the people who supported the opera and enjoyed travel—began to recognize themselves in print or on stage. Whether Benson sensed her readers' readiness or remembered Ogden Nash's suggestion from the preceding January, she decided to write her "Nutmeg series." Since Katharine White was away, Benson sent her proposal directly to Ross:

My dear Mr. Ross:

I have an idea for six stories about Connecticut, not *Desire under the Elms*, and I have done two of them. I didn't want to do any more if you didn't like the idea and the title, which may need explaining. I have to come to New York anyway and I would like to see you or Mr. Gibbs about it. I can come any day if you will let me know a day ahead.[32]

Gibbs replied for Ross on August 18th: "Ross wants me to talk to you about the Connecticut stories. Anytime except Tuesday afternoon would be nice. We might have lunch if you'll let me know when you're coming. Yours, Wolcott Gibbs."[33]

While Sally devoted herself to her writing in Madison, Babe continued working at Columbia and living at the Hotel Croydon. He wrote Sally telling her he was working so hard in the heat that "My best suit is soaked with sweat." To avoid temptation, he hadn't "seen Helen or the girls."[34] Months later, Benson transformed much of Babe's correspondence into "Room on a Court" (June 22, 1935). The piece begins: "When Mr. Roth came to New York . . . on business, he didn't care to drink or carry on, because drinking to him meant bicarbonate of soda which he disliked, and carrying on meant headlines in the newspapers and disgrace." Benson introduces the hotel—"a family hotel"—where he could get a room on the court (more quiet than a room facing the street) and describes a night when Roth is distracted by the goings-on in a room opposite his—the living room of a suite. Three women and three men, having imbibed a few drinks, are speaking loudly. Roth observes that one balding man repeatedly and vainly tries to get the attention of the rest by pathetically asking them to listen to something important—something he has never shared with anyone except his mother. They ignore him, he passes out, and they depart for a night of further adventures. Mr. Roth is left feeling "as though there was something he should do, but he couldn't decide what the best thing would be. So, after a while, he pulled down his shade and started to get undressed." So ends the piece, leaving the reader with a fabliau of sorts on apathy and meaninglessness. Coming so shortly after Agnes's suicide, the piece is especially chilling for anyone who knew Benson's circumstances. Katharine White liked "Room on a Court" and sent a note with Benson's check:

> I was delighted to see you have sent us a story at all as I hear you have deserted the *New Yorker* in favor of Ben Wasson and the high-priced magazines. This doesn't seem to be really true under the circumstances but please don't do it. I wonder if you will make more money in the end working through an agent . . . with agents' fees and all. Anyway, please don't forget us, and send us more manuscripts as we need them badly.[35]

Three days later, Benson replied:

My dear Mrs. White:

> Ben Wasson closed his office the day I sent him a story to sell. He has returned them to me and I am sending them on to you. There are supposed to be four more of them which I haven't done yet. Hence, I didn't resubmit them to anyone. If you don't understand the title, "A Yard of Nutmeg," I will explain. I have to go to New York Monday to pick out paint and I would like to stop in and see you.
>
> Sincerely,
> Sally Benson[36]

As for the "Nutmeg series," White forwarded Benson's material to Gibbs with the query, "See any hope in a series of this sort for summer?" When Gibbs concurred with White's negative appraisal, she wrote:

Dear Mrs. Benson:

> This is the way we feel about the nutmeg series. We feel that
> they are accurately observed and probably only too true, but
> that they somehow seem a little mild in interest and a little
> familiar. We have done the husband and wife business so much,
> and also the suburban atmosphere. We just don't think they are
> up to your usual standard.

White softened the blow by inviting Benson to resubmit the stories "as
they are really summer material and we might have a change of heart by
then." In the interim, she urged, "please be forgiving and send us some
more swell stuff."[37]

Undaunted, Benson did just that. With her next piece, "Formal Party,"
she requested that Gibbs send her check to Madison if they took the story.
She also asked, "When I come down again, if you are still reviewing plays,
I wish you'd take me to one," promising, "I will drink cups of coffee and
laugh with you. Sally." Like Babe, Sally was on the wagon. As an afterthought she appended: "I didn't put a title on this. I will. But I didn't
want to rack my brain for nothing. You are so clever about them, dear."
Gibbs thought the piece very funny, but neither he nor White understood
it and that "upsets us both," he wrote. You've got to clear up the little man
somehow," he advised Benson. "I don't know whether he actually knows
these people he's talking about—whether he's crazy or a practical joker or
what. . . . We can't print things that bewilder our own staff, although I'm
perfectly sure you don't see why not. Anyway, I think you can fix it quite
easily and I hope you will."[38]

Benson took the advice and clarified the "little man's" role—a psychologist—or so he claimed, marked by a head with "no back"—a sure sign
that "he had no self-esteem." The little man "kept bumping into people,"
eavesdropping and interjecting authoritative information on subjects of conversation—largely past acquaintances of the guests—at a party where Mrs.
Murdock, initially recognizing no one, gravitated toward the one person she
had always thought "terrible"—the way "you are very glad to get your supper in a hospital, even if it's junket."[39] Benson's satiric wit had claimed for
its target a pompous woman, whose insecurity and low self-esteem sparked
her annoyance at the "little man"—an apparent stranger—so confident that

he mingled with ease amid the guests. Thus did Mrs. Murdock explain his madness. She—not the little man—her foil—allowed Benson, the psychologist, to probe insecurity and its negative effects.

In November, because she wanted free copies of the mystery books she read nightly, Benson wrote to White offering to write mystery blurbs in place of the ailing Angelica Gibbs. In a memo to Don Wharton, managing editor, White recommended Benson—"I think she could do it as she is a bright girl with a bright way of saying things"—but felt the magazine should pay her. On December 7th, Wharton offered Benson five issues at the rate of nine dollars an issue, and on December 15th, he requested: "Let us have all the blurbs of the books that you really like. We will probably use three or four."[40]

Professionally, Benson had accomplished much in the five years since *The New Yorker* had published her first story. She enjoyed a strong, personal connection with Wolcott Gibbs, her editor, and had secured—besides a yearly contract with *The New Yorker*—recognition of her work by major publishers like William Morrow & Co. At the end of the year, *The New Yorker* would publish Benson's twenty-second piece, "Mr. Martin and the Hotel Child," in the December 23, 1933 issue.

Benson's correspondence with both Katharine White and Wolcott Gibbs shows that she felt comfortable with each one, but as the relationship with Gibbs developed, their letters quickly became informal and casual. Repeatedly, she submitted untitled pieces and often expected Gibbs to supply "heads" for them: "I'm lousy at titles, darling. I've thought and thought and can't think of anything very good. How about 'Formal Party'?" Many of her accompanying notes were handwritten in pencil or, if typed, contained a penciled afterthought and almost all her letters bore no time reference beyond the day of the week. As he had since 1930, Gibbs continued to sign all his correspondence to Sally, "Love, Wolcott Gibbs."

The following letter written toward the end of 1933 is a good example of their growing friendship: "I'm just leaving for New York right now. You might take me to lunch some day this week. I want to see if you have changed—so that I can go around saying, 'Have you seen Gibbs lately? Hasn't he changed though!'" In closing, Benson added: "Helen [Thurber] tells me you got married. How you do go on. Love, Sally."[41]

14

REFINING HER VISION

1933–1934

"Your notes upset Mr. Mosher. 'That waspish little party,' he calls you."

—Wolcott Gibbs

Babe Benson, high school and college athlete, was well suited to be manager of athletics at Columbia University. While Sally Benson was busily writing, Babe had been cheering the Columbia Lions to first place in their division. A week before Christmas, Sally took the train into the city to help celebrate the Lions' victory and bid farewell to Babe as he, the coaches, and the football team headed west. It was fitting that after attending all the Lions' home and away games, Babe should have the honor of watching history made on New Year's Day, 1934, as Columbia's championship team played in Pasadena, California's first Rose Bowl tournament.

As he traveled across the country, Babe spent some time each evening writing to Sally. The letters are reflective, revealing his sensitive, poetic side and his close connection to her despite their physical separation. During a stopover at El Conquistador Hotel in Tucson, Arizona, on Saturday, December 30th, 1933, for example, Babe wrote:

Hello Rabbitt [*sic*],

We rolled into ye faire town of Tucson this morning after many and varied adventures in our safari west. . . . St. Louis was exceedingly quiet—only a few Alumni down to meet the train—an impromptu luncheon and then practice at St. Louis University, a poverty-stricken Jesuit college. The field was in such

Figure 9. Reynolds Benson, manager of athletics at Columbia University, 1934

bad shape from recent rains and lack of care that the workout
was a flop and Mr. Lou (as the porters call him)[1] did his roaring
act. I didn't touch a drop and was in bed early Tuesday night,
but didn't sleep so hot and was a bit low on Wednesday.

Here and elsewhere, Babe alluded to his resolution to curb his drinking.
However, on this occasion, Babe made an exception: he "took two good
hookers" before dinner because, as he explained, it had gotten so cold and
his feet were so wet from "prowling around the field." He ate copiously;
played bridge with Stanley, Ike Lovejoy, and Paul Gallico until one; and
next morning was "feeling grand."

In Dallas, "great hordes of local firemen" greeted the Columbia players at the train station, the Southern Methodist Band played for them at the hotel, and the Columbia Alumni Club gave a gala luncheon. "After the boys had been fed and chased out, beautiful Texas gals did dances and we all had several gin bucks—the favorite local beverage, apparently. Several of my old college chums were in the group," Babe added. The team practiced at Southern Methodist University where "they were swell to us." Afterward, they rode around beautiful Highland Park before leaving Dallas in the late afternoon. He added cryptically, "The newspaper boys began to unlax [*sic*] at once as has been their wont as soon as the sun gets down every day." He does not say whether he joined them. Nor does he indicate that he tried to contact Jo Belle Smith, their sister-in-law, still living in Dallas or his and Sally's nephews—Champlin, Richard, and Sidney. Instead, his letter focused on the team.

Next day in El Paso, the Lions practiced in the Texas School of M [?] "up in them bare hills" before motoring through Juarez—"just another lousy Mexican border town"—which, because it was "rife with small pox," forced the Lions to remain on the train. Next morning he awoke "feeling better than I can remember. The air is like a shot in the arm." He described the hotel's Spanish architecture, its views of "barren mountains stretching to the north," and the air so "absolutely clear you can see . . . [mountains in old Mexico] 65 miles to the south [that] stand out so clearly that they seem only a few miles off." This poetic side of Babe was something that Sally never recognized publicly.[2] "I have to get to work now, Poos," he concluded, promising to "write more tomorrow. I hope Christmas was fun . . . write me all about it. Love and kisses to you and the fiends. Babe." But how much fun could Christmas in Madison have been that year, the first after Agnes's death? For all his waxing poetic, Babe apparently never understood the magnitude of Sally's loss, or worse, had forgotten about it. On the other hand, Sally appears to have masked her feelings so successfully that even her husband could not imagine what Agnes's death meant to her.

At *The New Yorker*, despite the warmth of their friendships with Benson, both of her editors were sticklers for detail and occasionally caught Sally in an inconsistency. She was glad to fix her pieces as suggested but only if a real mistake were involved. In matters of taste or diction, Benson often returned the galleys without correction and the story was printed exactly as the original had come from her typewriter. In May of 1934, Benson sent Gibbs "A Better Understanding": "Here's a little something for you. It has a funny ending which is something." She was willing to change the title if need be. "Maybe I can do better—I am coming to New York shortly, and will do my best to avoid you. But, don't blame me if you find me under an overstuffed sofa at Tony's looking more like a little wren than ever."[3]

Though some Benson stories might appear formulaic,[4] the majority are marked by originality and the best arose from Benson's lived experience. Notable examples of Benson's experience-based fiction are "Poor My Man" and "Farms Are for Farmers"—both emanating from confrontations with death. The first piece was inspired by a local Madison event—the death of Mr. Josifco—Benson's florist. The Josifco nursery stood adjacent to Anna Cora's little house off the Post Road in Madison, Connecticut, and may still be seen on the left when approaching Hammonasset State Park from the south. "Poor My Man," besides reflecting Benson's ability to transform lived experience into fiction, also illustrates her coping mechanism for dealing with loss—the repression of grief. Modeled long ago by Anna Cora at the time of Benson's first experiences of death—sibling John Perry and Grandpa Prophater—Benson's learned repression intensified at Agnes's death and eventually surfaced in the character of Mrs. Lewis.

Projecting her grief onto Mrs. Lewis, her alter ego,[5] Benson displays her character's repression of feeling as she simultaneously critiques upper-class pretensions to superiority and visits the flower shop to express condolences to "Joseph's" widow, finding herself in turmoil for three reasons. First, she visits from a forced sense of obligation rather than sympathy. Second, she fears that any expression of sympathy will provoke in the widow an open display of emotion, causing her, in turn, to lose her stoic control. Third, the flowers she would like to give as a token of sympathy seem redundant in the setting—like "carrying coals to Newcastle"—and she is uncertain what to offer in their stead. Benson supplies the nervous Mrs. Lewis with a young male companion for support and through their conversation allows the reader a glimpse into her protagonist's psyche. Lewis warns:

> For heaven's sake, be cheerful. Because we mustn't get her started. We really mustn't. I mean, what if she went to pieces on us or something? I couldn't stand it. I simply couldn't. I think I'd go to pieces myself. . . . I simply had to come. I wanted to get it over. You see he was delivering flowers to me when he got hit. And while I really don't think anyone could say I was exactly responsible, I feel funny about it. . . . sometimes I think I take things too hard.

Such fear of "going to pieces" is a good explanation for Sally's reticence in revealing Agnes's death to her *New Yorker* colleagues the previous year.

Besides hinting at how Benson had learned to handle grief, "Poor My Man" also reflects a stereotype of lower-class "Bohemians" that Benson possibly acquired from Anna Cora.[6] The florist's wife is a "Hungarian or a Bohemian or something, and you know how these people act," Mrs. Lewis reminds her companion. "They just haven't any restraint when it comes to people dying or anything. They just go to bits. I mean, you can't expect them to *act* the way you or I would. They don't know what it's all about, that's all" (emphasis mine).[7] In what may be a Freudian slip on Benson's part, her character—Mrs. Lewis—describes the restrained behavior expected from people of her class as "acting." Elaborating, lest her "young man" miss her point, Lewis describes being on a streetcar once when a "fuse blew out and kind of flared up" causing "all these poor people . . . absolute panic" because they "didn't understand, the way they don't." She, on the contrary, "sat perfectly still" while they all "were screaming and trying to get out." The conductor later complimented her: "Lady, I have to hand it to you. You didn't lose your head." One can sense Anna Cora's past insistence on her children's showing similar restraint in times of crisis, not foolishly making a public spectacle, but calmly, stoically, demonstrating strong inner faith—thus modeling upper-class behavior.

Benson's earliest personal crises were associated either with actual deaths or the metaphorical death of Alonzo's repeated absences. Outwardly, she displayed the controlled demeanor Anna Cora expected; inwardly, she feared losing control and exhibiting low-class behavior. Before concluding her somber "Poor My Man," as though to critique her learned repression, Benson injected ironic humor. Though of the lower class, the "tall and thickly built" widow demonstrates "upper-class" strength and inner composure, while handing Mrs. Lewis her "freshest and prettiest rose . . . for [her] coat." By contrast, the protocol-oriented Lewis is visibly ill at ease in explaining her intention to give "a little fruit or some kind of cake" for the widow's mourner-guests. The supposedly déclassé, foreign widow exhibits upper-class dignity and sincere feeling for Lewis whose pain is obvious. Rather than the display of unbridled emotion Lewis feared, Joseph's widow simply "sighed deeply," expressing sadness with the simple phrase—"Yes. Poor my man"—and smiled as Mrs. Lewis and her young man depart. Outside, having successfully maintained visible control, Mrs. Lewis reveals her vulnerability as, shaken by the "foreigner's" spiritual strength, and, longing to escape her own inner weakness, she begs her companion to take her "somewhere . . . anywhere" (most likely a bar), adding as a final comment: "Really, it was almost Russian, wasn't it?" Based on an actual event during one of Benson's summers in Madison, Connecticut, "Poor My Man" might strike the reader as a clever reframing of local news. In reality, the piece does more—it sheds light on Benson's character and the formative influences that shaped it: repressing emotion, dulling pain through distraction.

In July, Benson submitted "The Realist," a story rejected not only by *The New Yorker* but by other magazines as well. It is one of the few that remains unpublished to this day. On July 27th, John Mosher, the "magazine's principal first reader" (Yagoda 114), returned the piece:

Dear Mrs. Benson:

After a great deal of discussion, it seems that we are going to reject your piece. I believe that the chief objection to it is the young man. I guess he is a little bit overdone and the situation a bit unlikely. Also it is possible that the humor of the poetess spinster is a little exhausted. Mr. Ross thinks that you ought to try *Vanity Fair* with it. I am terribly sorry and I hope you will send us something else at once. Thanks a lot anyhow. Be patient with us.

Sincerely yours,
John Mosher[8]

Miffed, Benson fired off a letter the next day:

Dear Mr. Mosher:

I don't know why you've come into my life with your rejection slips so I'm flaunting you in the face with another story. And please don't keep it two weeks discussing it either because God knows I try to keep any suggestion of plot out of my pieces so as not to confuse all of you. You have a terribly polite way of turning things down. Personally, I just say, "Uh-Uh." But maybe you'll come out better in the long run.

Sincerely,
Sally Benson

P.S. Where is Gibbs? Lying down resting somewhere, I bet.[9]

When Gibbs returned from vacation, he wrote Benson requesting a few changes in her last submission, "Summer Is Lovely." One was that she delete a male character's bringing up divorce, the other, that she clarify another character's occupation. "If you fix these, we'll buy it. Like a shot," he assured her. Then, he offered a word of caution: "Your notes upset Mr. Mosher. 'That waspish little party,' he calls you."[10] A few days later Benson returned her story with the changes Gibbs wanted. She asked to be paid for it because she intended to go to Maine for a few weeks "if I can collect enough money from editors." She added:

> I have a story in the *Mercury* which will be out August 22nd. It's one you turned down ["Mental Cruelty"]. Also, do you know anything about Scribner's or Harper's and how much they pay? I have a story—about twelve pages—called "Farms Are for Farmers." It's very good but I don't think you would use it. It's pretty literary and sad. I would send it to you but you keep stories so long. It's like something Chekhov would do if he were weak-minded.

Unable to resist, Benson tacked on a retaliatory comment: "I bet nobody ever called John Mosher waspish. Love, Sally."[11]

Benson was struggling to establish criteria for judging her writing. In August, she complained to Gibbs:

> You are always bewildered and I don't want you to tell me that you are bewildered any more. I changed this story and I think it's clear. If you don't want it, may I have it back by Friday as I need another story and I don't know what else to write. I think it's a funny story and I hope the change suits you, you old fuss-budget.[12]

It is difficult to know how Benson decided what constituted a good story. Her next submission arrived with the following message for Gibbs: "I'm just as busy as a Sally-bee. Here's another story with no title. I think it's a very good one, but I have often proved that I am no judge. Anyway, Sally." At other times, Benson might question whether her titles were "too pretentious." Clearly, she was trying her wings but flying in a wobbly, uncertain direction.

Complicating Benson's problem of establishing her own criteria for judging her work were letters from editors and publishers outside of *The New Yorker*. One was from Bernard Smith of Alfred A. Knopf, Inc., who in a series of discussions with Benson and follow-up letters, added to Benson's confusion. On July 2nd, for example, Smith had encouraged Benson's proposal for a "book . . . in an E. F. Benson manner on Connecticut as she really is today" rather than "a volume of short stories."[13] On July 10th, Smith wrote, after "our conversation yesterday morning," which he "enjoyed enormously," he was "more convinced than ever" that Benson would be able to write an "interesting, charming, and saleable novel." His only hesitation, he warned, lay in the difficulties she would face because she had

> been accustomed to writing very short pieces. It will take you, perhaps, a little while longer than you think to adjust yourself to a piece of sustained writing. Your problem is to create some focus of interest or some character or some development in narrative that will carry both you and your readers along through a book. But I have confidence in you and am sure that you will be able to solve that problem. You say that you write very rapidly—which is probably a good thing, but I suspect that it will take you some time before you can really begin with the assurance that you have a theme big enough.

On August 16th, upon returning from vacation, Smith "looked eagerly" for a letter from Benson or "a few pages of manuscript." Disappointed, he inquired how Benson was "getting along with the novel."[14] Benson replied with petulance that Smith had "looked more eagerly for the manuscript than for the letter." Smith claimed he realized the difficulty of undertaking a "sustained piece of work" after writing the "sketches and short pieces . . . she had trained herself to," but he reiterated his confidence in Benson's potential. "What you did to Mrs. Leroy Mintie is the first step toward the solution," he advised. "The more women like her that you manage to put off the sooner you will finish your novel and the better it will be. I am the founder of a society organized for the purpose of annihilating social pests. Will you join?" On a more serious note, Smith concluded his letter with assurances of "sincere and serious advice" upon Benson's presentation of her manuscript.[15]

Suburban living, a positive experience for Benson, had provided a practical outcome: new material for fiction. The "Mrs. Mintie" allusion made by Smith derived from Benson's experience at a Madison, Connecticut flower show organized by Benson's sister, Rose Shuttleworth, and described by Benson in a letter to Gibbs:

> all the women got insulted. A woman named Mrs. Leroy Mintie was head of the committee and I was tipped off how to handle her. I was told, "You'll know how to handle *her*, Sally. Her name used to be Bertha Schrader and her father was a butcher in Waterbury." And I said, "Yes, I see. With a cleaver." It got back to her and things became a trifle strained when the begonias were being judged. I bet this makes your dwarf annual spirea look pretty cheap.[16]

The same flip tone and characteristic ability to see through people, as well as the unhesitating rashness of the comment—"Yes, with a cleaver"—would inform subsequent Benson stories. However, Benson's proposed novel was slow to emerge despite Smith's, Cain's, Hobson's, and others' encouragement. Then, one day, disturbed by a sense of inadequacy, Benson wrote to a former *New Yorker* editor, James M. Cain.

A former "jesus"[17] and managing editor at *The New Yorker* before he moved to California to pursue screenplay writing, Cain was also a crime novelist and had been particularly vocal in opposing Benson's writing of short fiction. Echoing Bernard Smith, Cain wrote a lengthy letter to Benson on August 25th to express his pleasure in learning that his "little tip to Angoff last spring had results." Once again he repeated, "I think you have a lot and I only hope that Angoff, or Knopf, or somebody gets it out of you." Cain specifically attacked Benson's complaining of "not being able to think up stories" because it gave him "more or less a pain in the neck." In Hollywood, he reflected, "where nobody ever thinks of anything but stories, and all the jumbled ideas finally superimpose on each other to make a gigantic shadow called The Story, you find out that nobody, ever, can think of stories." Even when you read the "prolific boys" who wrote "Literature," you find they had it "just as tough as anybody else" and produced only a few that were really memorable. Cain continued,

> Stories are tough . . . and you not being able to think of any doesn't make you an exception to the rule, but merely puts you in the same boat. . . . So what you need is to go to work. Brass tacks, sweetheart, a full meal of them every day. After you've sweated, and cursed, and wished you had gone in the interior decoration business with the clever aunt, then maybe you'll have a few written.

Cain offered Benson some tips:

> For God's sake, can those little *New Yorker* pieces and spread out. That magazine, excellent as it is, got out by a lot of precious amateurs, who are not the less amateurs because they are very gifted. Next: do as little magazine work as you can, and make up your mind to write books, plays, or something on the big stage. One book, even if it flops, does you more good than all the magazine pieces you can write. Next: Spend your juice on story, story, and story, rather than dialogue or descriptions of the scenery. Dialogue is fine and you write it beautifully, but what they pay their money for is a yarn—excitement—the only thing that can light up your characterization so that it really glows, makes the reader feel it. Be ready to go into the snow bank with it for three months, if necessary, to get it right. Next: Write, quit sitting around, grinning at thistles, and thinking about it. Next: Cultivate Angoff, or Knopf, or somebody who will be able to make it seem real, and not just a couple of other good intentions.

Cain concluded, "Well, so much for this installment. Let me know how it goes. I really expect a lot from you. Of all who submitted comical little things while I was on the *New Yorker*, you were the only one who got me much excited, and that was why I gave Angoff such a song and dance about you when I saw him. Yours, J. M. Cain."[18]

In a letter to Gibbs a few days later, Benson referred to Cain's letter as "very funny. I don't know him, you know, and it was full of good homespun advice. He thinks I should stop writing little pieces and go in for bigger things and I told him you all did, too." Benson, however, despite all the talk and discussion with publishers about her book continued to doubt her ability to write a sustained piece of fiction. She decided she liked Cain's passion for story and determined to try to "light up her characterization" with excitement as he had urged.

Within two weeks she submitted "Farms Are for Farmers," her second death-inspired story and one she had mentioned earlier to Gibbs. Stemming directly from Agnes's death, the piece opens with a prospective buyer arriving to look at a house. Benson introduces the house and its contents as though it were a character. Throughout the tour, its widower-owner comments on the décor. Items like the highly colored square of carpet "gleaming like an evil eye" on the shiny, black-painted, living room floor he attributes to his wife, Allie. She had liked this room, he explains, and planned to decorate it in "black, green, and orange." Proceeding on the tour, the two men pass Allie's player piano, which her husband demonstrates by inserting a roll titled "Little White Lies"—Allie's favorite piece, one she played "over and over." The melody continues to play for the duration of the tour, its title providing ironic commentary on the seller's sales pitch.

Continuing to guide his potential buyer, the owner allows the rooms to relate the history of their marriage. The dining room is in good condition—it "hasn't been used much" because "we kind of got to eating in the kitchen." Allie had lost her interest in fixing food because "it wasn't any fun cooking for two. Allie liked a houseful. . . . We used to have people up at first . . . but it's pretty far away," he explains, "And of course there isn't much for them to do. No movies or anything." Benson addressed the issue of social isolation in this piece, inspired by firsthand knowledge of her sister Agnes's progressive surrendering to the loneliness and boredom of her life in suburban Connecticut. Caring for a toddler, her only companion other than a servant, Agnes longed for her former Manhattan life writing reviews of plays and films. Like Eugene O'Neill's Mary Tyrone in *Long Day's Journey into Night*, Agnes sought compensation in alcohol and drugs. Benson reflects her sister's addiction by having the story's seller, an older man, offer his young, potential buyer a drink—only to discover that the "bottle of apple brandy hid away here somewhere" is empty. The reader infers that either the owner/narrator or his recently deceased wife had drained the bottle and forgotten about it.

Turning toward the kitchen, the owner points with pride to its pale-green porcelain dishwasher: "I wanted Allie to have everything she would have in the city." Outside is a small garden where she used to plant vegetables—a foolish idea, he comments—since farmers all around sell their produce at roadside stands. Satisfied that the sale is in the offing despite his cryptic warnings, the seller issues a direct caution: "You want to be sure you're going to like it up here." The local farmers are "kind of intimate with one another, but they don't seem to want to mix much with outsiders," he explains. It's "as nice a house as you'll find for the price. And easy to live in . . . the way I've got everything fixed. . . . You'd think anybody could be happy living in a house like this."

As the buyer declares, "I like it swell" and asks to bring his wife to see the house, the seller sighs deeply: "Are you going to tell her about Allie?" The buyer will, but not right away, because it might "kind of influence her about the house." The reader, assuming that Allie has either died or been divorced, is shocked to learn she has committed suicide. Benson, with her love of mystery books, displays her talent in achieving mild suspense by withholding that revelation until the next-to-last paragraph:

> When you tell her later . . . you might sort of explain that Allie couldn't have been exactly in her right mind when she did it. The doctor says people don't do those things in their right mind. Temporary insanity, he called it. I kind of hate to have anyone think that Allie would do a thing like that in her right mind. Because she never would have. Never in the world. Not Allie.

One can hear Benson's voice in the doctor's diagnosis. The sentiments expressed—especially the repeated insistence that Allie was not in her right mind—reflect the pain Agnes's suicide caused for Benson. Imprinted in memory, the doctor's words emphasize for present-day readers how misunderstood depression was in the thirties and how minimal and ineffective were the available treatments and medication.

Though Benson found the writing of "Farms Are for Farmers" cathartic, Gibbs and other *New Yorker* editors considered the story problematic. *The New Yorker* accepted almost all the pieces Benson submitted, but "Farms Are for Farmers" met with polite rejection. Gibbs explained their reasons for rejecting the work and made several suggestions. "It is a very good story," Gibbs wrote, "but there are things in it that need fixing." One was

> the little man buying a house without taking his wife along to look at it. In the second place, what is all this about a stain on the rug [suggesting] this girl shot herself, when it turns out in the end she was drowned? . . . Finally, couldn't you cut out the end, that talk with the taxi driver? I think it's an anticlimax. . . . You could put in a sentence somewhere in the body, making it clear that she did commit suicide—we don't care how.

The preceding comment seems insensitive on Gibbs's part, indicating that he may have forgotten about Agnes's death or, unaware of its cause, did not connect the piece to Benson's life. Though Gibbs may not have cared how the suicide occurred, *New Yorker* readers would have.

Despite her talent, Gibbs's referring to a meaningless stain shows that Benson needed occasional instruction in the craft of fiction. This piece was uncharacteristically lacking in clarity, possibly because it aroused so many negative emotions for Benson. Gibbs's mentoring advice continued: "The drinking doesn't seem very important, and I guess it would be better if this guy and the house had just driven her nuts." Given the pattern of heavy social drinking customary among his colleagues, Gibbs dismissed as irrelevant Benson's implication that drinking was connected to the suicide. But clearly, the role of drinking in this story mattered to Benson because, though her revision subtly downplayed the reference, she retained it. Gibbs ended, "I hate to send this piece back to you because I'm afraid you'll just send it off to some magazine that never asks questions. However, it's not much work really, and I'll trust you."[19] He also informed her in a postscript that "Ross has another story of yours—about planning a party. [You will] hear from Mrs. White about that next week." Gibbs, meanwhile, planned to go away for two weeks "to read O'Hara's book."

Benson accepted Gibbs's corrections, resubmitted "Farms Are for Farmers," and received a lengthy letter the following week from Katharine White:

Dear Miss Benson:

We like enormously now "Farms Are for Farmers" and here is our check for it. Mr. Ross had not read the first version . . . and finds a lot of new questions which I have tried to take care of in editing, but I want you to know about. One was . . . that the piano could not have been playing "Little White Lies" so long a time . . . unless the man put on a repeat mechanism. . . . I put in a phrase to take care of that. . . . Mr. Ross also wanted the suggestion of unpleasant breath underneath the spearmint taken out, so I simply cut that and I'm sure you won't mind.

Ross had questioned the seller's doing "just odd jobs now and then" because he did not understand how the man could finance himself, so White removed the reference to odd jobs, substituting "The old job folded and I'd saved a little. That's how I happened to get this place." White also changed the buyer's occupation from selling vacuum cleaners to septic tanks and the setting to Connecticut, but she allowed Benson the option of changing these emendations if she so chose. Though Ross had wanted the stain removed from the piece, White had "argued him out of that." She concluded: "This story seems to be one of the important pieces of work that Mr. Cain was urging you to do. All I can say is that the *New Yorker* likes it as well as Mr. Cain when you go in for stories in a big way."[20] In a postscript, White alluded to enclosing Benson's check at a flat rate greater than Benson's old "word rate." White also included a bonus for excellence and announced a slight raise in Benson's "word rate" effective from then on, hoping it would "spur [Benson] on to a great deal of effort."[21]

Benson's letter accompanying her next submission shows that she reacted to White's praise with a mixture of gratitude, awe, and self-doubt:

Dear Mrs. White,

I was staggered by my last check and flushed with success. . . . It's nice of you to raise my rates and I am very pleased. I have never got over that surprised feeling of being paid.

I have told Knopf that I will get them something by December, but I am not at all sure that I can do a sustained piece of writing. They are extremely encouraging and that worries me too.

In the spring and summer of 1934, as Benson wrote "Poor My Man" and "Farms Are for Farmers," her life in Madison revolved around gardening and writing plus occasional visits to her *New Yorker* office to catch up with colleagues and have lunch with Wolcott Gibbs. Most of her *New*

Yorker submissions were accepted, but one rejection was unusually blunt: "Dear Sally," Gibbs wrote in September, "We don't like 'The Overcoat.' It's hard to say why, except that those are O. Henry overcoats you've got in there, and we don't like them."[22] Disappointed but undeterred, Benson sent "The Overcoat" to *The American Mercury*, which had just published "Mental Cruelty" (also rejected by *The New Yorker*) in its September issue.[23] Benson offered to send the *Mercury* other pieces if publisher Charles Angoff were interested. Angoff responded with enthusiasm: ". . . 'The Overcoat,'[24] is excellent, and I am putting it into type at once. . . . Send me more of your stories by all means. I am looking forward to your book."[25] As a twenty-year-old, Sally had become engaged to several soldiers going off to the Great War; now a thirty-six-year-old, she repeated the pattern of toying with several men, this time publishers—Angoff, Hobson, and Smith—who might help get her book published at their firms.

When "The Overcoat" appeared in the November *American Mercury*, it caught the attention of Edward O'Brien, editor of *The Best Short Stories*, an annual anthology. O'Brien wrote on November 1st requesting a short biographical note for the forthcoming edition—*The Best Short Stories of 1935*—to accompany his selection of "The Overcoat." To the *New Yorker* staff's chagrin, Benson's story was reprinted there as well as in *The American Mercury* in both 1936 and 1941, and then in *The American Mercury Reader* in 1944.[26] "The Overcoat" was also chosen by J. A. Burrell and B. A. Cerf for *The Bedside Book of Famous American Stories*, and O'Brien would "certainly have liked 'The Overcoat' for a series" of twelve new stories by American authors that he was preparing for the *Pictorial Review*.[27] Instead, O'Brien included "The Overcoat" in *Fifty Best American Short Stories (1915–1939)*. With her unique blend of humor and sarcasm, Benson reported to Gibbs that Edward O'Brien had called on Mr. Angoff before leaving for London on December 5th wanting to know "what I looked like. Angoff told him I was a cross between the new Duchess of Kent and Emily Brontë and if you would say things like that about your contributors, you might get along better. I told Angoff if O'Brien was picking stories on the author's looks, he'd never run any of Martha Foley's. I'm at work on a masterpiece. I'm tired to death of it but I think it's art. It's dull enough to be."[28] Benson had come closer to defining herself as a writer, but she still struggled with what the nature of her writing should be. As for the intended masterpiece, she had serious qualms. The process of refining her vision and her craft was still in its first phase, despite growing recognition and increasing demands from publishers for more Benson fiction.

15

PERFECTING HER CRAFT

1934–1935

"She has the keenest possible eye for the small change in which women demand back the gold of their lives."

—Katharine Simonds, *Saturday Review of Literature*

Benson often had difficulty discriminating between the excellent and the lackluster. Writing to Gibbs in the fall of 1934, Benson reported that Charles Angoff had seen her story in the last *New Yorker* and concluded that she "must have done it with her left hand."[1] Puzzled, Benson continued: "And yet he loved that one I sent him about the overcoat that you all didn't like. Well, live and let learn as Ring Lardner once said." Though disconcerting, the conflicting opinions of two major publishers served to buoy Benson's common sense: she could not please every editor. She would be open to constructive criticism until she gained greater self-assurance and confidence in her own literary judgment. Her chief focus at this stage in her career was to balance her need for self-expression with the reality of her financial situation. Yet she seemed unconcerned at times with success or money as the letter to Gibbs accompanying her next submission indicates:

> Here is a story you won't like. Please don't keep it while you mull over it trying to figure out where to put the commas. You keep stories so long, especially those last two ones, that I think you must be building a nest or something. If this is true, write me and I will send you bits of old string. My stories would not make nests as you should know if you'd only stop to think but everybody tells me string is fine. I am glad Ross thought

so highly of that story. But don't let the length of them deceive
you. I am trying to get the hang of the adjectives.[2]

Clearly, though she viewed herself as a novice writer, she was sometimes
frustrated by the length of time powerful editors could take before making decisions. Her self-appraisal, however, as well as her financial situation,
were about to change.

New Yorker editors were interested chiefly in the magazine's financial
success and Benson's presence in the magazine played a significant role.
From that perspective, Gibbs admitted to Katharine White that he did
not always understand Benson's pieces, yet "hate[d] to send [this one] back
because she's getting so bright about Angoff etc. and is likely to turn it in
somewhere else, but I don't see how to fix it here, do you?" White, for all
her supposed friendship with Benson, was quite willing to manipulate her.
Replying to Gibbs, she confided: "I agree with you. Whatever she intends
doesn't get over. Why don't you hold the piece, write to ask her what her
intention is, and if she'd be willing to make it clear. Then send back the
piece if she will fix it. Might prevent her sending it elsewhere in a pet."[3]
The story in question was "Wild Animal" and, though Benson evidently
fixed it to White's and Gibbs's satisfaction, it appeared in the July 20th
issue as a mere "summer piece"—by definition, "one of slight interest or one
pertaining to summer activities."[4] Undaunted, Benson continued writing.
Her next piece—"The Witness"—evoked a laudatory memo from Gibbs:
"Mr. Ross thinks this is one of the best stories you ever did."[5]

Benson continued defining herself as a writer—often affirmed by
her *New Yorker* editors but sometimes challenged by *New Yorker* standards
regarding theme, type, and length. Further complicating Benson's difficulty
in clarifying her criteria for excellence was the escalating demand for her
stories from editors and publishers outside *The New Yorker*. As early as
January 1935, Benson had written to White regarding permissions needed
by a professor at New York University to reprint two Benson pieces in a
Harper & Brothers textbook for an Oral Interpretation course. Her letter
is modest in tone but it belies Benson's past writing success: "It seems I am
being considered literary, whereas you know and Gibbs knows that most
of my simplicity is due to an appalling ignorance in the use of adjectives
and a blank spot in my brain where grammar should be. I hope both of
you will have the decency to keep quiet about it."[6] Gibbs, answering for
White, explained that once the pieces appeared in *The New Yorker*, the
magazine had "nothing to say."[7] The author retained the copyright. He

advised Benson to say she would "appear free in non-profit-making books," but otherwise she should require a royalty. Benson replied, "Thanks for the advice. You're damned right I want to get paid for everything." In the same letter Benson informed Gibbs that some bright young man (Jonathan Edgar Webb) was starting a magazine in Cleveland and had contacted her. After naming all the "imposing people" who were contributing to his first issue, he asked, "didn't I want to be in Vol. 1 No. 1?"

When Benson wrote Webb to inquire about his requirements, she could not refrain from asking why he had signed his name "Jon Edgar," omitting his surname. "Are you tired already?" she quipped. Webb explained he was "Jon Edgar" to all his friends but admitted that the signature was perhaps "an affectation of some kind." He also congratulated Benson on her "appear[ing] in a textbook! That's a sort of honor . . . please don't send me a sketch. Watching for you, Jon Edgar."

Jon Edgar Webb, editor-to-be of *Sanctuary*—a magazine "For distinctive literary short stories of today"—had given Benson a January 25th deadline for a piece under four thousand words. He wanted "not one of those vague things with no plot," but one that would "be spontaneous . . . end with a click, leaving no want of further enlightment [*sic*] . . . a story [that] breathes movement." Benson ignored the request. Instead, pleased with Babe's Christmas gift of a "very fine" typewriter,[8] she promised Gibbs she would send "about ten stories written on it."[9]

February of 1935 proved eventful on many levels. On February 4th, for instance, Edward O'Brien wrote Benson thanking her for permission to reprint "The Overcoat." Interested in having a new Benson submission for the *Pictorial Review*, he wanted to meet her next autumn when he returned to America. February also marked Benson's moving into Gibbs's recently vacated apartment in the 33 West 55th Street Hotel. A perpetual in-bed smoker, Gibbs had set fire to himself continually, and when Sally sent him a piece reflecting her current relationship with Babe, she jokingly referred to the fire "still smoldering in the walls." What prompted her story, however, was far from humorous: Babe's discovery toward the end of January that Sally had added Demerol to her alcohol addiction. As Golseth recalls, "It was just too much for him and he left."[10] Characteristically, Sally Benson's response to Babe's departure was simply to weave personal experience into the new piece titled "Love Affair."

Babe was not the only one offended by Sally's addictions and their influence on her behavior. In an in-house memo to Katharine White regarding "Love Affair," Gibbs added a personal comment: "You'll be relived [*sic*] to know that she is not coming to the *New Yorker* party.[11] 'Too many little people with two heads,' she says, stealing a line from Mrs. Parker." While Gibbs's memo hints at Sally Benson's renewed effort to embrace sobriety, it also reveals that he and White were not looking forward to repetitions of Benson's prior drunken behavior at social events. Benson had become a difficult, embarrassing drunk and even when sober, annoyed others by disrupting conversations and catching, for example, men like Frank Sullivan and Jim Thurber, "in her orbit" (Kinney 784). At times, she even threw away *New Yorker* proofs—a behavior that, as Gibbs reminded her, "paralyzes the entire organization."[12] (Ironically, *The New Yorker* party instead witnessed St. Clair McKelway's fistfight with fellow staffer Morris Markey, causing Ross to hide in the men's room [Kinney 569].)

In rejecting Benson's "Love Affair" Gibbs explained: "It seems pretty familiar" and has "one of those ends you see coming from the beginning. . . . You confused the issue a little by writing it so well, but not quite enough, I guess." In the same letter, Gibbs alerted Benson to Ross's note on the proofs of "The Fur Piece." "It is your story, of course, and he doesn't insist on any change. Just trying to be helpful, he says. I have a feeling he's right though, and I hope you'll agree."[13]

The New Yorker's rejection of "Love Affair" prompted Benson to forward the piece to Charles Angoff at *The American Mercury* and it appeared in that magazine's May issue. Ruthie, the bored protagonist, attends a dance convinced that this night her Prince Charming will appear. Despite all her efforts to make the wished-for dream substantial, Ruthie's energies prove misguided. No one awaits her at the dance except the same old friend, Harry Sloane, whom she greets with: "Hello, Harry. Anything new or exciting tonight?" After kissing her lightly on the cheek, Harry returns the greeting: "Hello Ruthie . . . No, nothing . . . same old crowd. Come on, let's dance."[14]

Like many of Benson's stories, "Love Affair" is a virtually plotless, casual sketch. Her method was to establish a character, a mood, and a setting that produce a type of epiphany. In "Love Affair," for example, Ruthie's expectations are grandiose. In the tiny town and closed society she inhabits, the same residents will appear predictably at any given social function. Yet, Ruthie typifies the romantic, always hopeful that this time it will be different. Inevitably, she will have to settle for Harry's company, if not for Harry himself—the known, familiar, and uninteresting. Some might regard Benson's view as dismal and pessimistic. Rather, Benson is amused by human nature. Prince Charming is a rare fellow, more nonexistent than real. To be in a position to meet him at all, Ruthie needs to make major changes in her life and broaden her horizons, but she lacks the will power to make those changes. She is one of those unfascinating people that Benson encountered wherever she turned.[15] Benson's gift was to capture such people in their ordinariness, hold up their quirkiness for all to see, and allow ordinary readers a measure of comfort in recognizing kindred spirits.

As the reality of what appeared a definitive separation from Babe sank in, Benson's *New Yorker* pieces began to reflect the Bensons' breakup. "Really Living," published in the February 8, 1936 issue, introduces readers to Margot Archer, wife of a university professor. Benson presents Margot's interior monologue as she prepares the roaring blaze her husband considered "essential . . . unless his whole evening was to be spoiled." Reflecting on his usual behavior whenever the Morleys visit, she decides that he is "dry and unimaginative and . . . had no depth"—sentiments that Sally had begun voicing about Babe.[16] Examining Archer's disenchantment with her, Margot concludes:

> he had decided she was not worth impressing. Sometimes the tremendous show they gave together for the benefit of others astounded her . . . when he spoke to her his voice seemed to conceal an amusement, but it was no longer tender [but] cold and only grew warm on the occasions when she looked more pinched and clumsily put-together than usual. Then he paid her compliments, but she knew that he was ashamed of her at the moment and that his pride made him say things so that people would believe she was something rare and different . . . and she would stand there, her hands awkward and mottled at her sides, conscious of the unloveliness of her carrot-colored hair . . . her dress that struggled for a draped simplicity and succeeded only in looking bunchy.

The detail—"carrot-colored hair"—describes Benson's hair for much of her life as does Margot's negative introspection. The piece ends with Professor Archer arriving home distraught after learning that the Morleys—who "won't know what they are seeing"—are "going abroad, sailing next month, for a whole year," while he, because he has no money, must "sit here and rot." "Really Living" contains enough realistic detail in its evocation of a troubled marriage to suggest that Benson felt Babe was responsible for their breakup. Yet, her astute description of behavior often associated with alcoholics, namely Mrs. Archer's slovenly appearance, low self-esteem, and blaming someone else for her unhappiness, intimates that Benson recognized her role as contributor to the separation.

The following month, Benson's award-winning piece, "Suite 2049" (March 14, 1936), focused directly on an actual breakup, again reflecting Benson's life. The story opens: "It had never occurred to Lois Bentley that Don would ever leave her. . . . If there had been some sort of scene between herself and Don, tears and bitter words, it might have been easier. It was the way he walked out that left her stunned and lost." One can hear Benson's voice clearly: "It wasn't as though she had done anything to upset him; they were going along the way they always had, the way they had gone along for twelve years." The Bentleys (note the similarity to "Bensons") had been to a party and left with Lois feeling "uplifted and keen, the way she always did when she had talked about things of which she knew nothing"—as Benson the fabricator often did.[17] They "had about decided to go to Angelo's, a former speakeasy, hot, stuffy, and not too clean . . . when Don said he didn't want to go." His subsequent silence in the taxi was "not very odd, as he and Lois *hadn't much to say to one another*" (emphasis mine: Benson's exact words when describing her relationship with Babe [Kinney 513]). They return to their twentieth-floor apartment in a hotel where most of the furnishings belong to the hotel with a few "faintly personal touch[es]." Like Benson, Lois had always maintained, "The ideal way to live [is] . . . in a hotel in the winter, no lease, and have your own home somewhere in the summer"—Madison or Nantucket for Benson. The Bentleys had never "got around to buying a place in the country, although they talked about it every spring."

After Lois automatically hung up her wrap, feeling "comfort and reassurance" in this familiar act, she returned to find a changed Don in the living room. "Just what is the matter?" she asked "reasonably." Then, "like a lawyer stating a case," he expounded for twenty minutes "how little he had liked" all they had done in the last twelve years. "He resented . . . the very conveniences she had enjoyed." Benson elaborated with a catalog of hotel services and foods, culminating in: "he hated other people's things." Lois protests, "We have everything we want—a pleasant place to live, all sorts of friends; we have much more than most people we know. And we have each other." To which Don retorts: "Have we?" He would see that she had money to continue living as she has, but he had decided to "get a place and fix it up." Later they might "meet and talk things over sensibly like civilized people." Immediately in denial, Lois takes comfort lying in bed "as though the whole thing were too absurd to be taken seriously. Men didn't leave women for no reason at all, she thought. "He would come back and be sorry. She was almost asleep when she wondered suddenly and fearfully if, when men did leave women after twelve years, they ever came back. Or whether they came back to habits." Alternately switching the light on and off, Lois lay there with "the uneasy feeling of not remembering where she was." The powerful ending echoes Benson's feelings as she grappled with Babe's abrupt, definitive departure. Unlike Don Bentley, however, Babe would send no money. In fact, Sally Benson would need to motivate herself to produce more fiction than ever, leading to unimagined financial success. Ultimately and ironically, that success later enabled her to support Babe also.

In March, Benson was surprised to receive a solicitation letter from Herbert Block of Covici-Friede, Inc., Publishers:

Dear Mrs. Benson,

I had intended to write you some months ago after reading some of your stories in the *American Mercury*, but, unfortunately, I was told at the time that you had already signed a contract with another publisher. Charles Angoff . . . tells me that this is not so, and that as a matter of fact, you are planning a novel and another book. I am very anxious indeed to have a chance to discuss this with you and if you are coming into town again soon, I hope that we can arrange to meet.[18]

Benson's affirmative response to meeting Block led to an epistolary relationship (and more) with Pascal ("Pat") Covici. Born in Romania of Jewish parentage, Pat Covici and his business partner Donald Friede had initially made huge profits from publishing Radclyffe Hall's *The Well of Loneliness*. After the book's indictment for obscenity, the firm's profits doubled, but the Depression impinged heavily on its future success. By 1935 when Covici expressed interest in Sally Benson's work, the firm had published some of John Steinbeck's early novels.[19]

As soon as Benson's negotiations with Covici-Friede Publishers regarding publication of her first short story collection—*People Are Fascinating*—became public, a disappointed Bernard Smith wrote on March 27th:

Dear Mrs. Benson,

I read in today's *World Telegram* that you have just signed a contract with Covici-Friede for your novel.[20] Tell me it isn't true because if it is true it'll break my heart. I have nothing in the world against Covici-Friede, but I had hoped very much that we would have the privilege of seeing your book when it was ready. Yours faithfully,

for Alfred A. Knopf Inc.
(signed: Bernard Smith)

While various publishers strove to obtain her work, Benson continued submitting pieces to *The New Yorker*, some meeting with rejection and others with acclaim. One decision by Gibbs particularly upset her—his rejection of "One Fine Day"—and elicited a rare Benson admission. She had "muffed it" and could see "why it fell flat. I'm going to fix it and send it somewhere," she wrote, adding: "I work very hard nowadays." On another occasion, Benson admonished him: "If you are going to run this in summer, you had better not have that woman lying down in her bed at six-thirty." With a touch of humor, she continued: "I just got a letter from *Vogue* and they want me to write for them, but I don't know as I dress well enough." Knowing Gibbs's shared interest in gardening, Benson next mentioned that she had been to "the country for a few days and set out a lot of perennials." Incidentally, she added, "the insurance companies have cut their rates in half since I have moved into your place."[21]

In April, Benson admitted to having had the measles but cautioned: "Don't burn this [story] because I've been over them for a month. Helen told me she spread the ghastly rumor."[22] Actually, *The New Yorker* rejected "Hero's Wife" because, as Gibbs explained: "It doesn't seem worked out enough and suggests somehow that you changed your mind somewhere in the middle . . . the girl is vague and the whole story a little inconclusive, I'm afraid. We'd be delighted if you'd work it over, but I'm sure you won't."[23] What was innovative about Benson's style was her avoidance of plot and lack of character development. She wasted no time in needless descriptions, recording the facts after close and careful observation.[24] Her sketches should have suited the magazine, but Harold Ross preferred that readers should not have to grapple with meaning. As Matthew Bruccoli explains regarding *The New Yorker's* rejection of some of John O'Hara's fiction, O'Hara's "economical prose and tight control of detail troubled readers who were accustomed to having the message spelled out for them" (Bruccoli 139).

As Gibbs had predicted, Benson sent "Hero's Wife" directly to *The American Mercury* without changing it one iota. "I sold it without a quiver," she happily reported. In fact, to Benson's amusement, Paul Palmer of *The American Mercury* called "Hero's Wife" a "splendid piece of work [going] right smack into the October" issue with "cheers from compositors and editors alike. A check for $125" would be mailed that week, he assured her. "You are getting dangerously close to writing really remarkable short stories," he volunteered. "Your skill in observation and the ease with which you write—especially dialogue—all confirm my opinion that if you keep on improving it won't be long until there is no one better." Like Hobson, Smith, and Angoff—his predecessors—Palmer had entertained the hope that Benson would "do a long story . . . some day" and predicted "it will be a really great story." Before closing he inquired: "Will you have lunch with me in New York on Thursday so that I can flatter you further?"[25]

Gibbs, on the other hand, was not pleased with Benson's next submission and kept it "for a little while, as there are problems. A week, if you'll be patient," he assured her. True to his word, he wrote the following week explaining that he had "accumulated nearly seven pages of notes . . . giving the story a short lead of two pages . . . following queries from everybody, all mixed up." Set in Connecticut, the piece was titled "The Time Will Come." Gibbs's critique centered on "the mother, who seems very worldly for a native." She was more of a summer visitor, and Gibbs wanted Benson to fix her status at the outset and clarify whether the locale were Maine or Connecticut. Certain phrases—"great beauty" and "charm"—did not seem appropriate on the lips of small-town people. Nor did the mother's "push[ing] her daughter into the summer group," he explained. "Natives generally are suspicious . . . even patronizing about the summer colonists."[26]

Benson responded by defending small-town Connecticut society as opposed to urbane New York City life, a distinction she knew firsthand. Her argument derived from observation of her now fifteen-year-old daughter growing up in Madison: "Don't think the natives aren't worldly.

Many . . . the ones with daughters especially, try like mad to get away from the town life." She continued:

> The entire village lives on the summer trade, and while the men scorn the idea of mixing in, the women decidedly do not, and edge their way into garden clubs and other things that admit both shore and town people. This story couldn't be Maine, of course. Maine is more untouched, and their natives aren't as "classy" as our natives. This place isn't made up of a lot of James Gould Cozzens characters. It is too near New Haven, too close to the Post Road, and it has been influenced too much by the summer people.[27]

As for Ross's difficulty understanding why "the boys went cold on her" and his insistence on the importance of knowing, Gibbs reported:

> I presume it's because they are members of the club and don't want to be seen with this girl. But why? Because she's homely, or just because she's a smalltown [sic] girl? Two elements seem to get in it and confuse me. Of course, my firm opinion is that boys of that age aren't particular about looks, family, geography, or even color, once they get going. . . . What would have happened is that one of them would have tried to date her.

Because Gibbs considered Ross's reservations "unsound," he promised Benson he would "try to talk Ross out of most of his difficulties" with the piece. Gibbs's supposition was that Benson had both points in mind:

> They were cold on her before the club ever came up, just because she was a freak, but the club business clinched it. Perhaps you can make that clear somehow with a sentence near the end. If you can't, never mind and I'll argue. The mother will have to be fixed though, and I hope you'll try, because strangely enough, we all admire this piece very much.[28]

As is clear from the piece as published, Benson intended that "the boys went cold on her because they could see she wouldn't give them the sort of evening they had in mind. But they are nice boys and incapable of positive rudeness while they are with her. They just don't show up because that is a rudeness they do not have to meet face to face." Benson agreed with Ross's view that boys are unconcerned about looks, family, geography, or even color, but she maintained, "They are fussy about having to drag some unattractive little girl along to a dance where their friends will be. They are little snobs, as all young people are. They can't place her. She isn't one of them, and she isn't a waitress. They are not feeling too deeply about it, they just feel it's no go."

In July, Helen Thurber visited Benson in Madison and spent the night. A rarity for both, there was no drinking. Instead, they "ate candy and read detective stories" but didn't have a pillow fight. "I wanted to," Benson confided, "but Helen, like all you New York people, said she was *tired* of pillow fights. Imagine!" Helen filled Benson in on all the gossip, "all about mooey-mooey and people leaving their wives—things I hadn't heard about at all. I had a fine time." Though knowledgeable about Connecticut, Benson admittedly needed advice from Gibbs regarding how to answer *Vogue* employees who concluded telephone calls with, "It was sweet of you to call." In all simplicity she inquired: "What shall I do? Find out for me, will you?"[29]

Despite bouts of drinking and drug abuse, Benson's reputation as a writer was growing steadily. Part of her attractiveness to publishers like Henry Leech of *The Forum* was her ability to write a story that "does not end in disaster of one kind or another." For that reason, he inquired of Benson: "Our readers urge us to publish 'cheerful' stories. Can you help me satisfy them?"[30] The following month, Robert A. Pines of *College Humor* requested: "Have you anything on hand, or in mind, that I can use for *College Humor*, which is to make its re-debut shortly? About 3500 words—humorous or serious—with a college angle and a realistic (sexy) touch would fit like a glove. Please let me hear from you at once."[31] Such a flurry of interest and solicitations, initially overwhelming to Benson, began to pale in time especially as she became more involved with Covici-Friede regarding publication of her two short story collections: *People Are Fascinating* and *Emily*.

In addition to her professional relationship with Pat Covici, Benson developed a strong interest in him as a friend—especially because she was on the rebound from Babe. She and Pat corresponded frequently and toward the end of summer, he accepted her invitation to visit. In September, Covici wrote to thank her for her hospitality:

Dear Mrs. Benson:

I wish you would write oftener and longer letters. You're wise, witty, and mad. You are as volatile as a hummingbird, and wisely and delightfully irresponsible. You can't imagine how much I enjoyed my stay with you. I had lunch with your grave friend the other day [a pun on the surname of Oscar Graeve—who was interested in Benson's work]. Frankly, I fear you have dug quite a well there. However, don't worry about it. It will do him a world of good to be really in love. I know that's dangerous gossip, but you should welcome it.

After directing Benson to contact him in Kent Cliffe before the following Thursday, Covici asked: "When do we meet again? Please remember me to your very suave and witty sister [Rose] and to your glorious Barbara."[32] At this point Pat Covici appears to have become one more member of Benson's widening circle of friendships—or casual affairs. Some—like John Lawson—were well-known figures; others, like—"Auden" and "Jim"—remain unknown.[33]

After *The New Yorker* accepted "Upon a Midnight Clear" for a subsequent Christmas issue,[34] Benson sent it to Covici. He found the piece "very amusingly done. Your Mr. Parsons—chin in, chest out—is a priceless characterization," he offered. "Please don't worry about getting it done on schedule time, the important thing is to do it well, and with as much humor as you have in your letters. I would rather have the book delayed a few weeks than have you rush it"—words he would later regret. At this point Covici encouraged Benson and promised to read her story in the *Mercury* that night. "As to the serialization of your novel," he advised, "I have not quite decided whether we should do this. You can tell your friend Palmer, however, that he will have to talk to me about running *Emily* in his *Mercury* and not bother you about it." Covici agreed with Benson that "P.P. [Paul Palmer of the *Mercury*] admires you and everything that goes with you, your stories and your dog. I see no reason why you shouldn't sell him a Christmas story if he pays enough for it. $750 should be the minimum. When do I see you?"[35]

Despite her personal and professional involvement with Covici, Benson continued to write for *The New Yorker*. She submitted a Halloween piece with a note for Gibbs:

Dear Wolcott,

Am I too late for Halloween on this? I am moving back to New York toward the end of the month. Barbara is going to school there. Did I tell you that I was awfully sick? Do you know where Helen and Jim are? Will you let me know right away about this [the story]? I bought a new dog, a West Highland terrier. Do you love your new offices?

Love, Sally

Gibbs replied on October 10th with another rejection: "I'm afraid you've got us on this one. Are we supposed to believe in ghosts, or if not, how in hell do we explain the cat? It is a bothersome piece though the first four pages are very funny, and I'm sorry."[36] As was her wont, Benson simply added "Cat Ghost" to her *Emily* collection and sent Gibbs another submission—a piece he "may or may not like—[but] I think it has some funny lines." She also reported that she had stayed in all weekend and had been working very hard. Before closing, she added: "I am tired and need a finger wave. Tomorrow I'm going to have lunch with Helen, although I should stay in and work some more. Why don't you and Eleanor come down some evening when you are at your wits' end [a reference to their new life as parents] and I will run you ragged. Love, Sally."

On December 6th, Gibbs sent Benson another rejection: "They said no and I guess that's right. You leave the jokes to Thurber. Love, Wolcott." Almost immediately, Benson sent him yet another story, pleading, "Will you read this right away? I need some more money to spend for Christmas. I'll call you. Sally." Though she anticipated good sales of her Covici collections, she was not the best financial manager and could easily overspend. At this point, she seems short on cash but is not in real fiscal danger.

16

AFFAIRS, FINANCIAL AND OTHER

1936

"It has been clear for some time now that Sally Benson is one of the best of the *New Yorker* writers."

—E. H. Walton, *New York Times Book Review*

In January of 1936, upholding the strict standards he had set for the magazine, Ross objected to Benson's "I Love My Wife" on moral grounds: "I read it that she is on the town, a tramp, who is asking this man to her apartment for an affair, then and there." Gibbs passed Ross's objections on to Benson but softened the rejection by commenting:

> I'm sure you meant no such thing and were only suggesting that the girl realized how things were going to turn out in the end. The only change we can think of is that you have them get a drink somewhere and then have him take her to the door and leave her. . . . This sounds fairly lame to me, and perhaps you can think of some better way of getting around it.

Surprisingly, Benson agreed with Ross and told Gibbs: "It sounded too much as if they were both on the make, which I didn't mean. The man is a big SAP, but he isn't consciously on the make. At least not much. And he'd be much too sporting to start right in anyway." Benson suggested revisions of the man's name and urged Gibbs to let her know "right away" about the end because "the sheriff's men are at the door." Her revised ending, however, merely injected a bit of ambiguity—it hardly changed the piece.

Frannie Elliot, the girl in question, leaves her friend's apartment with Harry Page but rejects his suggestion of finding a nice, quiet place. Instead, she invites him to stop in for a drink at her apartment. Arriving, she "walked up two steps and looked down at him . . . with the strangest, kindest feeling for him. She stood smiling at him, immersed in tolerance, and it was only when she began to fumble in her bag for her key that she realized that, deep inside her, she was a little panicky." With this ambivalent ending so characteristic of modern fiction, Benson allows the reader to decide whether Frannie is a tramp or a kind-hearted ingénue. Yet, *The New Yorker* much preferred that its readers have clear, unambiguous stories.[1]

With Babe no longer contributing to household expenses, the need for money to support herself and Barbara—now seventeen—became a recurrent theme as Benson increasingly directed *New Yorker* staff members to advance or garnish her pay checks. Though Benson had a fairly steady income, she was not a good financial manager. She regularly overspent and ignored cash-flow problems until she became desperate. A letter to Katharine S. White in February, for example, reads:

> I heard Gibbs was away so I am sending this to you. It looks far from neat. For two weeks . . . I hovered around near pneumonia and I am still feeling dreadfully tired. I wonder if you would give this a quick reading as I am very broke and depetermined [*sic*] to get some money together so that Barbara and I can quit this God-forsaken city for a few weeks.
>
> Thanks sincerely, Sally Benson

The New Yorker rejected Benson's accompanying submission, "Private Sale." As Wolcott Gibbs explained in his letter to Sally on March 6, 1936: "I'm afraid they [the *New Yorker* editorial staff] didn't like this story. It has been widely read, but apparently none of the gents understand it at all, and the ladies only dimly. I'm sorry and hope you are feeling much better."[2] Gibbs had done did his best to soften the rejection, but even he saw no redeeming qualities in "Private Sale." (Covici-Friede would publish it two years later as part of Benson's *Emily* collection.)

Benson's "Private Sale" details the plight of a woman, formerly wealthy, whose failed economic circumstances lead her to sell prized *objets d'art* and other collectibles to raise money. The story illustrates Benson's willingness to address the reality of the Depression's economic effects on some upper-middle-class women. Since the story had emerged from Benson's own financial difficulties, its rejection was disappointing. The *New Yorker* staff either truly didn't understand the piece or found its realism potentially off-putting for the upper-middle-class audience it sought to attract.

Pat Covici soon reported good news. He informed Benson on February 11th that his "salesmen on the road [were] doing very well with *Emily*" and he believed the advance on this second of Benson's short story collections "would exceed our expectations." He had announced the publication of *Emily* for spring 1937 and needed her to set a date for the bookseller. Not knowing her plans, he didn't want to rush her. "Please drop me a line," he requested. "Better still, why don't you have lunch with me."[3] At this point, Benson trusted Covici and was still romantically involved with him, but all of that would change in the course of the year.

By April Benson's financial woes had increased and she laid bare her plight to Gibbs:

Dear Wolcott,

I have to pay a deposit on the cottage I rented this summer, and I wondered if you all would send me $200.00. I will send you a couple of pieces this week to make up for it and you can deduct it from my check. The reason I need it now is that Mr. Wade, the agent, is in New York and won't reserve the cottage without a deposit. I have been so busy reading the damned proofs on my story that I haven't done much writing. Will you let me know? Thanks a great deal. Sally Benson[4]

Another, more poignant letter in May demonstrates Benson's continuing inability to manage her money:

Dear Wolcott,

Hate to bother you but Bobs and I are trying to get our shopping done to get away by next week. Today she has to have shoes, shorts, and what not, also a dress to wear to Cornell this weekend. There isn't a soul near me who has enough money to cash a check. Adair doesn't keep this much on hand . . . has to

send way downtown for it. Like a fool, when the Mercury paid
me, I sent the money to the bank. If this is too much trouble
let me know. I won't bother you anymore about it after this
time anyway.

Love, Sally[5]

A memo of June 3rd, however, shows that Benson's May 25th check for
$150.00, payable to CASH and drawn on the Madison Trust Co. of Con-
necticut, bounced at Bankers' Trust in New York on May 25th and was
returned for insufficient funds. Yet, she managed to rent a place in Nantucket for the summer and remained there into December.

June also brought Benson ten copies of *People Are Fascinating* and
comforting news—the advance sales were good and Covici felt that "as soon
as the reviews come out and our ads begin to appear we will sell five times
as much."[6] In July, Benson's "novel"—forty-seven short stories and sketches
(forty-three from *The New Yorker* and four from *The American Mercury*) with
fifteen drawings by Perry Barlow—improved her financial situation and
restored peace of mind. Benson wrote to Covici, who replied, "You sound
more like yourself again. No doubt the sea and country air and isolation
have done a great deal for you. Or is it the isolation?"

As expected, reviews of *People Are Fascinating* were positive and sales
good, prompting several publishers to solicit further material from Benson.
William Rose Benet, for example, writing in the *Saturday Review of Literature* on July 11th, declared in opposition to most critics and reviewers that
Mrs. Benson was not a cynic. "In fact, she has an extraordinary sympathy
for human beings . . . seeing right through them . . . and exposing their
weaknesses. Hilarity lurks in her collection of observations, but she can also
present the minor tragedies of life with a sure touch . . . but the principal
victims of the book are women." Benet singled out "The Fur Piece" and
"More Like Sweethearts" as two of the best stories, concluding: "The people
of this book are all around you in New York, light-hearted or heavy-hearted,
old or young. More, please, Mrs. Benson" (14: 7). Samuel Sillen in *The
Nation* took a tack similar to Benet's, rejecting the typical blurb's "quiet
malice and shrewd venom" characterization as "unjust"—especially when
the collection is "read at a sitting."[7] E. H. Walton of *New York Times Book
Review* for July 5th was highly positive:

It has been clear for some time now that Sally Benson is one of the best of the *New Yorker* writers. . . . as one might expect—[all of the stories] have the virtues of conciseness, irony, and avoidance of the obvious. Her satire has point, force, venom; she is seldom guilty of rarified whimsy; only her poorest sketches are tepid and over-elusive. There is, of course, a general *New Yorker* pattern, but Sally Benson moves freely within those limits. (7)

Another Walton review ended with a similar point—that Benson had done "about as much as she profitably can with the *New Yorker* formula"—a good one but "there is enough vigor and feeling in the best of Mrs. Benson's stories to indicate that she could, and should go further." In this second review, Walton focused more finely on Benson's strengths—"a merciless ear for the fatuous speech, an eye as deadly for the foolish, betraying gesture." Weighing Benson's writing against Dorothy Parker's, Walton posited that Benson's stories were possibly "less brilliant" than Parker's, but that Benson had an "advantage over Mrs. Parker in that she is not so apt to be seduced by a wisecrack, nor so inclined to subscribe to the tradition of hardboiled gallantry." Though "slight" (i.e., "built around a conversation or a single illuminating incident . . . their suave brevity . . . half the secret of their charm"), the best in the book—about a half dozen—"transcend the limitations of a rather glib pattern. "If she is to make a name for herself," Walton advised, "it is this vein which Sally Benson must continue and develop."[8]

How much Benson was influenced by such a review is unknown, but the fact that she wrote because she liked writing and both sought and achieved publication in venues other than *The New Yorker* testifies to her inner conviction about the rightness of her fiction and her growing confidence as a writer.

The review in *Booklist* cited Benson's stories as presenting "the peculiarly urban levels of life in hotels, tea rooms, suburban clubs, bar rooms, remodeled houses, and other places where the basic flavors, the rooted values and the simple appetite for life have been almost entirely dissolved in a modern chemistry of deodorants."[9] William Soskin of *Books* focused on Benson's characters—"sad people . . . tripped by Mrs. Benson's tweezers, cut a bit with her scalpel, made to squirm, and finally fixed for a microscope slide, most competently." The writing of such pieces should be "forthright, bare, and understated. It is" (July 5, 1936, 5). The *Boston Transcript* reviewer, M.W.S., found that though Benson's stories often seemed trivial and shallow, there was "so much between the lines that they repay study. Her ability to leave equally as much unsaid . . . renders her work especially provocative" (July 18, 1936, 5). Only one reviewer focused entirely on Benson's stories, calling them "brilliant [but with a] knife-like cut, ruthless in their satire, and penetrating often to the point of tragedy. Mrs. Benson writes easily and concisely and her dialogue is astonishingly natural. The note of derision or gentle mockery is dominant in all the stories. Some . . . are beautiful burlesques . . . others are slightly bitter" (*Books*, July 5, 1936).

Benson, pleased with her reviews, was now more sure of herself and her writing than ever. A thrilled Covici sent Benson clippings of some reviews in case she had not seen them. He included an insightful commentary:

Dear Sally:

The one reason why I was anxious to publish your short stories is to give you confidence in your own powers. I wasn't at all doubtful at any time, as you know, of the critical reception you would receive. What is still more gratifying is that the sales will be better than you ever expected. Just this morning I received an additional order from Baker and Taylor for 300 copies, and orders from bookstores are coming in right along. . . . With all this genuine critical esteem your self-confidence certainly should be great enough to finish your novel, which again in my mind, will be a real contribution to American literature, and a best seller. . . . Am I going to see you? With the greatest of pleasure—nothing would please me more than to spend a couple of days with you on an island surrounded by cool, refreshing water. Do let me hear from you with a long gossipy letter.

Affectionately, Pat

P.S. By all means, write to the *N.Y. Times*, and to any other reviewer, that you are moved to write to. It cannot do any harm, and it will certainly do you good.[10]

By July 20, a Covici representative assured Benson that the sale of *People Are Fascinating* was growing apace. The second printing would be off the press "in a couple of days . . . and we'll soon see it on the best seller list."[12]

If Benson still lacked self-confidence, she was not shy about objecting to anything that would diminish her book sales. She complained to Covici about some of his ads and on July 23rd Pat wrote: "I'm afraid you're right—the ads starting 'For women only' and 'People with their clothes off' are not so good. Our advertising agent was a little bit off—he shan't do it again."

Covici reminded Benson of a personal bet: "I have to sell 300 or 400 more copies and then you shall have to buy me that bottle of cognac— and don't forget." He also informed her that one of the oldest publishing houses in England—Constable—"has accepted your *People Are Fascinating* and will publish it sometime in the Fall or Spring. They are very anxious to see your novel, of course. Who isn't?" Covici's letters took on a playful, even intimate tone. After encouraging Benson to "by all means, give [her] little talk—even about me," he teased:

> But if I OK this idea, will you OK my lecturing on you? I
> don't know what I would say about you but maybe you could
> give me a few lessons. Your place sounds damnably attractive,
> and your life exciting. No doubt you are the heroine of the
> whole island. But don't get too fat, and let me have that long
> letter . . . Yours with love xx. Pat[12]

All during her Nantucket summer, publishers continued to solicit Benson's fiction.

Marian Ives wrote in June to inform Benson that *Scribner's* magazine would have a new format with "extra room for fiction. We are interested in your writing and hope you will give us the opportunity of reading a good story . . . from 2,000 to 10,000 words. We are simply looking for the best that is being written. Any story from you will be given an interested reading."[13] In July, Mary Hamman of the *Pictorial Review* wrote: "I wanted to talk to you about doing a story for us. Our stories are, of course, a little more primitive and simple, perhaps, than the ones that you do for the *New Yorker*, but we feel that you might be interested in doing a ladies' mag yarn—and we are sure you could do a dandy job."[14]

The same mail brought a letter from Harry Hansen of the *New York World Telegram* explaining the O. Henry award and offering to send Benson a copy of the current anthology containing her prize-winning "Suite 2049." When the book appeared in December, Harry E. Maule of Doubleday, Doran & Co., Inc., sent Benson a check for $200—the amount of the second prize. "Since you have seen the reviews, Maule wrote, "there is no need for me to tell you that the award was a popular one with most of the critics. I do want to say, however, how much I personally enjoyed the story, and to congratulate you on it."[15] (Incidentally, the verso of Maule's letter became Benson's venue for a penciled list of her recent purchases: "negligee $10.50; bed and mattresses $67.18; sofa $74.95; chair $41.95; chest-on-chest $19.94; table $69.57." It is not clear whether she planned the purchases upon receipt of the $200 prize or whether it would be used to pay for items already bought. Her total cost—incorrectly tallied—came to $192.97—just a few dollars short of the prize money by Benson's faulty addition. The actual sum is $284.09.)

When Benson replied affirmatively to the *Pictorial Review* in July, Mary Hamman answered: "We are as pleased as pie that you will try a story for us and there's lots of eating in it if it clicks. . . . we want any kind of yarn except one with a juvenile in it. . . . If possible, we'd like something from you about people in their late teens." Hamman added, "I hope we'll be able to contribute to BENSON'S FOLLY. The gold door-knobs sound intriguing."[16] In August, Ernestine Taggard of *Scholastic*, the "American High School Weekly," requested permission of Covici-Friede to reprint Benson's "Wife of the Hero" and Pat Covici recommended that Benson grant permission. She did so and a month later they wrote again to request biographical data and a picture.[17] Benson was feathering her nest and looking forward to increasing profits.

Throughout her negotiations with these varied publishers, Benson was becoming an accomplished entrepreneur. From her early days as a film reviewer and the months she spent in Los Angeles while Babe was in Mongolia, Sally was fascinated by Agnes's work on screenplays. It was only natural that she and Agnes should envision some of Benson's books as film scripts. Now Benson moved her dream forward by actively exploring the possibility of turning her books into movies. She enlisted Covici's advice and he, in turn, discussed Benson's project with Edith Haggert, an agent he trusted. Covici wrote on August 6th:

> Edith Haggert convinced me that she has the right organiza-
> tion to handle the movies of your books. . . . she is really and
> honestly interested in you and in your work, and that's saying a
> great deal about any agent. I must admit you have a real friend
> in Mrs. Haggert.

In addition, Covici reported that *People Are Fascinating* was "still selling
nicely" and would for some time. His firm had appropriated more money
for advertising not on the strength of what the book has sold or will sell
but on the "build-up that the advertising is doing for *Emily.*" Benson's July
statement would reflect a deficit, he reminded her, since she had "drawn
quite a bit before publication," but her December statement would "show
additional moneys coming" and payment, as customary with all publishers,
would be made "twice a year . . . within four months after the statement
is issued."

Regarding Benson's request for more advance money, however, Covici
refused. Since the firm "is spending quite a bit of money on publicizing and
advertising you . . . I cannot . . . ask for additional money," he explained.
"It is just not in the cards. . . . when you finish *Emily*, I shall be able
to do something." Again, he signed: "With love, Pat." One can imagine
Benson's angry reaction to that letter. Whatever casual affair might have
been brewing, she nipped it on the spot. Her blistering reply to Covici
prompted his defensive but decisive response:

> I wouldn't attempt to toss you about "like a feather pillow"
> for more than one reason. Besides, I don't like strenuous exer-
> cise and I can think of far more pleasant things to do with
> you. . . . for an agent [Edith Haggert] to be so intense about an
> author is a rare thing. That's that, and I have no other interest
> in the matter. You know best what you want. As to your getting
> money when your book earns it and whenever you want it, that's
> not being done. . . . No publisher can afford a hit-and-miss
> method of payments.
>
> May I remind you, as gently as I know how, that you
> received an advance on *Emily* two years ago and we have received
> no manuscript yet. You also got your advance on *People Are
> Fascinating* long before the book earned it. So far the firm has

done more than it agreed to do. All I ask of you now is to allow the firm to live up to its agreement—and I guarantee you it will.

Affectionately, Pat[18]

Five weeks later Benson had a letter from Gibbs containing a little clipping that bothered him and a complaint: "When you get Benson it's time to look for Frost. We wish you would write some more pieces soon, or has Covici made you too rich?"[19] Benson hastily responded, "No, he hasn't made me rich. I haven't gotten any money from the book yet. It seems that publishers don't have to pay you for a while. When I get back to town I'll see about it." She loved his clipping about a talk she gave in Nantucket. With her characteristic humor she recounted that experience for him:

> I spoke to a group called the Nantucket Neighbors. First they had a band, then me, then a woman who sang about a robin on a bough and so 'twas spring . . . then the missionary talked about Peking . . . what stations he got on his radio, how good the plumbing was in the new city as against the plumbing in the old city . . . then the band played again. Then everyone dropped nickels and dimes into a quaint old iron kettle so that the Nantucket Neighbors can go on forever. I had to put in a dime too.

The selectmen had written her a note of thanks. There were "lots of old sea captains" there, but "I'd rather have you dear," she assured, "with or without the whale's teeth. They have a whaling museum here," she continued, "and I'm thinking of changing the name to the Whaling and Gnashing of Teeth Museum. I will have you down for the gala opening. Love from Sally." Benson added her new address: "4 New Dollar Lane (quaint isn't it?) Nantucket, Mass."

By October, Benson had patched up her quarrel with Covici and invited him to Nantucket. He was "all ready to go. In fact, I was quite excited about it," he wrote, but then "I discovered that I could not get away. I am terribly disappointed and hope that you are the same." He proceeded to answer Benson's questions about the sale of *People Are Fascinating*:

> Up to yesterday we sold 2,900 copies and the book keeps rolling right along. When you consider that the average book of short

stories sells 750 copies, *People Are Fascinating* is doing remarkably well. So, judging from these figures, you have earned about
$700. If you take off what you owe, the balance is not much as
yet. But you should finish *Emily*, and I am ready to do all that
I can to help you. Please tell me how long it will take you to
finish *Emily* by staying in Nantucket, and how much will you
require per week while there. If you can estimate the number
of weeks you require to finish *Emily*, and your weekly demands
are reasonable enough for the firm to meet, I am quite certain
that the firm will advance you the royalty. Now take your pencil
and sharpen it, look at your *Emily* and let me know at once.
With love, Pat[20]

Benson, disheartened by Covici's canceling his visit, let him know immediately. Trying to console her, he wrote that her letter had

given him the blues. If I could have boarded a flying machine,
I certainly would have come out to see you. You surely need
a good cheering-and-warming up. Not that I say that I could
do it, but I would try my damnedest. I am still hoping to be
able to get away to see you out there. Here's a check for $100,
on your royalties. By all means pay your bills but leave enough
money to pay for a couple of bottles of good Scotch for when
I do come out.

More importantly, he inquired: "Don't you want to tell me anything about
Emily—how it is coming along, how much you have done?"[21] But, Benson,
occupied with other business and personal matters, sent him no reply. In
fact, Covici had no idea that five months later he would be equally in
the dark.

Meanwhile, despite growing acclaim, October witnessed a change of
fortune. Paul Palmer of *The American Mercury* surprised Benson by returning a story and recommending that she try *Harper's Bazaar* or *Pictorial
Review*.[22] Two weeks later, another rejection came from Marian Ives of *Scribner's*. The piece was "Snake Story" and Ives objected to its storyteller frame.
What Ives wanted were "some fairly gay" stories of two to four thousand
words with "substance or significance. You are one of those few [authors]
who can write something that is not depressing, morbid, or tragic," Ives

encouraged. She also expressed interest in Benson's *Emily*.[23] Paul Palmer wrote again in November for more stories and an opportunity to see *Emily* when it was finished. He also offered to "print some of it in [*The American Mercury*] before book publication."[24]

On October 28th, Benson received another rejection letter from an apologetic Gibbs: "It is not in your vein or ours. I'm sure the *Mercury* and O'Brien will make us look silly about the whole thing, but we have to stick to our ideas. Sorry!" This rejection particularly stung Benson, so for six weeks she sent The *New Yorker* nothing. With winter setting in and the holidays approaching, Benson decided to move back to Manhattan, taking apartments first at 150 East 49th Street, then at 149 West 49th Street, and finally at 15 East 48th Street.[25] By December 14th, White was begging:

> There is little irony in this clipping which says you are on the staff of the *New Yorker*. I wish to goodness you were, or at the very least, a more active contributor. We badly miss your stories and I do want to know whether you won't have some for us in the very near future. Perhaps now that you are moving back to town you will . . . send us something. We have missed you.

17

TAKING CHARGE AND
BRANCHING OUT

1937

"Dear Mrs. White, I have not been in exile, but I have been busy."

—Sally Benson

Since her letters to Nantucket requesting short story submissions from Benson had been fruitless, Katharine White regarded Sally Benson's return to New York City as a most promising sign, but Benson, busy responding to requests from publishers and working on her *Emily* collection, wrote nothing new for *The New Yorker*. After Christmas, White telephoned her and reported to Mr. Hoyt: "I did get a rise out of her. She says she is through with the novel, has felt badly about that debt she owes the *New Yorker*, and will write two stories immediately."[1] In early February, however, Benson came down with the flu and was incapacitated for several weeks. While recuperating in her Manhattan apartment, she spent her days reading mysteries and by late February had still not sent anything to White.

Ever hopeful, White wrote in praise of *People Are Fascinating*:

Dear Miss Benson:

I wonder if you happened to see this flattering review of your book from *Punch*. I can only reiterate the last sentence from it and ask for some of these stories about fascinating people that you review so fascinatingly. Where is the story you promised over the telephone not so long back?

Please, please, do send us something.

Sincerely yours,
Katharine S. White[2]

On March 23rd White found it necessary to write again—this time to complain—but she also ramped up the pressure on Benson to produce by referencing *The New Yorker's* decision to offer Benson a raise:

> Where are those promised stories? I begin to feel that you have utterly deserted us. It is a bad time for you to stop writing for us because the business office has just been able to make a few raises in fiction rates, and yours is one of them. Your rate is increased by two cents a word, which doesn't sound like much, but which mounts up considerably in stories the length that you usually write. Do send us something soon.

Penciled at the bottom was: "Won't you let us see firsts on all your short stories in consideration of this raise?"[3] Benson was not impressed. She did not reply to White for over two months.

In the interim, letters—a mix of rejections and solicitations and occasional late payments from publishers—arrived regularly and occupied Benson. *College Humor* turned down "After the Ball" as "a bit quiet for us" but noted it was "excellently written . . . the psychology of youth authentic." Benson simply published the piece in *Emily* in 1938. Later it appeared in both E. K. Taggard's anthology as "Here We Are after the Dance" and in Maureen Daly's *My Favorite Stories* as "After the Dance." Daly's headnote compliments Benson's piece as "graciously written and blessed with a fine humor . . . neither slapstick nor deadpan, but [stemming] from a rather resigned fondness for people. . . . There is a very wise point to . . . ["After the Dance"] . . . but no one knows better than Benson that undiluted wisdom can be quite dull. So she has added suspense and humor to make it fun to read" (165).

Based on Barbara, Benson's then sixteen-year-old daughter, the piece portrays an attractive teen—"she might have been Joan Crawford . . . or the pampered daughter of a millionaire home from a winter on the French

Riviera"—who has convinced her mother to take a different vacation cottage from the usual "Spoondrift" in Monroe, Connecticut. She preferred "Pine Bluffs"—a place with "cabanas on the beach" where "no one would know how old she was." Benson wrote: "She began to fuss over her appearance, spending hours in the tub, hours over her nails, hours pressing her clothes and getting dressed." But, as an unknown newcomer, she had no social life "until she met Bill James." He rented a shack near the beach, "kept beer on ice," and was twenty-six. Impressed, she allowed him to "take her out in her mother's car." When he later found out that she was only sixteen, she was humiliated and resigned herself to socializing with her mother by going to the movies. Then, came the moment of truth. Bill arrived one night, "not tight, but just high," to take her to the dance at the club. She refused: "Who does he think he is? . . . What does he think I am? She smiled suddenly and gaily at her mother. "The old *cripple!*" Benson ended the piece, conveying succinctly, as was her wont, a decisive moment in a young teen's maturation from giddy, insecure ingénue to self-aware, self-respecting woman.

All winter Benson had been sprouting wings of independence by investigating the possible benefits of having an agency handle her project of translating stories into film. She contacted Sam Jaffe, Inc.—an agency for screen playwrights and likely a contact from Agnes's screenwriting days—and asked Sam Jaffe if his firm would try to get her a job in Hollywood. On February 16, Jaffe's literary agent, Mary Baker, wrote with enthusiasm: "Both Mr. Jaffe and I feel very confident that we can get an assignment for you. Let Bill Fadiman have a copy of your book," Baker advised, requesting a copy also for herself and inquiring whether Benson would sign a contract with Jaffe. She congratulated Benson on winning the O. Henry prize[4] and predicted that if Benson were to come to Hollywood, "a little gold statue would be dumped in [her] lap as the Motion Picture Academy Award."[5] Six years later the success of the Benson-inspired *Meet Me in St. Louis* came close to fulfilling Baker's prediction. The film won four Academy Award nominations and earned an Oscar for Margaret O'Brien as "Best Child Star."

As the weeks progressed, Benson's mail increased. *Short, Short, Short*'s James Hill invited submissions from Benson, offering $25 to $250 and promising to "report on solicited material within 48 hours."[6] *Fiction Parade* sent her a late payment of $25 for reprinting "Wife of the Hero" and offered a similar amount for permission to reprint "Her Own Things."[7] The same day, Laura Vitray of *McCall's Magazine* rejected "Local Girl Makes Good" because "the situation . . . was insufficiently developed," but Vitray encouraged further submissions. Benson promptly sent the piece to *Scribner's Magazine*, which published the story in its July issue. Next, *Fiction Parade* mailed Benson its delayed check for two reprintings—"More Like Sweethearts" and "Her Own Things"—and apologies for Mr. Bellamy's failure to answer Benson's letters. They also deducted $3.00 for Benson's ordered subscription to the magazine. Very likely, Benson wanted to analyze what *Fiction Parade* was buying.

In addition to handling the flurry of writing-related correspondence in the interval since White's last letter, Benson had "thought of the start of a mystery story with some quite funny characters" that David Selznick intended to turn into a film. In negotiating through Mary Baker, a letter of Baker to Benson went astray and Benson persisted in following up on Baker's apparent silence. Baker, of course, was "terribly upset" to think Benson had not received the February 16th Jaffe missive. It was now April 19th and Baker had assumed Benson's permission to represent her "for picture work." The lost letter was probably another Benson lie. According to an April 13th letter from William James Fadiman of Loew's Incorporated, distributors of Metro-Goldwyn-Mayer pictures, Benson had been in negotiation with him also. He had arranged to discuss the project with her but was called away. For that reason, he wrote an apology addressing Benson as "Dear Sally" and adding,

> It will help me a lot—and I know it will help you—if you will let me have a chapter or two of the new idea you mentioned, the one which is unsold. In fact, if you could possibly prepare a brief synopsis, my cup of joy would overflow. I'm going to haunt you about this so don't you dare escape to the vineyards of Vermont before letting me see it. Give my best to Barbara if my best is good enough for her.

The tone of Fadiman's letter suggests that Benson had established a personal friendship with him as well as a professional connection.[8]

Despite the amount of time spent in answering her correspondence, Benson continued writing mystery blurbs for *The New Yorker*. Editor St. Clair McKelway found them problematic. The blurbs "are running a little too long, girl," he commented, recommending that Benson read some of

Benchley's in "Goings on about Town" because Benchley was a master at "saying something bright in a very few lines . . . hard to do. We think they are fine otherwise, baby."[9] Two days later McKelway wrote again, modifying his advice: "I hope you won't take my suggestion about Benchley too literally. I just meant it might help you to get the knack of this particular kind of brief writing." A week later he had not received Benson's two promised stories. "Where are [they] for goodness sake?" McKelway inquired with some pique. "I will send you a Saroyan book if you have to copy out of that, but it seems to me that would be just *too* good luck for Mr. Saroyan."

When Benson finally did send a story, she submitted it directly to White with a long explanation and a request:

Dear Mrs. White,

I have not been in exile, but I have been busy. I thought of a set of characters which I told the story editor of Selznick pictures about, and they got very interested and before I knew it, they had me working away at a murder story which I am to have finished the first week in July. If you take this story, will you keep half my check on what I owe you, and I will be able to pay all of it when Selznick pay [*sic*] me. I have a contract with them, and they seem very pleased over my work. I have thought of several stories for you, and they get too long on me, which is unusual, but rather pleasing. And I've thought of a good New England story which I intend doing as a novelette when I get through with my murder. The Selznick thing is a gentle satire on such dopes as Philo Vance, and I think it's funny.

Sincerely,
Sally Benson

In the same letter Benson updated her contact information. She had moved to 15 East 48th Street—"where I usually am, but if you want to call me, you can reach me at Plaza 3-4718." Penciled sideways atop the left margin, as if an afterthought, Benson added: "I'm to get $10,000 for the story."[10]

By the end of May, White had complied with Benson's wishes by sending Benson a check for $95, credited her account at *The New Yorker* with $100 as requested, and added:

I was awfully glad to know why you had been so silent and the $10,000 scenario sounds like a very thrilling job indeed for you. I hope, though, that the work on it will let up soon so that you will have some stories for us. Please don't fail to send us stories even if they are too long because we sometimes do use longer ones, you know, and we wish you would give us first shot at all your work. I think you promised once to do this anyway, didn't you?[11]

If White wondered how Benson's contact with Selznick had come about, she might have been surprised to learn that like many other opportunities in Benson's life, this one had occurred through happenstance—this time because of Bobsie's friendship with Betty Knight. As Benson had shared in a lengthy letter to Mary Baker of the Literary Department of Sam Jaffe, Inc., Betty's father, Eric Knight, had remarried Jere Knight, "Eastern story-editor of Selznick." When the Knights and Betty came to visit her, Benson was surprised to discover their Selznick connection. She explained to Baker:

I didn't know Mrs. Knight was connected with Selznick and was just talking to hear myself talk. Shortly afterwards, she called me and asked me to come to her office where I saw Oscar Sirlin and Kay Brown. They asked me about my idea and wanted to know if I could write a brief outline, and an opening chapter. I did this and they liked it, and asked for five more chapters, and an outline of characters for Mr. Sirlin to take to the coast with him. I got it ready and they have taken an option on it.

Benson's work was especially translatable to the screen because of her apt characterization and her gift for rendering dialogue that resembled how people actually talked.[12]

With her *New Yorker* editors temporarily satisfied and the Selznick project under consideration in Los Angeles, Benson next turned her attention to finishing a 25,000-word detective story by July 15th. She decided to collaborate on it with Captain Joe Shaw because she felt she was "weak in plot." She planned to "[do] it in novel form and hope[d] to sell it serially to a magazine." If it were accepted, she would need to go to Hollywood for four weeks to complete the project and she would have to go before October 1st.

In mid-April Benson finally heard from Selznick-International, Incorporated. They had accepted her story and wanted her immediately to work with Ben Hecht for help with plot. However, Benson was uncomfortable with the offer for two reasons—first, in her words:

> because they wanted me to fly out and I am afraid to, besides it's silly; second because I knew that it would be Ben Hecht's story, and I don't think he's so hot. When I was sick, I read a lot of his stories that Covici sent me and I thought they were appalling. His earlier stories are good, but his more recent ones seem forced and stale. Besides, I have started working with Shaw who is quiet and helpful, does my writing with me, but straightens me out on technicalities and plot. He leaves me alone and I like him.[13]

Benson made her point, "the whole thing blew over," and she didn't have to go. Instead, she planned to finish the story in the allotted time and have ten chapters ready for Shaw to take with him when he left for the West in mid-May. "Not that Selznick will get a look at them," she added, "but simply so that we can send these ten chapters to *Collier's* or some other magazine with an outline of the rest of the story."

Besides developing greater self-assurance as a writer, Benson was gaining valuable experience as a businesswoman. She already had "another idea for a picture" that she intended to "fool with" during the summer. "It's pretty good," she observed. "I talked to Bill Fadiman about it and he was very interested," but she explained, "I can't take another job until I finish this one and know how I stand with Selznick." As for a contract, Benson was wary of signing one after her experience with the William Morris Agency. She had informed Morris that she

> would not renew [her] agreement with them, but . . . never heard a word from them, neither in answer to that letter, nor in any way during the whole year that they were supposed to get me a job. By signing a contract with any agent, I am helpless in their hands.

She regretted having to pass up the work that Mary Baker had in mind and offered, "If you have work for me which is satisfactory to us both, we may be able to come to an agreement." She hoped Baker would understand her attitude and preference for seeing "the whites of [Baker's] eyes" before making a commitment.

Benson shared with Baker how being treated "shabbily" by William Morris had "put doubts in my rather too trusting nature." She wanted to "work a while every year in the west" because she hoped to "buy a place in Vermont[14] and I would like to make more money. If I get any job in Hollywood," she would "work as hard as I can while I am there. I am really conscientious about work, and I think, with more experience, I would be quite good." Clearly, the conscientiousness demonstrated as early as her high school years remained an integral component of Benson's spirit and self-image.

Most significant in the letter to Baker is Benson's determination to write only what she saw fit. Though she needed the money her writing would bring, Benson had to feel her content was worthy of her and wanted her work to be top quality:

> It seems to me too many people let their writing flop by land-ing in Hollywood and staying there. If I can't get along under the conditions I have laid out for myself, I'll stick to magazine stories in the East. I am branching out and doing better with them, lengthening my work, and trying to make it less sketchy. I don't like doing it as well, though.

Before ending her letter to Baker, Benson made a rare admission. "You have been terribly nice," she confided,

> and certainly I would rather deal through you from what I have heard of you than anyone else who has written me. I am writing Friede to forget about me, as, between ourselves, he annoys me frightfully. He is the only other person beside [sic] yourself, I have even talked to, and I saw him when he was in New York because he had been associated with Pat Covici.

In closing, Benson invited Baker to visit her in Dorset, Vermont the next time she came East.[15] Somehow, Baker had won Benson's trust, and after Sally's disappointing business dealings with William Morris and Mr. Friede, she was glad to find a trustworthy agency representative. In

June, having reconciled with Babe once again, Benson agreed to move to Dorset, Vermont—a place Babe loved for vacations—and she stayed there until the following November. Bill Fadiman wrote with advice toward the end of June:

> I think you ought to put a hex on any motion picture company that prevents you from writing those delicious short stories and simultaneously accomplish the desired miracle of letting you and Barbara live on shortcake, spice-cake, devil's-food cake, and perhaps—in deference to Vermont—angel-food cake. I feel rather rueful at the thought that my own anxiety to read the HANDSOME STRANGER may be preventing you from lolling (do you loll under trees?) or developing superb Alexandrine rhymes about your neighbor, Cordelia de Schweinetz. . . . I lunched with Joe Shaw the other day and we discussed your collaboration warily, much as two fencers would do whose shoes were made of soap. In short, we said nothing inelegantly. However, I suppose the mystery will be finished one day and Selznick-International Incorporated will achieve the desired pinnacle of happiness.[16]

In July, Max Wilkinson of *Collier's* "most regretfully" rejected Benson's detective series because it "dealt so harshly with the established verities of detective fiction." Wilkinson ended by asking, "Give us another chance, won't you?" Benson did, but Wilkinson also rejected her next submission and dubbed it a "gag." What *Collier's* wanted, Wilkinson explained, was a story with "sympathetic people . . . with some emotional appeal, and conclusiveness . . . calculated to interest a large audience of readers without giving them the feeling that the writer has been having them on."[17] He offered to meet with Benson over lunch if she were "puzzled by all this. Maybe we can work it out together," he suggested. Benson requested samples of what *Collier's* wanted and Wilkinson responded: "It seems to me that you have your own peculiar style and interests, and what another writer has done would in no way help you to do your most successful work." He reiterated his description of the *Collier's* ideal story as one involving "a soundly characterized man or woman, sympathetically portrayed . . . its [*raison d'être*] in some incident which is dramatic, emotional, or both."

Though Benson was disappointed by Wilkinson's rejection of the series, she profited from his ideas by incorporating many of them in her forthcoming *Junior Miss*. Ironically, five days later Oscar Graeve of *Liberty* rejected Benson's "Woman's Intuition" and recommended that she forward it to *Collier's*. He added a personal note: Benson had been "sorely missed" at Madison that summer. "It's grand to hear of your movie successes. I hope they land you in the big money. Are you staying in Vermont indefinitely?"[18]

Katharine White, wondering the same thing, decided to contact Benson and wrote:

> Dear Mrs. Benson: (or do I call you Sally?),
>
> I am just back from an over-long summer vacation, and one of my first efforts here is to write to ask why, for heaven's sake, you aren't sending us any stories. In spite of all the promises of last spring, I hear you are up in Vermont collaborating with Eric Knight. Can't you take some time off and send us some stories? We need them badly. You'll be sick of my letters, but it's my job to be a gadfly, I fear.
>
> Sincerely yours,
> Katharine S. White[19]

Benson managed to fire off both a reply and a piece:

> Dear Mrs. White,
>
> Now what would I be doing in Vermont with Eric Knight? Collaborating on a great proletarian novel in Yorkshire dialect? The rumor is false, and Eric Knight is in Croton. I delivered my story to Selznick, they have asked for an extension on the option as Selznick is coming to New York in October and that's all I know about that. . . . Tell Gibbs I thought his book got good reviews and that I would like it because I still think he writes rings around Thurber. If you like this ["The Storm"], please keep half my check. I have a very short piece, too, but think it's poor and may do it over. I don't think you'll like it. It's too trick [*sic*] in a silly way.
>
> Sincerely,
> Sally Benson

A penciled annotation queries:

> Have you printed the story I sold you this spring? Also, can I sell
> it in England? They will buy all I can send them. My book [*People
> Are Fascinating*] went very well there. It came out in March and
> has been reviewed in the *Times Literary Supplement* and *Punch*.[20]

English reviewers were highly favorable toward Benson's work as
"Essence of Life," the *Punch* review illustrates:

> It is difficult to know how to describe all the segments of Miss
> Sally Benson's *People Are Fascinating* because the word *sketches*
> suggests something incomplete and *short stories* something too
> compact and rounded, so I think these little extracts from the
> lives of so many different types had better be labeled "snatches."
> Miss Benson knows exactly when to snatch. She pounces on
> the dominating wish, thought, or whim in a person's mind and
> from that builds up a complete picture, just as a clever doc-
> tor makes his diagnosis from symptoms that have been uncon-
> sciously betrayed. All her characters—"The Man's Woman," with
> a blurred face for which men are thankful "because it looked
> like almost any face they wanted it to look like," "Wife of the
> Hero," (in her hope only), "The Girl Who Went Everywhere"
> but seemed to get nowhere, "Mrs. Bixby," who tried to give
> "different" parties, and the man who loved his wife because it
> made a useful boast—are described ironically, shortly, and quite
> often in a kindly way. I defy anyone to read this book and not
> recognize himself or herself (the latter more frequently because
> the author writes more about women) and a great many friends.
> I hope Miss Benson will continue to find people fascinating and
> to introduce them so fascinatingly.[21]

Despite the reviewer's glowing appreciation, Benson privately commented:
"Are people fascinating? No!"

The *Times Literary Supplement* review of *People Are Fascinating* was
less positive:

> Most of the stories . . . are little more than sketches—pictures of
> people caught in a single instant, when their stories are implied

rather than told at length. Though many . . . are extremely funny, few are quotable, for Miss Benson's is the kind of humor that penetrates all her writing without very often coming out in high spots. She has an ironic touch that is particularly directed against a certain type of muddleheaded woman—though men come in for some sharp attacks too. . . . Some of the sketches may leave one with an uneasy feeling that their author has been unnecessarily unkind to victims who are pathetic rather than ridiculous; but that is not a very heavy price to pay for many amusing and penetrating portraits in a particularly American style of humour.[22]

The same day that White's letter arrived, so did one from Fadiman. "You were a peach," he told her, "to let me look at the brief synopsis of HANDSOME STRANGER." He returned it and agreed that Benson should wait before working on it further, until she saw "the glimmer of gold on your mahogany desk." Fadiman also encouraged her to meet personally with Selznick rather than rely on airmail since he "is obviously interested in any material you will write." Fadiman could not, however, "get excited in the screen possibilities of this story" because the central idea, "charming and nostalgic though it is, is too inconsequential to bear the burden of a seven-reel motion picture plot. . . . Your atmosphere literally smothers the story line," he explained, "so that the romance of Douglas and Chloe seems to be more inconsequential than it should be for screen purposes." He assured her he would "make certain the studio realizes how important dialogue would be in this story, smart, flip, sophisticated, and amusing," but he had "misgivings as to its being a picture for our studio. We seem to be more interested in material with greater emotional depth—whatever that is! . . . Anyway, I'll do all I can for this and will holler loud and clear all the way up to Vermont should one of our producers extend his right hand in welcome to your HANDSOME STRANGER."[23]

While her negotiations for *Handsome Stranger* continued with Fadiman, Benson had done nothing with *Emily*—much to Pat Covici's distress. Having given Benson a generous advance for the *Emily* collection in 1934, his last communication on that topic had occurred in October of 1936. After two years of vain waiting, Covici was understandably cynical about *Emily* at this point—almost a year later. On September 24th he wrote:

I have been out of town for the last few weeks, therefore my delay in writing you. As you know, I always love to hear from you as your letters are a delight to read. Tell me, who got your maid in the condition she is in. Was it one of your weekenders? Why don't you give me the lowdown on that murder mystery you have in work. Are you really going to finish it, or is it just another one of those projects that is going to be laid away with the late *Emily*? I am sorry you don't see your way clear to finishing that book. You are missing a good bet. Bookstores are still clamoring for it. Believe it or not, I have more than a faint urge to see you.[24]

Clearly, the relationship between Covici and Benson had gone beyond the professional and most likely they were romantically involved, but *Emily* would not see publication until 1938.

In her next letter to Covici, Benson proposed a "book around three women." Pat Covici thought the concept "superb" and encouraged her: "I sincerely believe you could do that book to a turn. . . . you would have lots of fun writing it, and I would enjoy publishing it. What's more, I think we could sell some copies. Why don't you forget everything else and go to it now. Please tell me in your next letter that you have started the book on the women."[25] Instead, Benson continued to work on stories for *The New Yorker* and in early October submitted "The Storm," a piece Gibbs considered "a beautiful story" but in need of some changes suggested by Ross. One of these concerned location. Feeling that readers "are bewildered when told about people who live in what appear to be unaccountable ways," Ross wanted a specific locale mentioned, and Gibbs suggested a "cabin in the Berkshires" purchased upon retiring from the molasses factory. Gibbs also related that the Thurbers were "having a fine time in Europe. . . . The capitals of the continent are at his [Thurber's] feet." Gibbs, showing his regard for Benson, closed with the playful comment: "I am, as always, at your feet."[26] Benson, despite the flattery, made none of the suggested changes and left "The Storm's" setting an unspecified, hilly locale. She returned the proofs on November 3rd with an explanation. Gibbs replied: "I loved your letter and am going to have it framed for Ross for Christmas. It will give him something to look at every time he wants to know too much about the past."[27] Gibbs also suggested that Benson write for "Notes and Comment" from time to time because though there is not much money in it, "it's steady." In the same vein, Gibbs passed on an earlier Ross comment: "I wish you would encourage Mrs. Benson to do some 'Onward and Upward with the Arts' pieces on radio. It is a rich field for a humorist who will listen to it and for anybody whose mind can stand up under it."[28]

Meanwhile, Benson's fiction earnings were helping to wipe out the deficit in her *New Yorker* account. In October, after submitting "The Storm," Benson promised White a Christmas story she thought would be "particularly good. At least, the more I think about it, the worse it makes me feel," Benson confided. (This softer side of Benson is not reflected in the serious, stern expression she wears in almost every portrait.) White was especially pleased that Benson had a Christmas story planned. "We need one badly and we want it just as fast as you can send it in. Please, please do deliver that," she begged.[29] Benson did, and on November 2nd, White sent her a check "minus what it took to pay off the balance on your account here. . . . From now on, no more deductions!"

Benson's next submission, "Little Woman," delighted White initially, but a week later she returned the proofs with a few queries.[30] Ross wanted the little woman's husband credited with more effort in arranging to get first-row theater tickets, and White had taken the liberty of assigning character Penny Loomis's critical comments to another female character to make Loomis "less gratuitously catty."[31] Ross's queries here and in other instances contradict Benson's later public statements that her stories came from her typewriter just as they were written. The reality was that though Benson sometimes held her ground, making no changes—as in the case of "The Storm"—she also rejected pieces that she found unsatisfactory. In such a situation, Benson was candid rather than proud and prepossessing toward her material. Responding to White, for example, Benson referred to a prior submission: "I read the very short story again and I assure you that you will throw up if you read it. I will try to fix it, but even the idea is rotten."[32]

When Wolcott Gibbs proposed to Benson a factual series called "American Pilgrimages" for "Onward and Upward with the Arts," she wrote to White and offered to do four pieces on the state of Vermont—"what city people have done to the state, the ruination of a not particularly interesting though very beautiful New England state by writers, artists, and city people who have tried to make it quainter than quaint."[33] White immediately sent McKelway an in-house memo to reserve for Benson's series such pieces as "a visit to Calvin Coolidge's grave," possibly one on Thoreau's Walden Pond in Concord, another on Buffalo Bill's grave, and one on Mark Twain's birthplace. White noted that Benson would think of others and asked Benson to "turn in the Coolidge one first as a sample to see whether we like the series."[34] The following Monday, November 22nd, White wrote again to McKelway:

> Sally Benson called up Friday in another fever and suggested still another series. Her title is "One Note Men" and it is about people who have made one splurge and then disappeared. . . . She doesn't want to write it herself . . . but wants to send it to another magazine [if we don't want it]. . . . I would hate to see the series started in another magazine. Would there be any honest way of buying the idea or stringing her along so as to prevent some other magazine using it?

McKelway felt Benson's idea was one that anybody would take for the asking. He immediately sent an in-house memo to White on November 30th urging: "Somebody will have to stall Benson somehow." When White sent Benson her check for "Upon a Midnight Clear," she explained that Mr. McKelway and others felt "One Note Men" resembled a series already being done ("Where Are They Now?") and that "various newspapers have run this sort of thing, including the *New York Post*. Thank you anyway for the suggestion."[35] Little did Benson realize how White was manipulating her for *The New Yorker's* benefit.

Upon reading Benson's Christmas piece—"Upon a Midnight Clear"—White immediately responded: "We are delighted with the Christmas story . . . [it] will certainly make our Christmas issue a distinguished one." White also expressed the hope that Benson was "hard at work on the birthplaces, and on other stories" that Benson, after Gibbs relayed Ross's request, had agreed to research for "Onward and Upward with the Arts."[36]

Though reviewers often cite Benson's cynicism and biting satire, most fail to recognize the sensitive, compassionate side that surfaced in such stories as this Christmas piece that delighted White. Full of sentiment, "Upon a Midnight Clear" describes Mr. Parsons, an elder resident of Madison, Connecticut, prodded by his sister to go to the annual pageant held at Miss Weatherly's home.[37] Miss Weatherly, wrapped in the blue shawl she had bought in Rome, sat center stage next to "a very fine early American pine cradle." Unlike the Madonna, however, Weatherly's eyes were not fixed on the cradle but roamed over the heads of the assembled worshipers as Christmas carols were played and sung. She had the most lines and in reciting them sounded to Mr. Parsons like a blend of New Testament and Miss Weatherly. Mixed with Benson's humor was her rendering of Mr. Parsons's nostalgia for life as it used to be in Madison before the tourists and New York folk moved in; for Christmas as it used to be celebrated—on the eve—not two weeks in advance; and, ultimately, for the joyful Christmas experience he had known as a child. Verging on the sentimental in this piece, Benson was consciously writing to please the *New Yorker* reader. She subsequently admitted to White: "I had to work on the pageant as the things I could have written sounded too sacrilegious—though God knows they were true. However, I knew you all wouldn't like that. . . . I have written for some more information on Plymouth and when I get it, will get to work on it."[38]

Also in the mail was a letter from Wolcott Gibbs, who had written to explain his inserting a sentence as a "necessary key" to understanding a recent Benson submission. "Some such remark needs to be there. We are that kind of a magazine," he explained, adding wishes for a "Happy Christmas, dear," and news: "The Thurbers have taken a villa at Antibes where the sun always shines." Benson replied, "I sketched out your line and added a bit that I think clears the point up. If you like your line better, leave it. You know I don't care." She praised his "profile on Beebe" as the "best the *New Yorker* has ever had. I loved it. You did it *well*. I may come to see you before I go away for Christmas. I think you ought to take me to lunch." Her relationship with Gibbs was one of great ease because Benson knew that he liked her.

Benson hardly mentioned Babe in *New Yorker* correspondence. Then, an unforeseen and unexpected reconciliation between the two occurred. Though she still relied almost completely on her arrangement with the magazine to support herself and Barbara, Babe's reentry into her life had an unwanted consequence: it interfered with her writing. On December 18th, Benson wrote White to explain:

> I haven't forgotten the story I was supposed to send but Reynolds fell down the steps at Rockefeller Plaza and hurt his back badly, and is at the Medical Center. He's coming home tomor-

row, the clumsy ox. He was ogling the skaters. I have been going there every day and having dinner with him. All he talks about is his diet. It has opened a whole new world to him.[39]

Benson had three stories started, she told White—"The House That Love Built," "You've Got to Hand It to Them," and a little thing called "Mouse Sanctuary." *The New Yorker* published only the first, the second—by Benson's own admission, being "not so good as I have an axe to grind."[40] As for the proposed series on "American Pilgrimages," Benson would not do any more on the Plymouth piece until Christmas when she would be in Vermont and could "find out a few things I want to be sure of. How about doing Wallace [*sic*] Simpson's home in Baltimore for one?" she asked. "They are announcing at the end of the tour through the house that she has engaged a room at Johns-Hopkins in February for a Caesarian." Thanking White for her check and Miss Terry for getting it to her, Benson added: "I was astounded! I did not expect so much. You all have been so nice to me that I will be glad to send you all my things before I send them anywhere else."[41]

White replied on December 18th, "I am now waiting for those three stories, waiting earnestly." She also approved Benson's Wallis Simpson piece and enclosed a previously done "Talk of the Town" clipping on Simpson so that Benson could avoid repetition. Best of all, White considered it "grand news" that Benson would send *The New Yorker* "all [her] things first." Though only two of Benson's pieces appeared in *The New Yorker* that year, 1937 had been very productive and profitable for Sally Benson.

18

BECOMING AN ENTREPRENEUR

1938

"The reviews I saw were marvelous . . . it must be very nice to get up early in the morning and find three publishers waiting alongside the milk."

—William Maxwell

As soon as the new year began, White reminded Benson not to forget the three promised stories. "I hoped you would be starting the year off with a bang by having two or three here to greet me. . . . We want fiction, we want the new series, we want everything," she pressured.[1] Three weeks later Benson received White's check for "Home Atmosphere" along with a forty-dollar bonus because "we thought the story was such a superlative one." White explained, "since [it] ran a little shorter than some of yours the initial payment wasn't big enough for the merit of the story, we felt. . . . We like brevity and will sometimes pay a bonus just for that." Though White still addressed her as "Mrs. Benson," the relationship between the two women was becoming more friendly. "Send along those other stories as soon as you can, and let's have lunch again. Will you call me up?" White invited, adding a postscript, "I see the anecdote is in print so a cheque will follow."[2]

Benson's next submission arrived on Gibbs's desk with her comment, "I love this story." In voicing this connection with her material, Benson strikes a remarkably different stance from writers like Dorothy Parker who detested writing fiction and almost always had to be coerced into producing promised material. Parker would often stare at her blank type sheet for hours and give up. She would string publishers along for months, even after receiving large advances from them. As Marion Meade, Parker's biographer, describes it, "Writing fiction was a torturous process for her. When she insisted that it took her six months to complete a story, it was often the case" (100, see also 163). Besides her genuine dislike for composing fiction, drinking accounted for some of Parker's procrastination. The "discouraging slowness of her work—the isolation, the claustrophobic silence" often caused her to "flee" (Meade 163). Benson, on the other hand, always a dedicated worker, plunged into writing with enthusiasm and could turn out a completed piece in three hours on average. What is more, Benson loved writing and often displayed a proprietary stance toward her material as shall be seen.

When White sent Benson the check for her "beautiful little 'Talk of the Town' anecdote," she shared that Thurber, in a recent letter, had said "many wonderful things regarding your writing."[3] A gratified Benson continued sending in pieces during February, March, and April, but unexpected surgery in May interrupted her productivity. Several *New Yorker* staffers telephoned their hospitalized colleague, and Katharine White sent stock and peonies—flowers Benson loved. She wrote to thank White for her sweetness and conveyed great disappointment at taking so long to regain her health: "I thought I would feel better sooner, but I am not up yet and still wear those little jackets. When I can type-write, I will send you several 'Talk of the Town' things and my story. Barbara is away again and I can't cope with longhand. I am frantic for something to do. You haven't any darning you want done, have you?"

May brought another change into Benson's life. Wolcott Gibbs had tired of editing fiction and resigned. His replacement was William Maxwell, an English professor from Illinois (Yagoda 160). Maxwell, knowing Benson was "not a reader of our popular periodical," sent her a copy of the May 28th *New Yorker* since it had her story, "The House That Love Built," "sitting on the throne."[4] A few days later, Benson asked Maxwell for an advance of $150, promising to cover it by sending two stories by Wednesday the same week. "I have found an apartment for next year," she wrote. "The leases are here, but I have to pay a month's rent in advance. . . . The stories are called 'Master' and 'Not in the Mood,' both are very good." As so often happened, neither story appeared. When she regained her health, Benson worked on completing *Emily*, her second collection to be published by Covici. Though she had received an advance for *Emily* in 1934, Benson had not yet produced the volume in 1938. When Covici wired her in Dorset, Vermont about needing one more story, Benson immediately wrote to

Maxwell. She would copy "On a High Hill" for him because she needed to send the piece to Covici. "I love it," she asserted, but:

> it has the word 'bitch' in it and Ross might not like that. He may not like it anyway as it is a little tougher than I usually am. It reads quickly. This is the last time I will bother you with stories to be squeezed in for the book. You have been very nice about them. I will mail your other story to you this evening and that can run any time. Will you use "On a High Hill"? . . . Let me know. . . . Never mind sending it back to me if you can't as Pat will have his copy and I don't want it for a memory book or anything.

(It may be well to recall the process of publishing in *The New Yorker*. As Wolcott Gibbs had advised Benson, once the magazine had published a piece, the rights to it belonged to its author.) Benson also told Maxwell she had bought his book (*They Came Like Swallows*) at Walter Hard's store in Manchester, Vermont and was so "crazy about it" that she would "finish it tonight" while Bobsie and her friend were visiting. She explained,

> Bobs has had a cadet who just graduate [*sic*] from West Point up here since we came. He wants her to marry him right away but she doesn't want to. They talk and talk and I go to bed and read. She came up the other night, closed my door carefully and laughed helplessly. She said, "Mama, if you had a dictaphone and could have listened to me this evening, you'd have lost your lunch."[5]

Maxwell responded with a congratulatory wire on June 24 for "On a High Hill," explaining he was "much too excited to write . . . only a wire or a birthday celebration would be adequate." It is "your most magnificent story," and "Mr. Ross is equally enthusiastic, thinks the story very fine, and we plan to use it in the issue of the 23rd of July." Maxwell added a personal note: "Thank you, thank you for your kind words about my book." The next day, Maxwell sent Benson her check for "On a High Hill" with an extra bonus of 10 percent because it was "so first-rate."[6]

Benson answered, still addressing him as "Dear Mr. Maxwell": "I was surprised when I got your wire. I was very pleased with it, too, even though I thought you might be tight"—a surprisingly personal comment given the formal salutation. "Take $100 from my check and the fifty off the next," she directed. "That should do it. You are all grand about giving the needy money and I am sure no other magazine in the world would be so nice. I finished your book and kept on loving it. It is a grand book."[7] (Despite the familiar tone of her letters to Maxwell, Benson omitted the complimentary close, ending with a mere penciled signature. Her letters to Gibbs, by contrast, had always ended: "Love, Sally").

While writing her *New Yorker* pieces, Benson resumed reviewing mystery books again. She told Maxwell she had "thousands of mysteries arriving by every mail. . . . I'm earning my keep *there*!" She had another story ready for him but couldn't get time to copy it. Part of the reason was:

> This place is a mass of Barbara's friends. Bobs and Frannie have just left for Albany to meet a boy—a boy they put on the train only yesterday about this time. He's back. I have no maid until the first and then I have one who is pregnant, but she still looks good to me. It is impossible to keep anyone here, up in the hills as we are. Arthur Bodanski came up here with five well-trained servants and they all walked out on him the next day. No movies. I do far more than I am supposed [sic] to, and heave coal into our damned hot water heater. Such things drive me nuts, and while I love to cook, I can't seem to throw rice and peas together and call it a meal the way the illustrators in Westport used to. I have to go in for hollandaise and stuff.[8]

Benson's letter suggests that she misses Nantucket and finds Dorset too rural. Without a maid she was forced to become domestic. She was also lonely. When Barbara began dating Robert Hamilton Binkerd, one of the Bensons' few neighbors, she introduced her mother to "Bird," Ham's mother. Discovering a shared interest in gardening led to a new friendship for both.

When Random House expressed interest in Benson's fiction, she asked Maxwell to send her pieces to Bennett Cerf, and Maxwell wired that his secretary, Daise Terry, would mail them—"which means that it is as good as done. And Lord love you for doing another story for early fall. And as for me, I love you for loving my story. It wasn't universally admired." He also commiserated with Benson "slaving away over the kitchen stove for God knows what hordes of young things."[9]

With her next submission of blurbs, Benson elaborated on her current situation for McKelway. "I have a houseful of girls and West Point cadets. They were talking about another cadet, a lad in henna pants, basque shirt, and quite a lot of beer, and they said, 'The trouble with Barney is he's much too Mid-Victorian.' Oh, well, oh God!" She had been impressed by Maxwell's "lovely wire," she told Mac, and asked that he correct her address and send copies of *The New Yorker* every week. "If I can't get it any other way, I'll subscribe to it," because "I like to read my mystery blurbs. They fascinate me."[10] This admission is another example of Benson's inner, childlike spirit. Unlike many writers, she was unashamedly pleased with her creations, even the blurbs. Equally unusual is her openness in sharing such feelings with *New Yorker* staffers, the majority of them, men.

McKelway, glad about Maxwell's wiring Benson, reported:

> He is one of your greatest admirers, you know, but I will joust with him as to whether he is a greater admirer of yours than I am. How do you know so much about the profession of housewife, for example, and furthermore, how do you know how a salesman feels when he stands on a doorstep? I really think you are wonderful. [The piece referred to is "Profession: Housewife."] How far up are you, anyway? I would like to drive by sometime and find out how you know about people who name their studios the Snuggery. That was really a honey. But you are probably too far north.[11]

Benson sent Mac some commentary on another set of blurbs and assured him, "I'd love to have you come by any time. We are six miles from Manchester, Vermont, and about twenty-five miles from Williamstown, Mass. So why don't you?"[12]

When Maxwell responded to Benson with a thank-you note on July 1st, he explained,

> I wasn't tight, just enormously excited. I showed your letter to Gibbs who, as you know, loves you dearly. We were both so pleased with the maid and Barbara's friends, and also Mrs.

Forman's vocabulary. . . . It pleases me to have you like my book. Somehow or other, I seem to have picked up the idea that you are choosy. Regards,

William Maxwell

Two new developments occurred in mid-July. Good news came from Edward Aswell of Harper & Brothers who reported that Hamish Hamilton, their London affiliate, had written: "For many months I have enjoyed Sally Benson's stories in the *New Yorker*. Do you think there would be any chance of getting a novel from her?" Aswell concurred with Hamilton's suggestion and invited Benson to meet and talk over her plans.[13] But July's auspicious beginnings and the pleasantries exchanged between Benson and Maxwell faded instantly when an unexpected storm broke in mid-July: Covici-Friede publishers had gone bankrupt.

Complications in abundance resulted. Maxwell immediately wrote to Ik Shuman, managing editor, that Benson had not released copyright and was expecting to see galleys of her book before it appeared. The problem, he explained, was that

the book is to be published July 29th, and it is already in the hands of reviewers. When Mr. Covici wrote her that he wasn't going to send her galleys to her summer home in Vermont, she came down to the city to talk to him about it but he wouldn't see her. He has, however, discussed the matter with her lawyer. Mrs. Benson objects to the way the book is printed and especially to the fact that at least three or four of the stories which the *New Yorker* has printed this spring haven't been included in it. All this, in spite of the fact that . . . Mr. Covici was writing her constantly for new material because there was not enough to make a book. Altogether, she thinks about sixteen thousand words were not included in the volume, and those stories are about the best she has written. Also, she at one time sent him, merely for him to read, a group of stories which she considers inferior and which have not been published, and which she says she told him she would redo for him if he wanted them. Now she finds they are included in the book without ever having been rewritten. She is trying through her lawyers to get an injunction against the publication of the book, and the lawyer wants to know whether we would go to court to stop publication of the book which, after all, doesn't have our copyright release. Since the publication is three weeks away, and since we have no particular reason for refusing such a request even now should the publisher ask for it, I don't see how we have a legal leg to stand on. Moreover, Mrs. Benson is an extremely temperamental woman whose word in matters of detail is not entirely trustworthy.[14]

When the second meeting of creditors convened on August 2nd at the Hotel Commodore to hear the report of the first creditors' meeting on July 25th, Little & Ives, the largest creditor, proposed to take over Covici-Friede's management and pay off their other creditors in monthly installments. As for authors like Benson, claims for royalties would be paid by August 20th and their contracts and options would remain in "status quo." Little & Ives intended to ask Pascal Covici to continue with the firm but not as its business manager. That responsibility would be "placed in the hands of an experienced person to be selected later."[15]

Benson wrote a "long and good letter" to Aswell explaining her "most complicated situation." He advised her that existing contracts with Covici could become void, and should that happen, he proposed talking over with her "a publishing program for any books you might write." Hamish Hamilton would be equally interested in having the English rights to such books. Even if the contract with Covici remained in force, Aswell suggested, "it may still be possible to make some arrangement that would give Hamilton the right to publish your novel in Great Britain," but the "Covici firm or its successors would undoubtedly . . . [want] to negotiate with Hamilton for the British rights." On a more personal note Aswell concluded: "It is most awkward for you . . . not knowing where you stand, and I do most sincerely hope that the whole affair will soon be cleared up. I shall certainly want to keep in touch with you."[16]

Despite the turmoil, Benson completed another story for Maxwell and reported that *Emily* had gotten good reviews, but Covici-Friede "are in a perilous state. . . . I suppose that's why Pat got the book out in such a state of confusion. But it was a pretty mean trick on me, as I suppose I'll not get a cent. He still owes me money on *People Are Fascinating*, too. Not much, though." At the same time, she mentioned that three other publishers—Doubleday Doran, Farrar and Rinehart, and Harper's—"want me . . . as they have been getting enthusiastic letters from a man named Hamish Hamilton in England." Her comment, "I don't care much," seems a curious response given her difficulty managing money. So also does her issuing Maxwell the humorous directive: "Take your filthy $50 out of my check, so I won't see your haunted faces in my dreams." In a playful mood, she ended with an anecdote related by her nephew, Toby Wherry:

> They were giving another one of those "I've Got Your Number" tests at his camp, and one little boy was asked "When poverty comesin [*sic*] the door, does love fly out the window?" And he said, "Oh, yes. It's happened to my mother three times."

One can appreciate Benson's enjoying such humor. In the same amused spirit she appended a penciled request after her signature: "If I can't own that picture of Thurber's 'He's so charming, it gives you the creeps,' I feel I can't go on. That's the best picture he's ever done."[17]

Maxwell replied with encouragement: "The reviews I saw were marvelous, and while I'm sorry that Covici-Friede are still in your hair, it must be very nice to get up early in the morning and find three publishers waiting alongside the milk." He added, "We like your piece 'Carry Me Back' immensely, and a check for it is enclosed, minus our filthy $50. Your request for the Thurber drawing has been put down first on the list. He is coming back early next month, as you perhaps know. Regards, Maxwell."[18]

As Benson modestly indicated, publishers were in a "feeding frenzy" trying to obtain her work. The next day she received an insistent letter from Donald S. Klopfer of Random House:

Dear Miss Benson:

> Should you decide to change your publisher at this time, Random House would do anything within reason to add you to its list. I know you are in Vermont now, so I cannot get in touch with you direct, but my partner, Bob Haas, has a home in Arlington, Vermont, and is there at the present time, and Bennett Cerf will be going up to Vermont in a couple of weeks. If there is any possibility of our talking over the chances of

Random House becoming your publisher, we should like the opportunity of doing so.[19]

In a similar vein, Charles Pearce of Harcourt, Brace and Company, Incorporated, wrote: "Most of the members of our editorial staff are great admirers of your work; those who aren't just haven't had the good luck to read your pieces. And that's a situation that would swiftly and pleasantly be remedied if we could see your next manuscript."[20] Donald B. Elder of Doubleday, Doran and Company, Incorporated, also wrote of his firm's interest in Benson's work—especially *Emily*—and invited her to meet with them to "discuss [her] future writing plans."[21]

Reviewers of *Emily* had whetted publishers' appetites for Benson's fiction. Dorothy L. Meyer's "Satirical Group of Feminine Sketches," for example, in the *Democrat Chronicle* of Rochester, New York, advised men they might learn "much about women from this sophisticated volume of short stories by Sally Benson." Like its predecessor, *People Are Fascinating*, the new collection, she continued,

> exposes the foibles of her sex in clever satire. Benson acquaints her readers with the so-called intricacies of the feminine personality, reveals the subtle workings of the feminine mind, and demolishes the idea that women were not made to be understood. She gently ridicules the pretense and arrogance cleverly characterized in her brief portrayals, most of which describe women in domestic surroundings.

Meyer had interviewed Benson and heard firsthand the oft-repeated Benson lies. "Since she started writing, Mrs. Benson has never received a rejection slip, nor been asked to revise or rewrite a story, something of a record," she reported. The last phrase—"something of a record"—implies Meyer's doubting Benson's account, but her report perpetuated the Benson myth.[22] Far be it from Sally Benson to correct her.

Stemming from Benson's insecurity and her need to cover it by lying, the myth was a distinct departure from reality. *New Yorker* records contain Benson manuscripts that editors both queried and corrected, yet Benson propagated the notion that she wrote speedily and flawlessly. As the *New Yorker* correspondence demonstrates, Benson was often advised to rethink or revise parts of her stories. In the early forties, the magazine rejected outright Benson's "A Toast to the Next Man Who Dies," and in the late forties editor William Shawn "killed" her "The Comeback" despite its being already in galleys. One wonders how Benson's *New Yorker* editors reacted when they encountered her exaggerations in print. Most likely, their affection for Benson and their understanding of the writer's ego enabled them to tolerate this foible of hers with the same mild amusement with which Benson rendered her characters. Even when she enjoyed popularity with readers, Benson needed to present herself as a flawless writer. One cause of such exaggeration might have been that lacking the college education her sisters enjoyed, she compensated by cultivating the persona of sophisticated writer.[23]

As her writing career met with increasing success, the critics also contributed to Benson's positive self-image. Frances Woodward, for example, reviewed *Emily* in *Books* and praised Benson as a "recognized satirist." Though the inept appellation "venomous" is the word most often applied, wrote Woodward,

> Benson is ironic, she is shrewd, she is too clear-eyed for comfort, but what she distills is not poison. And in the stories that deal with young girls—incidentally among the most successful of . . . *Emily*—she is compassionate in a way impossible to anyone except the very kind and the very wise.[24]

R. C. Feld presented a similar view in *The New Republic*:

> Sally Benson is a gentle satirist. She deals no brutal blows that leave ugly bruises, but with greater art, strips her subject of all pretenses and affectations and lets her stand naked, not as God made her, but as time and friends and circumstances have made her. Sometimes the creature that remains is likeable, sometimes not. But always she is human and understandable.[25]

Katharine Simonds of the *Saturday Review of Literature* voiced an equally positive appraisal:

> Mrs. Benson has all the qualities of the woman's mind at its best. She is light of touch, neat without being thin, deft in

construction, and quick to perceive pathos as well as absurdity. Her dialogue is so skillful that you can't resist the temptation of reading it aloud; her epigrams so satisfying that you catch yourself trying to work them into your own conversations. She has the keenest possible eye for the small change in which women demand back the gold of their lives. In spite of her skill and wit, she preaches as stern a moral for the women of her day as Maria Edgeworth did for her contemporaries.[26]

Such positive reviews of *Emily* gave Benson added strength in her struggle with its publisher. Responding to Charles Pearce of Harcourt, Brace and Company, Benson described her treatment at the hands of Covici-Friede in terms so graphic that Pearce hastened to assure her his firm would have treated her very differently. "If we felt that 15,000 words should be omitted from the book, we'd have presented our reasons for omitting them, but if you hadn't accepted our reasons, we'd have gone ahead and published your book as you prepared it." Admitting "It's none of my business," Pearce injected a "good word for Michael Sadleir of Constable." They, he felt, had done "intelligent and enterprising things with the work of American writers, and you probably would be happy to be published in England by them." He would be happy to offer her a contract for the next books she might write, whether "novels, collections of short stories, or short novels."[27]

Covici, meanwhile, had chosen an option other than the one offered him by Little & Ives. He wrote to Benson on August 17th:

Dear Sally,

Doubtless you know all about my joining Viking Press. John Steinbeck came with me and I hope a few of my other authors will join me soon. Not having heard from you since that unpleasant episode, I don't know how you feel about me. Do you think you can still love me well enough to permit my talking to my new associates about your present and future work? Drop me a line.

Affectionately,
Pat

Benson replied that she was still occasionally fond of Pat though there were moments when she "wanted to tear him to pieces." On the 25th he responded, glad she had written and hoping the "tearing to pieces" would be done "in a most affectionate way." Covici was remarkably recovered from the "terrific cataclysm" and cavalierly told Benson all was well, "even to a rainbow in the sky. In this new firm I hope to do some of the things I could only dream about." He also sent her a copy of *The Woman Who Could Not Die*—"to properly inaugurate you"—a book "somewhat depressing [but] . . . very brilliant. Tell me what you think of it," he requested, signing: "Affectionately yours, Pat."

Covici's letters, no matter how subtle or overt their sexual overtones, always contained a business subtext. Had Benson not seen it? Or was she so emotionally needy that she turned a blind eye? Perhaps, in retrospect at least, she saw that the friendship was a "love-hate" one. He never apologized for the significant financial losses he caused her, and Benson was furious at his handling of *Emily*—disregarding her wishes about selection and placement of her stories, so that she felt "misrepresented" by what he published. Worse, she never received the money Covici-Friede owed her.

Two days later, therefore, Benson was overjoyed when Bennett Cerf assured her that Random House would

> try to arrange some agreement whereby your contracts with Covici-Friede for both novels and short stories will be terminated by mutual consent, and the plates and entire stock of all your books turned over to us for a sum to be arranged. The whole deal, of course, would be dependent upon you and ourselves working out a contract that is mutually agreeable. I haven't the slightest doubt that we will be able to do this along the general lines of the letter I sent to you last week. Needless to say, when things get to a point where a decision is to be made, both the Lindey offices and I will get in touch with you immediately. I can't tell you how much I hope everything will work out because I really want you on our list—doing the kinds of things you want to do. Bob Haas leaves for Vermont this afternoon and I am sure that you will hear from him sometime next week. And I am looking forward to seeing you in Vermont sometime around Labor Day, although your concluding sentence

"but it won't be a holiday" sounds rather ominous to me. Just what have you in mind, Miss Benson?

Cordially, Bennett Cerf [28]

It is not clear just how Benson involved herself with Cerf, but subsequent letters hint that there may well have been a more than professional relationship between them.[29]

Toward the end of August, Benson was contacted by George W. Joel of Dial Press. His letter vividly detailed Covici-Friede's demise:

Dear Sally Benson:

The moment you walked into Covici's office, it was hotter than you thought. We had just received word that the "corpse" was to be buried. Now that the "wake" is over, I for one, am able to function. I know you have no publishing commitments. Before you make any, I should like to talk to you about the possibility of having you on our list. . . . What have you got to lose?[30]

Benson responded with her usual "honesty" that publishers were in "hot pursuit," evoking Joel's acknowledgment and equally honest statement: "I wouldn't want to rush you into anything because I know how far I'd get." Despite that, he reasoned, "because it was my original idea to have your first collection of stories published, I ask you to do one thing for me: talk to me before you sign up with a new publisher. Sincerely or Cordially, Geo (Joel)."[31] Because she liked his argument and because she trusted him, Benson made a commitment to Joel to write a children's version of classical Greek and Latin myths.

Entitled *Stories of the Gods and Heroes*, Benson's book proved successful. Published in New York City by Dial Press in 1940, this volume contained Benson's dedicatory note to Toby Wherry, her nephew,[32] illustrations by Steele Savage, and an introductory note. Since, aside from occasional comments on her writing found in the *New Yorker* records, little of Benson's critical writing exists, Benson's introduction to *Stories of the Gods and Heroes* is important. Informal yet academic in tone, Benson's introduction acknowledged her source—*The Age of Fable*, by Thomas Bulfinch, published in 1913—and praised his careful translation of the dialogue he had found in "Greek and Latin legends, or from Virgil or Homer." Benson continued: I have rewritten some of [the legends] entirely, and have cut, edited, and clarified others. . . . As stories of mythology are not simple, I have made no effort to write them simply, and have followed Mr. Bulfinch's grand, flowing style."

With her young audience obviously in mind, she explained: "Many of the stories used in *The Age of Fable* are not in this book. I found some of them dull, and some of them too involved. The tales of the Trojan War are considerably shortened, and I have left out the adventures of Aeneas altogether." If her reader wanted to know more about mythology, she recommended reading *The Age of Fable*—"the work of a man who conscientiously explored every source to be able to put into one volume myths that have been handed down by people to whom myth was reality." On a rare note of humility she concluded: "These stories are not mine. They belong to two races who lived and died, and to Thomas Bulfinch who brought them to life again almost fifty years ago" (*Stories* 12).[33]

Out of print today, Benson's *Stories of the Gods and Heroes* had gone through nineteen printings by 1977 and each edition had been received favorably and been given positive reviews. A. M. Jordan in *Horn Book*, for one, praised Benson's judgment in selection, omitting stories "too complicated," following Bulfinch "when he suits her purpose," and "rewriting when his style is formal or sentimental." Children "will find this easier and more compelling reading than many other versions."[34] The *New York Times* reviewer pointed out that the book "fills a real need." Children would "thoroughly enjoy it," and older readers would find it a "pleasant way of brushing up their mythological knowledge and . . . take satisfaction in giving it to young people."[35]

Two weeks after signing Dial's contract with Joel, Benson signed a contract with Bennett Cerf of Random House on September 13, 1938. When Covici learned of Benson's contract, he wrote immediately:

Dear Sally,

Of course, I feel sorry that I am not going to have the pleasure of doing your next book, but you have a very exciting publisher in Bennett Cerf. I am very fond of him. You two should get along magnificently. But you don't mind, do you, if I still hope that you won't get along with him quite as well as you did with me? Nevertheless, I wish you the best of luck and do let me see you.

Affectionately yours, Pat[36]

A week later Laurence Pollinger of Pearn, Pollinger & Higham, Ltd. (Benson's British literary agents) congratulated Benson on joining Cerf who had "left six [of her] stories with me." Five were now in Sadleir's hands, and the sixth—"Upon a Midnight Clear"—would be offered serially. There would be plenty of time to do that before her Constable book would come out in the spring, he assured her. "We must get *Emily* absolutely cleared before making a contract with Constable. As I see the position, half of her is owned by Covici, the other half by yourself! Perhaps my persuasive letter to Smith will result in his parting up with Covici's half to you." Should Pearn be successful with Smith, the contract with Constable need suffer no further delay. He would send her a list of the contents of Constable's book for her approval as soon as Sadleir had it ready. How different, Benson thought, from the sneaky proceedings of Covici. "What is next on the programme," Pollinger inquired, "the completion of that novel or another collection of shorts? . . . let me have duplicate copy of everything you send to Cerf for publication."[37]

Finally, on October 5th, Benson received a long-awaited letter from Pat Covici. After almost two years, he and Donald Friede had finally sent their statement releasing their rights to publish *Emily*. Meanwhile, Benson continued to produce pieces for *The New Yorker* and, after taking a short five-day break "riding around the country" and fearing she had missed proofs from Maxwell, she happily wrote him: "While I was away, Collier's have been wiring me about a proposal they want to make," and

> tomorrow a man from them is coming here to see me. On Sunday, too. I can't imagine why there is such a rush as I have been around for years and nobody's been spending money on wires.[38] And a man from Curtis Brown with a message from the *Saturday Evening Post* came to Manchester and called me and wrote me letters. Bobs said I was away. Then my English agents wired me that Michael Sadleir of Constable wants the book for publication

in England and will give me an advance if I will let them have my next two books. I tell you all this because my books so far have all been in Covici's imagination. . . . I was amazed at the speed you took this story. It's good though isn't it?[39]

A few days later, Benson sent another piece to White with a note: "The reason for my industry is that I have my state tax to pay, God knows how. I explained to Mr. Maxwell that the wolf was sleeping under my bed, so if I could get paid for these *if* you like them by Friday, I would be very well pleased. I think this is a very good story."[40] By September, Benson anticipated having more than ten stories accepted for publication in the magazine and questioned Maxwell, "What about the 20% on stories accepted over the ten [required by contract]? I'm as smart as a whip!"[41] Maxwell replied affirmatively and reviewed Benson's terms: "I should say you are. Twenty per cent on the first ten and as soon as we buy it, twenty per cent added to every check thereafter for the balance of the time covered by the aforesaid agreement."[42] Regarding White's response to her latest submission, Maxwell asked that Benson, "Read the attached and think about it, please. I bought your book," he added, "and I believe Ross did too, but neither of us has read it yet. . . . See what you think and write me or come in and talk about it. Love, Maxwell."[43]

Meanwhile, Bob Haas of Random House had written to compliment Benson as well as encourage her about her novel:

Dear Sally,

No other author has caused such a storm of paper work, and I think you should be very proud. . . . Your news about a short novel is simply swell. I don't see why you should be scared. I'm perfectly sure not only that you can do it but that you can do it beautifully. And it will put you on the map with a lot of people who may not now know of you. This may be of little, if any, interest to an aesthetic writer, but for a sordid publisher it contains implications which are gratifying to contemplate.

Cordially, Bob Haas[44]

Benson was clearly a woman of paradox. With public audiences with whom she had no personal ties, she could toss off her customary lies.

With individuals like Covici, she could be alternately loving and spiteful, depending on whether she had gotten her way. With her *New Yorker* editors, Benson seemed most true to herself, revealing awe at the fanfare surrounding her published collections, incredulity at the solicitations of publishers eager to bring out her work, and simple delight in pieces she "loved." She also respected her editors' judgment. Though she needed money for taxes, she wanted it only "*if*" Katharine White thought the story good. It goes without saying that Benson was especially pleased when she received a positive response to her work such as Maxwell's wire about "On a High Hill." Yet, she never showed this likeable, almost childlike aspect of herself in public. Worse, Benson was slow or too trusting to realize when publishers were promoting their own interests rather than hers.

Another impressive aspect of Benson's work at *The New Yorker* is one ordinarily overlooked: her mystery reviews. Responding to the galleys of Benson's reviews submitted for the October 1, 1938, issue, Maxwell, for example, waxed almost ecstatic: "I am speechless with admiration," he wrote, but reminded Benson, "And by the way, what, oh what, about that story for early fall? This *is* early fall." On another occasion, Benson's review for the October 15th issue of *The New Yorker* particularly praised Margery Allingham's *The Fashion in Shrouds*, calling Allingham the "best of the mystery writers" and her book the "best mystery ever written." Benson's commendation inspired William Shawn, the distinguished general editor of *The New Yorker*, to suggest to Ross a special "sub-department" on mysteries under "Books." In a long, in-house letter, Shawn wrote: "Here is a book, which though a mystery, is obviously news, and should be written about at greater length." They could have used the "Allingham book as a lead," incorporating the others in the body of the column instead of in blurbs. This might happen only half a dozen times a year, but "we should be flexible enough to provide the space whenever one [such book] appear[s]: something by a remarkable new writer, or . . . a peculiar discovery of Mrs. Benson's, or an unusually good book by an old writer about whom Mrs. Benson has interesting opinions."[45] Harold Ross not only agreed with Shawn's proposal but also passed it on to McKelway by typing at the bottom of Shawn's letter: "I heartily subscribe to the above. . . . By all means, tell Miss B. that she can have space to spread a little on special occasions. ROSS."

More success arrived in October via Nancy Pearn, who wrote Benson from England: "Such splendid news! *The Bystander* want four stories at their usual price of ten guineas each." In addition, the magazine wanted to "start running [Benson] as a sort of *Bystander* institution rather in the way the *New Yorker* does." The editor wanted to title Benson's sketches—"American Sketches"—to emphasize that "they are impressions of American life."[46] Pollinger gave details regarding the order and selection of Benson's pieces for the British collection and attached a list of the stories to be included. They would respect her wish to omit "Woman's Intuition," concurring with her that it was "poor." As for titling the collection, both Sadleir and Pollinger thought a "group title" would be stronger than "taking one story and saying 'So and So' and other stories." They invited Benson to "devise some phrase that would cover the collection and give it flavor."[47]

By November 21st, Laurence Pollinger had told another agent—Curtis Brown—to go ahead with the contract for *Emily*, making it quite clear to "Covici (now taken over by his printers, Little & Ives) and Constable" that "50% of all monies received from Constable is to come to us for you. The remaining 50% will go to the Covici office and I hope some of it will eventually find itself in your hands." According to the arrangement, the Constable book would contain only "about six stories on which you control the British rights." The balance of the book would contain "stories on which Covici control [*sic*] the British rights, drat them." Replying to Benson's prior letter, Pollinger commiserated: "Sorry about the hangover. Come over and drink some real whiskey or (as the posters say) 'Beer is best.'"

Given the two-week period it took for mail to cross the Atlantic in those days, Sally's hangover would have occurred around November 7th. Whether occasioned by the stress with Covici, who can say? A December 2nd letter brought the contradictory news that Benson reportedly had given Covici "control of the British rights of all of the stories in *Emily*." As a result, the new contract would have to be made with Little & Ives and cover all the stories. Pollinger still thought they had done well. The Covici business was a going concern and paying twenty shillings to the pound. If Benson could "dig up and send me your contract with Covici," Pollinger would have more solid ground to stand on.[48] Since Benson often annotated her business mail with shopping lists or recordings of how she spent her money, it is doubtful that she could produce a copy of the contract, but to the file folders in her *New Yorker* office, she soon would add a new one, titled "Bastards and Shysters." It would fill with correspondence to and from agents like William Morris, publishers like Covici, Little & Ives, and various lawyers.

The following weeks' correspondence discussed the potential title for the British edition of *Emily*. Contending were: *Friend of the Family, Shall We Join the Ladies?, The Feather Pate*, and *Folly*. These were succeeded by *Love Thy Neighbour, Women Must Weep*, and *Bourgeois on Parade*.[49] Finally, Pollinger had word that Covici and Constable had reached an agreement: "It is clearly understood by all that 50% of all sums of money . . . are to come to us to be passed directly to you." In the same letter, Pollinger reported that *The Bystander* would run Benson's stories serially before Michael Sadleir of Constable published them so she would be receiving even more money and royalties. Also, he had begun drafting an agreement with Constable for her next two books. He wished her "a happy Christmas and a jolly and prosperous New Year."[50] Two days later, Nancy Pearn wrote Benson: "I laughed and laughed to think of any so mournful a title as *Women Must Weep* being associated with *you*." She informed Benson that *The Bystander* would run her stories as *Americana*, starting in January and ending in February. *The Bystander*, moreover, was "behaving like a nice little brother to Constable . . . promising them to run a line making clear the fact that the series in question will shortly be appearing in volume"—something she considered "unusually brotherly on the part of the magazine" since it constitutes "free advertising for Constable." Best of all, the magazine would be paying as soon as the series began running, and Benson would have the checks in time to "buy some very early Spring hats!"[51]

Benson considered *Friend of the Family* a good title and wrote to tell Pearn. She included news of Vincent Carroll, the Bennett Cerf dinner, her *Collier's* success, and the family's recent excursion to Macy's to see Santa Claus—but no photograph. Pearn's reply of December 23rd asked for two Benson photographs early in the new year—"one for Laurence and one for me." Pearn also expressed her delight that Benson planned to visit England the following year. Michael Sadleir, she reported, upon discovering a Heinemann publication of the same title, had to reject *Friend of the Family* as the proposed title. Besides, it was not really a group title. Ultimately, everyone agreed that Benson's title should be *Love Thy Neighbour*. When the volume was reviewed the following April, the *Times Literary Supplement* spoke of Benson's work as "sharply entertaining."

> Venomous women with a spite against life are brilliantly featured
> in these lively and varied tales: the tiny helpless wife making a

business of looking peculiarly small and frail and useless until it occurs to her husband that she is indeed useless; the business girl who is sick of being a housewife and longs to get back to the office; the arty woman who dressed "in a suit knitted by herself, which made her look as though she were not only going backward but upside down as well." Mrs. Benson sees that pity and kindness sometimes underlie mistakes and absurdities. She describes adolescence with exactness, warmth, and humor.[52]

Clearly, despite the Covici problem, 1938 had been a banner year for Benson. With two collections in print and publishers on both sides of the Atlantic clamoring for more fiction, she was riding the crest of a wave. She had no idea how tidal it would become before it broke.

19

A WORLD AT WAR,
TURMOIL AT HOME

1939–1940

"I feel strange being so shot and wake up crying for no reason."

—Sally Benson

Until 1939, Sally Benson had published interviews, essays, book reviews, and fiction in newspapers, pulp magazines, college textbooks, and, most importantly, *The New Yorker*. Two collections of fiction had appeared in America and Great Britain, and a third was in the works. As the Second World War broke out, Benson's private battles with Covici-Friede publishers neared a truce, and she continued producing pieces for *The New Yorker* while attempting to sell her "one-note-men" idea (previously rejected by *The New Yorker*) to *The American Mercury*. The *O. Henry Memorial Award Prize Stories* had featured individual Benson pieces as had Edward O'Brien's annual *Best Short Stories* anthology. Additionally, several Benson pieces had been reprinted in textbooks designed for use at three universities: Colgate University, the University of Minnesota, and Columbia University. Within a year, a Benson piece would also appear in *Short Stories from the New Yorker*.

Though success had strengthened Benson's confidence as a writer, she still doubted the merits of an occasional piece and sought reassurance from "Dear Maxwell." Writing to him in February, for example, she complained:

> As a sharp contrast to my letter of a week ago, I am sending you this. I busted a gut on it. I was going to call it MAN OF LETTERS and decided that PATRON OF LETTERS was more

what I meant. When you read it will you telephone me what you think of it? I want at least a pat on the head. I am still laid up with a lousy cold. Last night I worked on this thing until almost ten. Then I began to feel tetanish from sitting at the typewriter so I stopped and listed [*sic*] to Toscanini conduct an all-Wagnerian program. It was grand. Then I ate a chocolate soda and crept quietly into bed with Mr. McFadden's *Master Detective Stories*. And will you tell Mac no books for this week.

With love from, Sally[1]

Despite Benson's misgivings about her writing, publishers continued besieging her for submissions. While writing "Patron of Letters," for example, Benson received an invitation from Lawrence E. Spivak at *The American Mercury* to meet the new editor, Eugene Lyons, and discuss doing some articles. Benson agreed, and after meeting with Lyons, received an affirmative letter: "Your bright idea about 'one-note-men' has stuck in my mind. I wonder whether a piece that polished off, briefly and vigorously, three or four such one-note geniuses wouldn't add up to a good full-sized article for us? Do call me about this."[2] Two weeks later, Benson pursued an invitation from George Waller to visit *Mademoiselle* and explore possibilities for an article. Waller sent a follow-up letter proposing two articles, one titled "Ye Compleat Siren," and the other "The Animal in Me." Each proposal delineated detailed, negative portrayals of women, but Benson committed to writing an article, and on February 28th, Waller sent her two copies of the photographs taken to accompany her piece. He explained:

> We have retained for publication the additional print of you in full-face and, indeed, it has already been sent to the engravers. . . . I can sincerely say you are just as appealing visually as your stories are mentally. . . . I'm still in the market for the one in full-face with one of your nice outspoken autographs.[3]

In March, Lyons again contacted Benson to propose another article on a "lady subject upon whom you could do execution in grand style if you cared to." Lyons offered to fly Benson to Washington or Chicago, if necessary, to meet Mrs. Dilling, the lady he had in mind. "Mrs. Dilling," he informed Benson, is "the female who operates the Red Network . . . a type if there ever was one. . . . The papers say she's good looking, which in itself is strange in a woman with a cause."[4] Benson, good looking herself and possessed of a cause—writing—did not miss the irony. She stored Lyons and his sexist comment away for a later piece.

Bennett Cerf sent Benson a copy of the forthcoming *Bedside Book of Famous American Short Stories* containing "The Overcoat." He hoped it would "bring a blush of pleasure to your cheeks (including the one on which the swastika is branded) and to those of your esteemed husband. Love, Bennett."[5] A second letter expressed his hope that she and Babe would be pleased with the biographical note accompanying her piece.[6] In an unusual move, Benson asked Cerf to give his opinion of a piece about a "big bad publisher" that she intended for *The New Yorker*. Cerf responded,

> There was just something about Mr. Martin that made me think, in that silly way of mine, of a boy I once knew named Donald Friede. Maybe you never heard of him. I loved the atmospheric part of the story, but the denouement struck me as a little bit flat. If I were Harold Ross, I'd ask you to sharpen up the ending a little bit but, of course, I am not Harold Ross. I am Bennett Cerf. And Bennett Cerf is waiting to hear when that Dartmouth-Columbia basketball game is going to take place. With a kiss smack on that swastika emblem of yours, I remain, As ever, Bennett[7]

With her next submission to *The New Yorker* Benson asked Maxwell to tell Ross several things. Interlaced with her messages is a mixture of humor and anger toward both Pat Covici and Donald Friede. Benson related, for example, that Covici, had

> spent one whole lunch telling me he was going to make me into another *Julia* Austen. . . . Also tell [Ross] that Bennett [Cerf] and Bob Haas read this story and laughed like fools because they thought I had done such a good caricature of Donald Friede. Will you also ask Ross (just one message after another!) if he did see the story about the Viennese murderess as if he has not I will bring it in. If there's anything else you want changed in the story, tell me, as I am feeling very soft toward all of you at the moment.[8] Did you like the opera? I am about to cook a

steak and make some salad for dinner, and five mysteries came today. I don't mind though, as one of them is a Rufus King and he's good.[9]

Maxwell continued to encourage Benson's strengths, and *The New Yorker* published a total of ten Benson stories in 1939, including the first two Judy Graves pieces, "Junior Miss" and "Madame La Marquise, Toujours Exquise."

Benson also heard from R. S. Hooper of *The Bystander* in London confirming that even though Nancy Pearn had given up on Benson's idea of a "New York Letter" because of war-related mail irregularities, *The Bystander* still wanted Benson to write an article for them. She should send it directly to Hooper at King's Langley rather than the London office, he advised, because, "We've evacuated London and are leading an odd rural existence hampered by distance and lack of paper, petrol and of course Advertising. It's a strange war."[10] What Hooper did not realize was that Benson had begun waging a war of her own toward the end of summer.

Benson's war was self-created: her drinking had escalated, her relationship with her husband was all but shattered, and her writing was all but forgotten. Babe had to arrange for her a short-term hospitalization followed by several weeks of recuperation at "the Farm," a rehabilitation center where he had been treated years before.[11] When released, though she returned briefly to her New York apartment on 93rd Street, Benson was advised to spend the rest of the year in Dorset, Vermont. She traveled with Bobsie to Troy, New York, and switched to a connecting train for Dorset, where her daughter had been living with Bertha Binkerd, mother of then–current boyfriend Robert Hamilton (Ham) Binkerd.

When she resumed writing in early 1940, Benson was working with a new editor—Gus Lobrano—who had succeeded Katharine White as fiction editor. After sending him her first story, he addressed a letter to her in Dorset: "Dear Miss Evarts: Here's the check for your story ("International Plot") which we all liked so much." Some minor editing, such as the introduction of three new characters had been done to "round out" the story, he explained, "but I think none of it will cause you any distress. Curiously enough, Mr. Ross recently had an experience very similar to the one you describe in your piece."[12] Mailed to Esther Evarts c/o Mrs. Sally Benson, the letter shows that Lobrano, as yet, did not realize that Benson used "Evarts" as her pseudonym whenever two of her pieces were scheduled to appear in the same *New Yorker* issue.

As was customary, the Evarts story was printed in the "back of the book."[13] In response to Gus, Benson wrote:

Dear Lobrano,

It is snowing up here again, and I am a little fit to be tied, but would far rather be here than around with too many familiar faces. I have had no mysteries—just when I would like to have them. . . . I felt ghastly on the train, and got into a dither switching about in Troy, but I am coming out of it. I have started "The Humorist"—three pages, and it looks very good, but I am frightfully slow. I wonder if Paladino would loosen up with $100 for me.[14] He will have the story next week, and he can take the $100 out of it in a bunch. I have some money, but not much, and pay Bertha Binkerd board for Bobs and me. The hospital and nurses rather knocked me. I found an ash receiver made of cigar bands which I am sending to Ross, and am writing him that I ma e [sic] it. Occupational therapy. If McKelway can carve little wooden benches, I thought I should contribute something.[15] Poor Ross! What he really wants is stories. I feel for him, and am quite pleased that the one I have started looks so fine. Reading back over it, I was surprised that anything came out of my head. It's just that the sound of knitting needles drives me to distraction, and a typewriter seems something to hang on to. God, but I am slow. It took me two days to grind out what I did. This afternoon I'm going to get through a little more. I feel strange being so shot and wake up crying for no reason. You are to write me a note, because the mild soft talk and muted voices around here sometimes make me believe that I've been lost with Byrd.

Love from,
Sally Benson[16]

This letter to Lobrano during Benson's convalescence is unusually revealing of her psychic, spiritual, and emotional state in 1940. Compared to the reticence she had displayed seven years earlier when her sister Agnes died, Benson's outpouring to Lobrano implies great trust in him and marks a distinct change in her. Having reached bottom, she seemingly no longer feels the need to repress pain, and for the first time she voices concern about her inability to produce fiction on demand. Rather than her customary three hours of writing at lightning speed, Benson now has to "grind out this story over two whole days." Vulnerable, lacking her wonted control, Benson has all the more reason to value Lobrano's guidance and style as fiction editor. Almost immediately, Benson and Lobrano had clicked as personalities, and their ensuing friendship surpassed Benson's prior relationships with Maxwell, Gibbs, and White.

Lobrano would write her little notes from his office even when no business was involved. As Ben Yagoda has noted, besides instituting the "first reading agreement," which gave writers a sense that they belonged "to a sort of family," Lobrano made *The New Yorker* a "home away from home" for many of its writers (161). Benson, already "at home" with her previous editors, Gibbs and Maxwell, nonetheless appreciated Lobrano's efforts on her behalf, and, Lobrano, for his part, though reputed to be "more comfortable dealing with men" (Yagoda 215), was particularly at ease in dealing with Benson. He had become another in the long line of male admirers stretching from Rich Johann in turn-of-the-century St. Louis to Benson's many Horace Mann friends, her "fiancés" of 1917, and finally, the various friendships—personal and professional—formed after her marriage to Babe. The most startling relationship of all was about to emerge.

20

BEHIND THE SCENE

1940

"I would like to have something to do so that I can stay in the city during July and August."

—Sally Benson

Since Babe had always enjoyed Dorset, Vermont, Sally had agreed to spend summers there starting in 1937 when Bobsie was seventeen, but by 1938, Sally found the place too rural and remote compared to Nantucket or Madison, Connecticut. She enjoyed the company of Bird Binkerd to a point, but in time, she became enamored of Bird's son, Ham. It did not concern her that he had been one of Bobsie's friends. By the summer of 1939, Sally—now forty-two—had fallen in love with twenty-two-year-old Ham. An experienced accountant, Ham initially served as Benson's personal assistant, going through her mail and paying her bills and taxes, but he traveled to New York occasionally to feed her cats—Pantsy and Molly Wuppy—and her terrier, Rover, whenever the maid had a vacation or extended holiday.[1] Benson's need for Ham's help was legitimate since increasing involvement with publishers and their projects for marketing her fiction had required some travel on Benson's part. Besides, mathematical ability had never been her strong suit. At first, Benson maintained secrecy about her affair with Ham. She installed him in an apartment and charged him with forwarding her mail. Benson's maid, Alliene Valentine, was one of the first to guess the nature of the Benson-Binkerd relationship, but in time, it became clear to his mother and even to Babe that the two were lovers. Neither appears to have disapproved, and even Barbara claims she was not upset. "I was not that interested in Ham," but I thought it "undignified of my mother to become involved with a man so much younger who happened to be one of my friends."[2]

Benson and Binkerd exchanged daily letters. Partly business and partly steamy adolescent-sounding expressions of love for one another, their recurring theme was each one's loneliness when apart and their longing to be reunited. In August of 1939 Ham wrote:

> Sally darling,
>
> I got your jewels this afternoon. . . . You left them there two years ago and it cost me seven fish to get 'em back. I won't tell you what is there except the ring which is very pretty and gold, and full of pearls, and one diamond. I see you are writing your letters double space now, but that is all right because it is hot and anyway you don't love me. I have *that* in writing. My house must be dirty and messy and there are some dirty dishes there. I will be home about 8:30 Friday providing the train is on time. . . . Darling, darling Sally, I love you anyway, which just goes to show, I always say.
>
> Ham
> I miss you darling.[3]

Each used terms of affection—"Darling, darling, Sally" and "My darling Ham"—but Sally's letters were particularly emotional and passionate:

> I got both your letters yesterday as we started off for Bennington, and I very nearly asked to be let off at Manchester to wait for the Flyer. The letters were lovely and I missed you so all day and all last night. . . . The minute you know about Friday, let me know. And if you can't possibly make it I will steel myself. I bought a new cotton dress in Bennington and your mother told [the saleslady] 'She has to allow for expansion, you know.' . . . Last night we decided my size was not normal and that I would probably pop out with a little one any day now. Bertha got very hilarious about it too. My laughter had a hollow ring.

Darling, I wish it were summer and we were lying around some-where together. I am on the side of being kissed until I can't move. I am hopelessly in love with you. Sometimes when I think of the things we have done together, I turn to jelly and haven't sense enough to do anything but sit and stare. Will you always love me, darling Ham? It's dreadful when I think you might not.

Momentarily, she assumes a mother's voice—"I bathed this morning and made my bed which looks pretty much a mess, and I think when the sheets are changed, I'd better be the one to do it"—before concluding:

Write me, darling. I saw that Colette's book has been filmed—*Claudine at School*—and I wish I were there to see it with you. Do you suppose it will stay until I get down? I bet Burchell has seen it. He loves Colette. I only love you and that's the end of that.

Sally

I love you. Bring me some paper! That's the payoff. I really only want paper.[4]

Eventually, everyone—friends like Robey Lyle and Lois Long at *The New Yorker* and Harold Ross and Gus Lobrano—learned of Benson's relationship with Ham. At a Stork Club celebration of Bennett Cerf's birthday, Robey Lyle, Benson, and Ham sat together at a table. Benson and Lyle, wearing hats and holding cigarettes, smile for a photographer while Ham, across from Sally, leans forward, smiling broadly, like the proverbial canary-swallowing cat.

No matter how emotionally involved she became with Ham, Benson did not let her feelings interfere with her writing. On April 11, 1940, for example, though she sent him two letters the same day, both were necessitated by work:

My darling, darling, Ham,

I am writing you again in the afternoon as I have done three pages of a story, and want to get up and finish before I get distracted tomorrow morning. But I will write you sometime tomorrow—in the afternoon or in the evening. I love you more than you'll ever know and I don't see a sign of slowing down. I don't know why I love you so much except that you are so darling with me and I've loved you right from the start, I am sure.

You can't think how I look forward to your coming. It is like a point in the whole week that I must reach somehow. The thought of not having you around scares the wits out of me, and I like it when you tag me from room to room. We haven't had so much time together, and I know why you follow me.

I wish I could have made a better sketch of you so that I could look at it. As it is, you repel me. Darling, tomorrow is Wednesday, and then there will only be three more nights until you are here.

I will tell you I love you as long as you can stand hearing it and from all outward signs, that will be a long, long, time. I mean I love you, too. I keep thinking maybe you don't know it.

Besides Ham, the other constant in Benson's life at this time was Gus Lobrano. Their correspondence indicates her growing trust in his friendship. At one point she told him she was

feeling rottener than you have any idea. I have been tottering about, reading, and jittering, and today I thought I would give Miss Evarts a little work to do and here it is. Maxwell cheered me up by writing that he had spent the entire month of March on a story which even he didn't like, and which you said needed a new motor. I have five pages done on THE HUMORIST now, and started a Judy story about Judy being one of the three little maids from school in an amateur performance of the Mikado [sic].

Referring to the newly finished Evarts story, Benson wrote: "I don't know whether or not you'll like this story, but I do." Next, she specified: "I would rather not have Ralph take any money off it, if it is to be used as an Evarts. If it is not used as an Evarts, he may have $75." Then, as though she could not resist making a jocose comment, Benson added: "If it is not used as anything you know what you all can do." Before closing, she requested sarcastically: "I wish you would write me a little news once in a while. God knows you sit around all day with nothing to do, and you might just as well be fooling with a letter. I am feeling better and have yearnings to work." Her conclusion, a final caveat, read: "Don't keep me in suspense about this, as I have to be HANDLE [sic] WITH GLOVES. With love from, Sally." In pencil, as an afterthought, Benson complained: "My typewriter sticks and is driving me nuts. Please give my love to Mr. Ross."[5]

The Judy Graves story was "Appreciation of Art" (May 25, 1940). When she submitted it, Benson told Lobrano she had changed the performance Judy appeared in from *The Mikado* to *The Tempest* "because I saw it at my nephew's school last Christmas."[6] The change of title, seemingly slight, is not insignificant: Judy is no longer playing Yum-Yum. Instead, she is cast as "Stephano, a drunken butler." Mr. Graves, reading the program, suddenly had

> a sharp memory of a talk he had with Judy a week before. "Daddy," she had asked, "how many drinks do you have to have before you get drunk?" And he had answered, "It all depends. A person might get drunk on one drink, and then again it might take twenty." "I suppose," Judy had persisted, 'if you were used to it, it would take twenty." He had said he imagined it would. And Judy seemed satisfied. (20)

Benson made a point of having Mrs. Graves anxiously worry aloud about a girl being assigned such a part. "I think," she comments, "it would have been nice if they had decided to give *The Mikado* [as] planned. . . . Except there weren't enough girls who could sing" (20). Next, Benson inserted a flip but subtle touch of ironic humor. The Graves family stand for the school song—words written by "Miss Dorothy *Brewer*" to the tune of "Flow Gently Sweet *Afton*" (emphasis mine). It is as though Benson needed to make light of her recent rehabilitation experience.

Particularly significant is the unquestioning way the adults respond to Judy's expert performance as a drunk. With the play dragging on, Mrs. Graves "sat tensely waiting for Judy's entrance." As Act I ended, the lights came up, and Mrs. Graves worried: "I don't see how Judy can be a *drunken* butler . . . I don't think Judy would know how to act drunk. As far as I know, she's never seen anyone very drunk." Mr. Graves concurred, "Of course, she hasn't. . . . A little high, maybe, but not boiled" (21). Benson built suspense until Act II, scene 2, when the audience heard the first "completely audible voice" of the evening—Judy's. She

> reeled onto the stage, a bottle in her hand . . . clothes awry . . . look[ing] tight as an owl [and] shouted: "This is a very scurvy tune to sing at a man's funeral. Well, here's comfort . . . and, lifting the bottle to her lips, she took a healthy swig.

The audience's "delighted laughter" prompted Judy to

> lift the bottle again, and stagger across the stage. . . . Each time Judy lifted the bottle to her lips the laughter from the lower grades got louder. Over the noise, Judy's voice rang out, blurred with drink, loud and insinuating. She spun around, crying, "Prithee, do not turn me about. My stomach is not constant."

As an added touch, wrote Benson,

> she put her hand on her small, firm stomach and hiccoughed. When the curtain fell, the applause was deafening. It continued until Judy stood alone on the stage. She lifted the bottle to her lips and reeled again. Mrs. Graves couldn't believe that her husband was smiling . . .

Through the next three acts, "Judy faithfully portrayed various stages of intoxication: she fought, she laughed senselessly, she was sad, she lapsed into self-pity, and her last line—spoken in a maudlin whine—'Oh, touch me not! I am not Stephano but a cramp!'—brought down the house." Her father immediately lauded her performance: "Judy was good . . . she was damned good" and, at the door, a parent congratulated him: " 'Best thing I ever saw, the act your daughter put on! . . . reminded me of you, Harry,' as he wiped away tears of laughter. Judy, then, trembling . . . buried her face against her mother . . . close to tears." Receiving their congratulations, she handed the papier-mâché prop bottle to her father: "Miss Smith says I can keep this for a souvenir." He "tucked it proudly under his arm" and sent her off to change. "We'll wait here for you. And take your time. There's no hurry."

In the letter that accompanied "Appreciation of Art," Benson told Lobrano, "I laughed over this piece and tomorrow I am having my hair done."[7] Her juxtaposing "laughter" and "hair appointment" raises the suspicion that very likely only the second half of Benson's statement is true. Written just weeks after her release from a long period of rehabilitation, Benson's "Appreciation of Art" is rooted in her experience at the farm. Needing to write about it as she had needed to write about Agnes's suicide, Benson allowed her feelings to emerge in this cathartic piece. (Was it coincidence, a stroke of irony, or deliberate, subtle symbolism, that the title—"Appreciation of Art"—shares the same twin letter abbreviation—A.A.—as "Alcoholics Anonymous" founded four years earlier?).

Benson had acquired in the New York City culture of the 1920s and '30s, an attitude toward alcohol common to many Jazz Age writers, including *New Yorker* staffers and contributors: heavy drinking was an accepted if not "integral part of social life." Like Dorothy Parker and F. Scott Fitzgerald, Sally Benson was part of a generation that "made the terms 'alcoholic' and 'writer' synonyms" (Douglas 23). Exacerbated by Prohibition, the prevalent attitude toward drinking crept gradually into *New Yorker* stories where, in some cases, even children could observe "drinking as a natural and congenial element of adult life" (Corey 1999, 184).

Following "Appreciation of Art," Benson thought of doing another piece about two sisters planning an overnight trip for Decoration Day weekend. "Friday I want to do an Evarts piece if I still feel all right, about two women who can't remember what they're talking about."[8] Her letter repeated prior requests: "Send me some money soon, as I am getting broke" and "I'm going nuts with my typewriter which doesn't work. It doesn't space right. Please tell Mr. Ross to express me a brand new Royal portable by September 3rd, which as he no doubt remembers, is my birthday."[9] Friday of that same week, true to her word, Benson sent Lobrano two pieces, and both appeared in *The New Yorker*'s May 25th, 1940 issue. Using the third person, she continued referring to herself by her pseudonym: "Here's a short piece from Miss Evarts. I am mailing it for her as she has trouble folding things with her fingers crippled up the way they are from the damp weather. You know that opal little finger ring, she always wears? Well, she can't get it over her knuckle, so you can see!"

Benson's letter concluded on a now-familiar note of financial-based anxiety mixed with concern for Lobrano:

What about the other stories? I am anxious to hear, as I am broke as hell. It is snowing again, and we are covered to the hilt. I wish Frueh[10] were here, and I could have some fun. I ate a package of raisins but only got as far as the garage. Mosher says you are being a saint. But he refers to me as a saint, too, at times, and that should give you an idea of his untrustworthiness.

    With love from,
    Sally

Benson appended after her penciled signature: "Are you working like a dog? I think of you being pestered, and hope you aren't sick."[11]

Except for letters to Katharine White, Benson's *New Yorker* correspondence is addressed to male colleagues and rarely refers to women other than her daughter. One notable exception is her correspondence with Daise Terry.[12] When Benson returned from the farm in April, she lost no time requesting of Terry "all stories, both Benson and Evarts, from 'Daddy Dear' (12/ 9/39) to date. They are to go to England so I don't want any stories that have not been published." The stories would be published individually at first—in publications like *The Bystander* and *The News Chronicle*—and later as the collection *Women and Children First*. On a personal note, Benson shared with Terry, that with seeds "planted in flats" and the garden "dug up," it was "so grand [in Dorset] now that [she couldn't] even think about going to New York." Benson's closing, however—"Is the office filled to the brim with new and indefinite faces?"—showed her curiosity about the goings on at *The New Yorker* despite her claimed preference for Dorset's tranquility.[13] In her next letter she asked for Maxwell's address and inquired whether Terry had seen Gibbs.

During the summer Benson produced a masterful story containing her most revealing insight into the rehabilitation experience. Published on October 19, 1940, and titled "Retreat," the piece merited congratulations from Gibbs for successfully bypassing *New Yorker* policy against publishing stories dealing overtly with alcohol. "This was an excellent piece," Gibbs wrote, "good enough to get by our prejudice against alcoholic stories, which is a triumph for you. Will you put a title on it please, when you get your proof, and send us some more?"[14]

Benson's "Retreat" began, "Although the sign on the stone gateway read 'Maplewood Farm,' the place was obviously not a farm. There were no fields of corn or wheat, no outbuildings, and, more particularly, no comforting smell of cattle and hay in the air."[15] (The rehabilitation center attended by Benson was High Watch Farm in Kent, Connecticut. It was begun by Bill W. who cofounded A.A. and the 12-step program.) A detailed description of the surrounding lawn, woods, and flower garden, Benson's first paragraph concludes: "Small tables, gay, striped-canvas chairs, and swings were arranged about the lawn, but they were unoccupied, and an atmosphere of futility hung over the entire place."

Marion Douglas, a Benson double, has been at the farm for five months and is thinner but her eyes are "clear and not swollen from crying." She is worried about a "little Madonna" she has been working on in the studio, but Dr. Scott assures her, "She'll turn out all right . . . Rome wasn't built in a day, you know." The little Madonna serves as a fitting symbol for Benson herself who in time may also "turn out all right." Strolling toward her cottage, Douglas sees "far back in the woods, Bardwell Hall, where she had been placed on her arrival at the farm. She remembered her narrow room—a hospital room really—and the quiet ruthlessness of Miss Frank, her nurse," who like the other nurses in Bardwell wore uniforms unlike the everyday clothes worn by nurses in the main house and cottages. As she left Bardwell, Dr. Scott had explained the difference: "You are our guest, Mrs. Douglas. . . . We want you to feel at home . . . free to come and go as you please around the grounds, and if you would like to drive to the village to have your hair done or do a little shopping, just let Mrs. Tennant know, and she will arrange a taxi and ride in with you." One can imagine Benson chafing at such a description of freedom, and in a pet, appropriately naming Douglas's "warden" Tennant, suggestive of the French verb *tenir*, to hold or have under one's control.

A paragraph depicting the busy life of a suburban housewife follows, ending with Benson's self-revealing comment spoken through Douglas, her protagonist and mouthpiece: "Leaving it all had made her hate the farm at first, and although she assured herself that she felt perfectly well physically, she had cried for two weeks." Next, Douglas enters the studio—a place she did not visit until her fourth week at the farm. She remembered how strange it looked to her—"statues of girls with leaves in their hair, their fingers and toes turning into branches . . . dozens of horses and minute ashtrays . . . paintings, mostly half-finished, of sunrises, still lifes, and others that merely expressed an emotion"—and how the sight had made her laugh. "I could do better than that myself," she said, "and I've never had a lesson in my life"—a statement easily predicated on Benson's lips. To her protagonist's surprise, plunging into creative projects proved enjoyable and much "better than sitting all day long in a canvas chair on the lawn, thinking of home, worrying about Jeanie, who was only eight, until the tears started and her eyes ached." Donning her smock, Mrs. Douglas approaches her Madonna and hears the instructor's praise—"I've been looking at her all morning. She's quite the best thing you have done." Mrs. Douglas pretends indifference—"She isn't too bad," she said carelessly. "But when she looked at the figure [the Madonna's hands were lifted in prayer, but her body was bent in submission], her heart raced and her cheeks flushed with excitement." Again, the Madonna-response might readily be ascribed to Benson in terms of her attitude toward her writing. Like Douglas, she had not had "lessons." She merely plunged into the craft, drawing upon her wide reading background, her power of observation, and her talent with words. Benson took secret pride in her craft, "flush[ing] with excitement at times," though she did not voice it beyond telling her editors, "Here is a piece I like." Finally, the very posture of the Madonna—hands lifted in prayer but body bent in submission—seems an apt symbol of Benson's feelings regarding her relationship with alcohol: she hoped for release from her addiction and she had, in entering the farm, bent her will in submission to the prescribed treatment of that time.

However, Benson's piece moves toward a horrifying conclusion. Tonight was the night of her husband's allotted weekly call. "Sometimes one needed a rest even from one's own family," explained Dr. Scott on Douglas's first night after being moved from Bardwell to the main house where there was a telephone in every room. She remembered thinking

> her heart would burst when she saw the one on the table by her bed. By lifting the receiver, she could call Pete and talk to little Pete and Larry and Jeanie. She closed the door of her room and lifted the phone. . . . "I'm sorry, Mrs. Douglas, but I have orders that you are to have no outside calls for a while." "Listen," she said, "I am just calling my home. I just want to know if they are all right. I just want to speak to them for a minute. I'm not going to tell them anything. Why, I wasn't even going to ask them to come and get me. I'm sorry, Mrs. Douglas. . . . And the telephone went dead.

Benson's vivid description of Douglas's attempted phone call and her frustrated response to its denial clearly emerged from a similar experience. Given Benson's temperament, the portrayal is highly accurate and credible:

She had flown into a rage and torn the telephone from the wall. With incredible speed she had rushed past Miss Davis and down the stairs and out the front door to the driveway. She was almost at the gates when they caught up with her.

In time, Douglas was permitted to receive her weekly phone call. "Stormy" at first, her talks with Pete "became calmer, until now it was almost as though she and Pete had nothing to say to one another." (The noncommittal dialogue of their telephone conversation, in fact, echoes several of Babe's and Sally's letters: "How's every little thing?" "Fine. How are you?" "I'm swell." "Well, be good to yourself." "You take care of *yourself*. And give my love to the children.") As Benson's story approaches its climax, her protagonist anticipates an evening playing bridge but is told "a big package" awaits her in her room. Full of curiosity, Mrs. Douglas attacks the "carefully wrapped"[16] package, discovering within it a portable victrola, a note from Pete, and an unlabeled record—the "only one" he knew she would like. Playing it, Douglas hears Pete's and her children's voices—"we miss you and hope you are lots better. Come home soon, Mummie. Come home soon." Snatching the wire from the socket, Douglas

threw herself across the bed. For a minute she lay quiet with her hands to her ears, and then she began to cry. "Oh, my God," she sobbed. "I've got to get out of here!" "Oh, my God, I've got to get out of here!" Her voice rose, and the door of her room opened. "Mrs. Douglas! Mrs. Douglas!" Miss Davis said. "Get away from me. Get the hell away from me!" She reached for her pillow and threw it at Miss Davis. And as she did so, she could hear feet running up the stairs. For some reason, the sound frightened her and she clutched her hands tightly over her mouth so that whoever was coming would not catch her screaming.

The Madonna image had ceased to have meaning. Faced with the wrenching separation from her loved ones, Douglas's prayer assumed a different form as prostrate in supplication, but no longer submissive, she demanded deliverance.

Benson's delineation of Douglas's contrasting inner responses—on the one hand to the agony of detention and loss of freedom—on the other to the desire for connection with family and familiar home surroundings—is powerfully rendered. Only one who had lived through such pain and possessed the skill capable of reproducing it could have written the piece. Benson was that person, and the excellence of her story was recognized not only by its achieving publication in *The New Yorker* despite the magazine's policy against stories dealing overtly with alcohol but also by Herschel Brickel's selecting it for inclusion in the *O. Henry Memorial Award Prize Stories of 1941*. In his introduction to that anthology, Brickel claimed to have chosen stories that "have been believed into existence" rather than "cunningly devised"— the former being superior, arising as they do from "the inner compulsion that is the source of all true art." Benson's "Retreat" is surely a product of "inner compulsion," though it contravenes Harry Hansen's appraisal as a piece showing "uncanny insight into the workings of alien minds." However unwilling Americans of the forties were to recognize Benson's personal story as their own, her story emanated from a kindred spirit rather than an alien mind. Bob Haas's evaluation best captures the power of "Retreat": "Dear Sally, I've just read 'Retreat.' You're a wonder and I'm not kidding. Bob."[17]

Since Benson's repeated complaints about her faulty typewriter had failed to produce a response from Lobrano, she wrote directly to Ross, declaring her need of a new machine. When Benson received a reply from Ross—who "never writes to anyone"—she promptly shared it with Ham because she was so pleased. In her excitement about Ross's personally responding to her, Benson overlooked the even more flattering encomium his letter contained. She wrote to Ham: "Darling, I got a letter from Ross today, and I was very, very pleased as he never writes anyone, so I will tell you what it says because I am so pleased." Ross wrote:

> The weather was dreadful in Connecticut yesterday but within the house all was sunshine because of the two stories you sent in. I spent the afternoon curled up before the fire with them, purring happily. We think they are the greatest things written since 'Kim' and Lobrano is sending you money for them immediately. $5,000 goes forward this afternoon and the remainder will be coming before the end of the war. This indicates our

sensitiveness toward your merest hint. In this connection, I have a portable typewriter which so help me, you are welcome to for the summer if you want it, or until yours gets fixed anyhow. It is on the little pipe table behind my desk (under the damask curtains) doing no one any good. It might do you some. We will have it reconditioned if necessary. Let me know if you want it.

I spent my lunch hour shopping, buying gloves. I got a pair of boxing gloves for handling O'Hara, a pair of gauntlets, one to be thrown down when warranted, and a pair especially for you. These are mauve gloves of nylon with black seams on the back and beautiful pearl buttons. I am wearing them as I write this.

Benson, understandably thrilled by this fine letter, hastened to inform Daise Terry that Mr. Binkerd would pick up her new typewriter on his next trip to Dorset. She "longed to hear how Maxwell [was]" and asked that Terry give Gibbs "my best love."[18] The same day's mail had brought a letter and check from Lobrano, a letter from Bobs, and one from Ham that, she told him, "was the BEST. And it made me want to crawl into your neck and stay there. YOU ARE TO HURRY UP HERE. I love you darling. Sally."[19]

The next day Benson sent Ross a lengthy thank-you, explaining:

Dear Ross,

The typewriter isn't for me really, it's for Miss Evarts. She has been using this thing and the words run together and that combined with the fact that she is working in a room called a study filled to the brim with begonias that have barely gotten through the winter is breaking even her brave spirit. I think it would be nice for you and for me if we could keep her from working up any temperament. There is enough temperament in that suite of offices as it is, and I don't think a B casual writer has a right to horn in. Let Moloney, Thurber, and O'Hara run the temperament end and let's just keep Miss Evarts the same sweet, pliant little body she was before she ever saw a typewriter. She's beginning to want her pencils sharpened *right now* and before long she will want you to send a boy up here to Vermont with

all the morning papers. Or, perhaps just to send a boy. She
made a present for you and I am sending it. I took her in your
office one day when you were fifty miles away, and she looked
so hurt at that picture of the Japanese girl that I know she had
an idea. Anyway, this little thing she made is to take the place
of that picture.

It would be grand about the typewriter and I can have
someone pick it up. I was very glad you liked the stories and I
thought it was nice of you to write. Take care of Lobrano, or
he may get an idea for a novel.

Sally Benson.[20]

In her thank-you to Lobrano for money he had wired, Benson complained and asked:

Are you getting so blasé that you don't even speak of the Miss
Evarts story which I hope you got? Anyway, will you tell me
the names of the two ladies I used in it? I want to do another
about them taking a trip. What is Maxwell [sic] address? I expect
a postal from him any day now. I loved the grand letter Ross
wrote me, and I think he is nicer than anyone. He really is,
isn't he? More work from me this week! AND I have only two
stories to go on my bonus.

Love from Sally.[21]

With the next Evarts piece, Benson again asked Lobrano to tell her the
two ladies' names. "If I've got them wrong and hear from you today,
I'll change them down at the post office before I mail this," she offered.
"Have you heard from Maxwell? Probably been scalped! My love to you,
Sally."[22]

The next day's mail brought the author's proof of the Judy piece from
Lobrano with a request that Benson return it as soon as possible. Her "lilac
bush piece" had gone to the printer and Lobrano informed her,

I've got Ross's OK on the Esther Evarts piece. He's a little bothered because the locale isn't made definite, but that can be easily

fixed. I guess we can't make it Times Square, but Scarsdale or Mount Vernon or New Rochelle might do. You care? . . . Maxwell must be in Santa Fe by now. The address he left here was, simply, Box 1624.

Love, Gus Lobrano

Delighted that Benson was still working, he added: "P.S. Ross told Winchell about special mauve gloves to handle you with, so maybe I'll have a clipping to send along soon. P.S. 2. Those ladies' names are Miss Harriet Clark and Mrs. Brainerd."[23] Days later, Benson asked for a "hundred dollars advance on 'Furtive Tear' " to pay for the victrola and records she purchased. She would mail another story the next day. "How were the fish?" she inquired. "You probably slipped on one, if I know your weekends. Are you in a cast? How is darling Ross?"[24]

Benson decided "the locale of the Evarts pieces will be Vermont" and she wanted as many pieces published in *The New Yorker* as possible, having calculated that she could double their earnings by subsequently sending them to England for reprinting in publications like *The Bystander*. More critical and assertive now, Benson even specified the *New Yorker* issues where she felt her stories fit: "I think the Evarts is too long. I will cut it if you like the idea. It can be cut in proof easily enough, or before. Except that if you do like it, it should make the Decoration Day issue." Impelled by the self-imposed urgency of sending pieces to London, Benson soon complained to Lobrano: "Why don't you run my stories oftener? You all have been publishing the Judy series far apart too, although you have quite a few other pieces. Your star authors get in oftener, and I *resent* it." Then, as though to excuse her unusual forthrightness, she added: "I am returning proof on Judy and it is raining so I thought I might as well devil you about something. If you don't want to bother about the other stories, to hell with it, darling Lobrano. Love from, Sally."[25] But returning immediately to her critical mode, Benson added a postscript:

Ross's bid for sensationalism and Winchell is going to get him into a peck of trouble one of these days. I think it would be nice if I went and stayed with him in Connecticut until I regained my full strength. I am no trouble, like hunting, dogs, horses, green vegetables, and my hobby is puttering about a kitchen.

> You might speak to him about it. I am good with children but
> they are not good with me.

Benson's writing, initially a matter of personal pride and financial necessity, had now become a means of bonding with *New Yorker* friends and editors, including Ross.

Throughout 1940, Benson continued to attract new readers. On February 26th, Colgate University requested permission to reprint "Daddy Dear," one of the *Junior Miss* pieces. On March 4th the Illinois-Indiana Home for the Blind asked permission to reprint Benson's "Suite 2049" in Braille. As scheduled two years earlier, Benson's *Stories of the Gods and Heroes* made its debut. In late July, Benson sent a copy to William Shawn and received an enthusiastic thank-you: "I've looked into your book, and it's a beauty; can't wait until I read more. Thanks for thoughtfully sending me over a copy."[26]

Benson's personal life took yet another twist. In late spring she thought it best to return to Manhattan—a move out of character for one who hated the city's heat and preferred the summer beauty of the countryside. However, Benson no doubt wished to introduce Ham to city life since Babe's expected arrival for vacation in Vermont at the end of Columbia's spring semester would make Dorset too confining. To acquire a separate Manhattan apartment for Ham, Sally pressured herself to earn as much as possible. After lunch with Lobrano toward the end of May, she wrote to thank him but also to complain, "I don't understand why the story wasn't measured up and I couldn't be paid for all of it.[27] Nor why I haven't been paid for 'No News Is Good' which you have had for three weeks or so. And don't blame Belgium as Belgium has only been in the front pages since Friday." She also reminded Lobrano, "When Ross is not too busy, will you ask him about me and this summer?" She explained,

> I would like to have something to do so that I can stay in the
> city during July and August. My Benson contract will be fulfilled
> by that time, and I don't know how many more stories you will
> be able to take from me. You have quite a few. Miss Evarts does
> all her writing in off moments, of which she has many.

Her letter continues with what might be construed as female flattery of Ross intended for Lobrano to share:

Isn't Ross nicer than anyone in the world? I really think he is, and you have no idea how much I like him. I think he makes most people look mighty feeble. You were lovely at lunch, and Mr. Collier was blue-eyed and had the appearance of a man who was flying in the face of providence.

Love to you, from, Sally.[28]

Just before July 4th, Benson sent Lobrano another story that she "liked. I will be back in New York Monday night," she informed him, "and I will call you on Tuesday [the 9th] or so. I hope you didn't get burned up with firecrackers over the holidays. Mrs. Brainerd has been worried," she teased.

Before long, Benson and Ham had settled in their apartment at 151 West 46th Street, first floor rear.[29] Ham's mother wrote regularly. Her correspondence shows her to be a jolly sort who harbored no resentment about her son's involvement with a woman more than twenty years his senior. In fact, Bird Binkerd appreciated the laughter that Sally and Ham provided when they were in Dorset as opposed to the doom-and-gloom atmosphere created by Bird's daughter (also named Barbara) and boyfriend, Judson Phillips. The gathering war clouds were particularly troublesome to Jud, whom Bird characterized as embodying the very bigwig politicians he blamed for leading the country down the road to war. Rather than argue politics with Jud, Bird preferred a drink with her guests now and then, admittedly getting "a little tight" on occasion. She welcomed Benson's return visits and praised the letters Benson sent after leaving.

Bird also read Benson's *New Yorker* pieces regularly. "I read Esther Evarts latest and felt a nice warm glow around my heart. Did she feel a little nostalgic when she wrote it?" Bird inquired. (The piece, "No News Is Good," is set in a country kitchen presumably based on Bird Binkerd's. Though Bird was her avid fan and friend, Benson, as was her wont, converted even the contents of Bird's letters into fiction.) Bird looked back on the preceding spring as "a great oasis . . . especially after we got the garden going. I wish we could do it all over again. Sometimes I feel there is nothing to look forward to and then again I take out the picture of the little house and really believe we will have it one of these days. But war or no war, I am going to be in New York next winter. . . . All my love to you both, Bird."[30]

As Anna Cora had a decade earlier in Madison, Bird looked forward to Benson's visits to Dorset and hoped she and Ham would come up for July 4th. "It would be heavenly to see you . . . now [or] any other weekend any time during the summer," she assured them, offering to meet their train in Pittsfield.[31] Benson and Ham did not go to Dorset for the fourth but telephoned instead. Thrilled by their call, Bird sent a long, newsy letter: "I sent a telegram to Reynolds. . . . It said, 'In Dorset for a few days. Will let you know when returning.' . . . I am awfully sorry that he is acting up so and I think you are damned well right in getting out. I hate to think that all the nice peace and quiet we enjoyed this spring is being disrupted for us both. It was so much fun and I certainly do miss it."[32] The reference to "getting out" appears to relate to the Bensons' home in Madison—the "hutch of our own"—anticipated so eagerly by Babe in 1932. Yet, Babe's "acting up" apparently did not signal a definitive separation for him and Sally, because a year later Bird sent Sally a joke that she wanted shared with Babe.

Possibly, Babe's "acting up" referred to his efforts to restrain Sally from drinking, since being in Bird Binkerd's company might well have weakened Benson's resolve to avoid alcohol. Almost every letter from Bird describes excessive imbibing on someone's part followed by Bird's cavalier response. Take for example:

> When I got home I found that Barbara and Jud had gone down to the Club for drinks with the Marshes. . . . They turned up about nine and Barbara was stinking. . . . I have never seen her look so pretty nor act as cute. I think she should stay drunk all the time. She had an awful hangover the next morning and was still very funny.

Worse than condoning drunkenness, Bird's cavalier approach to alcohol's effects would weaken Benson's efforts to reform—for Benson could easily join Bird and her guests in their "drinking and fun."[33]

Yet, despite carousing on occasion, Benson managed to continue writing feverishly for Lobrano. Fifteen of her pieces were published by *The New Yorker* in 1940, and when she wasn't writing, Benson was negotiating with agents, publishers' representatives, and radio programmers about a series based on *Junior Miss*. Another measure of Benson's success arrived in a *New Yorker* letter of September 6 announcing that Simon and Schuster planned to publish a collection of fiction, *Stories from the New Yorker*. A 10 percent royalty would be shared by the magazine with the authors selected. In collaboration, editors at Simon and Schuster and *The New Yorker* had chosen three Benson stories for the proposed anthology: "Home Atmosphere," "Profession Housewife," and "Little Woman."[34] September also brought Benson an inquiry from her English agent:

My dear Miss Benson,

Where, dear Sally Benson, is that new book of yours? We feel it would be just the thing to enliven us in our blitzkrieg. Seriously though, copy will be reaching us shortly, won't it? We should like to have it in time to fit into Constable's Spring list if possible . . .

Yours ever, Nancy Pearn

Benson decided to take a chance and sent Pearn the copy for *Stories of the Gods and Heroes*. However, on October 25th, Constable notified Pearn of its rejection, explaining "this cannot in any way be regarded as a novel."[35] Laurence Pollinger forwarded Benson a copy of Constable's memo with his commiseration: "Alas, alack. . . . Between ourselves, [Constable] are one of the extremely few British publishers that have got the jitters. . . . I [shall] go elsewhere with the stories and shall hope to have some good news for you before long." Pollinger included personal news of the war:

I am glad to say that despite the rather close attentions of Mr. Hitler's bombers both here and at home we are all well. We continue to sell a few books and a number of short stories. Did Nancy P. tell you about the big bomb that landed on our doorstep and the nasty mess it made of our offices? But we were soon back in them again, despite some of them being much draughtier than others. We are all cheerful especially so this morning as last night we did not hear the drone of Mr. Hitler's bombers from about 9 o'clock to about 3:45 this morning. Of course, they have done considerable damage, but not nearly as much as the newspapers and press photographers suggest. Hurrah for you, hurrah for us!

Laurence Pollinger

Benson was disappointed, but she fully realized the difficulties her British agents faced as they promoted her work. She responded to Pollinger's news by writing Nancy Pearn, "hoping to Heaven that she was all right," and sharing her decision to donate to the war effort the royalties on English sales of her most recent story. Pearn, impressed at Benson's thoughtfulness and concern, responded:

> We did love getting your letter and felt all puffed up by it. . . . we are not by any means "shaking like leaves" though I admit we might be at times and you must just suppose that it is that peculiar thing called British phlegm which prevents . . . being . . . as upset as leaves in the wind.

Pearn shared good news—another second rights sale from *People Are Fascinating*. Lilliput would be paying five guineas for "Love Letter," and Curtis Brown had sold some other stories to the *News Chronicle*. Pearn then praised Benson's "picture of Mrs. Maltby, the English nurse" as almost a short story in itself. "Send us," she urged, "more pen pictures in your own inimitable style, and more news of what the family is up to."[36]

21

AFFAIRS, FAMILY AND OTHER

1941

"To me you will always be the Gypsy Rose Lee of *Belles Lettres*."

—Bennett Cerf

By December 1940, Sally Benson had become a confident, successful writer and a shrewd business woman with strong ties to family and friends. Among the Christmas gifts she sent to family members was a business parcel containing duplicates of recent stories and the photo that Nancy Pearn had long sought. Now Pearn could write, "How doubly fond of you we are . . . we like your face as much as we like your letters!" Pearn added: "I have your indubitably attractive photograph now all beautifully framed in black and white on my mantelpiece, and many are the admiring comments it has brought forth."[1] As Benson had requested, Pearn directed that Benson's profits from English sales of "Love Letters" (published by Lilliput) would go to "the Spitfire Funds . . . for fighters" and both they and Pearn's agency were most grateful.[2] The first such payment, after deducting 25 percent for Constable and the 10 percent commission to Pearn, Pollinger & Higham, would be "three pounds, ten shillings, and ten pence."[3]

In January of 1941, thanks to her improved financial position, Benson rented a spacious Manhattan apartment at 26 East 93rd Street just off Madison Avenue and a few blocks away from her older sister, Esther. Benson's last *Junior Miss* piece had appeared in *The New Yorker*, and she continued her affair with Ham while negotiating with Bennett Cerf of Random House to finalize the details for the forthcoming publication of the *Junior Miss* series as a novel. Cerf promised Benson he would not compare her with "Dorothy Parker, Mrs. Miniver, Myrna Loy, or Elsa Maxwell. To

Figure 10. Sally Benson, circa 1941

me you will always be the Gypsy Rose Lee of *Belles Lettres*."[4] Earlier, Benson had tired of her teenaged character after the second "Judy" piece but she had wisely heeded Harold Ross's urging not to give up writing about Judy. Now the "Judy Graves" pieces numbered twelve and *Junior Miss*, her third collection, enjoyed an advance sale of forty thousand copies in the United States. In England, Laurence Pollinger, "keenly looking forward to receiving copy as soon as possible," inquired on March 19th whether Benson had retained the "British Empire except Canada volume rights" or whether they were "included in Cerf's contract."[5]

With the pace of her professional life accelerating, Benson hardly had time to keep up with her family's doings. Amid the activity and travel necessitated by her business dealings, Benson was surprised to hear from twenty-one-year-old Bobsie that she had fallen in love with Alexis Doster

Jr., of Litchfield, Connecticut, a graduate of Avon Old Farms School and a veteran of the war in Spain. Now a member of Squadron A of the 101st Cavalry, Doster was stationed at Fort Devens in Ayer, Massachusetts. They would shortly be married. Benson attempted to discourage Bobsie from further involvement with him by arranging a cruise for her.

Bobsie was thrilled to be sailing to Barbados and on to Brazil where she made the acquaintance of Charity, daughter of the Moore-McCormack Lines manager, whose American family lived in Brazil. Bobsie wrote from the *S.S. Argentina*, a Moore-McCormack steamer: "I drank four straight brandies going around Cape Hatteras and then didn't feel seasick and haven't since." She promised to mail Benson a "play by play description" from Rio or Trinidad. She was having a wonderful time and enjoying the fact that "everyone is reading your book [*Junior Miss*]. Even the head Admiral of the Argentinian Navy." A subsequent letter informed Benson that Bobsie, John Lawson, and another couple had gone ashore together and dined at the Copacabana.[6] Benson had known all along of Lawson's presence and counted on his giving Bobsie a measure of supervision.

A second family-related complication arose for Benson when her brother-in-law Fred Smith (Agnes's husband) remarried. The new Mrs. Smith proved incapable of caring for twelve-year-old Tony, now a troubled teen—out of control and suffering psychological issues. Feeling obligated in her sister's name to intervene on Tony's behalf, Benson became his legal guardian, and when the papers were signed, the boy moved to Madison to live with Benson's mother. Then, as the United States braced itself for war, Babe became increasingly interested in reenlisting so he could share the flying expertise he had garnered in 1917.

Professionally, Benson's Judy Graves character had changed her creator's life dramatically. By appearing in triplicate as best-selling novel, radio series, and Broadway show, *Junior Miss* attracted publishers, radio show hosts, academics, and Hollywood representatives—all eager to know more about Benson and to share a measure of her success. The phenomenon would be repeated a year later when Benson's *Meet Me in St. Louis*, after appearing serially in *The New Yorker*, would be purchased by Random House, become a best-seller, and be sold to Metro-Goldwyn-Mayer.

While doing her best to cope with the challenges facing her, Benson received two letters from Frances McFadden, managing editor at *Harper's Bazaar*, seeking submissions of "a love story lying heavy on your heart or light in a drawer." Benson had to send McFadden regrets since her top priority at the moment was completing her new *New Yorker* series—"5135 Kensington"—for publication as her fourth collection: *Meet Me in St. Louis.* She was also preparing for her lecture series at the University of Indiana Writers' Conference scheduled from June 9th to the 18th in Bloomington. With Benson so busy, a desperate Bennett Cerf wrote in mid-March,

Dear Sally:

For the love of God, how can one get in touch with you? I find a note on my desk that you are going to do twelve stories for *Good Housekeeping* that will certainly be a book for Random House. I am getting hoarse trying to persuade the Book-of-the-Month Club that they should send out *Junior Miss* for the benefit of the great American public. We are getting so steamed up about it that it should be a by-word in the nation by June. And I can't lay my hands on the author. Hands, I said, young lady. Don't you love me anymore?

As always, Bennett[7]

The last two lines are suggestive of a more than professional relationship between Benson and Cerf. Knowing Benson, this is not surprising, though little evidence exists beyond this letter's allusions and a formal invitation to a party at Columbia on April 8th with Cerf's message: "How about driving me up there in the new chariot?"[8] On the other hand, Benson had endeared herself also to Bennett's wife, Phyllis, who wrote to thank Benson for a birthday gift: "Pretty Sally, Your present is pretty like you. I love it and you."[9]

Whether Benson was involved with Cerf or questioning her relationship with Ham is not certain. However, in 1941, approaching the age of forty-four, she was apparently undergoing a midlife crisis. Benson's entrance into a period of introspection and soul-searching may well have inspired "Act 1, Scene 2" (or "Mrs. Crumbie's flat. The following morning"). Published on April 26th, this *New Yorker* piece features a female protagonist in the middle of an affair. Benson experimented somewhat by departing from her usual third-person narrator and inviting the reader into her subject's consciousness by employing a first-person narrator:

The whole effect was theatrical: the half-empty glasses on the table, the opened bottle of champagne wrapped in a white napkin and set in a bucket of melting ice, the soft glow of the lamps, and Dave in a dressing gown of dull green silk, leaning against the mantel piece, looking as though he'd speak if someone would only give him the right cue. It was hard to believe that . . . when they had gone in the other room together they had not stepped off into the wings, hurrying to their dressing rooms to change their costumes for the next scene. . . . It had looked exciting and strange when she had first come, but now as she stood at the door ready to leave, it seemed artificial and she was anxious for the curtain to fall.

Like her protagonist, Benson felt uncomfortable in her current affair with Ham and analyzed with depth and insight the consequent mixed feelings that arise:

Yet, she was glad she had come. Being with Dave, coming to his apartment, had given her the same sensation as acting in a play in which she was the leading lady and he was her leading man. . . . It was easy to ignore the rest and think of herself as a rather mysterious figure who appeared from nowhere particular to stay gracious and witty for a few hours before vanishing into the night leaving behind some subtle fragrance.

By closing the door she could shut out of her mind the "impersonal room" and the "nebulous quality" Dave had for her—"one as impartially as the other." Filled with a "terrible impatience to get away, she thought of the book she had started the night before." This last detail, so characteristic of Benson, is a good index to her feelings regarding Ham since she borrowed for Dave's subsequent dialogue phrases identical to those in Ham's letters: "When am I going to see you again? . . . How soon? Tomorrow? The day after? When?" In response to her "I can't think now," Dave persisted: "I'll call you tomorrow." Trying to discourage him, she demurred, "I'm not sure where I'll be. I may have to go out early." The whole room seemed incredibly unreal to her. She held out her hand, said goodbye, and avoided his kiss. "Goodbye, darling," he said.

Once outside in the cool air, she smiled to think of how pleasant the evening had been

> except for that moment at the end, when Dave had been a little too clinging. . . . Yet it amused her faintly to think that it was Dave who was anxious. Men were always going on about how such things should be. . . . always complaining that women did not take romances as lightly or sensibly as men. Pleasant interludes were all they were; brief moments of no consequence.

The preceding passage may hold a clue to Benson's cavalier dealing with men. As her daughter surmised, she "needed to punish men after the way her father had treated her. She could do this better with younger men."[10]

Benson, like her protagonist, viewed herself and Ham in roles that reversed the usual gender stereotypes. Though she struggled, Benson's character attained the cool objectivity usually shown by the male while projecting onto him the dependency typically associated with the female.[11] Once outside, the unnamed protagonist "felt independent and entirely free as she hurried along. She shook off the spell of the episode and became herself again." Unbuttoning her coat, she removed her gloves "as a gesture of relief from the strain of looking exquisite and desirable for so many hours." The story's second half, by introducing the threat of a strange man's pursuing footsteps, illustrates Benson's courting of danger in meetings with lovers. It also reflects her love of the mystery genre, as she builds an atmosphere of terror to accompany her protagonist's realization that her affair has become meaningless. Escaping unharmed to her room—but not without hearing her predator's soft, penetrating, and malicious laughter—she is unable to shake off her anxiety and telephones her lover, needing to hear his voice lest "her own familiar room fall to pieces under her feet." Danger threw Benson's heroine back to the dependency she had despised moments earlier. A powerful story because of its dramatic contrast and irony, "Act 1, Scene 2" gains greater importance when viewed as a revelation of Benson's ambivalence toward Ham in its first "scene" and her realization of the affair's damaging effects in the second.

Though Benson entered into some deep reflection in her quiet moments, the surface of her life was subject to the winds of publishing activity. On April 1st, she met with Cerf to sign the contract for *Junior Miss*. It would be published on April 23rd, Cerf decided, and its catalogue description and jacket blurb would be based on John Mosher's *New Yorker* piece, which "strikes just the right note." Thanks to Cerf's publicity strategies, the Book-of-the-Month selected *Junior Miss* as an alternate for June. In fact, as soon as Bob Haas, president of the Book-of-the-Month-Club, received his copy of *Junior Miss*, he immediately wrote Benson, "Everyone is crazy about the book. Cordially, Bob."[12]

Selection by the club meant that a book was marketed to reach those who read widely and had enough sophistication to realize that they always wanted to read the currently selected book. Announcing upcoming main selections in advance of publication allowed members the advantage of acquiring a book before it appeared in the stores. The author's advantage was a guarantee of huge advance sales; the club's advantage was that by absorbing the cost of competition with booksellers (who needed salespeople and an expensive shop), it acquired its books at a lower price.[13] *Junior Miss* quickly became a best-seller and as a Book-of-the Month Club alternate for June of 1941, vastly increased Benson's readership.[14]

More good news was in store for Benson. On April 30th, a week after the publication of *Junior Miss*, Simon and Schuster presented Benson with a progress report. The Book-of-the-Month Club had chosen *Short Stories from the New Yorker* as a "dividend." Since Benson had contributed pieces to it in 1940, M. Lincoln Schuster explained: "150,000 copies or more will be distributed through Book-of-the-Month Club in addition to the approximately 15,000 copies already sold in the regular channels to the book trade." So large a number of readers would in turn "stimulate the trade demand at the stores, and cumulatively extend the word-of-mouth discussion about these stories." As soon as the Book-of-the-Month Club issued its payment, it would be sent to *The New Yorker* for a "pro rata distribution" to Benson and other included authors. Each story would earn the author "between $100 and $150 in addition to the royalties earned in bookstore sales." Schuster concluded by thanking Benson again for her "share in creating this distinguished book."[15]

Benson was soon overwhelmed with requests for interviews and guest appearances on radio shows. Fueling the upsurge of interest in her was the ironic success of *Junior Miss*. The *New York Times* published Robert van Gelder's interview with Benson in the *Book Review* on May 18th, and *Omnibook Magazine* praised *Junior Miss* as a "deft, amusing book" with an "authentic ring." Judy, the reviewer noted, epitomized the forties' term "Junior Miss"—a girl "too young to be called a young lady but too old to be called a young girl." Judy Graves, "a little too impetuous, a little too tubby, pretty well stepped on by her own elder sister [but] look [ing] upon life with an eager, unprejudiced eye . . . recreates in the minds of adult readers of either sex, a sense of their almost-forgotten youth." Iris Barry appreciated the "uncanny observation, precise recording, delicate imagination that has drawn this nice ordinary girl and her nice ordinary parents out of nothingness and made them as permanent, pleasant, as revealing as a good, new mirror." Miss Benson's gift is rare—"to be at once . . . illuminating . . . and at the same time so neatly humorous and yet with the greatest possible delicacy, to capture the poignancy and terror that invest youth with its own transient and touching charm."[16] Gladys Graham Bates in the *Saturday Review of Literature* also noted Benson's "uncanny accuracy in catching the exact detail" but cautioned, "If you put these tales aside as children's stories simply, you will miss some extremely shrewd comment on human nature in general and our own day in particular." Readers would be amused by Judy's adventures, Bates predicted, but also "harrowed" for "Sally Benson's humor is based on the inherent conflicts between the ego and its environment, and not on any superficial 'quaintness' of children."[17]

In a perceptive, earlier review of *People Are Fascinating* for the *New York Times Book Review*, Edith H. Walton had favorably compared Benson with Dorothy Parker, citing Benson's advantage in withstanding seduction "by a wisecrack" or subscribing to the "tradition of hardboiled gallantry."[18] Reviewing *Junior Miss*, however, Walton focused on Benson's style:

> Though [Benson] has forsworn the sophisticated wit and irony for which she is so noted, these seemingly simple sketches . . . are no less adroit than her earlier stories. . . . Mrs. Benson is as pithy and concise as ever . . . a master of the perfect phrase, with an added quality of warmth and gentleness . . . until now . . . conspicuously lack[ing]. *Junior Miss* . . . is written with an artistry . . . one cannot sufficiently admire. On its own tiny scale, it is almost flawless. It makes one wonder . . . what Sally Benson would do if she were ever to turn ambitious.[19]

Like British critic Iris Barry, Dorothy Parker detected Benson's undercurrent in *Junior Miss*. Her review—"Stories about a 12-Year-Old Make Dorothy Parker Cry"—arouses suspicion, given Parker's penchant for sarcasm, but Parker quickly sets the reader straight. Far from the "distressing slickness" of

Booth Tarkington, "Mrs. Benson writes about her Judy without comment or interpretation . . . condescension . . . gentling, [or] self-indulgent memories of times past." Judy reaches the reader "through the eyes and the ears and the cool, calm honesty of her biographer. The result is that you remember, you laugh, sometimes you cry." Moved, beguiled, and "held by all of *Junior Miss*," Parker attributed the book's power to the "honesty and sureness of Mrs. Benson's writing"—two qualities of Sally Benson's that "put her and her book in the true necessity" rather than the luxury class, any time.[20]

Without question the best appraisal of *Junior Miss* appeared in *American Women Writers*. This reviewer found it ironic that despite its library classification, *Junior Miss* is not a children's book. Rather, each story humorously shows a young girl's attempt to learn about herself and the world; collectively, the stories reveal the human condition. Benson's light touch does not hide the seriousness of Judy's problems and the inadequacies of most adult strategies for coping with them. The dramatization by Jerome Chodorov and Joseph Fields (1942) achieved success by hardening the delicacy gained by Benson's stream-of-consciousness technique; it has the "rounded ends" and "climaxes" Benson disliked and creates a popular stereotype. Readers of the stories will perceive *Junior Miss* as a rare account of female rites of passage.

Benson captures a moment, wish, or thought in the mind of Judy Graves—in this case—and builds from that initial glimpse toward an epiphanic ending sometimes for the character, almost always for the reader. Today's young adolescents can relate to Judy's struggle for identity, despite the more glitzy, action-oriented media that attempt to shape young people's views and self-concepts.

The success of *Junior Miss* attracted the attention of New York University's Warren Bower, host of *Readers' Almanac*, a radio program broadcast over WNYC. On May 1st, Bower contacted Benson at Random House, inviting her to "talk about the book or whatever else [she] might like." Sponsored by the university and in its third year, *Readers' Almanac* was chiefly an interview program, Bower explained, and the current year's schedule included "authors William Dodd, Jr., Albert Maltz, Richard Wright, Maurine Whipple, Forrest Wilson, and Lillian Hellman." Since WNYC was a noncommercial station, Bower could not offer Benson a fee but promised, instead, "a large and . . . literate audience interested in books."

If Benson were agreeable, Bower would arrange a date at her convenience—"late this month, for example?" He would relieve her as much as he could of the "labor of preparing a script." His usual practice was to prepare a "series of questions which the guest answers" in advance of Bower's completing the final script.[21] Bower drew his questions "fairly heavily" from Benson interviews in the *Post* and with Robert van Gelder in the *New York Times Book Review,* but he gave Benson *carte blanche* to omit or change any of his proposed questions. If Benson wished to write out her answers, Bower would type them for her but she was also free to *ad lib.* He would expect her at the studio—Room 736 East Building on 237 Greene Street, one block east of Washington Square—between 7:30 and 7:45—"time enough for any final wrinkles to be ironed out." The program would air on May 27th at 8 o'clock in the evening.[22]

Unlike the more spontaneous van Gelder interview, Bower's method gave Benson the opportunity to make more thoughtful responses. Yet, she appears to have gone to the studio unprepared, answering "off the cuff," and worse, forgetting or contradicting statements she had made just a few days earlier to van Gelder. Benson claimed the success of *Junior Miss,* for example, seemed like an accident to her "because I feel a little as though I have been hit by a truck." She referred Bower to Bennett Cerf for answers—"he probably has a mimeographed copy." As for the story of her purchasing a new car when Cerf showed her the amount of Random House's advance on *Junior Miss,* Benson confirmed its truth:

> I took my nephew, Toby Wherry, with me to the Plymouth-Dodge-Chrysler salesroom across the street and I went around sitting in cars like a zombie. I only looked at the dashboards. When I found a car with enough gadgets, I bought it and charged it to Random House. Afterwards I took Toby for a chocolate soda and said, "Toby, what did I get, a Chrysler or a Dodge?" He answered, "a Dodge . . . maroon with a black top."

Given the advance preparation time Bower had allotted to her, Benson's responses and behavior are problematic. One explanation is that she had resumed drinking. Another, she was playing a game with Bower and lying. Replying to Bower's question about her schooling, for example, Benson claimed to have attended Mary Institute in St. Louis—a complete fabrication—as was her statement: "I couldn't have wormed my way into any college because during the course of my school years [at Horace Mann], I had dropped Latin, German, and a few more of the vital requirements." An exaggeration, the statement disguised the truth: the Smiths could not afford to send her. Asked whether she thought college would hurt a writer, Benson spoofed, "Not exactly. It may just slow him up for a time." Benson credited the *Morning Telegraph* for her writing experience and paid the paper a "left-handed compliment," claiming: "It's still my favorite paper. For escapist reading, it can't be beaten. Why, when the other papers have enormous headlines about the war, the *Telegraph* has equally large headlines saying, 'Whirlaway Kentucky Derby Winner.'" Benson was more than likely serious. A devotee of the track, she kept a picture of Man-o-War among her souvenirs and regularly placed bets on horses, notably Whirlaway, a favorite.

Asked what led her to write fiction, Benson responded,

> I wrote a story one summer when my daughter was away at camp. About Christmas time I let one of my sisters read it. She liked it and told me to send it to the *New Yorker*. So I sent it, and they bought it, and I have been writing for them ever since. I never thought of fame as a writer . . . I don't think anyone but Mr. Cerf would claim that I was a famous writer. He more or less has to. . . .
>
> I write quickly so as to get it over with, the way women wash dishes as fast as they can. I feel wonderful when I have finished a story. Just at that particular moment I think I have written the best short story in the world. I feel drunk. Then, before I lose that feeling, I take my story to Mr. Lobrano who edits me and needs a rest. I watch his face as he reads it, and I know by his expression how much I can ask for on an advance. I write because by now it is my business to write. It's the trade I know best.

Here, once again, Benson lied. Her *New Yorker* contract specified the fixed amount she received for each piece, and as noted in the preceding chapter, most of Benson's writing was done in Connecticut and mailed to Lobrano. (There is, of course, a kernel of truth in her statement. For example, Benson once heard Dorothy Lobrano, Gus's young daughter, talking at lunch about writing her autobiography, a recently assigned school project. Upon learning that one of her forebears was a pirate, Dorothy included him in her family tree and titled her story, "I Am Partially Pirate." Benson went back to her *New Yorker* office after lunch, sat at her typewriter, and submitted a

finished piece three hours later. Benson's "Les Temps Perdus" incorporated
Dorothy's story and even quoted it. As a sign of appreciation, Benson gave
Dottie a pen with a silver pirate's sword as memento.[23]

On the question of never having had a rejection, however, Benson
was surprisingly honest: "But I have had rejections, Mr. Bower." Yet, in the
van Gelder interview a few days earlier, she had stated in reply to the same
question, "Yes, it's true that I haven't had a rejection, probably because I
haven't tried other markets. My style fits here and it wouldn't most places."
With Bower, Benson continued with honesty and elaborated,

> *The New Yorker* turned down a story of mine called "The Over-
> coat." I sold it to the old *American Mercury*. It made the O'Brien
> collection, which you can take for what it's worth. *The New
> Yorker* was also cool about another story of mine, and I sold it
> to *Collier's*. I think I was in a prima donna mood and wouldn't
> fix it. Probably one of my genius days, when I feel too fine to
> be bothered with the riff and the raff, as Ring Lardner once
> called them.

Bower, like many previous interviewers and critics, wondered whether
Benson's daughter, Barbara, had been the inspiration for Judy Graves. Benson usually answered this question by describing an experience she had on
a Fifth Avenue bus. A little girl

> carrying three dimes [was] . . . dying to drop them in the slot
> to pay the fares for herself, her mother and her sister. She
> dropped the dimes, and I felt her day was ruined. You know
> how it is, scurrying around on the floor and getting your gloves
> dirty, exposed to tolerant smiles. I intended to do a short piece,
> but it got long, and Mr. Maxwell who edited me then, thought
> that I should do more stories about Judy. They were mostly
> wrung out of me, sometimes through poverty on my part, and
> sometimes through third degree methods on the part of Mr.
> Maxwell, who called me up once when I had bronchitis and
> told me I had promised him a Christmas story, and where was
> it? He called me at two, and I finished the story at half-past
> four.

(Here she appears to have misremembered: it had been Ross who encouraged the Judy pieces.) With Bower, though, Benson explained: "My daughter has some place in the Judy stories. She was once a fat little girl and went through a ghastly stage. She did make a cardboard house for a dying mouse, as I tell about in one story."[24]

In fact, *Junior Miss* is a blend of Benson's own adolescent experiences and her observations of Bobsie and her teenage friends. "Fuffy," Judy Graves's friend, for example, was based on Lorraine Adam, one of Bobsie's closest companions. Her Christmas story—"The Best Things Come in Small Packages"—(mentioned earlier) is another good example. In it Benson incorporated recent personal experience, parts of her girlhood diary, and a bit of Bobsie and friends. Judy, for example, bought her father a "gadget called a Scotch bartender, which measured an exact jigger of whiskey" and a special ashtray designed to ward off fire when smoking in bed (cf. the Gibbs apartment fire). Judy enumerated her Christmas gifts as Benson had listed hers in the diary of 1912. She later met Fuffy for a stroll down Fifth Avenue, "swinging their new bags," as teenage Sally had done as a Horace Mann freshman. Dipping farther back into her past, Benson ended the piece with Judy playing near a tree with little twin dolls, a gift from older sister Lois. Benson's story, though hastily composed, rendered a fine description of adolescent girlhood poised on the cusp between imitating fashionable adult leisure and retreating to familiar, pseudo-maternal play. Ironically, though her nostalgic piece recreated a world of innocence to be enjoyed at leisure, economic necessity had dictated Benson's speed of composition.

As to whether there would be a movie based on the Judy stories, Benson told Bower she might have been excited about a film adaptation a month earlier, but "now I have calmed down. . . . If I could sell the stories without the meetings over the lunch tables, it would be fine.[25] There is also enough love left in me for Judy so that if she were sold I would like to see that she were well and happy."[26] Bower next asked Benson whether she would write a novel. Benson replied, "I will never write a novel. I don't know how." Neither was she a "novel reader."[27] She preferred books "crammed with facts" (though she forgot the facts, she loved the books), "horror stories and novels based on real crimes," autobiographies, biographies, and old books "that I have read a dozen times." Currently, she was reading "Joseph Shearing's books as fast as I can find them in second-hand bookstores."[28] She admired Edith Wharton's *House of Mirth*, Willa Cather's *A Lost Lady*, and Sinclair Lewis's *Babbitt*, which she read every year, but her abiding interest remained mysteries—some weeks she read as many as seventeen—and detective magazines. "There is nothing more soothing to me than the sight of a body wrapped in a burlap sack," she claimed—a believable comment given Benson's childhood custom of burying her dolls.

Immediately after appearing on *Readers' Almanac*, Benson had a note from Bennett Cerf: "Your talk was a honey. In fact, come to think of it, You are a honey too."[29] Invitations to do other radio appearances multiplied. NBC's Alice Maslin planned to interview Benson on May 26th at eleven o'clock in Studio 557A on the fifth floor of NBC studios in the RCA Building in Radio City. Before the actual interview, Ruth Gould, Maslin's assistant, sent Benson a "rather dull version of what you told me about yourself yesterday," authorizing Benson to "liven it up in whatever manner you think most effective." Timing rehearsal would be at 8:30 a.m. in Studio 8-C on the eighth floor of the RCA Building, and the program would air at 9 a.m. the next morning, Wednesday the 28th, on Station WJZ.[30] The following day, a reminder arrived from Robin McKown of CBS about Benson's forthcoming appearance on Adelaide Hawley's program scheduled for Monday, June 2nd, at 8:30 a.m. Miss Hawley would conduct a preliminary interview with Benson on May 27th at eleven o'clock, McKown advised, and would call about the location "because I think she wants to come to your apartment" since her studio is being renovated. Benson, however, preferred to do the Hawley interview in her *New Yorker* office at 2:30 p.m. Benson was becoming more assertive.[31]

A fourth Benson radio spot occurred just a few days later. On May 28th, Parker Wheatley, radio director of Northwestern University, wrote in appreciation of Benson's manuscript for their "Of Men and Books" broadcast scheduled for May 31st. Wheatley "immensely enjoyed" Benson's answers to Mr. Frederick's questions and assured her she could "use another question or two, which would give her an opportunity to talk" or "double the length of [her] answers" in the program's second part. "We certainly want a full four or five minutes from you in each half of the program," he maintained. As early as May 15, 1941, Frank Cooper of General Amusement Corporation, Artists Representatives, had approached Benson about turning *Junior Miss* into a radio show. Convinced that Benson's "adaptation of *Junior Miss* . . . would make one of the high spots in the radio business," Cooper informed her, "I will call you next week. Maybe we can have lunch or cocktails—whichever is more convenient for you."[32] To Cooper's dismay, however, Benson, had already negotiated with Leland-Hayward for a *Junior Miss* radio series and was about to accept an offer of $1,500.00 a show. Apprised of Benson's prior commitment and disappointed at having "come in second," Cooper nevertheless offered to help if Benson needed "any information relative to radio. . . . I sincerely believe you have a lot to offer to the radio media and if you don't get full satisfaction from the Hayward office in the near future, I trust you will invite me to try to do something for you. The one thing that makes me feel that my efforts were not altogether futile is that I have had the pleasure of meeting a very charming woman."[33]

Despite a heavy schedule of social and business events, Benson agreed to several more guest appearances on radio shows. Among Benson's best supporters during this period of phenomenal activity was Bennett Cerf who assured her: "You will cover yourself in glory"—this as she prepared for *Information Please*, a program hosted by Clifton Fadiman and scheduled for a June 6th airing. Afterward, Cerf wrote again: "I cannot tell you how delighted I was with your performance the other evening on *Information Please*. I always knew you had it in you, kid, and now I hope I have your permission to match you with Joe Louis for the championship! *Junior Miss* is selling fine. Have a good time in Indiana and write me a love letter soon. As ever, Bennett." Whatever degree of romantic involvement might have occurred between Benson and Cerf, by December the relationship would cool over Benson's subsequently contracting to turn *Junior Miss* into a Broadway show. The sticking point was Cerf's betrayal regarding Benson's author's rights to the play version of *Junior Miss*.[34] Benson believed she had the rights to sell the stories to be used in a play; Cerf believed that Random House owned all the rights and that money from the sale would go to the publisher.

Benson's popularity spread from Manhattan to Ithaca, New York, where she was featured on Sunday, June 1st. "This is WBIX, the Voice of the Mohawk Valley" was a new program consisting of *Radio Book Reviews*. Dr. Strang Lawson, associate professor of English at Colgate University, had a portion called "Have You Read It?" Strang described Benson's Judy Graves for the listening audience and critiqued the author's style, praising Benson's "compact and subtle" manner of writing, her gift for the "right phrase," and her "capacity for economical suggestion." Largely positive regarding *Junior Miss*, Strang continued:

> I like Sally Benson best when she has a chance to show more of her wide range of perception, satire, and sympathy; and I hope one result of the popularity of *Junior Miss* will be to send readers to her earlier volume, *People Are Fascinating*. That contains some of her most brilliant cameos. . . . Mrs. Benson is at her best when she is looking coolly through humbug, as in "Really Living," about the college Professor who puts on a good imitation of humane living when there is company, but is actually a domestic and professional failure.[35]

In between her radio appearances, several publishers contacted Benson. First, Doubleday's Schuyler Crane congratulated Benson on "the appearance of Judy Graves in book form" and, unaware of Benson's occasional use of the Esther Evarts pseudonym, thanked her for the "wonderful letter to Mr. McCormick about Esther Evarts. . . . She sounds delightful and we'd like nothing better than to meet her [and] are following her career with interest."[36] Upon Ken McCormick's return from "a manuscript scouting trip to the coast," he was delighted to find "a Benson first in the form of a letter revealing the identity of Esther Evarts. I am not surprised that such excellent pieces turned out to be your work. . . . If you still are inclined to have that quiet little dinner with you and your mother in old Chelsea, I can assure you that nothing would give me greater pleasure."[37]

Second to approach Benson was Mary Louise Aswell of *Harper's Bazaar*. Reminding Benson that she had promised some pieces and even discussed outlines for them in Aswell's office but sold them instead to the *New Yorker*, Aswell pleaded: "How about some of those ideas that seem possibilities for *Harper's Bazaar*? . . . we are just as anxious, even if not as omnipresent as they [*The New Yorker*] are."[38] A third editor, Eugene Lyons of *The American Mercury*, announced plans to run an occasional story

> out of *The American Mercury* past—*Mercury* revivals. . . . I trust you will feel complimented that I'm starting the idea with "The Overcoat," a little story by Sally Benson we first published in November 1934. In connection with it I'm appending a little

note about *Junior Miss*, even unto the fact that it's published by Random House.[39]

A fourth request for Benson's fiction came in June from Kenneth Littauer of *Woman's Home Companion.* "What I have in mind is something rather more sentimental than your stuff in the *New Yorker*, but dealing with the humor of life among the very young." Littauer also invited Benson to meet and talk over the possibilities "face-to-face."[40] *The New Yorker*, meanwhile, had not been forgotten. Only two months after the magazine purchased "June 1903," the first piece in Benson's "5135 Kensington" series, she had submitted the second—"July 1903"—and on June 20th *The New Yorker* bought it.[41]

Benson's expanded market increased her profits. With her newfound money, she intended to build a new house in Madison, Connecticut and call it "Benson's Folly." Until then, when not in New York with Ham, she resided temporarily with her sister Rose in Madison and had mail delivered to Rose's address, "c/o Shuttleworth." One morning, she spotted among the many letters and advertisements, the brochure for the University of Indiana's Second Annual Writers' Conference. On its cover in alphabetical order were the names of presenters. Hers topped a list that included John Crowe Ransom and Irwin Shaw plus seven other writers and critics.[42] Inside the brochure, Ransom and his blurb received top billing, followed by Shaw. Benson was listed third—a rather prominent position, given that men still dominated the writing scene—and the blurb noted her *New Yorker* fiction and her collections, *People Are Fascinating* and *Emily.*

The ten-day program offered lectures and workshops. Besides its specific, writer-oriented agenda, the conference also provided two public lectures and several panel discussions, including one on "experiences in writing for the *New Yorker*" to be presented by Sally Benson and Irwin Shaw. In addition, Benson would lead a daily fiction workshop for students and other conference attendees wishing to submit manuscripts for evaluation and discussion. Benson was proud of having been selected and eager to participate, especially since Irwin Shaw would be there. Benson invited Ham to accompany her as far as Columbus, Ohio, but she traveled the rest of the way with Shaw. One of the first things she did after settling into her room at the Claypool Hotel in Indianapolis was to telegram Ham of her safe arrival. Ham's long letter of response addressed to "Darling,

darling Sally" provides a further glimpse into their relationship. Besides being humorous, poetic, and responsible—almost to the point of being parental—Ham was becoming a literary critic.[43] After telling Benson he was proud of her and hopeful that her trip from Columbus to Indianapolis had been pleasant, Ham wrote:

> Last night did you notice the beautiful full moon? It was almost as bright as day, and I kept looking out the window at the fields and the farms all the way to Pittsburgh. . . . I found out what that stuff is that we were wondering about yesterday. It's alfalfa. . . . I also read some stories in *Collier's* . . . the worst things I have ever read . . . Stuff like "His jaw jutted sternly out."

He described how Benson's cats—Pantsy and Molly Wuppy—greeted him when he returned to New York, but Rover, he reported, was missing. He left money for Alliene so she could feed them and "get something for herself." Then, he went to the garage to "straighten things out" before heading to Grand Central to mail his letter so Benson would get it via the overnight South Western Limited. Ham continued:

> Darling, it is very lonely here without you, but I keep looking at the calendar and I see that a week from the day after tomorrow I will be on my way back out to Indianapolis. Do you miss me, darling? You are probably too busy swanking around out in Bloomington in all your finery. I don't think that I like the idea that the whole state of Pennsylvania is between us. . . . You be very good, beautiful, and don't be getting into any card games . . . you must write me, darling, and don't forget and leave your medicine around someplace where you will lose it. Do you like Bloomington, darling, and do you love me, darling Sally? I love you so I think that it is only fair that you should. Darling Sally, I adore you, and I miss you very much.[44]

Concerned about her still missing Rover, Benson sent a second telegram on Friday and Ham wrote to her the next day. He was meeting his father and "some friend of his" on Wall Street to discuss over dinner a possible job in the Ordnance Division of the Navy. It "pays a nice salary, and you sit behind a desk, so I like it better than this running around the countryside chasing tanks." Ham had to give "this Naval commander" a report of his engineering and mechanical experience. A few days later, Ham updated Benson: "Apparently, the old man thinks there is a good chance that I will be able to get a job with Commander Buell in the Navy Ordnance which will automatically get me deferred in the draft." Both Ham and Sally would be glad of that.

On Sunday, Ham forwarded Benson's mail to Madison and reported, "I was promptly put to work on some charts for [Mr. Binkerd] to use on his case." After working with his father until twelve, Ham walked up to 45 Fifth Avenue and over to Bobsie's at 239 Waverly Place to see if Rover was hanging around there but he saw no sign of the dog. "Don't stay up till all hours of the night," he warned Benson, adding, "I have been very good, my darling, and I can hardly wait to get on that train. Don't write me after Tuesday, darling, because I won't get it till we get back. I miss you darling, darling, Sally. You be good, beautiful."[45]

That night Benson sent Ham another telegram claiming she had a cold. He responded the next day full of concern and repeated his eagerness to see her:

> Darling, you aren't finished with your lectures until the 18th, are you? My train gets into Indianapolis at 11:55 Central Standard Time on the 20th of June, Friday. Unless I hear otherwise, I will expect to see you at the station. If you feel terrible, darling, you don't have to meet me, just tell me where to go. . . . Darling, darling Sally I love you, and I miss you. Things are very dull around here without you, and I don't like it at all. Take care of yourself, darling, and there are only three days more. That's something! I saw in the *Tribune* that *Junior Miss* is climbing up the best seller ladder.
>
> Darling, I love you. Ham[46]

The following day Ham wrote another long, newsy letter about the cats' antics and Rover's continued absence. He wanted to know all about Benson's activities and how she liked it "out there. Are you in a dormitory where you have to walk a mile down to the john? . . . . Darling, darling Sally, I do miss you, and I wish that it was the twentieth now. . . . I hope that there is a letter from you when I get home. Do you miss me, darling?"[47]

Benson did not miss Ham as much as he missed her. As noted earlier Benson had already explored the inadequacy of her relationship with
Ham and reflected her feelings in "Act 1, Scene 1," a piece published in
the April 26th issue of *The New Yorker*. Busy at the conference, she merely
sent Ham telegrams, but she took time to write at length to Gus Lobrano.
Her relationship with Lobrano, though initially a professional one, had
developed into a friendship based on trust. She could and did share news
of a personal nature. She could also complain:

> Why haven't you written me? I am in Indianapolis and am
> going to have my hair washed. I had a fine time at the writers'
> conference. Here are two stories by a boy who is twenty and
> has lived all his life in a small Indiana town. . . . I had a fine
> time with Shaw. From time to time he would telephone me
> and tell me that he was madly in love with me. But that is his
> habit. Like a tic. He wanted to drive to California even telling
> me that it would set him back $150 a day for being late, but I
> said that by the time we got to Tucson, all I would be hearing
> was about the $150. He was wildly enthusiastic for the story
> on the new series.[48]

Whatever the nature of her involvement with Shaw, her comments to
Lobrano show that given her insight into people, she was capable of cutting
through Shaw's critical pomposity and discouraging his romantic overtures.
She attended Shaw's presentations and reported: "In his first lecture, he
attacked a lot of things . . . Gibbs, New York theater audiences made up
of overstuffed people who had come from 21 sodden, bad directors, awful
theater owners, actors, and successful playwrites [*sic*]." With characteristic
sarcasm Benson had demanded of Shaw whether "the only good one was
the author who was awful."[49] Ironically echoing Ham's letter, she continued: "we were riding in the country and the moon came up and he said,
'Look at that overstuffed moon coming in late for the theater.'" Shaw's
comment indicates he knew he had been had but he was gracious enough
to deflect Benson's incisive barb with self-deprecating humor. Curiously,
though Benson resorted to lying and exaggerating—often to bolster her
self-esteem—she was always quick to dispel arrogance in others.

Dismissing Shaw, Benson turned next to the upcoming Olivet College Writers' Conference to be held in Michigan in July. She had declined

Olivet's invitation to participate, she told Lobrano, because "They have Katharine Anne Porter and I feel I would just be a cherry on her fruit cup." Actually, Benson's letter of regret expressed strongly felt reasons and merited a lengthy response from Joseph Brewer, president of Olivet College. He was grateful, he asserted, for Benson's frankness. Though "sadly disappointed," he agreed with her "about writers' conferences." Benson had objected to the presence of so many "old ladies." However, Brewer argued, Olivet did not have "so many of the old ladies around; they haven't liked us very well. We have perhaps been too sharp with them." Rather, Olivet had witnessed its staff having the "opportunity to talk shop seriously" in a manner that had proven "pretty good and stimulating." Concluding, Brewer assured Benson he was not attempting "to persuade [her] to change her mind" and he welcomed her to visit if ever she were in the area, where she would "find a whole nest of [her] admirers."[50]

Once her negative response to Brewer was in the mail, Benson thought no more of Olivet. Intent on having Lobrano confirm her judgment on the fiction of Salem Shively, one of the student participants who had attended her presentation, she wrote:

> I just want you to read those stories and tell me what you think of them. I will be here until Friday and then will be at the Hotel Vincennes, Indiana, Sunday and Monday morning. I will wire where I'll be after that. Memphis, I think. I get my books all right.[51] Tell Miss Terry my Vincennes address. How is Ross?
>
> My love to you, Lobrano. Sally.

Benson's trademark—the penciled afterthought—asked, "What did you do to my second story? I like this city. I know a poetess here—Marguerite Young—she shows me around but gets lost herself."[52]

Lobrano explained in the return mail on Friday that he hadn't written because he knew that when Benson "had Shaw around to listen to," she wouldn't read letters. After mentioning some editing done on her "second series story," Lobrano promised to send the author's proof "somewhere along your way" and teased: "If there's some of it you don't agree with, please say so as kindly as possible. I'm awfully edgy these days, and burst into tears at practically nothing."[53] As for the fiction of the young man (Salem Shively) Benson had met, Lobrano was not impressed.

Benson informed Lobrano she would be leaving French Lick, Indiana, on Tuesday, July 1st, arriving in New York on the 5th of July or the Monday after. She agreed that her young "protégé's" literary efforts were negligible but explained, "I felt sorry for him. He looked like an owl." Benson did have her compassionate side, especially where young men were concerned. Coincidentally, she had won $9.70 "on a horse named React" by betting in a hotel she found—a "fine hotel for colored people . . . [where] they have wires to all the tracks in the back room" and where everything is reckoned as "three Derbies ago" or "before Derby" or "after Derby." Pleased with herself, she added: "I *understand* it."[54] Her big news, however, was, "I may be going to get $600 a week—no work—for *Junior Miss* radio rights." She had turned down $1,500 a week because she "would have had to do the scripts, and then where would Ross be?" She added, everyone in Blooming-ton, including Shaw, was surprised that she could tell one tree from another. "How do you know such things?" Shaw puzzled. In answering, Benson was misunderstood—"They thought I said that I sprang fully clothed out of Ross's head—not that anything out of Ross's head is fully clothed."[55]

The conference, besides occasioning Benson's telegrams to Ham and Babe, also prompted one from Ross on June 10th: "Did you get there comma please? H.W. Ross."[56] Benson replied in kind: "I am here comma. Shaw is here. We are going the way of all flesh. S. B."[57] Ross returned, "We just concluded extensive thanksgiving service over your safe arrival. Please keep in mind that the eyes of the Book-of-the-Month Club are on you. H.W. Ross."[58] A wire of a different nature arrived from Bobsie. Low on funds, she wired her mother asking for $100 just to be safe. Benson in turn wired Ralph Paladino, the *New Yorker* business manager, requesting that he send the money to Barbara, an amount Benson quickly repaid by having Paladino deduct it from the payment on her next story.

After the conference, its organizer, Ralph Collins, wrote Benson an appreciative note:

> I hope you found your stay at the Claypool a gateway to Hoosier hospitality. . . . At Bloomington talk is still warm in memory of you—even if we see ourselves as standing around open-mouthed and more than a trifle gawky. . . . This is very unofficial-appearing but do take my thanks for all that you did at the Conference. We appreciated it very much, and we think, if this is possible, that you are even better than your writing.[59]

Amid the fanfare of the conference and the friendly liaison with Shaw, Benson found time to keep her family abreast of her accomplishments. Anna Cora telegrammed her at the French Lick Hotel in Vincennes, Indiana, "bursting with joyful cries over your success. Please take care of yourself. Toby and Esther are coming here Wednesday for two days. Rose says come to Madison when you return."

When her Indiana sojourn was over, Benson did return to Madison. Sorting through the mail Ham had forwarded, she discovered a surprise— a letter from her old friend Bill Stayton, now a government employee in Washington, D.C.: "Dear Sara," he wrote,

> I have just finished reading "5135 Kensington." No wonder you were always so crazy about Lon. It is hard to say how much of my enthusiasm about the story was because I knew you all, but even discounting that, I still think it is the finest thing you have done. It is just as keen and dispassionate and unpretentious as your other things, but it is full of a careless, healthy, radiant happiness. It is so much like you were yourself when you came to Horace Mann that it is almost breath taking, and I am sorry for all those people who didn't know you then, and how lovely you were. Incidentally, this is strictly not bologna. It is the first time I have ever written you about your published stuff, and I do it reluctantly. Frankly, it is the first thing that I think is as good as your old Useless Ennelbesser stories. Anyhow, it gave me one of the nicest fifteen minutes I have had in a long time.
>
> As always, Bill[60]

Benson read Stayton's letter during a busy time in her professional life as she multiplied business contacts and increased financial assets. Bill's recalling memories of younger days at Horace Mann made her smile. As she read his critical appraisal of her work and of her youthful self, she must have had misgivings. She loved most of what she had written, despite Bill's praising a Horace Mann piece from 1915 and her recent "5135 Kensington" but scanting all she had written in between. In continuing the series, she wondered whether she could sustain the "unpretentious . . . radiant happiness" that Bill so admired. Current friends, family, colleagues—knowing her tenacity and determination in pursuing goals—had, however, no such doubts.

Benson's professional successes, major and minor, continued. On July 7th, 1941 the University of California requested permission to reprint Benson's "New Leaf." At the same time, the Kensington series was about to propel her to greater fame, and, already, requests had begun to arrive from Europe and South America for the rights to translate *Junior Miss* and other Benson stories.[61]

When Bobsie returned to Bangor, Maine, after her cruise, she and Alexis Doster were engaged and decided to marry immediately. The separation had helped Barbara make up her mind, but the larger motivation in the couple's decision was Doster's assignment to Egypt on a special mission for the Office of Strategic Services (O.S.S.). Though Benson had maintained sobriety for an extensive period, Bobsie's memories of painful scenes were still vivid. Fearing that a formal wedding might occasion her mother's showing up drunk, embarrassing her and the wedding guests, Bobsie and Alex eloped and were married in Groton, Massachusetts, on Friday, July 18, 1941. Reverend William Peck of the First Unitarian parish performed the ceremony. Benson responded to the news by sending the couple a gift check for $100. In Bobsie's thank-you note and subsequent letters, she asked among other things, "How is Ham's beard?" She also described life on the base. Ironically, Bobsie's social life had devolved overnight into rounds of bridge with older women, many resembling the women Benson treated in her fiction.

On August 6th, *The New Yorker* bought Benson's third Kensington piece, "August 1903." A 4,200-word story, it sold for $515 and earned a bonus of $114, bringing the total to $629. Ross, questioned by Paladino about the amount, admitted he had prematurely ordered that Benson be paid at the new rate ("18 cents a word for the first 1,500 words plus 9 cents after that and a bonus of 4 cents on the first 1,500 plus 2 cents after that). "September 1903," at 3,730 words, earned $470 and a bonus of $104.60, totaling $574.60. Ross explained he had mistakenly told Benson of the new rate before it took effect. "I remember her exulting in it," he said, implying the reason for his generosity.[62] Responses to the Kensington stories were positive, inspiring more fan mail than ever and justifying Ross's precipitous decision.[63]

Appreciated as a letter-writer by family and friends, Benson also pleased several fans by replying to their notes and letters.[64] The sympathetic, kind aspect of Benson's personality, though not perceptible to everyone, also revealed itself to fellow journalist Charles B. Driscoll, who invited Benson

Figure 11. Sally Benson in her *New Yorker* office

to lunch at the Ritz so he could interview her for his column, "New York by Day." Benson was "dressed smart, wearing a flamboyant, gaudily striped scarf," Driscoll reported. She "talks with a brittle, hard-surfaced humor but beneath it she is extremely humble and modest." As an example, Driscoll quoted Benson's reflections on public speaking: "I don't like lecturing. They want me to talk about prominent people and to bandy big names about. I don't know any big people and I won't fake them." As for writers, Benson stated: "Many who yearn for publication can't write. They just think they can write."[65] Driscoll is on target in his analysis of Benson's character as humble and modest beneath superficial hardness. Her complicated personality, however, as Driscoll illustrates, moves quickly from innate humility to apparent arrogance.

Though she kept in close contact with family, one fan letter piqued her curiosity. It came for her birthday from an "Auntie Whitaker" in St. Louis with greetings and gratitude for Benson's letters. Whitaker claimed to have passed them around and then posted them on the bulletin board of the Y.M.C.A. "All of St. Louis is proud of you," her aunt declared. Claiming herself a fan of Louella Parsons, the celebrity gossip columnist, Whitaker reported a rumor that "Fats" Lobrano and "Tiny" Maxwell would be given roles in the film of *Junior Miss*. "You're a very lucky girl to know them and not have to pay for your lunches," Whitaker commented, "since food is very dear in New York City on account of the World's Fair. I know you must be very busy tonight, your birthday night, and very happy and proud to be with all your lovely friends so I will sign off now. Just one last word to say we are going up to Manitowoc next week to ride on the bridge and watch the 'Pere Marquette' go by. Wow!" (As of this writing, none of Benson's family knew of the existence of an "Auntie Whitaker." The tone of the letter, I would suggest, is reminiscent of John Lawson's early letters to Benson. He very likely wrote in complimentary jest.)[66]

Taking her entrepreneurial skill to another level, Benson considered marketing some of her fictional characters as dolls specially made and named for them. By August 26, 1941, she had commissioned her good friend Robey Lyle to negotiate a contract with Margit Nilsen Studios at 71 Fifth Avenue to manufacture dolls "to be known as Judy and Lois." Based on *Junior Miss* characters, these dolls shortly went into production. When Benson rejected the first model for Lois, the Nilsen staff quickly cast a new head for Lois. The subsequent contract specified that Judy, about sixteen inches high, would sell at retail for $6.00 and twenty-two-inch Lois at $10.00—high prices by 1940s standards. Benson would receive royalties on each doll sold—5 percent of the manufacturer's wholesale price on the first 5,000 and 7 percent subsequently.[67] Lyle, who used Benson's office at *The New Yorker*, was pleased to help extend the profits from *Junior Miss* and kept Benson informed of progress made in this and other projects.

Two days after her birthday, Benson was delighted when Edwin Seaver of the Book-of-the-Month Club contacted her regarding some incredible copy excerpted from a radio script that a big publicity outfit had circulated as part of its "regular weekly service to women radio editors." Unable to resist mocking the excerpt, Seaver teased: "So you were delivered by a busy stork, eh? And you took a wedded husband? (Sounds scandalous to me). . . . Some day when you are free, let's have lunch together."[68] Benson's free time was becoming nonexistent as she accepted one invitation after another. September's mail also brought an invitation from Henry La Cossitt, fiction editor of *The American Magazine*, to discuss whether "the idea of magazine fiction appeals to you." Benson agreed to meet La Cossitt and proposed a piece in detail. A week later he wrote, "I am expecting to see the story we talked about next Monday, September 22nd, a week from today. Failure to remit will force us to charge you a rate of six per cent per diem until the story is submitted."[69] He had to have been joking. However, even before she could think of writing a piece for La Cossitt, Benson found herself involved in the second ugly battle of her career. This time the publisher was Random House and Benson's argument was with Cerf over—of all things—her rights to the play *Junior Miss*.

Benson's first skirmish had arisen over the requirement that she be a member of the Dramatists' Guild of America. Though she had agreed to allow *Junior Miss* to be made into a play by Jerome Chodorov and Joseph Fields, as its production by Max Gordon became actual, Benson made a disturbing discovery. For her play to appear on Broadway, Benson would need to join the guild, an essentially "closed shop." She could not "have any dealings with any manager who [was] not in good standing with the Guild," and since all three men were members, Benson would have to join. "If I do not join," she wrote,

> the members of the cast, the authors of the play, the producer, and all people connected with the play, will be out of work, will suffer loss of time and money. I do not feel I can withhold my signature to the Dramatists' Guild contract under these circumstances. . . . If I were the only person involved, I would not apply for membership, as I am against any closed shop organization.

What Benson found even more distressing was that she would also have to join the Authors' League of America and "be assessed on all income received from magazines, books, newspapers. . . . I do not understand," she wrote, "why I have to join the Authors' League, or why, because I may have a play on Broadway, I will be assessed on all my writings." Benson reiterated her reason for signing the "blanket agreement"—that she felt an obligation toward authors, producer, and cast members. Under protest, "torn between my principles and the obligation I feel toward others," Benson scrawled her distinguished back-slanting signature, enclosed a check for the required $8.00 fee, and mailed the application.[70] She was not happy.

Once she became involved with the production of her play, Benson had to neglect other commitments. On October 10th, having received nothing from Benson, an angry Henry La Cossitt wrote: "LOOK HERE,

BENSON. WHAT THE HELL?" The same day a more positive note from Bennett Cerf arrived.

> . . . the play's really fine and has every chance of success though it seems a little skimpy in length . . . the last half of the last act strikes me as having been done a little bit hurriedly. The rest is ship-shape. . . . I didn't object at all to the character of J.B. Sure it is a stock characterization, but it is always good for laughs!
>
> Bennett.[71]

Junior Miss continued to be marketed in a variety of venues. In October, for example, Benson accepted an invitation to an author's dinner hosted by the Art and Library Department of the Women's Republican Club of Massachusetts. The event occurred in the ballroom of their clubhouse at 46 Beacon Street, a fashionable section of the city. There would be no speeches, but if Benson wished "a few minutes to talk about [your] book, we shall be glad to hear you." While in Massachusetts, Benson also addressed a large audience at Boston Garden on October 23rd at the annual *Herald* Book Fair. The *Boston Herald* reprised the event the next day in an article titled "Defense Needs Will Curtail Book Production, Publisher Says." A photo shows a smiling, corsage-wearing Benson seated next to Alice Dixon Bond, the *Herald* book editor. Behind the women stand Harry Maule, Percival Wilde, Bennett Cerf, Max Schuster, and Clifton Fadiman. The accompanying article reported favorably:

> Cerf found himself talked back to by his prettiest author, Miss Sally Benson . . . when he characterized her as the "one beam of sunlight" on the staff of the *New Yorker* magazine. Certainly, one of the most pulchritudinous of women authors, she made a charming picture in a striking gown of black crepe and electric blue sequins that were effective contrast for her red curls. Her assertion that members of the *New Yorker* staff were "perfectly normal" persons who might, on occasion, have fun rolling a water cooler along the floor, or by setting fires in waste baskets, was backed by Fadiman, literary editor of that publication.[72]

No one who knew Benson would have been surprised at her talking back to Cerf or her painting a picture of playful *New Yorker* colleagues. From Massachusetts, Benson traveled next to Madison, Connecticut for a presentation to the Women's Club. Then she returned to New York where additional invitations awaited her.

Mabel Search of *Liberty*, despite knowing how busy Benson was and that *The New Yorker* "had a corner on everything" she did and that she "didn't like seeing [her] name elsewhere," urged her to write some stories for *Liberty*. Search suggested that Benson could do "something that would be up our street, and while, of course, I would love to have your name, I think a good story under a *nom de plume* is nothing to sneeze at. When you have a moment, let me buy you a cocktail and we'll talk the thing over if you are interested."[73] The very same day's mail brought a solicitation from Sarah Rollitts of Music Corporation of America (MCA) regarding "an SOS from their Hollywood office asking whether you would be available to do a script job on a very important picture dealing with adolescents . . . to be directed by one of the top Hollywood directors." Rollitts hoped Benson would "permit [her] to talk . . . more about this in person" and offered "all good wishes to *Junior Miss* which I hear is terrific. I am so glad." Somehow, Benson made time to answer both Search and Rollitts. She would let no opportunity for success or financial gain slip through her fingers.

As the November 18th opening of *Junior Miss* at the Lyceum Theater on Broadway drew near, excitement became palpable. Throughout the day flowers and congratulations poured into Benson's *New Yorker* office. Among the attached cards was one from Mabel Search, thanking Benson for her note and extending

> best wishes for a long run for your show. I hear it's a honey and I hope you make a fortune out of it. Do let me know when you have a minute for lunch or for cocktails. I would love to see you even if we don't do any business. By the time *Junior Miss* has been going a little while, you won't be interested in making money but even so, don't let any nasty editor get you to work for nothing.[74]

So captivating a personality could Benson project that even over a business lunch she had won a friend in Mabel Search.

Telegrams addressed to the Lyceum Theater Stage Door, 45th Street East of Broadway, arrived from all quarters. Among the more memorable ones was Andy (E. B.) and Katharine White's, which read: "Four and twenty critics / Sitting in a row / Conjuring superlatives / While Sally counts the dough. White and White." Jim and Helen Thurber wrote: "Best of luck.

We know you have a hit. Sorry we cannot be there to join in the cheering." Babe also wrote: "Hello Hello Hello. The show can't be anything but Absobloominglutely Posouddyvtively wizard all the luck in the world old dear. Babe." Betty Bryant, Benson's milliner, ordered: "Hold all your hats, draped and otherwise, for a stupendous success. Lovingly, Betty Bryant." Paul Streger, Benson's agent at Leland Hayward, offered: "I am sure the electric sign will be blazing for a long time on 45th Street and all points west. Best wishes. Paul Streger."[75] Even Edna Ferber sent greetings: "Congratulations on *Junior Miss*. Every good wish in the world. Edna Ferber."

For opening night, Anna Cora, Rose and Sam Shuttleworth, and Esther and Henry Wherry joined Babe, Ham, and Benson's *New Yorker* colleagues—Maxwell, the Rosses, the Lobranos, Daise Terry, Gibbs, and others for a light, pre-theater supper to celebrate Sally's success. Only Bobsie was missing (travel from Bangor being prohibitive), but she sent a telegram and followed it with a letter saying how sorry she was to have missed the occasion. As the curtain rose, an audience already familiar with Benson's fiction sat back with delight as Judy and the Graves family came to life. When Act III ended and curtain calls began, bouquets and applause greeted Benson, Chodorov and Fields, director Moss Hart, set designer Frederick Fox, and others involved in the production. Momentarily, Benson wished Agnes and Lon could have been there, but she was quickly swept away by flashbulbs going off in quick succession and journalists angling for an opportunity to get her ear. It had been a great night, and no one objected to continuing the celebration afterward at Bleeck's to await the morning newspapers.

Reviews were highly positive but paid scant attention to Benson as the inspiration for Chodorov's and Fields's drama.[76] The one exception was John Mason Brown's in the *New York World-Telegram*. Broadway, Brown began, already indebted to *New Yorker* sketches for successes like *Pal Joey, Mr. and Mrs. North, My Sister Eileen, Having a Wonderful Time*, and *Life with Father*, had

> turned to that delightful magazine once again last night for what should be another success. This time it is Sally Benson's charming stories . . . vignettes [of] two average parents whose fortunate misfortune was to have two daughters. . . . With a brilliant mastery of her medium and infinite gentle humor, Miss Benson told about the impact of Judy and Lois both on their parents and on each other while on a family automobile trip, when trying to

mother a mouse, at Christmas time when childhood would out, at the moment of writing a diary for homework, when making New Year's resolutions, acting in an amateur production of *The Tempest*, or going to a first party. Miss Benson's writing was as quiet as it was perceptive. Her sketches were incidents observed with a fine eye for detail. [Plotless] the only climaxes were the constant jabbing truths which they managed to get stated.

Brown observed that Chodorov and Fields, on the contrary, had come like Guy Fawkes "bearing a regular theater plot . . . to plant the gunpowder of action in these sketches." The result is "much more understated and gagged than the *Junior Miss* that Random House published, but the play is nonetheless a genuinely rewarding one."[77] Focusing less on the production's merits and more on her stories, Brown's review cheered Benson—though she was genuinely happy for the play's success. *Junior Miss* ran on Broadway for almost two years before taking to the road for Boston, Baltimore, Chicago, Philadelphia, and Washington, D.C. Royalties from these productions added significant sums to Benson's bank account.

Just two weeks after *Junior Miss* opened, the Japanese attacked Pearl Harbor. However, Sally Benson and Bennett Cerf were privately embroiled in a strife of Cerf's own making. Random House had sent Benson a pre-publication copy of her play, *Junior Miss*, with her name on the dust jacket but Chodorov's and Field's names on the spine. As soon as Benson saw the error, she wrote to Cerf. Her letter speaks for itself—its tone polite and calm—its well-chosen, clear phrasing exuding thinly veiled anger at the injustice done her:

Bennett,

When you sent me the play of *Junior Miss* I only looked at the jacket but did not take the jacket off. On the cover of the book itself, it is *Junior Miss* Chodorov and Fields—both on the front cover and on the side. This is a breach of the agreement they have with me, as you know. Also, in the inside of the book on the page opposite the picture of Judy in her party dress, the names of Chodorov and Fields are in larger type than mine, and as Paul Streger pointed out to you, the copyright is wrong and the agency listing is wrong. Now, I have no idea what you can do about this. As I wrote you, I hope that you have something in writing from Chodorov and Fields. In any event, I never heard of anyone publishing a book without the consent of all the parties concerned. You must have made a contract with Chodorov and Fields, but you have made none with me. I am not complaining about my 5%.

How can you make changes in this book? It is on sale and advertised in the theatre programs here. How can you recall these copies? As for your good faith, I haven't questioned it. I think you have been unbelievably careless, and in a manner which hurts my interests. I am also very much tired of having these things occur between Chodorov, Fields, and myself. You know of the situation existing between us, and of the way my name was left out of the Washington papers when the play opened there. You should know the whole story. I think it is up to my agents, Joseph Tiefenbrun,[78] Chodorov and Fields, their agent, and Random House to come to some sort of satisfactory arrangement. I am very sorry this happened, but Bennett, I am not willing to overlook it. I see no reason why I should.

> As ever,
> Sally Benson[79]

Benson was woman enough to stand up for her rights and to point out the shoddy treatment dealt her so often by men. Previously stung by Pat Covici's mishandling of *Emily*, a now experienced Benson knew what had to be done. She hired the legal counsel necessary to win compensation in the present case and avert future injustice at the hands of Cerf and on the part of Random House.

In December, facing litigation initiated by Benson, Cerf telephoned her but got nowhere. He followed with a letter distinctly different in tone from his previous correspondence:

> Dear Sally:
>
> As I told you over the phone, it was my impression that you knew all about our plans for publishing the play version of *Junior Miss*. I am sure that I don't have to tell you that we wouldn't dream of proceeding with anything in which you were so obviously concerned without your full approval. Any-

how . . . I hope it is now understood that when and if we do publish the play, the royalty of 15% will be divided in three equal parts: 5% to Fields, 5% to Chodorov, and 5% to you. Write me just a line okaying this arrangement and we can all forget about the whole thing.

We won't go ahead with play publication until the threatened lawsuit is resolved in one way or another, since there is obviously no point in involving you or ourselves in a legal tangle in which I don't think we are the least bit concerned at the present moment. I will keep you posted on developments.

Cordially,
Bennett[80]

Much as Benson might have wanted to preserve a cordial relationship with Cerf, she was not going to. She had already run into too many "bastards and shysters" as she termed them in labeling her file folder. Now Cerf would be relegated to the same file, and Sally Benson would turn to a more cheerful project.

Reflecting on the year gone by, Benson knew that she had achieved much despite the difficulties she had faced. She looked forward to completing the Kensington series for *The New Yorker* and subsequently having it published under the title *Meet Me in St. Louis*. That was not all: Metro-Goldwyn-Mayer, in the person of Bill Fadiman, had waited a mere three days after *Junior Miss* opened before announcing "in his own fumbling way" MGM's interest in having Benson work for them:

> May a Junior Mister talk to a Junior Miss? What troubles my usually serene soul is the electric news that you are finishing a book with the intriguing title *Meet Me in St. Louis*. Is there any chance, however miraculous or remote, for me to read the manuscript and see whether it is the knockout movie I am hoping hard it will be?

Fadiman admitted he wasn't sure whether "this is a collection of your latest *New Yorker* stories or a sparkling, full-length novel." Could Benson add to his knowledge in any way, he wondered.[81] Benson's response is unavailable, but Fadiman's proposal was most attractive and she most likely gave it some consideration.

PART III

22

BECOMING A CELEBRITY

1942

"Little by little, I get what I want."

—Sally Benson

As 1942 dawned, Benson continued to garner attention from various media representatives. Joseph S. Batt invited her to be part of a broadcast featuring former St. Louisans who had "reached eminence in one of the arts, theater, screen, radio and Belle Lettres." If she agreed, Benson would be joining the ranks of Betty Grable, Fanny Hurst, and Morris Carnofsky, among others. Representing the Associated Retailers of St. Louis, Batt would be in New York on January 10th to complete plans for the broadcast. He hoped Benson would agree to meet and discuss the matter further. Though pleased with Batt's recognition of her success—and that just a month before Random House announced the publication of her new book, *Meet Me in St. Louis*—Benson decided to decline the invitation for lack of time.

After completing the Kensington series for *The New Yorker*, Benson had agreed to go to Hollywood to work on the *Junior Miss* radio show scheduled to air on March 4th. Benson's family and friends, though excited about her success, bemoaned her absence in advance. Esther, for example, had written on February 20th: "Darling, I want to be funny but I can only think how much we will miss you. Good luck and even more love than I hope you make money. If you know what I mean. Ess." However, on February 20, after a dinner party to celebrate both Ham's twenty-fifth birthday and Sally's *bon voyage*, Ham escorted Benson and Ariane Ross (Hal's wife) to Grand Central, settled them in a compartment aboard "The Chief," and waved them off.[1] Paul Streger, Benson's agent, telegrammed:

"Dear Sally, Ten minutes after you left, New York went into a blackout with no air raid. Love, P. Streger." Later that night, "A Friend" (Harold Ross) wired Benson's train as it headed for Santa Fe: "Only three days more and you will meet Shirley Temple personally. Just think." Benson was clearly loved by family, friends, colleagues, and acquaintances. Not yet forty-five, she had already touched many lives.

In Harold Ross's night letter to Benson he had recommended the Garden of Allah "when the Champs-Elysées palls."[2] He also asked for a part in the film: "Could you work me in for the part of Lon, the brother in the picture, and I could marry Shirley Temple the nut-brown maiden for the big Roman scene? We are having your curtains done and the carpet cleaned."[3] Ross knew that Shirley Temple had been selected to play Judy Graves, a fitting choice given Temple's popularity as a child star. When Bobsie heard that Shirley Temple would be playing the part of Judy, she wrote from Maine, "I am quite pleased and excited about Shirley Temple. If you come home saying she's a sweet little girl, I'll be sore." Bobsie also shared an anecdote she knew would please her mother:

> A soldier I met up here . . . heard me say to a woman who had a dog named Sally, that my mother's name was Sally and later I said that you wrote, and he said, "Oh my God! Not Sally Benson?" and fell writhing to the floor. He is an admirer and his family lives near Ross's family.[4]

Benson would shortly come to regret the choice of Shirley Temple. At this stage though, she was optimistic. In her first letter to Gus Lobrano after settling in at 450 North Sycamore Avenue in Los Angeles, she shares her delight in California's warm, sunny weather and beautiful hills. She was picking sage and enjoying the garden—admiring its "strange plants" and "marvelous" flowers. The "main streets look like Coney Island, but I don't mind that," she wrote. "I like where I live. There is an olive tree in the courtyard" and a place called the Farmer's Market where "you can buy wonderful vegetables, fruit, and honey." As for her project, she went into some detail:

> The radio show looks all right. I had the final say so on the casting, which I think was nice of them. The director is nice, and Ed Wolf has been wonderful to me. I have fifteen scripts all lined

up. I had to go to the Temple's [*sic*], but that was kind of awful. Her playhouse is as big as Radio City. And then Mrs. Temple wanted the coat script changed so it would be for Easter, but I was firm.[5] You have to listen in next Wednesday—WABC—and please write me truthfully how it sounds. If it doesn't sound all right, then I will have time to change it.[6]

The train trip had inspired a new piece: "I've thought of a lovely story about the train which was full of tycoons. You would have died at them, tycooning all over." Her friendship with Lobrano was blossoming, and she promised to tell him upon her return all about "that place where they wanted me to stay. It was a very funny place. I have never seen anything like it." Her penciled afterthought complains, "No books have arrived yet. Give Farrell a poke." A second postscript penciled at the top reads: "Give my love to Maxwell."

As soon as Benson had arrived in Los Angeles she became the subject of Louella Parsons's gossip column in the *Los Angeles Examiner* for February 28th:

> Just talked with Sally Benson who is here to adapt *Meet Me in St. Louis* for MGM. I have known Sally since she was a little girl and she is in Hollywood both on her MGM job and to supervise the writing of *Junior Miss* for Shirley Temple's radio series. Sally tells me that *Meet Me in St. Louis* is all about herself and her sisters, Agnes (who used to be with me on *Morning Telegraph*), Esther (the beauty of the family), and Rose (the older sister). This is Sally's first visit to L.A. and it is one of the pleasantest things in life—to this writer, to know of the great success of her *Junior Miss* on the stage. *Meet Me in St. Louis*, published in five installments in the *New Yorker*, will also be brought out in book form.[7]

The quality of Parsons's reporting—already questionable by virtue of its categorization as a gossip genre—becomes more dubious given its inaccuracy. In fact, nine of the twelve "Kensington" pieces had been published before this Parsons column, and Benson had lived in Los Angeles as early as 1922 while Babe was pursuing his business venture in Outer Mongolia. On March 1st Sally had telegrammed Babe to let him know of her arrival in Los Angeles and to be sure he knew *Junior Miss* would air on March 4th. That very evening, Babe responded with a newsy letter:

> Hi! Your telegram just came. . . . So *Junior Miss* is on for Wednesday! All the New York Sunday papers carried it. Enclosed is *Times* photo; no doubt forty-two of those "Yes, Miss Bensons" have shown it to you already. I was thinking of flying out with it but could only think of four people to say they would come along and work with me, so we had to call it off.
>
> I have been the acme of decorum and am on the wagon— thought that might please you.
>
> Do you remember who wrote *Hide in the Dark*? And do you think it would make a good movie? I always thought so and still do. If you do and I can get the rights, which oughtn't to be too difficult, do you want to go 50-50 in trying to get it sold? I don't remember it too well, but isn't there a good part in it for Bill Powell? Write when you get a chance. I know you are frightfully busy.
>
> PipPip
> Babe[8]

Babe's effort to engage Sally in a film deal seems like a ploy to win her attention. There is no existing evidence that she entertained or took Babe's suggestion seriously.

On the night of March 4th as soon as the program ended, telegrams began to arrive. Babe's read: "Radio *Junior Miss* wonderful script meaning you, Blue Moon, and you're tops. Collaborator superb as always. Miss Shirley super, super. Keep her flying. Just threw out box of Lux. Love, Babe." (In all of his letters to Sally, Babe used unusual pet names and tried to be humorous. In this case, she was "Blue Moon" and he joked about disposing of the soap [Lux] whose manufacturer sponsored the show.) Esther's message was: "*Junior Miss* wonderful. Terribly proud of your writing, dearest. Love, Esther and Harry." Bobsie's telegram arrived the next morning: "Heard *Junior Miss* through static last night. Story wonderful. Temple wonderful. You're wonderful. Bobs."

As for the proud author at the receiving end of these congratulatory sentiments, though alcohol ordinarily fueled celebrations of success in show business, Benson had gained ground in her struggle with addiction. No alcohol flowed because, like Babe, Sally was on the wagon. A proof lies in her response to a courteous gesture on the part of Ross. When she and Ariane Ross were leaving for Los Angeles, Harold Ross had pressed into Benson's hand a hurriedly written, blue-penciled note for his friend Dave Chasen,[9] who owned a popular Hollywood restaurant: "The bearer, Miss Benson, is practically a life-long pal. One bottle of your very best wine for her pls." On the back of the note, in ordinary pencil, Ross wrote:

Dear Dave,

We can't get Miss Benson to take a drink. Therefore, we ask you to also include any and all steaks she wants. This does not cancel the drink—I'm saying this badly—but you understand, Dave. If they change their minds—and you can ask them—they can have a steak as well as a drink on the Rosses.

Thanks a million. H. W. R.

Benson had remained alcohol-free and was both proud of her self-control and grateful for the support of friends like Ariane Ross. Benson's next letter to Lobrano reinforces her new attitude toward alcohol: "I went to Chasen's but I didn't give him the note from Ross because I really didn't want the bottle of wine. Tell Ross the food's good here, and that he's a dandy little cook."

After listening to the *Junior Miss* broadcast on Wednesday, March 4th, Lobrano wrote on Friday, "I fear I have no helpful comments to offer." He continued,

You're doubtless pretty sick of hearing by this time that little Miss Temple is almost spectacularly drab as a radio personality. There were, of course, occasional bright spots that were obviously wholly yours.

I note with enormous pleasure and reassurance that you miss your office and will be glad to get home. Your room is being dusted and aired regularly, and we can have it ready for you at a moment's notice.

Love, Gus [10]

The show cost $12,000 a week to produce and would stay on the airwaves until 1954.

Initially a welcome three-month respite from Benson's Random House litigation, the Hollywood experience would prove to be lonely and vexing. As Benson continued work on adapting *Junior Miss* for radio, she missed her *New Yorker* colleagues and they also missed her. William Shawn inquired in early March, "How are you out there, and how is the Oppenheim lead?[11] The book is aging so probably we ought to run something on it soon. If you decide to drop the idea of the lead, you might send us a blurb? I don't see how you can concentrate on such things in the midst of the glamor."[12] Other business also began to intrude. From England, Laurence Pollinger wrote how pleased he was to learn that Random House would be bringing out "another book by you entitled *Meet Me in St. Louis.*" He asked for a "set of proofs followed by complete copy as soon as possible so [he might] get to work with the book here as quickly as possible."[13] A few days later Benson received a request from Ken McCormick of Doubleday, Doran, and Company for permission to do a booklet that would "run from 4,000 to 6,000 words" on a Christmas motif. Specifically, Ken asked whether she would "be willing to do a Judy story" for the series of booklets, but suggested she might also "angle one of your present *New Yorker* series in that direction" so that Benson could "use it in the *New Yorker* and have it perpetuated in the booklet form . . . [thereby] mak[ing] the effort doubly worthwhile." Though it would not appear for more than eight months, he wanted the manuscript within six weeks.[14]

Benson had Ham answer McCormick to explain that the current *New Yorker* series was scheduled to appear in book form on May 20th. When Ham wrote McCormick, he added that Benson was presently "tied up with a contract with a movie studio" and cannot write anything for publication, but "she suggests that you get in touch with Miss Terry at the *New Yorker*" to learn what might be available. For any non-series piece Benson grants permission, Ham advised, but any series pieces would require permission from Bennett Cerf of Random House. Ham also pointed out that Benson pieces "do not run anywhere near 4000 or 6000 words."[15]

A similar request for a Judy story came from *Harper's Bazaar.* Intended for USO publicity, the publication would offer no pay and the deadline, like McCormick's, was at the end of April. Benson telegrammed Ross asking what he thought, and Lobrano answered for him in a night letter:

We are not clear about the *Harper's* project but with no intention of being unpatriotic or unreasonable would be dismayed at the appearance in *Harper's* of an orthodox short story in an orthodox manner. If some kind of stunt article for special distribution, no argument here. We fear you might be promoted and advocate you use your vigilant, good judgment.

Ross/ Lobrano[16]

Benson telegrammed the next day: "Will do piece on Judy Graves at USO camp. Don't know how they'll use it. Came as charitable appeal. To me. Are you kidding about being promoted? Am practically at end of rope now. This sound ok? Answer collect. Sally"[17] Lobrano replied the same day, "If Judy piece is short story, we hereby offer space in this magazine to USO. Can't see releasing established series idea to *Harper's Bazaar*. Love, Lobrano." Benson answered the following day, "Thanks for good advice. Think you are right. Called deal off with *Harper's*. Will write. Love, Sally."[18]

Meanwhile, "5135 Kensington, March 1904" had captivated Fred Finklehoffe, one of Leland Heyward's hottest writers, who telephoned his friend Arthur Freed: "I have just read a short story that is absolutely fabulous! The writer is a client of Leland's by the name of Sally Benson—it's going to appear in the *New Yorker* magazine." Freed, a songwriter with MGM, read the Kensington piece and became equally enchanted. He telephoned Benson immediately to make "a deal for the property" and bought it at the flat rate of $25,000. Additionally, he negotiated a separate contract for her to work for him in Los Angeles at MGM (Fordin 69). As if juggling the *Junior Miss* negotiations with one hand, Benson simultaneously began preparations with the other to write the screenplay for the film version of *Meet Me in St. Louis*.

Knowing she needed to jog her early memories of St. Louis and the Fair, Benson asked Ham to have her secretary, Miss Terry, forward a photo-book published at the time of the St. Louis Exposition in 1903. Accordingly, Ham wrote to Daise Terry on March 3rd:

She is busy right now writing next week's *Junior Miss* radio script, but she has been to her producer at MGM and he is particularly interested in any book material about the St. Louis World's Fair. On top of the filing cabinet in Sally's office, there is a large green book, *The Forest City*, which is all about the fair with a great many pictures. In the rush of getting away from New York it was forgotten. Please send it so she'll have it before going to MGM on April 1st.

Sally sends her love and will write to you when she gets a chance.

Before closing Ham also asked Daise Terry to send along all the proofs of the Kensington series.[19]

When Daise Terry sent the proofs, she also pressured Benson about Nancy Pearn's request for a feature article. Terry explained that as Benson's train had headed toward the West Coast, her English agent, Nancy Pearn, had cabled Benson's *New Yorker* office inviting her to write a monthly feature of twelve to fifteen hundred words. Its purpose would be to stimulate British-American understanding through descriptions of the war's effects on American domestic life. Pearn cited Benson's "outstanding letter-writing gifts" and enticed her with an offer of "Twenty-five guineas each"—an amount equal to $105.00.[20] Pearn had followed the cable with a letter expressing the strong hope that Benson would accept the offer. Benson agreed to do the letter but she had some reservations about her ability to reflect American domestic life—especially after her California experience. In a letter to Gus Lobrano she explained:

> If I have to write about the war spirit out here with N.T.G., a moth-eaten master of ceremonies[21] who drags the officers out on the floor where they caper about with the chorus girls, and the newspapers that have headlines three inches high, and about the man who is being divorced because he liked to dress up like a maid, and the children's cemetery where nursery rhymes are played and of Utter McKinley's burial advertisement[22] where you can get the works for $68, I don't know what my propaganda will do for England. There is a lovely story in how to be buried here. One cemetery—Forest Lawn—is full of statues, stained glass, organ music, and people go to spend the day there. Most of the places, though, advertise Jewish funerals, so I guess the Christians are put in Potters Fields.

Just a few weeks of Hollywood living had soured Benson's outlook.

To Lobrano, Benson could always vent her negative feelings. In the same letter she complained of having had a "bellyful" of radio. "About eighty people have ideas and nothing happens. But I hope you heard last week's show, because little by little I get what I want. This means fighting for six days and knocking myself out." At first Benson had been

> concerned over the fate of the radio, but the shows are getting better and better. The Temples got mad because Shirley got a bad notice in *Variety* and wanted to leave the show. I wanted her to leave, too, but the sponsors didn't. So they got a writer (who did Shirley's scripts during her Christmas broadcasts) to do scripts. He was to help Doris put more of Shirley into the show and less of the rest of the cast. He is *not* doing scripts though.[23]

Benson had become possessive of her "Graves family." When the temporary writer did not understand the humor in a long segment of dialogue Benson had written for Judy and Hilda, the maid, Benson told him "it was just like Mark Twain." Changing the subject, she exclaimed, "So wait until you see Judy Garland as Rose!" (Actually, Garland was cast as Esther.)

Lobrano's letter in reply informed Benson that Ross had been to Quebec and found the "whole experience pretty profitless." It had taken a busy and ailing Harold Ross several weeks to share his news with Benson, but he finally wrote on March 11th a lengthy and frank letter. He'd been trying—"damn it"—to get a letter to her for weeks, but "beset by so many things," he not only lacked time, but he also hadn't "been in a mood to say a pleasant word to anybody in the world." Ross described his health problems, the futility of his two-week hospital stay, a "rigorous period of straight living," and now, despite all, a doctor's decision that an operation was necessary. He was in a mood to have it done so he could "take a drink and be like other men." This information is confidential, he told Benson, not even to be shared with Ariane, lest her reunion with her sisters be spoiled. Most of their husbands were going off to war.

Ross continues with a detailed account of his health issues followed by a compliment:

> The operation wouldn't be much, evidently, and what the hell? Everybody is a sissy about them, I guess. And another thing is

positive: I haven't got anything malignant, including leprosy.
And another thing is positive: I'm so damned old that they won't
get me into the trenches this time and I probably have much
to be thankful for, although the Benson bank is getting down
to almost nothing, one story of yours having been used in the
back of the book last week, and causing considerable comment
by its merit, I will add.

He explains that Ariane is mad because he won't telephone long-distance
and confides:

> I was doing it to discipline her and to save $18 which I needed
> and no joke. By God, women have got to realize that there is a
> war on, and taxes. I didn't wholeheartedly approve of her going
> out there and spending several hundred dollars . . . although she
> had it coming after nursing me through the last several months
> of ulcers. I guess I've been a bastard and am a little of a bastard
> still. I'm willing to concede outright that I am a crank. . . .
>
> The war situation worries me—generally and in the office.
> McAllister, our art idea man, is gone. He went over to Gov-
> ernor's Island with Maxwell. Maxwell came back later in the
> day, rejected, but McA. went on and hasn't been heard from
> since. . . . I don't know how many more will go . . . in my
> mood I don't want to be bothered with anything, especially as
> most of the people in the office are cross and treat me bad. I'm
> not cheered by the prospect of sitting through several years with
> Mrs. White, Miss Terry, and a few other women, children and
> old men, but it is the lot of the age, I guess. . . . Tell Ham I
> have had several conquests at gin lately, the most . . . $123.40
> of pure Hollywood dough. . . . They say you'll be back in three
> or four weeks . . . I hope to God that it is true . . . I read
> about you in *Variety* and other publications from time to time
> and think how I used to know you and am proud.

Ross also includes advice and a critique of Shirley Temple:

> Whatever you do, don't enroll for any long periods out there.
> They'll think you're trash if you do. I listened twice to Miss

Temple etc. and formed a very unfavorable impression. . . . The weakness seemed to me to lie with Miss Temple. I don't know how she's worked out since, for I haven't listened . . . Some *World-Telegram* writer had a piece about mystery writers and mystery reviewers and said they were all second string people. He didn't mention you by name or anything, and I guess, had newspapers in mind.

Before closing, Ross asks that Benson give regards to "Ham and to my wife if you see her. . . . With the old admiration, Ross."[24] It is not clear when Ham arrived in Los Angeles or how long he stayed.

Concerned about Ross's health, Benson immediately responded. Despite its length, her letter merits inclusion in its entirety for two reasons: it sheds light on her friendship with both Ross and his wife, Ariane, and it provides glimpses of self-revelation:

Dear Ross,

I think if you go on dieting and messing around the way you have to now, you will go nuts. How good is your doctor? [an echo of Anna Cora's attitude when Benson was hospitalized in 1932 for appendicitis]. I mean, can the old fool *do* an operation or is he some old doddard? If I had an ulcer, I think I would just have it chopped up, because I hate to drag around, so I imagine you will decide to. I won't tell Ariane.

Last night we went out with Ham and Barron Polan who is with the Heyward Agency, and who is nice enough. We went out to the Players and there was Louella Parsons, tight as a mink, and when I would get up to dance, she kept on blowing kisses in the direction of the chair I had been sitting in, still thinking I was in it. Then, Ann Honeycutt came over. It seems she got a sudden urge to come out, but she, too, was vague. I like Ann, though. She was with Dorothy Parker, Alan Campbell and the Perelmans. We did not go over and speak to them. I don't know Dorothy Parker. Benchley was there too. After that we went to hear a colored girl sing. We had a nice time and Ariane looked pretty. Tuesday we are going to a fortune teller. Keep your shirt on.

Next she gives an account of her progress. Note how the letter reveals Benson's commitment to hard work and her disregard for slackers who do not match her standards as well as how proprietary she is about her writing:

> I have almost finished my *treatment* of the Kensington stories. That's what they call it. I have done a whole novel really. A treatment is supposed to run forty pages and it takes these underworld characters out here two months to do one. Mine will be about 180 pages, and I will have it done the end of next week. Then it goes to the script writers who did *Little Women*. One of them, Sara Mason, is nice. Deaf too.
>
>   The scripts Doris [Gilbert] and I did on *Junior Miss* were all right, but they were not all right by the time eight people had changed them around and put in a plot. I don't listen to them any more myself. Mrs. Temple is a horror. It was nice when I had to come here as I couldn't work on any of them. You will be glad to hear that I haven't signed any contracts with Metro yet. They are nervous about it. I have done all the work on the stories, and they don't own them. The main point was that I couldn't tell them about my mysteries, simply because I didn't want to. It is none of their business. They have thousands of readers, and why should I let them have things that were written for you? You were a big fool to tell Bill Fadiman you didn't care. I cared. These people are too cheeky. Anyhow, now I don't have to turn them over here, and I am now bickering because they have an idea they want me to stay over six weeks, and I won't. I want to come home.[25]

Considering how many times Benson had moved during adolescence—from St. Louis to New York to Texas and back to New York—one readily understands why home had become so important. Yet, the sense of home she projects is centered in her circle of *New Yorker* editors—friends and colleagues whom she invested with ties of loyalty and affection normally reserved for family members. Most of all she felt she owed special loyalty to Harold Ross. As daughter Barbara Benson Golseth explained, the *New Yorker* staff were like family to her. They really took care of her during her marital difficulties, financial straits, and emotional rebounds from her "quiet little affairs."[26]

23

THE WAR ESCALATES
AT HOME AND ABROAD

1942

"If I had written a book with characters like these, it would not have been accepted by any magazine or publisher in the country. I feel these radio shows are doing me a great deal of harm."

—Sally Benson

Determined to make up for his previous oversight with Benson's *Junior Miss* play, Bennett Cerf asked Benson to send pictures on April 9th, well before the scheduled publication date. When he received the three photos Sally sent him—along with the bill—he wrote with sarcasm: "We didn't have in mind a painting by Leonardo da Vinci. Is this a gag, or was the bill sent to me in error, or what?" A retaliatory Benson had charged expensive photos in revenge. Cerf continued, "I will hold the pictures here locked in the safe along with our bars of radium and autographs of Harold Ross. One of the pictures sure is beautiful and we'd like to use it, if we could get permission, for the usual fifteen or twenty bucks. I await word from you with breathless interest. As ever, Bennett Cerf."[1]

Feeding Benson's discontent were some annoying financial issues and artistic concerns that she had to straighten out with Ed Wolf. First, Benson sent Kirby Hawkes, her agent, a list of thirteen detailed objections to one *Junior Miss* radio script. Some examples are listed to illustrate how carefully Benson attended to details of speech, dress, and gesture in developing her characters' upper-class status. Benson wrote:

I have read the Paragon script through very carefully, and no matter what you think about the construction, I think this is a cheap story for the following reasons:

1. Why is Judy looking for a taffeta dress in the first place, and why does Mrs. Graves gayly contribute her own wedding dress for Mrs. Bates to cut up into little pieces?

2. People go to sleep at night, they don't retire.

3. Why isn't the quarrel with Fuffy planted where it would make some sense?

4. Why does Judy have to talk to herself all the time? She is not Maurice Evans.

5. How in the name of God can a little girl move the furniture from an entire living room, and pack it into a small maid's room? Is she a professional mover, or do the Graves family have nothing but end tables? . . . Do the Graves buy their furniture on the installment plan? Do they have a living room *suite*? You mean the sofa and two chairs that match. CHRIST! . . . .

Mrs. Graves's social manner slays me. She has all the artful simplicity of Bella Gross.

10. Is it funny to sneeze?

. . .

13. Do you think for one minute Mr. Bates would turn on Mrs. Bates and try to slap her?

Other items Benson objected to were the use of expressions like "Mr. Smarty Face" and "My dressing table is positively nude." Summing up, Benson complained, "The whole thing is "heavy-handed and unbelievable." In particular, she could not understand why "Mr. Kronman didn't use a single line of dialogue from either the script or the book. Is this what he calls cooperative? These people are not the Graves family. This little girl is not Judy." Obviously angered, Benson advised with controlled sarcasm:

> Take Kronman's script and sleep over it, or on it, or with it. Boil down its plot, consider its motivation, read the dialogue, and tell me what you've got. When you put this script on the air, don't put my name with it. I would rather fall on bad construction than on bad writing. And I object to Mr. Hurdle telling me he had to cut dialogue from my script that was "offensive." There is no dialogue in my book that is "offensive," and I have used the words "lousy" and "stinker."

Regarding her financial concerns, Benson wrote Ed Wolf [2] to explain that Paul Streger, her agent at Leland Hayward, reported that their lawyer, [Mr.] Tiefenbrun, had instructed Ed to withhold $150 due her for script work from the April 8th broadcast payment, though the $600 she received was marked "Paid in Full." She had to remind Ed,

> My agreement with you states that I only have to supply ideas, if I think of them and edit scripts. It does not specify that I have to do any writing. Now, the April 8th script was done by Doris and myself, and the whole idea was worked out with Kirby Hawkes present. This was done before I started work at Metro, before you left Hollywood.
>
> The ideas since then have been based on ideas suggested to Kirby Hawkes by me, and these ideas were in the hands of my agents many weeks ago. I receive the scripts every week, make my comments on them, turn them over to Heyward, and they are then sent back to the agency with my comments. There is nothing in my Metro contract to prevent my doing this. I think you had better read the agreement you had with me again.
>
> I was brought out to the Coast by you, and worked here on *Junior Miss* from the day after I landed until the day I went to work here. I still have supervision of the scripts. Whether or not Benton and Bowles pay any attention to my suggestions is their business. It does not affect my deal with you. Tiefenbrun has never received any instructions from me about withholding

any checks. Also, my checks are due every Saturday—that being ten days after the broadcast, and I am not receiving them on time. Will you please see that I do?

After spelling out her dissatisfaction regarding payment, Benson turned to the issue really troubling her—her perception that *Junior Miss* was being distorted beyond recognition. Her description of the problem is poignant:

> I feel that you have taken *Junior Miss* which is a valuable prop-
> erty to me, and have mishandled it disgracefully. As it stands
> it is not *Junior Miss*. It might be any show. You brought me
> all the way to the coast, and I have extra rent to pay for over
> a month, extra expenses, simply to be pushed aside. I do not
> understand your attitude in any way.
>
> When I talked with Mr. Rogers, he asked me particularly
> to see that the characters of the book, the tenderness and quiet
> action of the book were kept intact. This I tried to do. I even
> worked on this show, which I did not have to do, in an effort
> to get what I wanted and what I thought was wanted. I hope
> you have not forgotten that the scripts Doris and I did in New
> York were approved by you, Benton and Bowles, and Proctor
> and Gamble.
>
> You have taken a property which could have gone on for
> years and changed it into a third-rate show, which had no char-
> acterization whatsoever, and no warmth. You did not help either
> Doris or me. We had to fight for a stenographer which Benton
> and Bowles paid for. We were told that Shirley Temple's part
> was not built up enough; and now the scripts are running with
> practically no dialogue for Shirley.
>
> I have never been treated so unethically. You even made a
> plea to me to take a $50 cut when I had worked like a dog on
> the show. This, when you were paying your star $300 a week.
> I refuse to take any cut as long as this show is on the air. And
> my agents will act for me. If you would like the remainder of
> the money due you, you may have it in the next mail.
>
> In the meantime, I expect my full payment paid on time
> every week. It is small compensation for the material I had

which has turned out to be something that has been twisted almost beyond recognition.

I hope you will answer this letter.

Sincerely,
Sally Benson[3]

Though Benson's complaint was legitimate, she had not defined the terms of her original contract clearly and her attachment to *Junior Miss* seems amusing because of her letter's emotion-laden diction. Yet, whatever her authorial interest in Judy, Benson's eye was also on the bottom line. She valued her work and had grown savvy regarding her right to protect her artistic vision and to receive just compensation.

Benson was also miffed at the slow pace of her fellow script writers. She complained to Ross in a long letter on March 17th:

> The writers here would send you crazy. They are as pale as ghosts, and we all sit at a special table at lunch. Doris and I come to the table singing over our work and none of them like us. Richard Connell is here, and a lot of people I never heard of. There is one woman named Mary McCall *Junior!* This is God's truth. You will also be glad to hear that Bennett brought out the play *Junior Miss* without any permission from me which makes it arson. It also makes chopped meat out of Chodorov and Fields because by doing this, they have broken their contract with me. I have written the Hayward office to gouge their eyes out, the crooks.

She repeats, "I am very homesick" and adds: "I see a lot of funny people. This is a terrible place and will soon blow away, I think. Evereybody [*sic*] makes a lot of money, but no one works very hard." Once again, she expresses appreciation for hard work and deprecates those who, by her standards, are deficient.

In Gus Lobrano's next letter to Benson he reported the army's acceptance of McAllister and rejection of Maxwell. His short note mentions Ross's new x-ray, McKelway's office renovations, and the emptiness of Benson's office. He notes the warm weather (65 degrees) and asks: "When *are* you coming home?"[4]

During the next two weeks Benson continued working on *Junior Miss*. Finally, on March 30, 1942, having resolved some of her differences with Random House and after receiving a letter from Leland Heyward, her agents, Benson signed the movie release on her Kensington series. Coincidentally, Cerf wrote the same day:

Dear Sally,

I had hoped for a letter from you before this telling me what is happening to our Little Nell among the fleshpots of Hollywood. If you can find time to send me a line, I'd love to hear something of your adventures and impression.

    I thought the last three stories in MEET ME IN ST. LOUIS were the best in the whole collection. They end the book with a terrific bang. I am having several sets of extra galleys made up and will do our darndest [*sic*] to intrigue one of the book clubs again, although I am sure I don't have to tell you what the odds are against lightning striking twice. The bookstores are showing tremendous interest in the new title and there isn't the slightest doubt in my mind that the book will be a big seller from the start. I thought you might just want to hear a little bit about the book business in the midst of your radio and motion picture conferences!

As ever, Bennett[5]

Two days later—as scheduled—Benson met with an MGM producer on Thursday, April 2nd to discuss the St. Louis World's Fair. As soon as she returned to her bungalow that evening, she telegrammed Daise Terry requesting all the diaries from her desk at *The New Yorker*.[6]

A week later Benson wrote to Lobrano and seemed pleased:

I am almost through with my *treatment*. It is good, too, and Mr. Freed and Mr. Cukor like it, and don't want a word changed. Now it goes to the script writers, but they are very good ones. They did *Little Women*. . . . I work hard because I want to get through. I am sick of it here, although Metro is probably the best place to work. The office is nice and so are the people I have to see. They are impressed with the amount of work I have done, and that makes me feel good. Track fast! There isn't a track open here. You knew that. The roses are all out, though, if you care for still life. Tonight I am cooking dinner for Doris and a man named Noel Langley, and tomorrow I am eating with the McKennas. He's the story editor. I think it is a move to break me down into signing my contracts. I am glad no one is in my office. Robey goes there once in a while. I have a lot to tell her. Get her to show you the present I sent her.

Love from, Sally

I get more homesick every day and the people I see are the damndest.

Benson had no idea that the complications she had faced thus far were only the tip of the iceberg.

Since Freed felt it was difficult to adapt autobiographical material for stage or screen, he wanted Benson to collaborate with experts. His choices were script writers Howard Lindsay and Russell Crouse, who had worked on *Life with Father*—a film based on an earlier *New Yorker* series. Crouse, however, had to decline because of a prior commitment: "I know Sally's stories and like them," he said. "In fact, they are probably a little more interesting to me than to most people because I knew the family, including Agnes, whom they largely concern."[7] To her dismay, by June 9th Benson found herself "eased out of any further work on the treatment." She had been replaced by Sarah Mason and Victor Heerman, but the dialogue script produced by this new team proved equally unacceptable to Freed. He then approached George Cukor and William Ludwig but the former had been inducted into the army. Freed next offered Oscar Hammerstein a two-year contract but he declined. Circumstances seemed to dictate that Freed put the project on hold (Fordin 78–79). However, though Benson's plotless novel seemed an unlikely candidate for a film, Freed would not give up.

Enamored by the Smith family and the theme of "no place like home," Freed contracted with Judy Garland to play Esther Smith and then tackled the task of bringing Louis B. Mayer on board. Since Mayer never read scripts, Freed counted on Lillie Messenger, a "soft-spoken, knowledgeable, lady" with "intimate knowledge of Mayer's tastes," to capture his interest and sell him on the project. Predictably, Messenger succeeded—to the dismay of most of the staff—who were unimpressed with "this dull family moving to New York." Messenger's enthusiasm convinced Mayer: "I think the story is very exciting, there's a lot of action . . . those girls who have to leave their home and their sweethearts . . . it nearly broke my heart!" With Mayer's approval, Freed summoned Fred Finklehoffe to write the script and agreed to have Irving Brecher work with him.

To take on the task of creating a screenplay for *Meet Me in St. Louis* both men had to renege on their prior agreement to produce *Anchors Aweigh* (Fordin 93). As soon as that was done, they studied all the previous scripts, including Benson's treatment. They decided to start anew. Like Freed, they had fallen in love with the characters and wanted the film to succeed. Just six weeks later they submitted their screenplay. When he read the Finklehoff/Brecher script, Freed realized that the "simplicity, warmth, and sincerity" of the Smiths and the "emotional impact of daily life, with its laughter and sorrow" could only be brought out by music. He told Mayer, "I'll make a plot with song, and dance, and music. That's the way my characters will come to life" (Fordin 93).

At this point, as the movie was about to become a musical, Benson's characters had been appropriated by Freed, but, unlike her outraged response to the radio script writers' mishandling of the Graves family in *Junior Miss*, in this instance Benson refrained from interfering because she trusted that Freed's adaptation would be authentic. Being practical, she also anticipated a good financial outcome.

As her days on the West Coast continued, Benson began to love "the way everything [in California] looks," and she was happy to be getting "wonderful letters" from her nephew "about how my field is flooded, with maps to show me where." Tony also reported the "last two *Junior Misses* were good."[8] The one aspect of Hollywood that Benson consistently disliked, however, was the caliber of the people she met socially. Never one to mince words, especially when writing to Lobrano, Benson described her reaction to Los Angeles:

> The people really stink. I don't like any of them. I went to tea at Dame May Whitty's. She is called "Dame May" like "Princess, honey." You know, have a muffin, Dame May. It sounds sort of off-color. Every single night someone has to talk about

something. No one talks during the day, and I get home feeling ragged, and am glad to see the mysteries . . .

Dame May drew Benson's satiric ire for taking on airs. Whitty, daughter of a Liverpool journalist, had become famous on the London stage in 1882 and been recognized by the title "Dame Commander of the British Empire" for performing for the troops during World War I. She had retired to Hollywood where money could be made for easy work. Assigned upper-class roles for elegant women, Whitty assumed an imperious air on and off the set. Then starring in *Mrs. Miniver,* a film in production at MGM, she was active in Hollywood social circles despite her advanced age. Little did Whitty suspect while hosting her teas, that one of her guests—Sally Benson—was repelled by her snobbery and would punish Whitty by recreating her in "V Is for a Lot of Things."[9] Incidentally, *Mrs. Miniver* became the top-grossing film of 1942 and an important propaganda piece. An adaptation of Jan Struther's novel, *Mrs. Miniver* succeeded in swaying American isolationist feeling into pro-war sentiments. Its depiction of families in London having to send their school-age children to outlying, rural areas evoked American sympathy powerfully.

In June, Benson was moved to write again to Wolf regarding the radio scripts about to be broadcast. This time her complaints were even more specific and reflected her concern for realistic detail, especially as it related to class-appropriate diction and lifestyle:

> I find these scripts so badly done . . . I can't believe that anyone could write them. No one says tuxedo, certainly not in the Graves family. And is Mr. Graves the sort of bore who won't listen to a violinist on general principles? Is he down on the farm or does he live in New York and go to the Metropolitan once in a while? Does he say shindig? Why do the script writers play up this Mouse-Meat gag every script? I should think Mr. Graves would wear a dinner jacket often, men do, you know. And going formal is just plain New York University fancy talk. No one says going formal but a lot of half-breeds from the Bronx.[10]
>
> These plots are incredibly bad. It seems to me that the show is being deliberately ruined week by week. I can't believe that two script-writers at the money you are paying them could

be so bad. This script, like the scripts Mr. Kronman has had a hand in, are simply not *Junior Miss*. They bear not the faintest resemblance to the characters in my book. If I had written a book with characters like these, it would not have been accepted by any magazine or publisher in the country. I feel these radio shows are doing me a great deal of harm. I still can't believe, Ed, that you can allow this distortion of my ideas to go on.

These letters reveal the tenacity with which Benson pursued her artistic principles. They also underscore what critics have praised—her attention to detail and her powers of observation. Though free-spirited in lying about the facts of her life at times, Benson zealously defended artistic truth in writing. Or did she?

Complicating the story is another view of Benson and her art found in a letter from Robey Lyle, Benson's good friend and *New Yorker* colleague. Lyle wrote to complain about her dismal social life with Arthur Windsor and all his friends "at the loveliest possible dinner parties" where they proved themselves to be "colossal and crashing bores." The most recent was a dinner for eight at the Persian Room after which "we were taken to see *Junior Miss*." The following week, Windsor intended to do the same— another party with *other* California people, to be followed by a performance of *Junior Miss*. "So, you see, the play is becoming practically a career with me," Lyle reported. Then, she observed, "The first act has been gagged up so you'd never know the place, but what do you care. I never have forgotten how you felt about it from the beginning, so I know that whatever they do to it will not distress you." Had Benson been lying about "how she felt from the beginning"? Lyle might have been referring to Benson's statement that she had tired of Judy after the second *New Yorker* piece. Or, had Benson disowned the Chodorov and Fields version of Judy? In any case, Benson's letters to Wolf and Hawkes strike a note of sincerity, if only because the anger expressed is genuine.

Lyle's letter is of interest for another reason. It highlights Benson as seen through the eyes of her best friend. Even before Benson set out for California, Lyle had described for her the two "utterly different worlds" she would find—"all those places [that] were the bunk" as opposed to "something *you* wanted. . . . I am sure you will find Hollywood itself with all its straggling loose ends more interesting than the suburban orderliness of Beverly Hills." Lyle envied Benson the "mimosa and wonderful walks and drives and bumming about" that California would provide. Knowing her friend, Lyle added: "I don't envy you at all the amount of work you are going to do while you are there, but I do know darn well that you will get everything there is to be got out of the people and the place and your work." After expressing delight with the Victorian figurine Benson had sent her, Lyle told her friend how pleased she was that Benson's "crack to Parsons about going home to cook dinner and money not being everything was literal fact and not a mere crack." It pleased Lyle "because it said pretty darned plainly that Sally hadn't changed. So [Lyle was] sitting here on [her] backside cheering." Lyle enclosed the Louella Parsons clipping that would have "opened up a lot of elaborate speculations" for her had not Benson's crack made clear that the Parsons' statements were false.

Lyle also had been following the *Junior Miss* radio broadcasts and offered a critique:

> Timing seems to be off and your most characteristic lines do not seem to be given value. They register, but not as they should and as they do in print. This is due to insufficient rehearsal or incompetent playing or something, but it is obvious that you have had your hands full. Nevertheless, I honestly believe this program can shape into the most civilized of the family programs if *everybody* will work at it.

Lyle's last comment raises the distinct possibility that Benson was motivated by more than financial or artistic concerns in trying to preserve the character of her original *Junior Miss*. She may well have viewed the radio *Junior Miss* as a means of raising the level of family radio programming as well—a subject for further study.

Lyle had heard from Barbara several times and forwarded Benson's address since Sally had apparently neglected to send it. In one letter Lyle speaks of missing Sally and their usual activities—"doing the races, eating a banana on Third Avenue, or just window shopping." Lyle continues,

> You are in a divine spot at the perfect time of the year and as for battles with dopes I know who will win. As we hoss people say, you've got plenty of heart and will stay the course. And God help those guys who think they can ride you into the rail. Darling, I want you to have *all* the fun and *all* the perfect

Figure 12. Barbara Benson and Sally Benson, circa 1940

weather and thrills that California and the Pacific are capable of giving you—and I don't mean movies nor yet radio. . . . I'm glad you're getting hats you love. Do every damned thing you want. It's good for you like anything.[11]

Throughout her months in Los Angeles, Benson continued to write occasional pieces for *The New Yorker*. Some were published close to submission; others remained in the "Benson bank" for as long as a year. For this reason, it is difficult to identify the piece Ross referred to in this affirmative note:

Miss Benson:

Wow! As Lobrano remarked, the new piece will completely confound those who had been complaining because you have been

on lavender and lace so long. I wish to say I think you are one
of the greatest dialogue writers of all time. It was thrilling to
read this. The arrival of your piece nerved me up and encouraged me generally as nothing has in several weeks. I am happy,
thankful, and proud.

H.W. Ross[12]

Since Benson's correspondence with her editors frequently contained no
mention of her submissions by title, one must rely on other clues to identify specific stories. In the latter case, they are slight. "Going Home" is a
strong possibility since it is not a "lavender and lace" piece. Rather, Benson
incorporated her own experience in returning to New York from California
by creating "Evelyn," an African American maid traveling to visit her Atlanta
home for Christmas. More importantly, Benson dramatized her sensitivity
to racial prejudice. Benson draws a fine contrast between Evelyn and her
upper-class employers, the Careys, in terms of their living spaces, their dress,
and their speech—employing black dialect for Evelyn. The greater contrast,
though, is the one Evelyn realizes as she tries to buy dinner at a restaurant
in Washington's Union Station while awaiting her connecting train: her life
in Atlanta will consist of the same segregation and racism she encountered
in D.C. Though longing to be reunited with her family, Evelyn instantly
decides that being treated with equality in New York is more important. She
had become a "Northern nigger" and New York had become "home." For
Benson, the experience of being in Hollywood was the obverse of Evelyn's.
While in California, Benson had enjoyed a position of power and privilege
and attained a small fortune through her work, but her sense of separation from family and *New Yorker* colleagues was such that, like Evelyn, she
had to go "home." Though the year is 1942—two decades before the civil
rights movement—Benson's piece is a harbinger of an emerging civil rights
consciousness—especially given its placement in *The New Yorker*.

On a more personal level, Benson had a warm relationship with her
maid, Alliene Valentine, who wrote from her Harlem apartment at 409
Edgecombe Avenue:

My dear Mrs. Benson:

I hope you had a pleasant trip out. I followed you in my mind
every bit of the way. . . . We have been right on hand for both

of the broadcasts of *Junior Miss*, and have really enjoyed them. I really got a kick out of the last one, the Southern drawl and all.

Everything at 161 [East 46th] is alright [*sic*], I've been down at least three times each week. And just between us, I've begun making ready for your return. Please tell Mr. Binkerd that I didn't know that we had left his evening shoes out until he had reached his destination. I hope he did not curse me too loudly . . . I felt terrible about it. Please give my best regards to Mr. Binkerd. Take good care of yourself. Dezelle [her husband (a detective)] sends his best. . . .

My very sincere best wishes.
As ever, Alliene[13]

As the time for Sally's return drew closer, Alliene reported:

I went right down to Mr. Benson's. He did not answer. I had written a sealed note to leave in such an event. Maybe he will let me come in and help in some way. . . . You have quite a few letters from China Relief, Russian War Relief, etc. Gee! But I'll be glad when you folk come back to New York. . . . I dreamed not long ago that I was talking with you and during the conversation you mentioned Mr. Benson. So Mr. Binkerd's letter suggesting that I go by Mr. Benson's was my dream.[14]

Alliene repeatedly inquired about Anna Cora in her letters to Sally. Showing how well she knew Sally, Alliene offered advice: "Be real sweet (Ha, Ha) but don't let anybody infringe on your sweetness. . . . You know I send lots of love." Alliene took care of planting Benson's yard with morning glories in readiness for her return. She clearly loved and appreciated Sally Benson as a person and not merely as her employer. Undoubtedly, Benson had her in mind when she wrote "Going Home."

Another candidate for Ross's high praise was Benson's "V Is for a Lot of Things," a piece that appeared in *The New Yorker* a year later. A combination of Benson's responses to meeting Dame Whitty and reading Bird Binkerd's and her nephew Tony's letters describing his and Anna Cora's gardening efforts,[15] this Benson story acknowledges that while the country was at war abroad, class skirmishes continued on a smaller scale at home.

Though busy with her work and seemingly removed from the war, Benson had responded personally to the war effort by donations to the Spitfire Fund in Britain prior to America's engaging in the conflict. Now, she reflected the war's impact on American life through a description of a "Victory" garden (as small plots for homegrown vegetables were known during the war). Benson's piece begins with Mrs. Buell, a suburban Connecticut housewife ordering from Sears Roebuck a special denim suit—jacket, trousers, and denim cap—merely to wear while planting cabbages in her garden.[16]

The winter had been harsh, and Buell was determined to can her own vegetables and save "our points" for things that we "can't grow ourselves, like butter."[17] Conflict enters the story when Buell realizes she has lost her gardener, Andrew Sini—a Sicilian who had worked for her for ten years—to a neighbor who paid him ten cents more an hour. The preceding Christmas when Buell delivered wrapped presents for his eight children, she was shocked to discover that Sini had never applied for citizenship. A study in class ensues with Buell pestering Sini about getting his papers and Sini, ignoring her efforts, pronouncing her garden, "no good." Benson mocks the snobbery of Buell types. Dressed in her newly purchased garden clothes and focused on aesthetics—in this case, a symbolic, cornflower letter V in red, white, and blue—Buell fails to notice the sickly character of the produce, a symbol of what she is unable to create. Buell has missed the point of the garden entirely: authentic citizens focus on the vitality of the garden. With or without papers, they respond like Sini—"I fix"—and plunge into work. Like Anna Cora tending her garden in Madison, a diminutive figure dressed in black, Sini stoops over the cabbages, allowing his hands to "move quickly among the plants," transplanting them out of the Buell-imposed V letter pattern, watering them back to life—as immigrant labor then and now enriches America's food production. Buell's heart softens under her special denim jacket as she reframes her assessment of Sini. Now a *"good man,"* Sini has achieved victory, as Benson's piece neatly skewers the sterility of Buell's social pretentiousness and her ridiculous symbol of patriotism.[18] The saying—"V Is for Victory"—now has a double meaning.

While Benson pieces like "V Is for a Lot of Things" reflected the wartime background, the content of both *Junior Miss* and the forthcoming *Meet Me in St. Louis* was as far removed from the subject of war as possible. A relief from war's threatening reality, these Benson collections and their translations into radio and film ironically owed some of their success to the nation's need for temporary escape from the war's grim reality.

As the weeks passed Anna Cora and the family increasingly missed Sally and their sadness intensified at Easter. A telegram from Rose reported, "The family are having Easter dinner with us. We shall miss you sadly. The golden egg, chocolate marshmallows and jelly beans to you. Love, Rose." Esther also sent one thanking Sally: "Your flowers a staggering surprise. Easter love, darling. Miss you." And Robey Lyle's stated: "Happy Easter bunny angel. Your flowers are sweet like you. Love and trimmings." In May, close to Benson's expected return, Anna Cora wrote: "Dearest Sally and Ham, Thank you for your letters. They mean everything to me. Now that your homecoming is in the offing, I have been thinking of the best way to arrange our living comforts—better say our sleeping problem." Benson's mother offered several options—a neighbor "about a quarter of a mile above us towards 'The Circle' keeps summer boarders" for four dollars a room for a week. "It might solve your sleeping problem." But, she offered, "I shall be very glad to give my room to Bobsie or Ham. This is just a suggestion. You may have other plans." Tony was trying harder at school, she reported, and it was wonderful to have Bobsie with them. "She is a very busy girl what with helping Rose . . . doing air warden duty—motor corps work, etc. She is a true soldier's wife. Darling, it will be wonderful having you home again. I'm counting the hours." Anna Cora was also happy that Sally "loved [her] working surroundings" and had sent snapshots of her "delightful bungalow," but the "Tabor Street one got me down"—a reference to one of the addresses where Benson's father once lived.

While her family eagerly awaited Benson's return to the East Coast, the business and publishing worlds anticipated her presence at book signings and other public appearances. In late March, for example, Doubleday & Doran's St. Louis representative, Robert Sachs, inquired whether Benson would be in St. Louis when the book came out as they wanted to arrange "an autographing party" for her.[19] On April 7th, Benson replied: "I expect to be through at Metro-Goldwyn-Mayer not later than May 10th and leave here before the 15th. As the book does not come out until the 20th of May, it seems improbable that I will be in St. Louis at that time. . . . I will let you know definitely before I leave here. Very truly yours, Sally Benson." Sachs received the galleys from Random House on April 9th, "enjoyed them greatly," and informed Benson that Doubleday already had seventy advance orders. Sachs had even telephoned the current occupant of Benson's former Kensington home to inquire about getting a photograph of the house. The new owner agreed but warned, "the neighborhood *has* degenerated."[20]

Benson did leave Los Angeles by May 15th (as her riding teacher there, Ernest Vogt, learned with disappointment) but could not attend the book signing in Missouri because "an unexpected difficulty in manufacturing . . . [had] delayed the completion of the printing and binding" and moved the publication date to June 2nd. Instead, Benson returned directly to New York where her days were filled with professional activity and catching up on correspondence. Among her top priorities was sending her nephew, Toby Wherry (Esther's son), tickets to a Boston performance of *Junior Miss*.

As Benson checked her mail, she found several positive pieces. One was a flattering invitation from Professor John H. H. Lyon of Columbia University to speak to his writing class. She accepted and in his thank-you note, Lyon promised: "You will have a good time; everything is going to be most informal." He would put Benson on his calendar for January 6th but contact her again in September to confirm the date.[21] A second letter from Martha Foley, the new editor of *The Best Short Stories*, requested permission to reprint Benson's "5135 Kensington, August 1903" in the Edward O'Brien memorial anthology. Foley offered an honorarium of $20 and wanted information for a biographical note.[22] Sally had Daise Terry reply: "Miss Benson has just returned from the West Coast and . . . grants permission. Get any biographical material from Random House."[23] A third letter delighted Benson—a thank-you note from her nephew Toby:

Darling Sally,

I was very surprised yesterday to find someone who didn't like your play. When I asked why, he said it was because the book was so much better. I liked your "Brownie" Kensington story very much and loved "Best Foot Forward."[24] You were sweet to get such good seats and two of them at that. . . . I go back to Exeter the fifth and hope . . . to see you before then. I am telling everyone I meet that I am really "Junior Miss" and that you've just translated me into your own sex because you thought you could write better there. . . . Please come back in time to see me, and thank you again for the wonderful evening.

Love, Toby[25]

Benson was understandably touched and pleased.

From New York, on May 23rd, 1942, the day her last Kensington piece appeared in *The New Yorker*, Benson took part by telephone in another on-air discussion for Northwestern University. Critic John T. Fredrick conducted the interview. Since the book's delayed publication prevented his acquiring *Meet Me in St. Louis*, he had read only some of the pieces in *The New Yorker*, and after stating these circumstances, Frederick made a few points before raising questions. He liked Benson's work particularly because it possessed one of the rarest qualities in literature—"real, sound humor." By Frederick's definition, this humor was "an appreciative, joyous recognition of the comic elements in people and life—free from malice, free from meanness." In Frederick's opinion, *Meet Me in St. Louis*, in addition to humor, brought a rich recreation of past experience with its "real people, lively incidents, and richly realized atmosphere—a combination that appeals to young and old." After three questions—why had Benson written the book? What were some of the good things she had left out? What were some of her experiences in writing it?—Frederick turned the conversation over to Benson. Evidencing more reflection than she had in the *Junior Miss* interview with Barrow, Benson spoke at length. Perhaps a major reason for the difference in the two interviews lay in Benson's new sobriety.

Benson "had not left out anything." As to why she wrote the Kensington series, she claimed, "I suddenly got stuck with *Junior Miss*"—a statement never explained but implying Benson had tired of the Graves family. The transition to the Smith family was easy. Benson needed her sister Rose's diaries from 1902–1904 to clarify the facts, and they were "simply marvelous for telling me of dresses, what they went to see, and things of that sort—facts. The stories aren't true." The last statement her truest, Benson continued, fabricating as she went along. "The characters are [true], the house is; the neighbors are sketched in. They're not true." Katy, the maid, was put in because she had been so much a part of the family, though she did not work for us in 1904." Benson explained, "I changed the ages of the family around to make it, well, right. I wanted the three older children to be nearer the same age which they weren't." (In fact, Lon, Rose, and Esther were only two years apart from each other—rather close!) "I made my sister Agnes older than she was, I made myself older." Agnes, twelve in the story, was actually nine in 1903; Benson was six in 1903—the same age as in the story—but since she claimed 1900 as her birth year instead of 1897, it appeared "true" that she "made [herself] a

little older." Though the diaries were full of slang, Benson "was quite spar-
ing of the slang because I think if you use too much slang of the period,
you horse it up . . . make it quaint . . . a tin-type." She wanted readers
to think the stories "could be written now" rather than

> have the horrible feelings of these quaint people leading this
> rather foolish life. . . . I wanted what happened and how these
> people felt to be the way it would be now, and all I wanted to
> get in the whole thing was the spirit of this family who really
> liked one another. There are so many stories about families who
> aren't happy—little girls who are monstrous and little boys who
> are dreadful and too prankish—that I desperately wanted to
> avoid that. I simply wanted to do a perfectly ordinary family
> who were happy, didn't have much money—they went to private
> schools, not that that makes much difference—but I wanted to
> give the sort of life struggle to keep a family like that going.

Benson made a point of saying, "I did it in third person," claiming
she didn't want to be "put on the spot" by people asking, "Which one are
you?" Yet, Benson rarely used anything but the third-person point of view
in her fiction and reveled in telling *Meet Me in St. Louis* audiences, "I'm
only six in the book, but I'm smarter than the older ones." Was this a
case of delayed sibling rivalry? She magnified the anomaly by quoting her
exchange with Harold Ross who had said: "You certainly made yourself
good and smart." So, "I said, 'Well, why shouldn't I? I wrote it.'"

As to why she used humor, Benson explained, "I couldn't tell you,
except that I like light things. But the terrible thing about writing humor
is that it goes out of date." The only exceptions she could think of were
"Ring Lardner and Mark Twain [especially] the beautiful arguments Jim has
with Huckleberry Finn . . . because they are basic arguments and perfectly
beautiful ones." Writing during wartime, Benson claimed, made her turn
to the past and to children, the only other alternative being to do a war
story with a hero in the army and "I don't want to put all my people in
the Army. . . . I want them to go on as they were . . . to do this I have
to look back to another day." Benson's remarks are provocative. "To go
on as they were" is an unachievable, even undesirable, dream, and in her
fictional attempt to preserve the Smith family as they were, Benson compromised even as she unwittingly fabricated. Examining the nature of that

compromised, fabricated, idealized story, one comes closer to discovering the real Sally Benson. It is not without irony that her novel should be called *Meet* Me *in St. Louis* (my emphasis).

As she had the year before with *Junior Miss*, Benson agreed to appear on the New York University broadcast over WNYC. This time, Leah Daniels, not Bennett Cerf, wished her well: "I hope your broadcast will sell hundreds of copies of *Meet Me in St. Louis*."[26] On June 10th, Benson was to appear on a panel broadcast over WGY in Schenectady, New York. Martin Goldstein sent train tickets, informing her she would be sitting "next to Princess Paul Sapieha, Orville Prescott of the *New York Times*, and Granville Hicks, author of *Only One Storm*."

With Benson in New York, Doris Gilbert (Benson's treatment partner) sent gossipy letters full of studio screen-writing news. In the first, Gilbert gushed over losing Benson:

> It's been the most wondrous three months of my life," she declared. . . . I sure do love you. What would the writers' table think? . . . When you get to your so beautiful New York, I hope you find your family in a happy dither over having you back. Maybe by this time Tony bit Pants and all is serene at Benson's Folly. Give my best to Barbara whom I do not know but it was damned sweet of her and Ross and Rose and Esther and the Algonquin and your little milliner and your maid and Robey and Maxwell and Lobrano to lend you to me for a brief beautiful while.

The relationship was apparently one-sided as might be expected. Benson rarely mentioned Gilbert in letters to family or friends, and Gilbert, in her next letter, attempted to impress Benson, promising to "snoop around to see what I can find out on the *Meet Me in St. Louis* script" because "Cukor was non-committal about it." A young ingénue—at twenty-eight—just five years older than Bobsie, Gilbert unwittingly reveals her unawareness of Benson's distancing from her: "What's with *National Velvet?* Berman says you're doing your treatment on it, but you didn't say nothing about it no how." Yet, despite Benson's minimal correspondence with her, Gilbert announced she was going to New York to work with Benson. Her next letter claimed that she had an idea for a story titled "Madam, Will You Waltz?" After two more letters, Gilbert could finally thank Benson for a response. She continued planning the trip to New York and it materialized eventually.

Figure 13. Sally Benson, 1942

Sitting in Benson's "Doris Gilbert" file is the story, "Madam, Will You Waltz?" Gilbert had counted on Benson's influence at *The New Yorker* to promote its publication, but though the piece was rejected, two other Gilbert pieces were later accepted, and Benson continued briefly to collaborate with her from a distance.[27] Their only coauthored screenplay—*Destination Unknown*—was the "story of America and World War II." Its protagonist, Nellie Sperry, lived at home with her family, worked in an office, and was so ordinary that she "was the one girl fitted to become an American Mata Hari."[28] At summer's end Gilbert virtually disappeared from Benson's life.

For about a month Benson enjoyed some leisure with the family, including Babe and Ham. The country's involvement in the war, supported by more Americans as a result of Pearl Harbor, propaganda, and the impact of news headlines, had begun to take a greater toll on everyone. Ham's mother had written to Sally and Ham in mid-April, "we feel that the war is very real and that it will not be long before we will all feel it begin to pinch us pretty bad. I have not licenced [*sic*] my car because my tires are none too good and also because I have not the money to either pay for running it or to insure it. . . . Please call me up as soon as you return."[29] After a hard winter Victory gardens cropped up everywhere, rationing complicated food purchasing, and fuel shortages limited automobile use.

The war had affected many Americans, one of them Benson's son-in-law, Major Alexis Doster, who was now deployed in Egypt for surveillance work with the O.S.S. The other was Babe, who surprised Sally by reenlisting at forty-nine. Though she tried to dissuade him, Babe signed on as an officer of the 45th Combat Bomb Wing in June of 1942. As a major in the U.S. Army Air Corps (now the U.S. Air Force), he was sent to England where his World War I flying expertise proved invaluable on British reconnaissance flights. He served as gunner observer and combat staff officer on forty-five missions over Europe. Major Reynolds Benson was awarded the Distinguished Flying Cross at the war's end. For her part, Sally Benson began to weave the war into her fiction.

"Men Really Rule the World" conflates both the actual war and the less prominent war between the sexes with its resulting fallout—inner conflict. In this story, Katherine Foster of Scarsdale drives into Manhattan

Figure 14. Major Reynolds Benson, 1942

to pick up Dorothy Craig, newly arrived from the West Coast on the Twentieth Century. Their first topic of conversation is a mutual friend's husband, Jack Russell, who "is awful . . . [and] gotten *much* worse." Katherine explains, "I think it's affected his brain . . . really affected it. I don't see how Isobel stands it. After all, he brought it completely on himself with all that drinking, and now he's completely shot. . . . He just putters around." As the women visit with Isobel later that evening, wearing "printed evening dresses," they are oblivious of Jack settled in a corner with his radio program. While the three women engage in spirited conversation and reminiscing, Jack Russell sits in the corner, "his skin thick and blotched . . . a gray, dead color . . . his hands rough and dry, but his eyes an intense and wonderful blue." The women speak mostly of California, shifting attention slightly to the war by calling themselves "war widows" as they discuss Dorothy's husband's job—committee meetings involving "all this fuss about oil"—when suddenly, a siren sounds, the radio stops playing, and they assume Jack is merely being thoughtful in turning it off for them. Unaware that an air raid drill is in effect, they resent Jack's insistence that they darken the house by pinning up the black curtains and dousing the candles. "We're not going to sit here in the dark," Isobel said. "Yes, you are!" he shouted—"You damned silly fools!" In a somewhat conciliatory manner, he later adds: "You can talk if you want to," but Benson concludes: "The women couldn't think of anything to say."

As summer ended, Benson tried to arrange nephew Tony Smith's transfer from the local public school in Westport to the Emerson School for Boys in Exeter, New Hampshire, but she was hospitalized for a throat infection and had Ham attend to Tony's financial and legal affairs in her absence. In September, she enrolled Tony at Emerson where, on the basis of "intelligence and achievement tests" given on September 25th, he was assigned "to our highest class, which normally prepares boys to enter the second year at Exeter," the headmaster wrote. However, he wanted Benson to help decide whether that were the best arrangement since Tony was "younger than the average of his classmates."[30] Now in control of Tony's estate, Benson paid his tuition for the year and advised the headmaster that Tony should decide on his class placement. When he read his aunt's letter, Tony chose to remain in his class for a "two-weeks' trial," but a week later, Emerson's headmaster raised the question of placement again because Tony's grades were a "B," two "C's," and a "D." Benson supported Tony's desire to stay at the level assigned, especially since she knew how important it was that he "learn to live with other boys." *Junior Miss* was scheduled to open in Boston in October, and since she had already sent tickets to his cousin Toby Wherry, Benson wrote Emerson suggesting that Tony and another student or a master attend a performance in Boston. Emerson would try to arrange the trip, she was assured, since the suggestion appealed to Tony.

Babe and Sally continued to correspond regularly all during the war. By November of 1942, Babe had written several detailed letters from England describing his experiences and telling Sally of his love. One expedition involved a two-day search up in the mountains for a missing plane that Babe and Captain Smith found. "Except for the grim aspect," he wrote, "that country was eighteen Palisade Park roller coasters plus. The ravines are too steep to fly up so we climbed up and skipped through the wisps of cloud just at the bottom of the overcast, which was flirting with the tops of the ridges. Many of them were wooded and the trees were beautiful with heavy snow on the branches." Again, as he had when writing from Arizona, Babe demonstrated his poetic side. The letter continued in this vein, almost a short story in itself, ending: "While we were cruising around, we saw three beautiful deer standing on a hillside watching us."[31] Though their daughter claimed her parents had nothing in common and Sally has said the same, it appears that on the deeper level of experiencing the natural world and expressing their capacity for wonder in words or storytelling, the Bensons shared much.

In November Sally telegrammed Babe from Exeter and sent a detailed letter a few days later from Madison about Tony's progress at the Emerson School for Boys. Four years later, Sally Benson would publish in the December 21, 1946 issue of *The New Yorker*, a story titled "School Boy," based on the relationship between a prep school senior and his homeroom teacher. The boy, like Tony Smith, is "a clever boy, does well in his studies" and means "no harm" but "distracts his fellow students." He embarrasses his teacher by presenting a monetary Christmas gift, unaware that his teacher has just reported his recent misbehavior to the headmaster. As she had before, Benson would capitalize on her experiences with people she knew—in this case her nephew and ward—to create a story for her *New Yorker* readers.

When Babe responded after Thanksgiving, he shared details of a cold that had turned into a grippe and required him to be in the infirmary. "I have seldom felt lower and lousier," he wrote, "but things will be looking up once we get the hell out of here. . . . Take care . . . enjoy yourself and have pretty things while the going is good. I'll write soon again. Love, Babe."[32]

At about the time she received Babe's letter, Benson resumed drinking. She arrived at Rose's house in Madison on Christmas Eve (as she had on several other occasions) so drunk that her nephew, Albert, had to drive her to the "the farm" for yet another period of rehabilitation.[33] Despite all her professional success in 1942, Sally Benson had yet to win her battle with alcohol.

24

THE WORLD AT WAR, BABE AND HAM

1943

"Can you blame us if we soak ourselves in beer? When . . . the horror of our fall is written plain . . . Do you wonder that we drug ourselves from pain?"

—Rudyard Kipling

On the home front, after emerging once again from rehab, Benson needed to deal with her finances and unmet obligations to *The New Yorker*. In February of the new year—1943—she visited Harold Ross's office. Looking up the statistics, Ross verified and shared with Benson, his suspicion that

> there was a long, terrible cold spell (which I now distinctly recall with a shudder) when you wrote practically nothing. Between February 19th and November 24th—a period of nine months and five days—you turned in only one story—on July 2nd. You were comparatively, a miraculous whirlwind the other two months plus twenty-five days of the year but, my God!
>
> H. W. Ross.

In a follow-up letter, Ross reported Benson's 1942 earnings as $6,578.94. Nine of her pieces had merited $4,739.80 and her mystery and crime blurbs brought in $1,300. Royalties from the Book-of-the Month Club accounted for the rest ($539.14).[1] Ross's letter sparked renewed energy in Benson, and she produced eleven pieces for *The New Yorker* in 1943. In addition, Benson assembled a fifth collection of short stories to be published by Random House in November. It would be titled *Women and Children First.*

Of the eleven new submissions to *The New Yorker* only one—"A Toast to the Next Man Who Dies"—met with Katharine White's rejection. Despite its having been revised and gone to galleys, White had two objections—it was "too tough on the reader" and its ending was obscure. To Maxwell she complained that Benson should make clear in the first paragraph, for example, that Las Lilas was located in New York City. She should also clarify her intended outcome:

> To this moment I don't know whether the Major is going to be sent overseas and into action, and hence, feels and acts the way he does, or whether he is about to commit suicide. My surmise is the former and that is the ironic point—the night club ladies' assuming he is a desk man. But why should the reader have to guess? The words of the song don't help. It maddens me to read a story so obscure as this one—obscure for no good reason. . . . Usually, Benson is crystal clear and I hate to see her doing an O'Hara on us when clarity has been one of her big virtues.

In her memo White was voicing the official *New Yorker* policy requiring pieces to be located in New York, but Benson was moving in a new direction—toward a universal, nonspecific place.[2]

Ironically, the obscurity White cited reflected Benson's mixed feelings as both Babe and Ham had enlisted in the military. Substantiating this claim is Benson's "Young Man," written about the same time as "A Toast to the Next Man Who Dies" and published in *The New Yorker* on March 6, 1943. Taken together, the two pieces illustrate Benson's confusion as she reevaluates her life. Besides Benson's having grown disenchanted with Ham's youthful ebullience, the major factor causing her ambivalence was her deep regard for Babe. The frequency of Sally and Babe's wartime letters and the care represented by the many gift packages Benson sent to him indicate their closeness despite the geographic distance separating them. One can imagine Benson reconsidering her involvement with Ham, especially when one recalls her multiple engagements during World War I and her explanation of them.[3]

"A Toast to the Next Man Who Dies" clearly was based on Babe. Its protagonist is a major who regularly visited the bar at Las Lilas where Xena, a fortuneteller, and Irina, a singer, regarded him with mild disgust because he arrived "loaded." His previous "know-it-all" behavior included protesting vociferously that the Basin Street Trio employed at Las Lilas had misquoted the lyrics to "Gentleman-Rankers," a tune he accused "lousy Yale bastards" of swiping. The Major performs as expected, and when the trio offers to do "Roar, Lion, Roar" (a Columbia song) for him, he asks for "the new song." Reluctantly, they sing: "Stand, stand to your glasses steady, / This world is a world of lies, / Here's a toast to those gone already, / And a toast to the next man who dies." As the Major moves toward the phone booth, Irina comments, "Don't let it get to you. He's still fighting the last war. Why those stripes on his sleeve are from the *last* war. Those fancy ribbons are from the *last* war. *He's* from the last war." She finished her brandy. "To the Major!" He left and walked across town in the mist. Benson wrote, "At first his legs seemed hardly able to hold him, and twice he lurched slightly. But as he walked he became steadier." In this piece, Benson incorporates Babe's alcohol problem, his aging, and his disregard of her insistence that he not reenlist in the air force. (An Esther Evarts piece two years earlier also focused on Babe—his drinking and stories. "Been all over the world, and can he tell you things that would make your hair curl!")[4] But there is more.

The "Gentlemen-Rankers" song was composed by Rudyard Kipling and, typically, dealt with class divisions. The speaker is a son of privilege—the officer class—but, as an enlisted man in the British army, served among the lower classes. Such a descent could only come about through sin, mere poverty being insufficient to degentrify.[5] The sin in this case is defined by the reference to the "Curse of Reuben"—adultery—committed with Bilhah, Jacob's concubine. The poem's midsection may be an insight into Benson's thinking as, in the middle of an affair with Ham, she reflected on her alcoholic binges and explored their cause:

. . . Can you blame us if we soak ourselves in beer?
When the drunken comrade mutters and the great guard-
    lantern gutters
And the horror of our fall is written plain,
Every secret, self-revealing on the aching white-washed ceiling,
So you wonder that we drug ourselves from pain?

We have done with Hope and Honor, we are lost to Love
and Truth,
We are dropping down the ladder rung by rung
And the measure of our torment is the measure of our youth.
God help us, for we knew the worst too young!
. . . And the curse of Reuben holds us till an alien turf enfolds
us
And we die . . . We're little black sheep who've gone
astray . . .
Gentlemen-rankers out on the spree, damned from here to
Eternity . . .[6]

The Yale parody resulted in the "Whiffenpoof Song"—a rendition far less pessimistic. Yet, Benson's Major prefers the original. Before leaving Las Lilas, like William Faulkner's Quentin Compson, he removes his valuables—"a gold watch and chain, a gold pen-knife, a gold basketball engraved 'Eastern Inter-Collegiate Champions, 1916,' [Babe's class at Columbia], and a ring of his college senior society." Putting all into an envelope, he gives it to the hotel clerk to be stowed in the safe. "If you don't hear from me again, sell it for gold." His parting words are, "Don't worry about *me* . . . Jesus! I don't want anyone to worry about *me*. He pulled his cap over one eye and stepped jauntily out into the night." Benson's piece is stark and provocative communicating something of despondency in the face of death. Sadness at his and Ham's going off to war fed her fear that Babe might not return this time—the same fear that had motivated her multiple engagements in World War I.[7]

"Young Man," on the other hand, is based on Ham. Its setting in a small Manhattan apartment is reminiscent of one described in Benson's 1940 letters. She had taken a one bedroom, first-floor apartment in the back of a building in midtown. "The room was large. It had been the kitchen of the big brownstone house before the house was remodeled, and it had a back door that opened out onto a yard, enclosed by a high wood fence which Martin, the protagonist, had painted blue. In the room was a box spring and mattress covered with soft blue denim and bound in white."[8] Martin's wife worries that the sheets will be "mussed" when he sits down (as Benson had complained in a letter to Ham about his not making the bed properly).[9]

Martin Rogers, modeled on Ham, arrives breathless after a day at work, six minutes late. "I must have missed a train" or "walked slower," he explains as he feverishly kisses his wife, who "pushed him away." As she disappears behind a screen to dress, he moves the screen—to see her. Her annoyed mood, it develops, has resulted from his plans to enlist in the navy: "You were doing defense work and you said yourself that they wouldn't take you, especially since you couldn't breathe out of one side of your nose. . . . I don't see why you had to give up a good job to have your nose fixed and enlist." When he calls her "my beautiful darling" (a direct quote from one of Ham's letters to Benson in 1941), she pulls away and berates him: "I wish you'd stop saying that. You've said it every minute for six weeks." She will return to her job when the navy calls him because "It'll be more fun." He offers to put in a garden for her—as Ham had done for Sally. Their evening ends with a trip to the movies "and a coke afterward"—a hint that Benson had returned to sobriety—and that Ham's efforts to wean Sally away from drink had been successful.

The two stories, companion pieces, are evidence of Benson's reevaluating her life in 1943. The warm tone of Babe's letters may have contributed to her confusion, but they may also have facilitated the break-up with Ham. Her daughter Barbara, however, believed Ham left Benson because she had resumed drinking, but the truth may have been the reverse—he left her for the navy—and she once again sought comfort in alcohol.

Amid her writing and reevaluating her life, Benson also had been attending to her teenage ward and nephew, Agnes's son Tony. Before long, plans for Tony's graduation were being made and headmaster Everett Emerson asked Benson to forward the names of guests she wished to invite. Emerson also made reservations for Benson and her mother "at the Inn for the night of June third." In California, meanwhile, Barbara gave birth to Alexis Doster III, making Sally and Babe proud grandparents. Sally immediately wrote Babe and made train reservations for a visit to Barbara and "Dusty." Babe answered on July 31st: "I expect you are home now and perhaps are working in your garden at Madison at this very minute." Babe shared details of the Allied effort against "the Hun . . . he is beginning to bend." Babe was getting one or "possibly two hours of sleep twice a day," and it was unusually hot. Journalists he knew from New York, Corey Ford and Alistair MacBain, had visited his station for several days on special assignment for *Collier's*, he reported, and "one of the boys loaned me five

New Yorkers the other day . . . and I read them from cover to cover and back again. There wasn't anything of yours unless it may have been the mystery reviews. Do you still do them? Are you allowed to send books?" Babe made a list from the reviews and hoped Sally could send one at a time "if it's not too damned complicated."[10] If these three mysteries are lousy, Babe added, "don't send them. You know the type I like." He asked that Sally let him know "how best to get in touch. You will have peace and quiet over the holidays. I'd love to hear from you when you get back to town. God bless and keep you always. Babe."[11]

On August 7th, as soon as she read Babe's letter, Sally replied. Bobs and Dusty were flourishing, she told him, and she would send the pills Babe needed. Sally enclosed a photo of their grandson in her next letter and Babe responded, "I loved getting the picture of Butch.[12] He is a swell looking baby, but will probably cause his mother a lot of trouble. Don't let him sleep with his ears the wrong way—they're enough of a handicap now. . . . I like to hear from you so do write when you have a chance. Love, Babe."[13]

In addition to the common bond that Dusty represented, the Bensons had a reading connection (though their tastes in books differed), and Babe even "tried to see *Junior Miss* in town, but London is a mad house." It took him "five hours of hoofing it in the dark to find a hotel with a vacancy. I finally got what must have been the Prince of Wales suite at the Ritz—sitting room, veddy French bedroom, and a bath you could swing a mastodon in for three pounds *per diem*. London is not glad to see young America—but how they love our dough!" He had had a horrendous week recently and had "been quite on the ropes . . . I can go fine for three days with practically no sleep or food, but seven days gets me. Guess I'm getting old," he admitted. When he returned, he "did a kitchen prowl and caught two eggs, fresh mind you, some bacon and coffee—God was it good! We probably have enough food but it's hard to look in the face most times and army cooks can murder the best intended grub." He had changed quarters and described the furnishings, including the calendar Sally had sent. He "changed the picture so the mood varies. . . . All in all it's very homey. We have a bath tub and sometimes hot water—it's not a half bad war at that." Referring to war photos, though, Babe reported:

> You've undoubtedly read of the socking the German cities are taking. It's no exaggeration . . . you can't realize the devastation without seeing the photos as I have—hundreds—of absolute

ruin, God damn their stinking hides! We love it. Keep in shape and try not to work too hard and don't fret about old man Benson—he was born to be hung. Cheerio and write soon, tho I know it must be a hell of an effort after hitting a typewriter all day for 1/8 you and 7/8 Uncle Sam. Babe[14]

In California, six weeks later, Barbara received sad and shocking news: her husband of two years, Lieutenant First Class Alexis Doster II, had died of polio on October 1st in Egypt[15] and was buried with full military honors at the American cemetery in Heliopolis, a suburb of Cairo. When Sally conveyed the news to Babe, he replied, "Poor baby, I'm glad she was with you. Being staunch like your mother is in many ways, seems to entail having all the family burdens descend on you but I know you were glad to be able to get Bobs through the worst of it. God knows you have had your share plus of having to maintain broad shoulders."[16]

Though Babe offered his condolences immediately, it is difficult to accept that they constituted his opening paragraph—a mere one-sixteenth of his letter. The remainder, while fascinating in its vivid detail of war-time living, was narrated with a degree of excitement inconsistent with the sympathy Sally and Barbara might have expected. The letter confirms Golseth's assessment of her father: "He was very cold and distant."[17] Sally, nonetheless, continued to send Babe care packages of books, Fanny Farmer candy, candied fruits, assorted jars of jelly, and "condensed vitamins." In February, he wrote,

Do you suppose you could arrange to send me some bittersweet chocolate? I would give practically anything to receive some. I am well and have stopped losing weight as skin and bone is difficult to work off. . . . All I crave is unsweetened choco-late. . . . The food is so monotonous that appetite departs at sight of same. . . . If you read or hear on the radio that our boys are happy about all the nourishing food they are being inundated with, kindly remark "horse . . . and the second word begins with 's.' " Also, I don't know where all the big shots such as Bob Hope play, but it ain't here. . . . Two more *New Yorkers* came—Jan. 8 and 15—so they are evidently coming through regularly. Thanks ever so much for everything and write when you can and keep well. Love, Babe.[18]

Figure 15. Major Reynolds Benson, circa 1943

From California Bobsie wrote a long letter revealing her anger toward her father:

> I'm sending you a letter I got from the old man. I suppose he thinks I should get some stupid Mexican woman to look after Dusty and go to work in a war plant and earn enough to pay her salary or maybe he thinks Dusty is old enough to take care of himself.
>
> I don't know what the hell right he has to lecture me anyway—what has he ever done for me? You are the only one who has the right and if you don't, by God, he shouldn't. I haven't answered it yet. I'm waiting for my ire to cool down. I've bought about $2,000 in war bonds and I bet he never saved that much in his whole life. I notice that he hasn't so much as

sent Dusty a dollar bill for his future education. In other words, I'm burned up. He'll probably be full of advise [*sic*] about I have to send him to college on someone else's cash. However, I did send him a Christmas box and I refuse to fight with him.

Love to all, Bobsie

The letter is significant because it shows another side of Babe and indicates the difficulty Sally faced in dealing with him over the years. It also shows that she had been a caring and considerate parent to Bobsie.

25

MEET ME IN ST. LOUIS— THE FICTION, THE SOURCES

A LOOK BACK, 1941–1942

"It was a real wake, and the best funeral we've ever had."

—*Meet Me in St. Louis*

Sally Benson had drawn upon her 1912 diary, letters from teenage friends in St. Louis, and memories of raising Barbara to craft the *Junior Miss* series. In the wake of its popularity, it was logical that Benson should explore her sister Rose's 1902–1904 diaries for further material, and the time—1941—seemed ripe for the family series Benson had toyed with as early as 1933.[1] A great incentive for Benson—besides the predictability of financial gain—had been Clarence Day Jr.'s *Life with Father* pieces—first published in *The New Yorker* and then produced in 1939, as an enormously successful Broadway play.

Like Rose's diaries, Benson's new "5135 Kensington" series spanned the year prior to the opening of the St. Louis World's Fair in 1904 and appeared in *The New Yorker* from June of 1941 through May of 1942. The twelve stories introduced each of the Smiths, including Grandpa Prophater, but its central character was six-year-old Tootie whom Benson self-styled as the "smartest."[2] In actuality, most of Tootie's fictional capers were based on those of Benson's older sibling, Agnes, who was nine years old at the time of the fair (Sally was only five).

The first segments—"5135 Kensington, June 1903," "July 1903," and "August 1903"—focused on Rose and her suitors, while Esther attempted to win their new neighbor as her next beau while their mother prepared for the family's annual vacation in Manitowoc, Wisconsin. "September 1903" focused on Benson's oldest sibling, Lon, and his departure for Princeton University; "October 1903" introduced Halloween rituals unusually violent for the time; "November 1903" centered on Tootie's and Agnes's pranks; "December 1903," on Lon's return from Princeton with an "Eastern" girl-friend and the preparations made by Rose and Esther for a spate of holi-day parties. "January 1904" and its thaw allowed the Smiths to visit the fairground's muddy construction site; "February 1904" gathered Rose's and Esther's friends for a party hosted in their parents' absence; and "March 1904" took the Smiths to Madame Roditi's "at-home" for foreign and local dignitaries planning the fair. As the longed-for fair's opening approached, "April 1904" shocked the family with news of Mr. Smith's promotion and their imminent move to New York, but, "May 1904," after elaborating on how each of the Smiths participated in the fair, culminated with a sur-prise—Mr. Smith's announcement that after considering his family's wishes, he had turned down the promotion—the family would remain in St. Louis. With its happy ending and nostalgic survey of a family's trials and joys at the turn of the twentieth century, *Meet Me in St. Louis* entertained readers and moviegoers during World War II by relieving them temporarily of the stark reality of wartime. Paradoxically, however, a close reading of Benson's novel reveals much that is dark.

Writing her memories of a St. Louis childhood in 1941 at forty-three, Benson tapped into feelings of past and present loss—especially that of her sister Agnes—as she recreated her family environment and revisited her youth. In reliving her joys and sorrows, Benson had significant choices to make. Most significant was her decision to begin "5135 Kensington, June 1903" with a literal awakening that, in light of Benson's life story, is also symbolic. The first paragraph sets the tone of the novel by introducing joy and pain, as six-year-old Tootie Smith, Benson's fictional counterpart, without opening her eyes, knows that the sun has flooded her room but "feels the scab, a really good one, on one knee." In minutes, older brother Lon, she knows, will tell her a lie about a white pony in the backyard, just as yesterday he had told her of a nonexistent black pony. Before long, all came to pass as Tootie had anticipated, but Lon's deceptive muttering—"anyone who would tell a lie to a six-year-old is a cad"—baited Tootie to believe one more time. Then, as he had the day before, Lon paid for his deception with money, his second payment—a quarter—tucked inside a poem he had written and hidden in Tootie's shoe. The gesture is curious for two reasons. First, it signals Benson's identifying a pattern initiated by her brother Lon and woven through her life—using money to assuage feelings of guilt. Second, the poem's negative content suggests the source of Benson's low self-esteem: "Tootie is a bad girl, / Tootie is a fraud, / Tootie is the worst girl, / I ever sawed" (*MMSL* 9).[3]

In the last piece, "May 1904," Benson presented Tootie led by Grandpa to a "place on the Pike"[4] where she watched in fascination a girl in "spangled dress that came to her knees. She had on a lot of ruffles too. And she had her face all painted up to look pretty. We stayed and saw her three times," asserted Tootie, who memorized the whole act and all the words to the song, ironically titled "Teasing." Tootie intended to repeat the song-and-dance routine for Lon "because he'll like it" (287). In paralleling but reversing the teasing Lon dispensed in the first episode, Benson unconsciously exposed the root cause of the lying pattern that shaped her life. On the surface, the two pieces appear to represent typical sibling teasing within a large family. But, Benson introduced images whose subtle connotations suggest possible psychological abuse.

"June 1903" contains a third example of Benson's "victimization," this time at the hands of her older sisters. Rose, disappointed because her expected marriage proposal did not materialize, deals with her feelings by drawing Esther into a scheme—"torturing" Tootie by "kidnapping" Margaretha, "Tootie's favorite doll"—and leaving a ransom note signed "Mafia." The plan enabled Rose to displace her annoyance with her noncommittal hoped-for "fiancé," and the piece's abrupt concluding statement—"New York seemed very far away"—may be prophetic of the nostalgia Benson often experienced after leaving St. Louis.[5] Earlier, Rose had chided Esther, "I can't see . . . how you can all spend your time thinking up ways to fool Tootie. I should think it would be beneath you. . . . I think it's childish now. . . . And I must say that if I were married and had children, I wouldn't want them *teased to death*" (16, emphasis mine). Rose's reversion to the immaturity she had earlier berated in Esther indicates Benson's adult awareness of fickleness in those she admired. A classic example of displacement of feeling, the episode suggests that the "torturing" Benson experienced at the hands of her older siblings had unintended effects on the sensitive six-year-old. Later in the piece, Benson describes Katie, the Smiths' maid, who also "took out her feelings"—but in a different manner—"by baking three cherry pies and two dozen cinnamon buns" (22). If, as Benson claimed, the material included here were rooted in actual fact, her using these examples demonstrates that she learned to deal with pain in two ways: first, as she had in her youth, by "torturing" others—witness the multiple engagements in 1917—and second, the more adult method of transforming negative feelings into creative projects. Benson's fiction, like Katie's baking, provided release and a measure of joy. Significantly, as the adult Benson drew upon Rose's diary, she created dialogue that condemned habitual sibling teasing and illustrated in Katie's creative response a better alternative.

Other thematic strands—death and drunkenness—introduced in this first of the Kensington pieces, echoed in Benson's personal life and other fiction, revealing her subconscious awareness of demons that plagued her sporadically. Whether survivor-guilt stemming from John Perry's death, difficulty achieving a sense of personal identity, low self-esteem, or a combination of the three—something threatened and gnawed at Benson's inner peace. One consistent manifestation was the recurring problem with alcohol that developed in her thirties, another, the many quiet affairs that compromised her integrity. A third was her lavish spending. All three were rooted in Benson's childhood, and whether consciously or unconsciously, Benson allowed them to surface as she wrote the Kensington series.

The death motif in the first piece is introduced at the dinner table. While Esther and Rose sit silent and tense, awaiting the telephone call from New York and its hoped-for marriage proposal, Tootie recounts her day spent riding with the iceman.[6] As twelve-year-old Sara Smith voluntarily helped her Uncle Jay's young farmhand at harvest time—crossing class lines—so six-year-old Tootie did the same. Telling the family about her day on the ice wagon, Tootie focuses on death and drunkenness—once directly—once metaphorically. She recalls for them a story told by her driver. "The iceman saw a man get shot," she said. "He was a *drunken* man and the blood spurted out at least three feet" (19, emphasis mine). Scolded mildly for the inappropriateness of this morsel as dinner conversation, Tootie then asks to eat the mashed potatoes her way: "squeez[ing them] in her fist until they came out like fat white worms between her fingers" (23).[7] Mrs. Smith, of course, refuses permission and the reader might dismiss the incident as childish orneriness. However, the "fat white worms," suggestive of death and decay, are a second example of Benson's morbid streak. A third instance, Tootie's "quiver[ing]" at the thought that her sick Mrs. Rockefeller doll might die ends her story and the piece.

By inscribing memories of intoxication and morbidity into Tootie's rendition of her morning's conversation—hardly what Rose would have recorded in her diary—Benson offered clues to her own emotional state in 1941. "August 1903," like the preceding episode, besides developing the morbid strain in Benson's self-characterization, also hinted at Benson's early exposure to alcohol. Tootie began,

> I've been having a wake. . . . A real Irish wake like Katie told me about. Maude Rockefeller died this morning, and Bunchie and I buried her. She was one of the richest dolls so we put her by herself nearest the little pond. Her leg came off and she bled to death in about a second. . . . We put her in her coffin and stood it on end and made a clay pipe out of a piece of clover and stuck it in her mouth. Katie says that's what they always do. It was a real wake, and the best funeral we've ever had. (59)

Then, taking a swig from a bottle, Tootie sings: "Consumption has no pity for blue eyes and golden hair." Esther, horrified, demands, "What's that stuff you're swilling?" Tootie replies simply: "It's a little bit of everything [a mix of squeezed raspberries and peaches, lemon juice, and water]. . . . It was part of the refreshments. *After*, you know" (60). The ritualistic drinking, the song's lyrics, and Benson's emphasis on "after," reflect the stereotypical behavior associated with an Irish wake. Perhaps young Benson learned about such adult customs from listening to Katie's stories, but she may have witnessed drunkenness at actual wakes in neighbors' homes. In any case, Benson's inscribing here her memory of wakes and drunkenness resonates with the difficulties she experienced with alcohol during her thirties and forties.

Two years before, in 1939, Benson's *Junior Miss* had presented a similar depiction of adult behavior after a burial. Entitled "Bury Me Not," the piece centered on Mr. and Mrs. Graves upon their return from a funeral. Somberly, Mrs. Graves initiates a discussion about burial sites while Mr. Graves offers everyone—including preteen Judy and seventeen-year-old Lois—a "spot of sherry." Mrs. Graves wished to be buried near the pond in Manchester, Vermont, but her husband preferred a high hilltop in Danby Four Corners where there was plenty of light and air and a view. Judy's choice was more romantic—to have her ashes "scattered to the wind . . . over the sea," while Lois preferred a vault in the "place down on Wall Street . . . where there were a lot of people around" (22–23). Judy reminds Lois that the Wall Street place no longer allows burials, but Lois counters with, "For all you know, I may be famous, and they'd let

me in just the way they would in Westminster Abbey" (22). Such a discussion—possibly inspired by an actual one at the time of Agnes's death
in 1933—shows that Benson contemplated the effects of fame and the
impact of her own death. (She returned to this theme in "Spirit of '76,"
which *The New Yorker* published in its 1954 December 25th issue when
she was fifty-seven.)

Writing the "Kensington" pieces in her mid-forties, Benson obviously
embedded an ironic subtext into what appear to be humorous, nostalgic
renderings of halcyon, childhood days. Yet, despite their being touted as
autobiographical, the "Kensington" pieces reveal little about Benson directly. Her alter ego is, after all, only six years old. Rather, Benson recapitulated
in these pieces some general patterns that shaped her life—the fun she had
with her siblings, her mother's religious sensibility, her grandfather's quirkiness, her conflicting passions for the novel and exotic, on the one hand,
and rootedness, on the other, in a home far from the glitz and glamour
of either New York or Hollywood. Into numerous other stories, as has
been seen, Benson wove specific aspects of her adult life, which, though
concealed, invite discovery.

Besides Rose's diaries, Sally Benson tapped other, unacknowledged
sources—family correspondence and several scrapbooks of stories, songs,
and plays, some written in collaboration with friends. For example, in
"For Posterity," one of her *Junior Miss* pieces, Benson's Judy Graves opens
a scrapbook similar to the one Benson had compiled during her years at
Horace Mann. Among the memorabilia, Judy discovers a play and Benson
incorporates the work in its entirety, including childish misspellings. Its
characters are Father, Mother, and Jean. The first "scaen" centers around
a conversation about a sleeping baby who awakens and is given brook
"watter" newly fetched by Jean. In the second brief scene, Jean is told that
the baby is sick and she begins to weep. Scene three focuses on a nurse's
diagnosis—"She has Ty.P."—which causes Jean to faint. Learning that the
brook had provided the water, the nurse exclaims: "Oh, no wonder. She's
done for." Mother "falls on the crib, Baby dies, and Father falls to the
floor. Jean is allready [*sic*] dead." A narrator pronounces: "Poor family.
They all died of T.P. . . . . I'll have the funeral tomorrow. [8] This is such
a bad case, oh dear. She faints." Having finished reading the play, Judy
Graves stares at the ceiling and asks her sister Lois: "I don't guess you'd
really get typhoid fever from the brook in the country, would you?" Lois
answers reassuringly, "Of course not. . . . It comes straight down from the

mountain. It's the same water we drink." As though still unbelieving, Judy adds: "I used to think you could."

Introduced into a story based largely on reading about one's father's life as scrapbooks tell it, this segment on "T.P." is rather bizarre unless explained by Sally's memory of the death of John Perry, the infant sibling who lived only twenty-four hours. Almost four years old at the time, she was pleased to retain her status as baby of the family but some guilt feelings may have ensued. Judy's concluding comment is cryptic: "I think I'll never forget anything as long as I live." Unlike Mr. Graves who forgot the formerly prized baseball that symbolized a moment of fame on a champion team, Benson would literally never forget her brother's death. "For Posterity," designed to sentimentalize an adolescent's growing awareness of memory's role in forming identity, represents Benson's striking a chord of sympathetic vibration.

A case in point may well be a letter from her good friend, Helen Yule, written shortly after Benson's departure from St. Louis for New York. Yule's letter was full of newsy tidbits: the concert to be given by Mrs. Strauss and Fritz, complaints about the hot weather, and gossip about "the biggest flirt" who just moved into "those stone flats across the street." Next came an ominous hint: "I don't know what Mary and I will do this summer. There used to be four. Now there are only two." More small talk follows and then a startling

> P.S. Florence died Monday at three o'clock of diphtheria [*sic*]. She was out on my porch with me a week ago Tuesday and didn't go to school any more that week and a sign was put on the door at ten o'clock Monday morning: "Died in Mother's arms." Her real mother came and she looked dear. Mary and I sent flowers.[9]

Benson must have puzzled over Helen's inconsequential news and her delayed reference to their friend's death. Withholding this major piece of news suggests that Helen had difficulty in accepting Florence's death and feared that Sally would as well. One can only speculate about the impact of Florence's death on Sally. Possibly, it made her more determined to enjoy life to the full and, therefore, more willing than ever to take risks.

In *Meet Me in St. Louis* Benson succeeded in masking what were essentially personal painful experiences under a nostalgic veneer. For example, her description of the vacation trip from St. Louis to Manitowoc, Wisconsin, was couched in endearing, familial images—a packed lunch, a carriage ride at dusk, a parrot and her grandparents awaiting her arrival. Summers in St. Louis found most of its inhabitants staying close to home. "Life was precarious, for health care and public sanitation were primitive or non-existent. . . . Terrible epidemics swept the land . . . yellow fever, spread by mosquitoes [being] the worst . . . ravaged the population" (Cuthbertson 12). Tuberculosis was another threat. Alonzo's early letters to Anna Cora urged her to leave the city—head north for Manitowoc—to avoid the threat of illness.

Turn-of-the century St. Louis was anything but pleasant in summer. As Emily Hahn—a *New Yorker* writer and colleague of Benson and another St. Louis native—noted in *Times and Places*, "St. Louis was a hell of a place for a summer resort. It rests in a topographical hollow, and the air is unusually quiet, growing humid to an extreme degree in summer, except for the times when everything blows up all at once in a cyclone" (4). Thirty years earlier, humid St. Louis air drove Benson's father to position himself in the "girls room by the window [to catch] all the breeze [one] can," as he wrote to Anna Cora. It was August of 1886 and he had given up his vacation at Manitowoc to care for his mother-in-law—Rose Smith—then close to death.[10] "The day is very clear," Alonzo noted, "and I can see all over South St. Louis, and a very pretty view it is too."[11] Both Emily Hahn and Alonzo Smith recognized the beauty of the city while admitting its brutal summer heat. Yet, Sally Benson—except for a reference to delaying supper "until it is cooler"—omitted all negative aspects of St. Louis.[12] In another letter, Alonzo addressed the danger of St. Louis summer conditions more directly:

> Let the children have plenty of water while the weather is warm. As your father would say, 'Turn the hose on them.' Don't worry. Keep cool as possible. Keep plenty of ice in the old ice chest. Eat all the ice cream you want and it won't hurt the children. Get on a Northern Lines packet if the children get sick and go north on the River. I will be home soon. Yours with love and kisses . . . I would give anything for a hug right now. Lonny.[13]

Benson chose to sentimentalize the city of her birth—as an analgesic for painful memories—or, more likely, with an eye to the marketplace.[14]

Benson presented her city and neighborhood positively and Tootie Smith as highly active regardless of the weather. Emily Hahn, on the other hand, recalled being dismissed early from school when the thermometer hit ninety. Like Hahn, who lived on Fountain Avenue just three-and-a-half blocks from the Smiths' home, Benson may have walked barefoot after school over melting asphalt, its "mushy consistency" streaking her legs. If such were the case, Benson at midlife chose to omit such an unpleasant reality in *Meet Me in St. Louis*. Hahn, by contrast, wrote: "The parched grass of Fountain Park was easier on the feet . . . but the backyard was best. There we could turn on the garden hose and wallow." Remembering her backyard, Hahn fills in details that Benson might have corroborated, had she so chosen:

> When I pulled myself up to stand on the rim of our ashpit and peered over a wall into the alley, what I saw was almost rural. The alley was cobbled, bounded on one side by a vacant lot and a couple of wooden outhouses and a stable. In the stable lived a horse, who kept his head resting on the lower half of his divided door and always regarded me amiably. The whole place smelled of horse, cold ashes, garbage and open ground.[15]

Hahn's memory of an almost rural Fountain Avenue, so close to Kensington Avenue, makes plausible Lon's promising Tootie she would find a pony in the yard. It also raises the possibility that Benson's conversations with Hahn at *The New Yorker* echo in the "Kensington" pieces.[16]

Like Benson, Hahn had come to *The New Yorker* in 1929 with encouragement, in her case, from Harold Ross and the caution to write "just a little clearer" (Yagoda 73). Why did Benson distance herself from St. Louis, omitting negative details and creating a romantic, nostalgic aura?[17] What Benson was actually thinking in 1941 as she wrote the pieces that became *Meet Me in St. Louis* is, of course, matter for speculation. Deep down she knew her fiction would sell. Even Benson's remembered summer trips from St. Louis to Chicago are rendered in romantic terms unlike Emily Hahn's account of a similar journey. Hahn, seven years younger than Benson, described her summer getaways from St. Louis with realism:

> We traveled on a train, taking with us a big trunk and many suitcases, getting aboard in the late afternoon and sleeping in

flimsily constructed rooms of green cloth. The moldy smell of that cloth is still evocable in my nostrils. Arriving in Chicago next day, we rode across town in a Parmalee horse-drawn bus to another station. The bus was upholstered in something shabby and slippery, and the streets were bumpy. . . . I was looking out with horror at the streets . . . towering height of Chicago's buildings . . . black all over with grime . . . dreadful buildings, and ramshackle wooden sheds, and the brick facades of miserable tenements. (6)

Hahn's memoirs specify the negative aspects of train travel and connecting via Chicago—moldy smells, bumpy streets, grimy buildings. Benson's rendering, by contrast, seems sheer nostalgia, even escapist. She omits all specific details regarding the Chicago transfer except a reference to riding on the "Parmalee bus" and Tootie's comment: "I wouldn't like to live in Chicago" (47). Benson focused instead on arriving in Manitowoc late at night: "There would be the ride in the carriage in the dusk over the brick streets, the different sounds the horses' hoofs made when they crossed the bridge. . . . And then there would be Grandma and Grandpa's house, and Grandma . . . in the doorway with Polly perched on her shoulder" (50).

As Fred Davis observes in his essay on nostalgia, almost anything of one's past can emerge as an object of nostalgia provided it can be viewed in a pleasant light (viii). Essentially formed from the Greek *nostos* (to return home) and *algia* (a painful condition), nostalgia denotes a painful longing to return home. Yet, homesickness alone does not express nostalgia's meaning. Rather, the word connotes a mood "more contemplative than active," accompanied by alternating tears and laughter. Benson's recollections of her natal city as presented in *Meet Me in St. Louis*, while superficially pleasant and comic, plunge the prober of her text into subtle undercurrents of sadness. The trickster, Benson, apparently sentimentalized her childhood in this fictional memoir, but the discerning reader cannot fail to detect Benson's bittersweet subtext and pick up clues to its author's lack of inner peace.

Although Davis notes that nostalgic feeling is almost never infused with negative sentiments—unhappiness, frustration, despair, hate, shame, abuse—he does allow that it may be tinged with melancholy. Indeed, he writes, "the nostalgic mood is one whose active tendency is to envelop all that may have been painful or unattractive about the past in a kind of fuzzy, redeemingly benign aura." Hurts and disappointments are "filtered forgivingly" or omitted. In addition, nostalgic experience contrasts sharply with "bleak, grim, wretched, ugly, deprivational, unfulfilling, frightening" present experience. Always, "adoration of the past triumphs over lamentations for the present . . . for to permit present woes to douse the warm glow from the past is to succumb to melancholy or, worse yet, depression" (16). In Benson's case, melancholy occasionally gave rise to bouts of binge drinking. Whatever the cause of that melancholy, Fred Finklehoffe's reading of "March 1904" introduced him only to a lively, fun-loving family. So, too, moviegoers enjoyed Finklehoffe and Freed's *Meet Me in St. Louis* and basked in its sunny warmth—unaware of the clouds overshadowing Benson as she wrote the book.

26

THE MAKING OF
MEET ME IN ST. LOUIS

1943–1944

"I get more homesick every day and the people I see are the damndest."

—Sally Benson

As Babe dealt with illness and deprivation at the front, Sally began fighting battles of another sort at home. In June of 1943, when Benson began negotiating to have her play, *Eight Cousins*, produced, she met an unexpected obstacle: Frank Orsatti, the producer, began referring to it as "our" play. Benson immediately contacted Paul Streger, her representative at Leland Hayward, who advised her to be very specific and firm in handling the problem. She followed his directions carefully, writing:

Dear Frank Orsatti:

I got your wire about "our play," *Eight Cousins*, and there are a few things about this play that I want you to understand. This is not *our* play. It is *my* play. . . . negotiations for this play will have to go through the Hayward office as I told you. I am under contract to Leland Hayward and accept and recognize this obligation. As to any producer commitment on this play, Jack Skirball is my producer, a condition I recognize and accept also.

I just want to be sure that no sordid matter involving business gets mixed up in our correspondence. How are you and your trees and your mother? I have been working in the garden like crazy and have a fine crop of rocks. I will be in California for a week and I imagine I will see you then. My best to you.

> Sincerely,
> Sally Benson[1]

In an earlier *New Yorker* "Profile" on Frank Orsatti, Benson had described him as a

> literary and dramatic agent in Hollywood, California. He looks and walks like a big, black bear. He is one of the "dese" and "dose" guys, and a close friend of Louis B. Mayer. One brother, Vic, is known as the "Sheik of Hollywood," and is introduced as such by Frank. Another brother, Ernie, was an outfielder for the Cardinals about six years ago. Frank was Shirley Temple's agent for many years. He called her "de Baby." In answer to a question from someone who was doubtful of Shirley's ability to play a certain part, Frank said, "De Baby can do anyting." His mother who weighs about four hundred pounds and has trouble getting through doorways, goes to Saratoga every year, where she cooks spaghetti for all the jockeys. She wires hot tips to Frank and L.B. Mayer.[2]

With her good sense of humor, Benson appreciated Orsatti's colorful character but she was not about to allow him to take possession of her play. (Incidentally, Benson's *Eight Cousins* was not produced until Jose Quintero adopted it in 1956.)

Amid these difficulties, Benson was also enjoying the acclaim won by *Meet Me in St. Louis*. The film had gone into production in November of 1943, was completed on April 7, 1944, and had its first preview two months later on June 5. It was hailed as an "unqualified success" (Fordin 117) just as Arthur Freed had expected. Having envisioned "the most delightful piece of Americana ever," he had arranged special expertise for every department no matter the cost. He hired Lemuel Ayers, Broadway set designer for *Oklahoma*, to do sets that exceeded four times the projected budget but were free of Hollywood clichés (96). Music and lyrics required the best talent, so Freed hired songwriters Hugh Martin, Ralph Blane, Kerry Mills, and Andrew B. Sterling—among others.

In preparation for the world premiere of *Meet Me in St. Louis* scheduled for November 22, 1944, Sally Benson contacted childhood friend Helen Yule—now Mrs. Al Rowan—and invited her to attend at the Loew's State Theater on Washington Avenue in St. Louis. In turn, Helen insisted that Sally stay at her home rather than book a hotel room. Local newspapers made much of Benson's arriving in town a few days early and published major articles about their city's native daughter. Journalists also interviewed Helen, who reported that she and Sally had walked through their old neighborhood to look at the ashpits and have a chocolate soda at the drugstore.[3] Helen also recalled Benson's first return visit in 1913 when they were both sixteen. "I remember she stepped off the train looking so New Yorkish and all the boys fell madly in love with her."

On opening night lines of people stretched over four blocks long, hoping for admission. Despite the 3,100 seats in the Loew's State plus 200 standing-room places, 2,000 disappointed customers had to be turned away. The next day brought an announcement: the proceeds from the premiere of *Meet Me in St. Louis* had broken the record previously set by *Gone with the Wind*.[4] Everyone involved in its production was elated. Judy Garland, who had balked initially at reverting to playing a teenager (since she regarded herself as mature), went from being the star of *For Me and My Gal* and *The Wizard of Oz* to being hailed as a *superstar*. Vincente Minnelli's career as a director had been launched, and his developing relationship with Garland culminated in their marriage the following September. Scene-stealer young Margaret O'Brien was awarded a Juvenile Oscar by the Academy in 1945, and the film garnered four Academy Award nominations: George Stoll for musical score; Ralph Blane and Hugh Martin for music and lyrics in "The Trolley Song"; Irving Brecher and Fred Finklehoffe for best screenplay; and George Folsey for Color Cinematography. (Fifteen years later, *Meet Me in St. Louis* was presented as a CBS television special on April 26, 1959. A stage version with additional songs by Hugh Martin and Ralph Blane premiered at the St. Louis Municipal Opera on June 9, 1960 [Fordin 118] and enjoyed a Broadway revival in 1990.)[5]

Back in New York, Harold Ross sent Benson a night letter at the Rowans: "Reviewers say picture is sensation and that your family was affluent and I am giddy with gratification. Stop. Congratulations and a long

life to you in technicolor. Please get busy on next series immediately."[6]
A second letter from Ross arrived three days later: "I tried to send you a
congratulatory telegram for the movie's premiere, but it was turned down
because of that word. A jewelry clerk likewise refused to deliver a string
of pearls to you on grounds they were not essential. I am stymied but will
find some way of expressing my admiration."[7]

The *St. Louis Post-Dispatch* quoted Benson the next day in a feature
article: "I know the usual trend is to write about unhappy childhood, but
mine wasn't that way," she proudly claimed. Then Benson shared with the
reporter her plans for a new series about war wives

> inspired by her daughter, Mrs. Alexis Doster, Jr., whose hus-
> band, a paratrooper, died in the service. It's about my daughter
> and the two girls she lives with in a terrible cottage in Car-
> mel, called Shangri-La, about how they have to get the coffee
> grounds out of the sink before they can bathe the baby and the
> most important furnishing in the living room, a box of Kleenex
> which occupies a position of a bowl of roses. Those girls do well
> though. They have a lot of courage.

Benson, ever modest, also made clear that *Meet Me in St. Louis*, the film,
had elaborated on her family's modest circumstances: "Our house was much
smaller . . . because we didn't have much money and lived in a modest
neighborhood. But that isn't good to see. It may be realistic, it may be
Russian, but it isn't good to see."[8] True to form, Benson refused to put
on airs. She had done well by worldly standards but she remembered her
St. Louis roots.

While the movie's elaborate Victorian mansion clearly magnified the
Smith family's circumstances, at least one part of Benson's fictional rendition
lends the modest home a degree of distinction: "The yard to the house at
5135 Kensington Avenue stretched back about three hundred feet to the
alley, down which the trolley cars ran . . . a wooden walk led to the wood-
shed and chicken house . . . there were cherry trees, the pear tree, and the
two peach trees . . . the lilac bush, the clump of peonies, the rose bushes,
and the snowball bush; there was the lawn of grass and red and white
clover" (8). A more detailed picture of the alley occurs in Eisenkramer's
The Boy Next Door: "The alley was very wide. . . . The Hodiamont streetcar
tracks ran down the center . . . with separate paved alleys on each side.

The tracks weren't embedded in cobblestone; they were like train tracks, fastened to wooden ties" (5). The proximity of the tracks explains Benson's childhood fascination with trolleys and horses. It also renders plausible the episode in "November 1903," where Tootie and Agnes try to make a trolley stop short by placing a make-believe body (their mother's stuffed dress) on the tracks.

In its wake, the success of *Meet Me in St. Louis* left Sally Benson a much-sought-after screenplay writer. Caught up in a whirlwind of negotiating with potential producers, Benson jeopardized her *New Yorker* income because her regular fiction writing had been disrupted. The *New Yorker* staff—more than she realized—regularly watched out for her interests. On November 1, 1945—almost a year after the world premiere—Forster of the accounting department staff sent Harold Ross a memo pointing out that if Benson did not do a story by December 13th she would lose "all right to her $399.93 annuity for life." Ross wrote immediately to Benson: "Please see enclosed. For the love of God, get in one piece at least, before December 13th. . . . I will do something about you socially soon."[9]

Another factor in Benson's diminished fiction production was her resumption of drinking. In 1946—after agreeing to Babe's request for a divorce—Sally Benson entered yet another rehabilitation facility. One happy result—in keeping with her talent for turning life experience into fiction—was the emergence of several new stories. Most notable of these pieces is "Lady with a Lamp," published in the January 18, 1947, *New Yorker* and chosen in 1949 for inclusion in *55 Short Stories from the New Yorker*. Here Benson's protagonist is Miss Robbins, a temporary night nurse summoned to the home of a woman alcoholic who "got scared and called the agency herself" rather than wait for her doctor to make arrangements. The piece opens with Robbins's view of her charge—fully dressed and sleeping "heavily" on a couch, her "dress pulled up above her knees," her stockings twisted, soiled and full of runs, her eyes swollen from crying. Robbins takes the woman's pulse, but disgusted by her dirty hand and cracked, broken fingernail, allows the limp arm to drop "heavily across the woman's breast." Robbins next picks up a blanket and throws it across the woman's legs, noticing in the process, "dust everywhere," a stopped mantel clock, an empty glass that smelled of whiskey . . . the woman's handbag." Though unwilling to touch anything in the apartment, Robbins nonetheless examines the purse's contents item by item. The reader, already aware of Robbins's righteous, superior attitude toward her patient, becomes privy to

Robbins's thoughts directly when she converses with her replacement. Both women agree that alcoholics "just don't seem to care or have any pride."

Robbins relates that on arriving she found the alcoholic passed out and blocking the open apartment door: "I could hardly push her aside. She was a dead weight." Personal comfort is clearly Robbins's priority as, unwittingly condemning herself, she proclaims: "I always ask for them. They're no trouble when they're as bad as she is. There's nothing you can do, so I just bring along the *Mirror*, and some nice little sandwiches, and make myself as comfy as I can." On these cases, "you usually have a chance for a good nap," she explains. Robbins has just made a pot of coffee, its "warm, comforting smell" pervading the "dreary, little kitchen" where she and the replacement make themselves "comfy." Addressing a question, Robbins adamantly advises, "*Don't* lift her. . . . She can manage all right. I wish you could have seen her last night. It would have given you a laugh." Robbins's comment on her patient's "uncombed for a week" hair, elicits "Maybe that's my job," from the new nurse. But Robbins justifies her neglect and discourages such personal attention:

> I didn't touch it. . . . If they can hold a glass, they can hold a comb, I say. . . . I just got that door open and took off my hat and coat and read my paper. You have to get used to these cases. She was kind of crying, but you couldn't make any sense out of her, so I thought . . . there's no use trying, and I put my things away and put my sandwiches in the icebox, so they'd stay nice and moist. I always bring my own sandwiches. You never can tell what you'll find to eat. They never eat.

When the replacement asks, "Hasn't she had anything?" Robbins coldly responds, "How should I know? . . . She was in no shape to eat last night. . . . She couldn't move for a while. She lay there all the time I was reading my paper . . . over an hour . . . and rolled around a little." While Robbins admittedly feasted on her snacks, the patient tried to get up off the floor. "You should have seen her! I watched her the whole time I was eating." Robbins's callous description of a two-hour process during which the patient repeatedly gets halfway up, falls over, and starts to crawl, elicits her replacement's ironic comment, "It makes me ashamed to be a woman when you hear things like that." Robbins further denigrates herself by admitting to doing nothing when the patient asked for her doctor.

Instead, she berates the patient, simultaneously revealing herself to be a monster: "Why should I wake up a man in the middle of the night for a thing like you [who does not] look human?" While the woman crawled all the way to the couch, Robbins "just sat there" thinking, "Look at you!" Her final advice to her replacement is, "Oh, she isn't dead . . . I took her pulse." Smiling "as though deeply amused," Robbins claims authority: "I ought to know. *Nothing* ever kills them."[10]

Benson's convincing story stems from personal experience and highlights perceptions of alcoholics common at the time. Her title, "Lady with a Lamp," a phrase associated with Florence Nightingale—model nurse—sheds ironic light on the cold, callous Robbins as it invites pity for the afflicted woman who, despite her addiction, deserves to be treated with respect. In 1946 when Benson wrote the piece, she did not know that her binge drinking was an inherited trait. As David Roberts notes in his biography of Jean Stafford, the clinical understanding of alcoholism in 1947 lacked the fruit of later research that considers alcoholism a disease transmitted across generational lines. Sally, Agnes, and Lon were alcoholics as Alonzo, their father, had been before them. In addition to the genetic factor, Benson, as an American writing during the first half of the twentieth century and living through Prohibition, may have been doubly susceptible to the disease.[11]

When Benson completed her rehabilitation program, she resumed her career as screenplay writer and resided in both Hollywood and Madison, Connecticut. Though she continued to write for *The New Yorker* and planned to complete the new "Shangri-La" series, her correspondence with Gus Lobrano shows that fiction writing was no longer her top priority. In 1946, for example, having forgotten the names of characters she had used earlier in the first of the "Shangri-La" pieces, she had to ask Lobrano to send them. By late March of 1947, her failure to produce the second promised piece occasioned a letter from Harold Ross stating that both he and Lobrano were worried about the proposed series—seriously worried:

> This series is different from the *Junior Miss* series. They were independent pieces, didn't carry a series title, and had no pressing time element. . . . It is different from the St. Louis stories. They had a series title and were interlaced but they were based on a period so long past that it would stay put. The present series are on a transient, fast-disappearing period of American life that will go dead soon. They're not reminiscent pieces, but

topical and timely ones. Gus says that you propose to do a story in the next day or two, another in the next few weeks while on the Coast, and more after you get back some weeks hence. That will be just fine if you follow through, but I'll continue to worry until you get enough stories in for us to be safe in starting to print them, and by "enough" I mean a sufficient number to insure our not being out on a limb if you are hit by a truck and incapacitated. I wouldn't sleep nights if we should start this series off without a minimum . . . to see us through, whatever happens. I always felt unsettled when the St. Louis stories were running, but we could have suspended them and not been too much embarrassed, but that's not true of the present pieces and my uneasiness would be cubed, which would mean a state of jittery paralysis, for . . . these are much more in the nature of a serial; much more interlaced, and . . . the first two are pretty much introductory. We don't even have a smell of what's going to happen—not enough, for instance, even to begin to wonder what the series title should be. You haven't got down to the episodes yet. For God's sake, please stick to your schedule. I think the stories are in danger of going stale and perishing if you don't.

As ever, H.W. Ross.[12]

As Ross feared, the "Shangri-La" series never materialized. Benson had succumbed to screenplay fever, and another relapse into drinking led to confinement in yet another rehabilitation program—this time at Pinewood in Katonah, New York.

In May, Benson wrote Maxwell that she was finishing "*Pride and P.*—as we call it. It looks very nice except that I am tired of writing like Jane Austen and not succeeding," she complained. Then, addressing the "Shangri-La" issue, she advised: "Tell Gus that I am rewriting both stories of what we used to call my new series, and taking out all time elements . . . in fact, all time, space, and everything. So they will be cosmic and have no more relation to us as we are today than the atom bomb. . . . I will be home about the middle of June, probably having sold the series to the movies. . . . As I re-read the last story . . . I thought it was lousy, anyway."[13] Benson never completed the series. Instead, she completed the screenplay for *Little Women* and wrote Lobrano: "Everything is lovely. All those four girls are all sweet and Marmee is glad everybody's happy."[14]

By August, Benson had returned to writing fiction for *The New Yorker* and received a check from the magazine's Robert Henderson for "Nothing Serious"—a "nice, funny piece we're delighted to have. It's the sixth in your bonus cycle, so I'm enclosing your 25% bonus check." On the 8th, Ross telegrammed: "Second piece received. It's fine and God bless you. Your starting up again is the most hopeful thing that's happened this summer."[15] On the whole, however, Benson's later short stories lacked the vitality of her earlier work. "In All Due Respect," for example, struck White as "not much of a story" and Ross corroborated White's judgment: "The ending seemed awfully weak. . . . Make clear that Madge is a Protestant and the offense to the religious might be removed but I couldn't be sure whether Madge was meant to be Roman Catholic or Protestant." By contrast, Ross praised Benson's next submission, "A Number of Things." "Those ladies are rare and sweet, and the piece is quite an accomplishment. It is wonderful for you to be writing again . . . especially short, light stuff which we need terribly at this juncture. I always say, 'God will provide.' I'll buy a lunch or dinner most any time."[16] Ross also liked "A Totally Different Person." He thought it was "a cute and clever idea and very expertly done and some wonderful talk . . . I'm very glad men fill a need."[17]

27

HOLLYWOOD, PINEWOOD, BROADWAY, AND BEYOND

1947–1957

"I loved her talent as an artist and respected her self-worth as a woman."

—Marshall Jamison

Most of Benson's late 1940s fiction centered on alcoholism—with a twist. Tucked into what appears to be a slight story is a revelation of Benson's having gained some understanding of her drinking. An Evarts piece—"In All Due Respect"—features Madge Ferris and Millie Potter who meet for lunch in a restaurant. Millie has arrived first and is already halfway through a cocktail before her friend arrives. "How many of those have you had?" asks Madge. "One," says Millie, "But I think I'll have another." Madge double checks: "Are you sure you want another?" Madge laughingly explains that she was just thinking of Millie's diet but adds,

> It was so odd to see you sitting here drinking alone. There's something about drinking alone—well even doctors who *advise* taking a drink *normally* would soon put a stop to it if you ever told them that you drank alone. . . . now that we're all being educated with these wonderful books and moving pictures, we *do* know where the danger lies. There's nothing to be ashamed of, anyway, because it's all a disease.[1]

This story also suggests that Benson is coming to grips with signs of aging and rediscovering an interest in religion. The women will visit the cathedral as Madge has planned. She had earlier that morning visited its statue of St. Elizabeth but needs to return because her intended lighting of a votive candle to honor the saint had been interrupted by meeting a priest. "You've got the sweetest St. Elizabeth here, and you've done her so beautifully, wrinkles and all," she tells him. Then, since Millie knows nothing of the saint, Madge explains: "You'd love her. . . . She's about our age—not young, you know, and not old . . . there she stands with some *faint* wrinkles, just as all women have when they're a bit older . . . the sort that come from laughing." First, though, both women need to shop for hats. The piece ends with Millie assuring her friend that she will surely love St. Elizabeth—"It's such a *difficult* age."

If "In All Due Respect" existed alone, the reader might agree with Ross about its slightness, but Benson followed this story with others that repeat her concerns about women, alcohol, and aging. The next—"A Totally Different Person"—centers on Madge and Millie again, this time at Madge's home having tea.[2] Their conversation turns to a mutual friend whom Millie presumes to be leading a lonely life because she is single. On the contrary, Millie discovers that Katherine Pritchard entertains each evening a group of younger men who live in her building. In fact, Millie reports, they are "Very young. In their twenties." Madge tries to explain that boys "like to have a place where they can drop in and feel at home." They probably look on her as an "older woman who is *kind* to them." Unconvinced, Millie retorts: "I can tell you how *she* looks on *them*. Avidly is the way she looks, as though she'd never seen a man before. . . . asking them to light her cigarettes and pawing them every chance she got. . . . They loll around on the floor . . . and they don't talk at all. They just laugh and scream."[3]

The piece concludes with Millie's admission that the boys fill a need for Katherine just as her husband does for her. She would be just like Katherine were it not for Harry and so would Madge, she asserts. But Madge disagrees. "I wouldn't, without Sam." Millie's next concern is Katherine's age—"forty." Again, Madge tries to bring her to reality by reminding her, "So am I . . . and so are you." Madge finishes the discussion by advising her friend not to show too much how she has missed her husband when she picks him up at the station. It is as though Benson is reconciling herself to being middle aged and rethinking her affair with Ham.

A third story is "Seeing Eye," set in a restaurant where Ruth Hardy and Ellen Russell await the arrival of Ruth's husband.[4] Both women order martinis and discuss Don. He didn't look well the last time Ellen saw him—

just before he joined the army. Ruth agrees, blaming him for enlisting (and reminiscent of Babe): "Then the war came, and he *would* go, although they never would have drafted him at his age. Poor, foolish Don." Ruth claims they are happier now than before, "Busier and happier. You see I have to be his eyes." The cocktails arrive, and the women down them quickly so they can have another when Don arrives. "He'll want one to celebrate seeing—being with you again." Again, the piece focuses on aging, this time shifting to a male whose faulty vision led many to identify him as James Thurber, claiming that Benson was paying Thurber back for his negative portrayal of Babe in *The Male Animal* (Kinney 610, 1187). "Nothing Serious" followed with a discussion on death, centering on Millie's illness and Madge's unwillingness to associate illness with death. Madge cannot even say the word "death" or hear anyone else use it.

In May of 1949, Benson's "Just Depressed" appeared.[5] Here the two friends discuss Frances Mabee who has been "put away in that place in Westchester for two years. She's out of her head, but completely," reports Millie. Madge counters, "She was never out of her head. She was just depressed." They put her there as a "protection to herself." Millie argues, "She was far from depressed . . . until she spent every penny" of the money left by her husband. It was good of her relatives to keep her in "that place in Westchester, *which* I understand is just like a hotel." Madge is incredulous: "A hotel! . . . I hardly think a hotel would lock one of its guests up at night, or have a psychiatrist calling in every day. And I understand that's what happened to Frances." Their next problem is what Frances will do "now that she is out of that place"—or more to the point, how will she behave at lunch in Rose Anne's?

When Frances arrives at the restaurant, Millie does not recognize her in her expensive clothes and perfume. She is further surprised by Frances's news that she has found an apartment. It belonged to a little old lady about to be sent to the Cedars (Benson's rehabilitation site was the Elms). The women order drinks, but Frances can no longer abide martinis, which "taste of paraldehyde," and chooses a Daiquiri. "With all the paraldehyde I had for all those weeks—every four hours, if you can believe it—I cannot touch anything that reminds me of it," Frances explains. She recounts an experience at the Cedars in occupational therapy. She can't remember doing it but she threw an ashtray at a girl, causing her to need six stitches in her arm. Millie, when asked by Frances what exciting things she's been doing, is at a loss. "Nothing exciting at all compared to you," she states, earning Madge's admonition: "I don't want you to get it in your head that being depressed is all beer and skittles, is it, Frances?" Benson concludes with Frances's well-intentioned, "If you're feeling depressed, I couldn't possibly recommend a nicer place to go to than the Cedars. Heavens! I should know, shouldn't I?" In typical Benson fashion, an experience that most people would regard as horrendous— spending time in an institution for depression—is transformed into an occasion for humorous satire. The newly released "inmate" not only looks happy and healthy but recommends the experience to friends who had previously thought they were happy.

In June 1948 Benson submitted "Third Time, No Sound," a rewrite she had done for Sidney Sheldon. Lobrano rejected it and encouraged Benson to do her own writing rather than work on someone else's material. He promised to see that her work would get a "careful reading."[6] However, Benson entered once again into a period of rehabilitation. Her next contact with Lobrano would be almost a year later in the spring of 1949:

> I'll be in New York Sunday, March 13th for eight days. Put a big red circle around that date on your calendar because you'd be taking me to lunch. Don't get sick, for God's sake. I've noticed you've used that form of escape. Just keep spraying your nose and throat. I'm dying to see you but I don't want that to make you nervous. Tell Ross so he'll be steeled.
>
> Love, Sally.[7]

Later in the year, Benson sent "The Comeback" to *The New Yorker*. Though it was set up on October 17, 1949, it sat in the "bank" for three years. Finally, it was "killed" on December 9, 1952 by then managing editor William Shawn. An excellent piece, it was apparently too graphic and raw for Shawn's taste. This time Benson's protagonist is a male who has enjoyed the companionship of fellow patients during a rehabilitation program but is about to be released. After packing his bag, he meets his wife and gets into her car but by the time he gets home, he realizes he can no longer deal with her predictable, bland responses. After dinner, he goes into his room, takes out a poison-loaded syringe hidden in the back of his radio, and injects himself. Probably Benson's most graphic piece on depression, "The Comeback" went to galleys and would have been published had it not been for William Shawn's squeamishness. Benson did not try to publish it elsewhere.

Meanwhile, Benson was still using her creativity for screenplay writing. In the fall of 1949, she had proposed a "Hobo idea" to Sam Goldwyn at 20th Century-Fox but he rejected it as more appropriate for a Bing Crosby musical or a Bob Hope or Danny Kaye comedy. "Sorry darling," Sam wrote comically explaining: "I jest cain't handle the hobo idea. . . . To attempt to tell the story as a straight drayma [*sic*] with a sterling actor like Cornell Wilde in the principal role would cause my cup of bitters to runneth over."[8] Next, Benson proposed "the Bainbridge matter" to her agent at MCA, Roy Myers, who vetoed it with reluctance and softened the rejection with a compliment: "Of course, Sam [Engel] doesn't think anyone can write like you . . . I hope I can work out something for you, to do something for him in New York one of these days soon." He encouraged her to promote *Eight Cousins*, assuring her Hayward was still interested. He was glad she was "having such a good time with her Spanish dancing lessons and such." Benson, it would seem, was now a fading star. *The New Yorker* published only two Benson pieces in 1949 and nothing more until December of 1954.

As for her daughter, in 1946, Barbara Benson—now twenty-seven—had married Robert Webster (Soup) Campbell in Carmel, California and moved to Hanover, New Hampshire where their daughter, Sara Taber Campbell, was born on February 19, 1947. Barbara and Soup went on to have two more children—Robert (known in the family as "Booter") and Susan. They shortly moved with Dusty (Barbara's three-year-old son from her first marriage) to Canada where Campbell managed a plastics factory. Benson rarely heard from Barbara after that move—a separation prompted by Barbara's inability to deal with her mother's addictive behavior.

From the end of 1949 and into the fifties, Benson alternated between Broadway script writing, rehabilitation programs, and Hollywood screenplay writing. She gave minimal attention to fiction writing but in May of 1950 she returned to Madison, Connecticut for the summer and received from Lobrano some checks and a renewal of her first reading agreement. Then, in February of 1951 William Maxwell tried to pressure Benson into putting down on paper the "five stories all finished in [her] head." Pull the telephone out of the wall, he urged. Four stories "is all it takes for all sorts of remunerative bookkeeping to start grinding away, and the checks mount up surprisingly these days," he cajoled.[9] Hollywood, however, where she enjoyed a luxurious home complete with swimming pool, had claimed her. She wrote or collaborated on screenplays for the next four months, returning to New York only to work on the play script of Booth Tarkington's *Seventeen*—a saga of adolescent romance.

When *Seventeen* opened at Broadway's Broadhurst Theatre on June 21, 1951 reviews were mixed. Blame for the production's weaknesses lay evenly on the Tarkington subject matter, Benson's failure to give it vitality, and the music. "The story line has little substance and even less suspense, so its frail plot is padded with . . . innocuous dialogue about youth in love. It has a tendency to be too precious at times, and too often lacks kick," noted Marie Torre in the *World-Telegram* (June 22, 1951). Sally Benson's book is "paper thin," wrote Robert Coleman in the *Daily Mirror*. "The Benson libretto is slight and fails to catch the nostalgic charm and juvenile heartbreak of the Tarkington original . . . [the script is] low horse-powered." By contrast, Brooks Atkinson in the *New York Times* was positive: "Sally Benson has preserved the integrity of the old-fashioned fable." Otis Guernsey of the *Herald Tribune* was negative: "It is all much too bouncy to believe, and without enough keenness or variety of humor to gain any great comic validity."[10]

Benson was disappointed but plunged into the project of moving from 93rd Street to 45 East End Avenue on the East River at 81st Street. She continued writing for *The New Yorker*, and Maxwell sent her two checks in October. He sympathized as he acknowledged their paucity: "Time was when by putting these two checks together you could have got something that dangled, from B. Harris, but surely not anymore."[11] On December 7th, Benson called Lobrano but he did not take her call. She wrote immediately to complain, explaining she had gotten through to Maxwell but,

> he seemed cross with me. I told him I would be in but he didn't believe me. Anyway, here is the story I had started and now have finished. I have some more I've thought of too. I am in a new apartment and can spit into the river. Where is Sandy now and Dotty? . . . Barbara and her four children are living in Canada. There is a plastics factory there that Soup runs. I'll be in next week.
>
> Love, Sally[12]

Benson did submit a piece titled "A Long Way from Home," but *The New Yorker* rejected it and Lobrano explained, "It's a pretty convincing glimpse of senile dementia but it seems to us to be interesting as pathology rather than fiction. Please give us a chance at something else soon."[13]

Somewhat disillusioned, Benson returned to Hollywood and spent the next three years working on screenplays. She completed *The Belle of New York* for MGM in 1952 and *The Farmer Takes a Wife* in 1953 for 20th Century-Fox. For all her involvement in Hollywood, Benson avoided the political controversy surrounding the Screenwriters' Guild but could not conquer her drinking problem. She fell into debt, worsening her difficulties until, in the summer of 1954, Benson was admitted once more to a treatment program at Pinewood in Katonah, New York, where her financial straits pushed her to rediscover her muse. She produced one piece, "Spirit of '76," for the December 25th issue of *The New Yorker*.

In the weeks before Christmas, Benson complained to Maxwell:

> I did not get my check in time to get off a few things for the kids . . . here is how it was spent: overdue bill here [Katonah] $412.31; extras $29.95; bill here paid to Jan. 7th $190.00. This [leaves] me $150.79—not quite enough to go on that 'spending spree' that the doctor here told me you were all worried about. I have had no winter clothes . . . and as all I came with was a few summer things, I have to get sweaters, cold cream, and things of that sort. Also, I do smoke and buy cigarettes, candy, and go to the movies.

More poignantly, Benson continued:

> The holding up of my check made me feel very badly, and I will send my other story on when I get over the feeling that I am not thought of as an idiot child. I was excited over the story, but amazed at the hullabaloo. I'm not Lillian Roth and this is not my life. I am grateful to people and will continue to be, but cannot go around in sackcloth and ashes. The kindest thing that can be done for me is to let me go ahead and write, not to tell anyone where I am until I can get somewhat out of debt. The back bill here which had to be paid, took a large

part of this check, but I will be able to get more from the next. Also, will you let me know if I still have an agreement with the *New Yorker*? I would also like to do their mysteries again, as god knows I have time. Merry Christmas and love to you, and stop putting your heads together. Tell me for a change, and you will see that nothing dire will happen. Sally[14]

On January 5th William Maxwell, gentleman that he was, sent Benson "contract and consideration." Maxwell's "consideration" sparked a year of productivity for Benson. She began writing once again in earnest and had seven pieces published that year. Dr. Wender upgraded her to outpatient status, requiring a weekly visit to his office in Pinewood. Since Benson did not want to go back to Manhattan, she rented a place in Bedford Village. She wrote Maxwell, "It's a sort of tourist place, but I have a clean room with a little alcove and a shower. I can walk to the Village and there is a movie there." On nice days she walked into town for diversion but when it snowed she thought nothing of calling for a cab. She continued, "The place is run by an old man and his wife, and there is a hamburger place across the road where I get my breakfast. The truck drivers eat there." Before long Benson's new residence had inspired a piece called "Hospitality" that appeared in the March 19th *New Yorker*.

With her first check, Benson paid the sanitarium all she owed them and the rent for five days in Bedford Village. This left her with $30.00, so she asked Maxwell for a $100 advance because she wanted to

see *Waterfront* and have a place to stay over the weekend. It got so crowded at Pinewood that there was no place for my typewriter. People are evidently cracking up all over the place. After breakfast today when I got back, carrying a carton of coffee, the woman who runs this place gave me a large piece of apple pie to go with it. I am fat. I have a radio I listen to. I have a lot of mysteries that I got at the library, everybody talks to me, and it's nice to be away from people talking sick all the time. My best to Gus. Love, Sally[15]

On February 7th, Benson went over to Pinewood to get her check and mailed "Hospitality"—"I really love it," she confessed. She also had started another one called "The Other Side of the Island." It's about a little boy, she explained, "as I'm trying to vary them and not have them all about old people." She had bought *The New Yorker* and liked Salinger's story. "But the Saul Bellow one I didn't understand." After seeing *On the Waterfront* and *Barefoot Contessa*, she paid her rent ($42.50). That meant she had about $35.00 left so she asked that Maxwell send her check before Thursday when she would next go to Pinewood.

Benson's letters to Maxwell during these months were chatty and breezy. Often, she offered advice on child-raising: "Please don't look at your baby and think who she looks like," Benson advised. She remembered that she had alienated Barbara by staring at her and asking, "Where did you come from?" Benson—five foot two—could not adjust to her daughter's height—five feet, nine inches—and large frame since both her parents were short (as were Anna Cora and Benson's siblings). She continued:

> Esther grew up being told she was like all the Champlins (kind of fat). I have Papa's nose (the Hyde nose), Rose has the Maguire teeth (braided), and I've known since I was a baby that any weight I got would be right in my belly (the Prophaters). So don't! And as for taking the baby back, take care she doesn't take you back and go off with Peter Pan. My God! I just looked at one of my shoes (for inspiration, I guess) and it's coming all out on one side. So you'd better send me some money. I sound very grasping when I write, and I am. My best to Lobrano . . .
>
> Love, Sally (Sally Benson).[16]

Each of the seven stories Benson wrote in 1955 was accompanied by a similar long letter to Maxwell. Sometimes, in addition to stressing her need for money, Benson offered observations on her experience as a young mother. One passage is particularly touching:

> Yes, I kept staring at Barbara. I was pretty young and sort of felt that she'd been left on my doorstep. I loved her, but I think it was Dusty [her grandson] who took the heart out of me. Bury this secret with me. Barbara was sort of calm, whereas Dusty *quivers*. . . . For God's sake, say something about "Hospitality." I loved it so, and all you say is that you have it, that it came, and stuff like that.[17]

Often, Benson referred to her pieces as though they were offspring. She "loves" them or "really loves" them. In this letter, Benson's comments on her feelings about Barbara and Dusty parallel her feelings about her story.

As though to atone for neglecting to comment on "Hospitality," Maxwell shared an observation made by Sylvia Townsend Warner, an English contributor of fiction to *The New Yorker*. Warner couldn't think of a story and had written Maxwell:

> I cannot think you would have a wish in the world left, after that Sally Benson story about the couple on the way to Boston. It is like heaven to read stories by her again, or more accurately, like purgatory: torments—and yet an overwhelming consciousness of the paradisal admiration one will feel at the end of the story. *Mon ange, ma gouge.* Tell her so with my love. . . .[18]

Benson enjoyed Warner's compliment and wrote Maxwell with advice about the type of doll to purchase for his daughter.[19] Considering her early childhood relationship with dolls, Benson's directives are instructive:

> . . . get a pretty one. Dolls don't look like dolls any more. They look like *people* and I think that's too bad. After all, if a child has to be with people all day long and look at their silly faces, she shouldn't have to have the same sort of face looking at her when she plays. Now, honey, they have dolls all dressed, but if you'll look at the inside of their clothes, they are stitched badly and fall apart. I dressed one for Sara and I knitted her a skating dress and made her clothes. You see a doll needs nightgowns, towels, a washcloth, her own soap, her jewelry, her handbags, bathing suits, winter coats, sweaters, capes and hats. Don't get a baby doll—they have that wrinkled look, modeled as they are after real babies. Get a doll with hair. When you get her, send her to me here and I'll start making her clothes. I love to do them. Then, you see, she'll eventually have a trunk and a bed and a little chair. . . . At the rate I sew, your baby will have the doll when she starts school.[20]

When Benson sent Maxwell "The Rummage Sale" she thanked him for the check for $500.00, which "did a lot to dispel the clouds."[21] Then, she confessed: "I bought two pounds of Candy Cupboard chocolates and *ate* them." She begged him to let her know about her submission soon "just to quiet my anxiety over *anything* I do. And, of course, I am broke again." After inquiring about the baby, she volunteers: "Soon she can lie out on the grass. Dusty used to sit in his play pen out in California when he was seven months old and eat olives that fell from the tree." In closing, she promised to send her nearly finished "The Other Side of the Island," but first, she had to go to the movies for a Sunday matinee.

In June, Benson began working with Marshall Jamison on a script based on a compilation of F. Scott Fitzgerald's "Josephine" stories. Titled *The Young and the Beautiful,* the play was scheduled to go into rehearsal in mid-August and "come into the Plymouth about the first of October." When she finished the script, Benson wrote Maxwell, "Now I'm going to do several stories. I finished this one yesterday ["The Artist"] and I started one today called 'Arrangement in Silver.'" She was staying "for this week at the Elms Inn in Ridgefield, Connecticut" because

> the sand pit in Katonah got too much for me with all the win-
> dows open. . . . Baron Pollan found me this place to stay and
> cool off—God! Katonah is hot—and he lives at West Redding.
> How's the baby? And why haven't I gotten proofs on "Rummage
> Sale" and "The Pet"? I thought "The Other Side of the Island"
> looked good, and people said they loved it.

She was heading for the drugstore to get a chocolate soda. "I'm hot and I've *typed* for five days solid, but tonight . . . I'm going to the movies, *The Sea Chase.*" One of the doctors was renting Benson's place in Katonah, and she wished she could "stick him with it for the summer" because she liked the Elms Inn where she didn't have to cook.[22] By Monday, the 11th, Benson learned that her stories had gone astray. She had to type them over and it "killed" her to do it again. Her whole schedule was "knocked" and she had to postpone a trip to Guilford to see her mother. She would send the next package "registered and special delivery. Do you think God is test-ing me?" she asked. "Believe me, I felt like it." As she grew older, Benson began to sound more like her mother. More and more, God came into her conversation, though simply as an exclamation or to express vexation.[23]

In the middle of a heat wave, Benson went over to Pinewood and moved all her stuff because she no longer had to go back. She kept reading the newspaper reviews of her play, *The Young and the Beautiful*, but confessed to Maxwell:

> I have no more interest in it than if I'd never even seen it. I don't think it's very good, but I hope to God I'm wrong. I was wishing the other night that you had a magazine and I had a magazine, and you'd write for me and I'd write for you. And there would be no embarrassing questions. I figure with our original backing we could last six months. But what a six months! Just Heaven![24]

In August Benson sent Maxwell "Onward Christian Soldier" and wrote:

> It's so lovely here now. The dust flowers and black-eyed Susans are all in bloom along the roads, and when you go through the shady spots, you can smell the pines. When those people call me from New York, I tell you that play seems a hundred miles off. I eat like a wolf and I'm fat, and I just want to stay in the country. I can't think why I used to like New York so. Maybe by winter I will.
>
> Love, Sally.
>
> Call me when you get this. No matter what you say I can tell by your voice.[25]

The Young and the Beautiful opened at the Longacre Theatre on Saturday, October 1, 1955. Benson had enjoyed working with Director Marshall Jamison whose first impressions of her were that she was a "tough old broad." He liked her because she was "gutsy. She didn't take any crap from anybody, including me. She was far from a shy flower. She knew what she could do, and she could do it well." Asked what motivated Benson, Jamison replied, "Desire for self-expression." As to whether Benson had betrayed her talent by switching from fiction to Broadway dramas and screenplay writing as many *New Yorker* editors viewed it, Jamison disagreed. He considered the switch "a budding out, growing her talent, showing her ability." In sum, Jamison admired Benson (now fifty-eight) and even his mother was fond of her. He explained:

They were both old ladies and they got along great. Sally had a lot of great ability and was sharp as a tack. She was an animal who had been hurt and she fought back in the only way that she knew: she became a bitch. I didn't see her as a bitch but others saw her that way and she liked it that way. Sally was the kind of person you'd go to hell for. She was okay. She was a million bucks. Boy, could she write.

Jamison knew Benson for the duration of the show—seventeen weeks of rehearsals—from the first stages of production until it closed—and for some time after. They occasionally had a few drinks together, but alcohol "never affected our relationship." In his experience, Benson was a

fascinating woman. She was ugly. She was horrible. But she was one of the most wonderful women I ever knew. We hit it off. A playwright and a director don't always see eye to eye, but we cared about doing the job the best way we knew how. We respected each other, and that, too, is rare in the theater between a playwright and a director. We made the effort to get along. She liked me a lot. I have no idea why. As years go by, your opinions of people change, but my feelings about her have not changed and will not change: I loved her talent as an artist and respected her self-worth as a woman.[26]

As for the show, Benson's *The Young and the Beautiful* intrigued reviewers. Its main character was an appropriate one for Benson—a virtual alter ego—since, in Brooks Atkinson's terms, the adolescent Josephine Perry was a scheming flirt who, in her greediness for men, cheated and lied. Benson's multiple fiancés in 1917 had fitted her with expertise in bringing Josephine to the stage. Atkinson credited Benson with achieving more than "another comedy of adolescence." She "mixes a little gall with the romance." He continued,

Although Josephine is patently outrageous, she is also a desperate . . . frightened, pathetic young lady, headed for the sort of doom that Scott Fitzgerald coveted. Although he was fascinated by sin, he had a puritanical sense of the punishment that sin extracts from . . . transgressors; and *The Young and the Beautiful* represented him faithfully. . . . An old hand at the humors of adolescence, [Benson] sketches in some amusing scenes with the young and the insufferable—the premature decadents, the premature courtesans, working hard to make their little world wicked and glamorous.[27]

Richard Watts of the *New York Post* was surprised to find *The Young and the Beautiful* had captivated him with its

curious combination of nostalgia and bitterness. . . . All humorous nostalgia and smiling-contemplation-romantic boy-and-girl love on the surface, but at heart sardonic, chill, and disillusioned . . . its youthful sentimental dream turning inexorably into a nightmare . . . the cute child isn't what she seems [but] . . . a minor monster . . . shamelessly lead[ing] the young men on, throw[ing] herself at them when they show a lack of interest, and flee[ing] in dismay when they take her pretense for actuality. . . . Her tragedy is that she is utterly incapable of affection or genuine emotion of any kind . . . a pathological case, in desperate need of masculine admiration but unable to respond to it.[28]

John McClain of the *Journal American* praised Benson's weaving of Fitzgerald's stories into an "incisive and poignant consideration of a golden girl who loved lavishly, if not well," capturing the "flair and flavor of Fitzgerald's generation." Since that generation was also Benson's, her recreation of 1915 Chicago could not fail to be accurate. Her "unerring ear" created characters posturing and prattling "against a background of upper bourgeois luxury . . . riddled with the atmosphere Fitzgerald created with such mastery"—a world Benson knew well from her high school days in New York City. Walter Kerr in the *Herald Tribune* called Benson's play a

perfect production . . . curiously honest, achingly bitter, dry and devastating . . . a piece of genuine observation . . . written with a shrewd and unsparing hand. Scott Fitzgerald might well have been pleased.

Despite so many positive appraisals, the show survived only two months. It had not found the right audience. Two reviewers, Robert Coleman in the *Daily Mirror* and William Hawkins in the *New York World Telegram*, barely mentioned Benson's script and gave the play mediocre reviews.[29] The reviewer for *The New Yorker* offered some perceptive comments regarding Benson's appropriation of Fitzgerald's material. Admittedly, he had not read the "Josephine" stories, but he could appreciate that

> Mrs. Benson [was] clearly attempting something a little more ambitious than a study of a shallow adolescent egocentric. . . . she thinks of Josephine as a victim of a time of peculiar spiritual chaos for the young (the action of the play takes place in 1915) and that she believes there is a small but authentic tragedy in the story of a girl whose enormous vitality might have found some satisfactory outlet under almost any other social conditions but who is now condemned to a series of easy conquests that she finds dismayingly empty without knowing exactly why.

Fitzgerald, the reviewer acknowledges, was "a remarkably exact social historian," so he accepts his view of the prewar period as "a sort of moral vacuum, when everybody's goal was only a state of perpetual excitement." Benson's underlying theme is the same, but "never comes through very clearly or convincingly" because of her "extraordinary gift . . . manifested in *Junior Miss*—for writing so charmingly and wittily about adolescence." The resulting tenderness and humor "defeats the serious purpose of the play almost absolutely."[30]

In November 1955, before the show closed, Maxwell sent Benson a "first reading" contract with a note: "As you know from other years, this isn't precedent-establishing, but it does establish some kind of a record, by God."[31] Miffed that her involvement in theater kept her from writing fiction, he queried: "How long is this going to go on?"[32] Benson, however, produced only "Rummage Sale," published in March of 1956. In April 1956, Maxwell sent Benson a royalties check for $47.00 for British and American editions of short story anthologies.

In September she contacted *The New Yorker* from Hollywood because CBS-TV had called and wanted the dates on her Madge and Millie stories. She explained to Maxwell that all were Esther Evarts pieces but one that Ross had "put it in the front of the book *against* my better judgment."[33] Daise Terry sent Benson the list of her nine Madge and Millie stories the next day along with a request from George Bennett, a teacher at Phillips

Exeter Academy, for permission to use three Benson pieces in a pamphlet to be used in an English course—specifically, "The Artist," "The Guest," and "The Other Side of the Island"—all published the previous year.[34] Terry inquired whether Benson approved and what fee she wanted for each. Given Benson's continual shortage of funds, she presumably agreed but no record exists of the fees she asked.

Financial reasons caused her to resume writing and by September 22nd she had finished "Birthday"—a "story for the Christmas issue, if you like it. I would have made it Halloween to hurry you, but it didn't fit. Anyway, if you think you are going to like it, would you send me an advance? I just learned that I have to pay the money I get from MCA and Random House in back taxes—all of it—for years, I think."[35] To Benson's dismay, Maxwell sent unwanted news:

> It's a "No." Be patient with us for God's sake. The people didn't have any faces on them, and reading along it was difficult to be sure whose side you were on. I don't think it is easy to switch over, instantly, from script writing to stories, but you have done it over and over. Just don't get annoyed and go off and sign up with some fool movie company before you hit your stride.[36]

The next day she sent in "Enter Mr. Brown" but that was not accepted, Maxwell explained, because "none of us found the talk or the characterization of the children convincing." Maxwell, who had replaced the ill Lobrano, feared that Benson would

> get provoked and wash [her] hands of the whole business, and it will all be my fault and what would Gus say? The truth is, you have been working in a different medium and it shows. These people, children and adults, are generalized, like characters on the stage or in the movies. A little more time, and you will revert to your own deadly eye and accuracy.[37]

To soften the blow, he added: "I suppose it isn't true that it hurts me worse than it does you, but I feel as if it does."

Before Benson had a chance to adjust her fiction as Maxwell had advised, she was back in Hollywood working on screenplays and living at

6376 Yucca Street. In December she sent in her signed contract and told Maxwell:

> I have been very busy. I went over and made Mr. Magoo into his first full-length picture . . . and he is going to be Don Quixote! . . . Then I went and did Mother Cabrini for which they hope to get Anna Magnani . . . and Tuesday I go to Disney to do *Babes in Toyland* . . . Also Jose Quintero is going to produce and direct *Eight Cousins*, and it will come in this April, and Mr. Quintero will be here the 22nd or 27th to see me. We have signed with him and I am very pleased. He likes it.

As though to explain her productivity, Benson added, "I just got tired of not having any money with people barking at my heels, and I wanted something sure like a salary."[38] She added that Anna Cora was still alive and, though ninety-six and showing some signs of dementia, still had clear moments. Esther had written that they had gotten her up in her chair after a nap and her first comment was: "I feel so sorry for all those people in England and France with more gas rationing." Benson wished Maxwell a "lovely Christmas. I am spending Christmas Eve and Day with Joe Justman and his family. Some time I will tell you all about the Cabrini nuns and how darling they are . . . and about the Christmas plays I went to see that their orphans gave. The costumes were so beautiful that I felt the Motleys ought to hire the sister who designed them. My love, Sally." Maxwell's long letter of response included a plea: "For God's sake don't you get so interested in all those goings on out there that you forget there is any such thing as a short story, or that you ever wrote one."[39]

Benson and Maxwell continued to correspond throughout 1957 while she worked on Hollywood screenplays. Then, in August, Katharine White asked specifically that she write a story. Benson replied to Maxwell that she had "just finished a thing for Universal yesterday. I have been wanting to do *Fourteen Fifth Avenue*, about which I've thought for years. And I will start it. But, of course, you don't take series until four or more stories are in. And you may not like it anyway. But, I'll fool around with the first one." On a personal note, Benson added:

> I like being here overlooking the Pacific, but I do get homesick once in a while. I bought the *New Yorker* a couple of

weeks ago . . . but it was thin and read only one story which I couldn't get through. The stories run so long! I think the magazine looked better when there were more stories . . . and shorter ones. And there are no very short, funny ones in back. And I go crazy trying to see if there are any recommended mysteries. There has been a wonderful crop of them, which I buy . . . Harper Suspense and others, but I can't find them soon enough in the *New Yorker* and have to go to Martindale's and pick them out cold.

In all of her letters to Maxwell, Benson continued sharing ideas about raising his daughter, Kate. When Maxwell's second daughter, Brookie, arrived, Benson commented: "I know how those new babies are and how you feel about Kate. But you will like that new baby, although Barbara's other children never meant so much to me as Dusty." In her last letter, Benson observed, "Kate should be at the age where she's trying to run everything about now. And Baby must be having it tough. I will never forget Dusty on the little merry-go-round at a cheap little carnival in Madison. The look on his face! As though he'd seen a vision."[40]

EPILOGUE

Benson continued her screenplay writing until 1966 as collaborator or sole author of fifteen successful Hollywood films. These include: *Shadow of a Doubt* in 1943 for Universal Studios; *Experiment Perilous* in 1944 for RKO; *National Velvet* in 1944 for MGM; *Anna and the King of Siam* in 1946 for 20th Century-Fox; *Come to the Stable* in 1949 for 20th Century-Fox; *No Man of Her Own* in 1950 for Paramount; *Conspirator* in 1950 for MGM; *The Belle of New York* in 1952 for MGM; *The Farmer Takes a Wife* in 1953 for 20th Century-Fox; *The Adventures of Huckleberry Finn* in 1960 for MGM; *Bus Stop* in 1961 for 20th Century-Fox; *Summer Magic* in 1962 for Walt Disney; *Viva Las Vegas* in 1963 for MGM; *Signpost to Murder* in 1963 for MGM; and *The Singing Nun* in 1966 for MGM.

Babe Benson died on April 23, 1969, at Roosevelt Hospital in New York and was buried in West Barnet, Vermont. There is no evidence that Sally attended his funeral. In 1970, illness caused Sally Benson to spend the last two years of her life as a resident/patient at the Motion Picture and Television Hospital—a retirement home established in 1948 in Woodland Hills, California, for members of the film industry—whether actors, directors, producers, or crew. Some paid a modest sum; the needy resided free.

Since Sally and her daughter had been estranged for many years, Barbara never visited. She had severed connections with her mother after Benson resumed drinking in the forties, and she discouraged her children from having contact with Sally. The move to Canada had been part of Barbara's effort in this regard. However, thanks to her longtime friend, Marian Selby, Barbara and Soup Campbell returned to the United States and settled in Tucson, Arizona, where Barbara began working for the *Arizona Sun* as editor of the Women's Column. Granddaughters Susan and Sara Campbell managed a visit to their grandmother while they were in college but did so secretly, against their mother's wishes. Benson, of course, was happy to meet these grandchildren, though she really did not know them. (They remember that she introduced them to Groucho Marx, a fellow resident.) Lon's grandchildren in Texas had been frequent recipients of Benson visits, especially at Thanksgiving and Christmas when she would arrive laden with gifts like a true "Lady Bountiful." No record exists of their visiting her. Rose's grandchildren also remember Benson but apparently did not keep in touch.

After divorcing Soup Campbell, Barbara married her third husband, Ralph Golseth. He was the one who persuaded Barbara to visit Benson during her final illness. Barbara reluctantly yielded to his coaxing and enjoyed a time of reconciliation with her mother and visited her mother every day at the hospital in Woodland Hills during the last three weeks before Benson died on July 19, 1972, at the age of seventy-four. Obituaries appeared in the *Los Angeles Times*, the *New York Times*, the *St. Louis Post-Dispatch*, the *Shore Line Times*, and *Time* magazine. All praised Benson's rare talent of combining incisive wit with humorous compassion, especially in her portrayals of adolescents.

Looking back over her life, one realizes the prophetic accuracy of the handwriting analysis done for Sally Benson in 1920:

> She is full of color—warmth—and really more dependent on people . . . though her spirit is balky at times. She likes companionship. It is in that which she is dependent—not what people may say. As a friend she would be loyal and true and staunch as the Rock of Gibraltar. . . . She's a little amusing and very appealing. She tries to be so independent and different, yet all the while she loves people as she finds them, is affectionate, lovable, very artistic. . . . She is quite intuitive—ought to be a good linguist but would never make a good lawyer.

The positive qualities Benson possessed—warmth, loyalty, humor, generosity, compassion toward people—endeared her to many. On the flip side, Benson's flighty, temperamental nature allowed her to be mean and ugly at times, causing her to alienate people, even those close to her. How, then, should Sally Benson, be remembered?

Sally Benson should be remembered for her contribution to American literature and twentieth-century popular culture. From a woman's perspective, Benson illustrated her times, a period extending from turn-of-the-century St. Louis through the Jazz Age in New York to suburban, post–World War II Connecticut in the fifties. Her fiction focused on women's experiences, presenting ordinary characters, often trapped by societal and cultural pressures. Nicola Beauman writes, in "imaginative literature woman is of the highest importance . . . in everyday life she is insignificant" (2). Benson, however, brought to life insignificant but real women, satirizing their situations and challenging readers to break out of patterns that bind.

Liar that she may have been, Benson hated hypocrisy in all its forms. She particularly detested class pretentiousness. Siding with the underdog and the oppressed, Benson delighted in her characters' triumphing over their oppressors. Using raw material from everyday life, she applauded the efforts insignificant people make to improve conditions for themselves and others. Whether a campaign to fund an ambulance for Madison, Connecticut, or a wake-up call to "care-givers" like Nurse Robbins, Benson addressed social concerns while critiquing pettiness and poking fun at human foibles with her unique blend of wit and sympathetic humor.

Appendix A

GENEALOGICAL GUIDE

Warner Prophater
b. 5 September 1803, Harper's Ferry, WV
d. 12 October 1891, St. Louis, MO

John Sidney Prophater
b. 11 June 1838, Allegheny City, PA
d. 15 January 1905, St. Louis, MO

Eliza Korns
b. 18 May 18 ?
d. 24 December 1860, Cumberland, MD

Anna Cora Prophater
b. 23 October 1860, Allegheny City, PA
d. 1956, East River, CT

Patrick Smith
b. 1802, Vinegar Hill, Co. Wexford, Ireland
d. 3 October 1890, St. Louis, MO

Rose Smith
b. 1842, Ireland
d. 20 September 1886, St. Louis, MO

Ann Maguire
b. 1810, Ireland
d. 19 March 1890, St. Louis, MO
Nicholas Smith
d. Victor, NY

Ira Smith
> b. 1785, West Stockbridge, MA
> d. 6 February 1854, Manitowoc, WI
>> Abigail Boughton
>>> b. 31 July 1757, Stamford, CT
>>> d. 23 January 1817, Victor, NY

Peter Perry Smith
> b. 15 February 1823, Victor, Ontario Co., NY
> d. 24 January 1906, Manitowoc, WI
>> Joel Redway
>>> b. 14 June 1757, Rehoboth, MA
>>> d. 1 July 1837

Mahala Redway
> b. 21 April 1791, Lanesboro, MA
> d. before 1837
>> Hannah Clark
>>> b. 5 March 1755, Thompson, CT
>>> d. June 1824, Cheshire, MA

Alonzo Redway Smith
> b. 29 August 1852, Manitowoc, WI
> d. 23 May 1923, Dallas, TX
>> Paul Champlin
>>> b. 19 July 1774, New London, CT
>>> d. 7 August 1853, Middlebury, VT

Hiram Hyde Champlin
> b. 18 September 1798, Middlebury, VT
> m. 29 March 1828, Corinth, VT
> d. ? 1853, Manitowoc, WI
>> Esther Hyde
>>> b. 9 November 1777, Salisbury, CT
>>> d. 15 January 1874, Middlebury, VT

Esther Almira Champlin
> b. 29 January 1830, Addison Co., VT
> d. 16 May 1912, Manitowoc, WI
>> Amos Boardman
>>> b. 17 November 1763, Portland, CT
>>> d. 31 July 1854, Corinth, VT

Almira Boardman
> b. 5 December 1797, Fairfield, VT
> d.   4 July 1876, Manitowoc, WI
>> Prudence Chapman
>>> b. 3 March 1768, Chatham, CT
>>> d. 21 July 1851

APPENDIX B

THE SMITHS

Family History

When twenty-nine-year-old traveling salesman Alonzo Redway Smith met twenty-one-year-old chambermaid Anna Cora Prophater in the fall of 1881, he knew his solitary nights of reading in boardinghouses had finally ended. The next morning, on Dodd, Brown & Co. letterhead, Alonzo penned in neat, ornate calligraphy a letter to be hand delivered by Miss Hoffman, receptionist of Hurst's Hotel in St. Louis where Anna Cora worked.

November 2, 1881

Dear Miss Prophater,

I intended to have seen you last night for a few moments at least, but other matters necessitated my being elsewhere. However, this evening (Wednesday) if agreeable, we will go the "Olympic." Be ready in Ladies Parlor about 7:45.

Your friend, Alonzo

That night at the Olympic initiated the two-year courtship that culminated in their marriage on October 23, 1883 in the Fourth Baptist Church.[1] For the bride it was a double celebration: it was Anna Cora's twenty-third birthday. In marrying Alonzo, Anna Cora rose in class and status, but she could not foresee how the phrase—"other matters necessitat[ing his] being elsewhere"—would become a repeating pattern throughout their married life, nor how Alonzo's absence would affect their children: Lon, Rose, Esther, Agnes, and Sally.

389

Before their first wedding anniversary Anna Cora gave birth on September 18, 1884, to their son, Alonzo Champlin Smith Jr. On September 27th Granny Esther sent congratulations to her son from Manitowoc, Wisconsin, but expressed concern regarding Anna Cora's health—"the poor girl has had more than her share of suffering lately." (The reference is to Anna Cora's combined responsibilities toward both her aged grandparents and her ill mother, Rose.) On Moore and Smith letterhead from the San Francisco office of his brother, Hiram, Uncle Ira Smith also wrote. Dated October 8, 1884, Ira's note read: "Uncle and Auntie congratulate Father, Mother, and *Son*. May he live long and prosper." Thorvald Solberg, a business associate of Alonzo at Dodd, Brown & Co., also sent congratulations but on September 23rd—just five days after the birth—four days before Granny Esther's and two weeks before Ira's. Announcing his son's arrival to his colleagues had taken precedence over telling the family.[2]

Two years later Anna Cora gave birth to Rose Sidney on June 30 in Manitowoc, Wisconsin. Alonzo was traveling. Employed by a succession of dry goods firms in St. Louis, Los Angeles, Chicago and Texas, Alonzo frequently left the family alone as he plodded along on a checkered career path.[3] In the early years of his marriage, though he wrote voluminously and frequently to his wife, he often sounded lonely and self-pitying: "It seems to take a letter so long to get . . . here. I am still, of course, hard at work and sweating myself all to pieces as the extreme sultry weather continues. . . . I want to see you and have a good long talk." Written on July 8th, 1886, a week after Rose's birth, Alonzo's letter underscores the fact that Anna Cora is virtually a single mother, raising an infant and a toddler without her husband's companionship. At best, Alonzo expresses mild concern: "Ma [Granny Esther Smith] writes the baby is colicky which is quite a serious matter. I hope you won't have the long siege you had with Loney. Have you thought about a name for our daughter? My choice is Anna. . . . Do you hear from your mother and father?"

Alonzo's proprietary stance in wanting to name the baby might be amusing were it not so insensitive: "As you know this baby is mine (you remember our agreement). It is quite possible I may insist on my rights as owner to name her without consulting you."[4] Somewhat flattered by Alonzo's desire to give her name to their first daughter, Anna Cora took the upper hand and named the newborn "Rose Sidney" in honor of her own parents. When forty-four-year-old Rose Smith died three months later on September 20th, Anna Cora felt she had rightly chosen the baby's name.

As was customary, Anna Cora arranged with her father's help for the wake to be held at her home where she hosted her grandparents, her uncles, and their families. Two days later, on September 23rd, all of these relatives attended the funeral Mass with Anna Cora, John Sidney, and Alonzo who—to his credit—had spent much of the summer in St. Louis caring for the dying Rose. Afterward, all accompanied Rose's body to its gravesite in St. Louis's Calvary Cemetery.

Home alone with a toddler and an infant, Anna Cora was alternately comforted and piqued by her husband's letters (all of which she saved and Sally Benson later read). Alonzo's repeated complaints of homesickness and "hugging pillows all night" plus his protestations of finding no relief except "by the sight and presence of your own darling self, the sweetest, best, and most precious old love in the wide, wide world" at best compensated his wife for his absence, but in later years, similar avowals would heighten Benson's realization of her father's insincerity. Once during her childhood, he sent her a postcard of an excursion steamer from Keokuk, Iowa, without writing a message. If she initially considered the blank card a joke, she soon associated that blankness with his absence and unconcern. She began to realize she could not trust him.

In a subsequent letter Alonzo indicates some awareness of the effects his absence is having on the marriage. He asks Anna Cora to forget "the pains, sorrow, disappointments, sickness, troubles, and tears of the first years of your married life and look with eyes of hope on the future." Like a classic alcoholic, Alonzo promises "happiness in store . . . and plenty of it." Since his only ambition "is for the family," that happiness is sure to come, he argues, waxing more eloquent as he concludes: "With our love towards each other, what can stand in our way?" Before closing, he asks her to "kiss the two cherubs for their father" and to write to him: "A letter from you is better than $1,000 and I would pay that for them if I were rich. Your own darling, Loney."[5]

When Esther, their third child, arrived on June 19, 1888 in St. Louis, Alonzo wrote two weeks later from New York City. Timing and text reveal his characteristic mix of caring and irresponsibility:

> My dear darling Anna and children, I was very sorry to know you were obliged to call Dr. Bond for Rose and I sincerely hope to hear she is much better in your next letter. I am glad to know more than anything else that my dear darling girl is

sitting up again. You will probably improve fast from this [time] on. I didn't go to Vermont as I wrote you—got left by two and a half minutes.

Alonzo had missed his train. Five years into the marriage, Anna Cora had three children and an absentee husband whose whereabouts she often did not know, even as she went into labor.

Besides this irresponsibility, Alonzo's self-centeredness also becomes more obvious as he bemoans the city's awful dullness: "It is ten times worse than St. Louis . . . barring, of course, the seaside attractions. The city itself is deader than a doornail." Obviously, Alonzo frequented the seaside attractions at Coney Island. His complaining, apparently designed to elicit his wife's sympathy, continues: "Upper Broadway, usually the center of the swim, is positively, painfully, quiet, and it is a relief not to go there, so I don't go." Contradicting himself in the next sentence, Alonzo adds:

> I went Saturday night to see the McCaull Co. at Wallack's in "*The Lady or the Tiger.*" The cast included Dr. Wolf Hoffer Klein (the fat Friar in *Falka*), Madeline Lucelli (Caterina Marco) whose real name is Kate Smith another daughter of Mark Smith, the formerly well-known actor of St. Louis, and others that I don't think you know. The play was awfully funny, extremely so, and I nearly "died a-laffin."

Wallack's Theater, one of the largest playhouses of the city, had moved in the 1860s from the heart of the theater district to a "new and splendid home uptown" on the northeast corner of Broadway and 13th Street. Its "architecture and furnishings, its handsome lobbies and lounges, represented the last word in elegance" and "first nights there brought out the most distinguished audience to be found in New York. . . . You attended Wallack's, like the opera, as much to be seen as to see" (Morris 65). Although by the 1880s the "Four Hundred" had shifted allegiance to the Lyceum on Fourth Avenue near Twenty-third Street, Alonzo was, nevertheless, not among the hoi-polloi at Wallack's. In spite of his complaints, he knew how to entertain himself in his wanderings.

Benson's father had, indeed, been fortunate in choosing Anna Cora for his wife. She remained faithful and devoted to him throughout the forty years of their marriage, raising their five children unassisted except for occasional household help. Perhaps she believed Alonzo's epistolary assurances, "I am thinking of you all the time, wondering what you are doing . . . and what the children are doing. How is little 'Esther Anna' (the two sweetest names to me in the whole vocabulary of feminine names)."[6] It is difficult to comprehend, however, how Anna Cora endured continuous financial insecurity coupled with Alonzo's cavalier stance toward her lack of cash: "Casey will give you all the money you want. Just send word down or telephone. Get the receipt for the rent but never mind. I will attend to that." In an era when women were highly dependent on their husbands, Anna Cora coped with loneliness, confusion, and anxiety while Alonzo, miles away, enjoyed city night life socializing with friends. To his wife he merely sent poems and platitudes:

> Be a good girl. Keep cool. Don't worry about anything. Keep Mrs. Albertson as long as you like. Kiss all of the cherubs, and don't make any mistake about my loving you always and forever. Yours, Loney[7]

A similar letter arrived a week later. Again, Alonzo bemoaned Anna Cora's shortage of cash, advising her to "go to Mr. Casey" if the children got sick. "Get any amount of money you want and go to Manitowoc. . . . The Froliche and Dunker bill I overlooked entirely, but you will be paid for it when I get home," he assured her.

Sally Benson's observations that her father was rarely home, leaving her mother virtually a single parent under a cloud of financial insecurity while he indulged in drinking sprees and enjoyed "the good life," led Benson to develop a negative attitude toward men. They were not to be trusted, they aroused her suspicion, and they sparked an unconscious desire to punish their behavior. More importantly, they, along with her mother's example, convinced Benson to become her own woman. Having witnessed Anna Cora's devotion, thrift, and reliability, Benson incorporated her mother's determination to succeed by establishing patterns of hard work and persevering effort almost in spite of her father. Though Benson would spend money freely in adulthood and suffer occasional cash-flow problems, she developed the resources necessary to supply her wants. Unfortunately, as she built her writing career, Benson also fell ironically into her father's pattern of alcohol abuse.

When Anna Cora's grandparents died two years later—Ann Maguire Smith on March 19th and Patrick Smith on October 3rd, 1890—she was relieved of the responsibility of caring for them, but she still had to manage the household and three children, six-year-old Lon, four-year-old Rose, and two-year-old Esther. Alonzo, meanwhile, changed firms and addresses regularly, continued his travels, and returned to St. Louis from time to time. After three such visits, he left Anna Cora pregnant again. The Smith family welcomed Agnes Wickfield Smith on April 1, 1894, and three years later, on September 3, 1897, Sara Mahala Redway Smith, the future Sally Benson. John Perry, born on June 25, 1901, died shortly after birth. He was interred the next day in St. Louis's Calvary Cemetery with his maternal great-grandparents and grandmother, Rose.

Though Anna's and Alonzo's five children had become a sizeable group to have for summer guests, Granny Esther Smith never hesitated to invite them every year to her Manitowoc home on Lake Michigan. For Sally and her siblings, these Wisconsin summers at Grandma's were treasured times for playing with cousins. A letter from nine-year-old Rose to "Papa" on July 23, 1895 describes the fun that Benson's older siblings associated with Manitowoc:

> We arrived here Friday and I must say it was delightful. Polly was glad to see us and Grandma and Grandpa as well. Yesterday we went to the lakeshore. Esther found 64 shells, Alonzo 66, and I, 108. . . . Grandpa has put up the swing and it broke down on Alonzo but it's up again. . . . Today we climbed the ladder and ate cherries. . . . Every night we have the fiddle or the music box and all dance, even the baby.[8]

However, when Sally was old enough to partake of such activities, she strangely took little interest in them. The prime object of her summer was the doll cemetery she constructed next to the asparagus bed. A sensitive child, she would relive John Perry's death and burial by repeatedly engaging in her doll cemetery ritual.[9]

Recent research on the effects of death on a surviving sibling emphasizes the importance of the survivor's expressing thoughts and feelings in play. Often such play may constitute a reenactment of events such as the funeral.[10] Betty Davies writes: "Unstructured play . . . enhances the child's feelings of control and predictability [and] serves as a temporary escape . . . and as a vehicle for resolving emotions" (Davies 65). In another view, the child, "quick to equate the death of another with his own possible death," employs defenses such as "displacement of anxiety on to . . . obsessional ritualized behavior"—like Benson's doll-burying.[11]

Lon, Rose, Esther, and Agnes had regularly corresponded with their Grandpa Prophater while he was at sea, but Tootie, too young to write, was merely mentioned in seven-year-old Agnes's letters.[12] She loved receiving postcards from the various river ports where his steamer, *The City of New Orleans*, docked. When her grandfather joined the family, she became fascinated with the quaint hats he had collected from around the world.[13] She loved wearing them and created personalities to match. Later in life, Benson honored Prophater's hat fetish by developing her own—as may be seen in many photographs and in comments made by friends.

A second letter referring to Tootie is more significant because it contains a clue to Benson's religious development. Agnes wrote on a rainy, Saturday morning from Granny Smith's home to thank Grandpa Prophater for writing to her and Sara: "We (Tootie and I) got your letter yesterday when we were out playing. . . . The girls are going to church as it is a feast today. We went out wading yesterday afternoon and played in the sand with a bucket and spade. I wish you could come up here. Even a day would do, any old day, it doesn't matter at all . . ." August 15, feast of Mary's Assumption, was a holy day of obligation requiring attendance at Mass. Strangely, Anna Cora did not take the two younger girls to church. Such a departure from Catholic practice suggests that Anna Cora was not so strict an observer of Catholicism as granddaughter Barbara Benson Golseth claimed. This episode partly explains why the Smith children's adherence to their faith diminished as they reached adulthood.[14] As each one grew up and encountered anti-Catholic prejudice—first among peers and then in society at large—they abandoned Catholicism as an inevitable first step toward acceptance by the white, Anglo-Saxon, Protestant upper class.

In later years, according to Golseth, Anna Cora, did not always get to Sunday Mass in Connecticut because there was no church in Madison and access to St. Michael's in Guilford, the neighboring town, was difficult if not impossible. "We left for Guilford yesterday morning at eight-thirty (standard time) to attend nine-thirty Mass. We got back home at twelve—all of that time spent in trying to get there and back with the bus service," Anna Cora complained.[15] However, a native of Madison, Maria Elena Pignatelli, remembers that Madison had a Catholic chapel close to the Village Green where Mass was celebrated every Sunday for the Irish servants employed by local Madison gentry. Possibly, Anna Cora shunned attending Mass with Irish servants to disassociate herself from her past. A property owner in 1930s Madison, Anna Cora could disguise her Catholicism from Protestant neighbors and dim the memory of her humble roots in Galena, Illinois. This class consciousness was imparted to all of her daughters though it least affected Sally. Or, characteristically, because her mother and sisters were so class oriented, Sally rebelled.

Benson's later fiction often satirized such snobbery and hypocrisy. Going against the upper-class tide, Benson retained an admiration for Catholics, especially nuns.[16] Several stories for Christmas issues of *The New Yorker* reflect Benson's fondness for Catholicism, though regular church attendance was not part of her life.[17] In "Midnight Mass," for example, the main character, Martha Hornsby, hosts a Christmas Eve tree-decorating party and serves her guests brandy but refrains from joining them because she wants to attend Midnight Mass at St. Francis Church. Once there, she basks in the atmosphere of the crowded, beautifully decorated church. She considers everything "just perfect" from the Latin hymns and the boy choristers to the "clean, serious faces of the men . . . the relaxed, calm faces of the women," and the "Christ Child in His cradle." After the Mass, Hornsby lights a candle "before a kindly, richly-tinted saint," and walks out into the night "conscious of feeling heavenly." Arriving home, however, she encounters her guests arguing over the melody of a Christmas carol. They are all "feeling good" from the brandy consumed. In characteristic fashion, Benson's story ends with one guest's incomprehension of Hornsby's experience: "You could have stayed at home in your nice warm house and heard the whole thing over the radio." Such a view misses the point and reinforces Benson's satire: some people immerse themselves in the trappings of an experience but miss its essence. To such people, it is futile, if not impossible, to explain the difference.

A second incident sheds light on Benson's lack of faith development. As a teenager attending the christening of her nephew, Champlin Smith, Benson was invited by a Mrs. Vandervoort to "come to their church." Reflecting that night on the invitation, Benson wrote in her diary simply, "Yes and No." This ambivalence toward institutionalized religion, well established in her adolescence, characterized her adult life. Among the many Christmas cards she sent and received each year, not one depicted a religious icon.[18] Every card bore a generic holly wreath, blazing fireplace, or snow scene—nothing specifically Christian. However, Benson's attitudes and actions often embodied religious values, and, as she reveals in "Midnight

Mass," she was drawn at times into the celebration of religious mystery. Most importantly, she was open, just, and compassionate in her dealings with others.

In her early parenting Benson's mother, inspired by her mother-in-law, emulated Esther Smith's openness to people of all faiths and classes and tried to instill a similar tolerance in her children. With Sally, she had partial success. Benson acquired in early childhood Anna Cora's disregard for social ostentation and Grandma Esther's ability to see beyond class differences. Like young Tootie—her fictionalized self—Benson was equally happy helping in the kitchen and listening to tales of Ireland spun by Katie, the Smiths' maid, or engaging the local iceman in conversation during the frequent rides she hitched with him.[19]

That her sisters, unlike Benson, were more overtly class conscious is apparent in *Meet Me in St. Louis*, "March 1904." Here, Rose and Esther meet visiting fair dignitaries from several countries. When asked by Chinese visitors what school they attend, Rose answers with pride, "Oh, at Mary Institute, of course. I'm a senior and Esther's a junior. We have a brother named Lon, who's at Princeton" (237). In actuality, Agnes also attended the prestigious Mary Institute as did her older sisters, but Sara did not.

NOTES

CHAPTER 1. THE WRITER'S ORIGINS

1. In her May 1941 interview with Robert van Gelder, Benson voiced her attitude toward war in terms of male novelists: "Why must they go trucking all over the world and slaver with delight at wars?" (184).

2. Sara Smith, letter to Alonzo Redway Smith, 27 August, 1903.

3. A lock of Sara's honey-colored blonde hair, cut when she was eight, remains among the memorabilia kept by Anna Cora and later by Barbara Benson Golseth in her home in Tucson, Arizona.

4. Dorothy Lobrano Guth, telephone interview, 7 July 2001.

5. Alexis Doster, telephone interview, 9 February 2001. The diary Benson kept during her freshman year at Horace Mann contains references to her having read several Dickens novels: *Dombey and Son, Great Expectations, Hard Times, and David Copperfield.*

6. Barbara Benson Golseth remembered how her short skirt allowed the seat's woven pattern to imprint itself on her "rear end. And it was awfully itchy," she added, hastening to explain that none of the children ever left the table "because those women were so funny." Interview cited in *St. Louis Post-Dispatch* via Bigchalk. com 7 June 2000.

7. Some of Agnes Smith's articles include: "Dressing Is an Art with Florence Walter" and "Pearl White to Act in Thrill-less Film" (*New York Herald*, 10 December 1916 and 9 July 1916).

8. Anna Cora Smith, letter to Sara Smith, 18 August 1910.

9. Sara Smith, letter to Anna Cora Smith, undated c. 1909–1910.

10. Herpicide was a common lotion for scalp and hair.

11. Katherine Pierce, letter to Sara Smith, 11 April 1910.

12. Helen Yule, letter to Sara Smith, 2 December 1910.

Chapter 2. Manhattan Daze

1. On March 4, Sara's friend, Mary Johann, who lived nearby at 5157 Kensington Avenue, wrote her a "train letter," as was the custom, addressed to "My beloved bed-fellow." Writing in a circular pattern—a preteen fetish of the day—she began at the circumference and spiraled inward:

> Dear Darling,
>
> How I will miss you. I can't sleep night or day knowing you are not under my care. . . . Do not be surprised if you hear I have gone mad in your absence. Have a nice time there. Get acquainted with nice girls. Oh, you Davis Jordan, Richard Kline, Charlie Swingley.
>
> From your ever-loving friend,
> Mary Johann

A second train letter, written in the same, almost illegible, spiraling pattern, was presented to Sara by Helen Yule with specific instructions on the envelope: "Do not read until you are on the train." Helen spoke for several friends:

> We all hate to see you go, but if you must, you must. You keep my ring and I'll take good care of yours. . . . We have a holiday Friday so I won't have you to play with and Mary and Florence won't be home so I am going downtown. Whoopee . . . I will send you the Easter eggs if you send me your address and when I should send them so you will get them Sunday. I think it takes three days, I am not sure. You will have a perfect picnic with your doll on the train, I know. We will have a picture of trips and send them to you so you will remember the little idiot.
>
> Helen Yule
> 5157 Kensington Avenue
> St. Louis
>
> P.S. Don't forget the national Hymn so we can sing it together this summer.
>
> P.S. You will be pretty busy with all your letters and books to read. Don't forget the candy you are to send me. All le ai (meaning "Good Day").

2. See Smith College Archives, Class of 1910, Fifteenth Reunion Book, 1925.

3. The diary Sally kept in 1912 makes no mention of using public transportation to get to school. It also refers to a tenth-floor apartment "one block from Broadway." Therefore, the Smiths most likely lived on Claremont Avenue, since Amsterdam, the only other possibility, was largely owned by New York Hospital and not residentially zoned. See Diary, 31 January 1912.

4. Now part of Columbia University, the Claremont buildings constitute luxury living today and provided the Smith girls with easy walking access to Horace Mann's campus and the tennis courts.

5. In a biographical blurb written for *Junior Miss*, Benson added proudly that she studied English with "Heywood Broun's aunt in Horace Mann school."

6. In Benson's freshman year, for example, *The Horace Mann Record*, Vol. 10, No. 6, reported that on December 19th her class party, held in the Thompson Hall gym on Friday, December 8th, was unusual in striking a "happy medium" between the games of the younger classes and the dancing of the juniors and seniors.

7. Horace Mann referred to its eighth graders as "first years," its seventh graders as sub-freshmen, and its sixth graders as sub-sub-freshmen. See *The Mannikin*, 1912.

8. Actually, Alonzo wrote to "Sally" in 1909, but it is the only time that form of her name appears in all the correspondence preceding 1910.

9. These figures are based on the 1914–1915 brochure of the Horace Mann School for Boys. There was no corresponding girls school brochure available in the school archives at its West 246th Street, New York location as of July 2000. My assumption is that fees were the same at the girls school.

10. Dolkart notes that this policy included exclusion of Jews. However, a separate experimental school, the Speyer School, was established by Teachers College a few blocks north of Horace Mann in the middle of a poor Manhattanville neighborhood. It was to be run in conjunction with the University Settlement House and aimed to train poor children in both traditional subjects and domestic and fine arts, thereby rendering them good citizens of upright moral character (234). Yet, when established in 1887 as the Model School, a department of Columbia University's Teachers College, the Horace Mann School building had been home to students of many nationalities and social levels. Myra Rice, for example described its 1903 celebration of "Decoration Day when the marching line held French, German, Swedish, Irish, and pure American children in numbers; Bettini di Moise, our little Italian count, Irving Hue Kin, son of the Chinese missionary around the corner . . . proudly carried . . . the Stars and Stripes and sang with fervor 'My Country 'tis of Thee.' "

11. On January 1, 1912, Sally dutifully recorded the first day of the new year with a full-page entry:

Got up rather late after seeing the new year in. Didn't do much of anything until I got dressed for Lon and Jo's. We had a fine dinner. After dinner we started home and met Jack Molthan coming in. He came upstairs and we talked together. I think he is fine. He tried on my hat. Agnes told me the only thing that could make him change was reference to me.

Jack, a senior at Horace Mann and classmate of Agnes, was actually Emil Henry Frederick Molthan. In his formal *Mannikin* portrait he is a handsome, darkish blonde wearing a Buster Brown collar and tie. The quote accompanying his picture matches the twinkle in his eye: "And the ladies call him sweet" (1912, 24). Besides playing varsity basketball and baseball, Jack was president of the Dramatic Society, athletic editor of the *Record*, and secretary of the GAA—the Horace Mann General Association—which managed all athletic and social activities.

12. If their classes ended before 2 p.m. students were required to attend study hall. In December of 1911, Mr. Prettyman "startled the school" by requiring seniors to monitor the study halls, promising to back them up as if they were teachers. Strange to say, study hall 411-12 had only three or four students present, yet any student waiting for a game or club activity was required to attend a study hall and keep silence. See the *Horace Mann Record*, 11 October, 3 and 19 December, 3.

13. Ice cream parlors in 1911 were ubiquitous like today's fast food restaurants. The Horace Mann crowd could choose among Wasself's Pharmacy on the northwest corner, Charles L. Pope's drugstore directly across the street, Friedgen's Pharmacy at 120th Street and Amsterdam Avenue, Halper's Drug Store on the southeast corner, or the drugstore in Whittier Hall (the new residence for female students of Teachers College), which offered concoctions like the "Horace Mannikin," the "Co-ed Frappe," and the "College Yell" ("a very yellow, long-drawn-out drink"). Eva Elise Vom Baur, "Dwellings in High Places," EP, 17 May 1913, 9. Quoted in Dolkart 433n173.

14. See the advertising section of *The Mannikin*, 1912–1915. See also advertisements in *The Horace Mann Record*, 1912–1915. Friedgen's did such good business that in 1914, when Sally was a junior, it opened a second store on Amsterdam at 114th Street. Each one boasted long, high counters with barstools.

15. Benson's diary mentions a combination of classics and mystery thrillers: Charles Dickens's *Hard Times, Dombey and Son, David Copperfield,* and *Great Expectations*; Nathaniel Hawthorne's *The House of the Seven Gables* and *The Scarlet Letter*; Charlotte Brontë's *Jane Eyre*; Mark Twain's *A Connecticut Yankee in King Arthur's Court*; *The Bolted Door* (author unknown); A. K. Green's *The Woman in the Alcove*; *The Window at the White Cat*; and O. Henry's *The Trimmed Lamp*.

16. *The Horace Mann Record*, 8 November 1911, 1.

17. *The Horace Mann Record*, 19 December 1911, 3. The Florence Crittenton Mission was a home for young girls awaiting trial for minor crimes or as runaways.

18. *The Horace Mann Record*, 17 April 1912.

19. A fuller detailing of the league and its activities appeared in the 1915 *Mannikin*. Two divisions, a senior league for the three upper classes and a junior league for the three lower classes, comprised the league. Each group entertained the other with special parties. Prominent men such as Dr. Jefferson, Dr. Wise, and Commissioner Kingsbury were guest speakers. Foreign students from Teachers College would also speak about their countries.

20. "Machine" was a common term for automobile in the early twentieth century. (Incidentally, only a small percentage of Americans owned cars at the time—their cost equivalent to an average person's yearly salary. Sally's friends are among the highly privileged.)

21. "Hump" was the nickname of Horace Minear Humphrey, a handsome senior whose yearbook quote expresses something of what Sally disliked in him: "We know jes' how to treat him: you mus' *reason* with a mule" (*Mannikin* 1912, 21). When she first met him, she recorded in her diary: "We met Hump . . . I don't like him at all. He calls me and Margaret 'Tubby Belly'" (January 9).

22. The "Irish Mail" was a type of three- or four-wheeled wagon propelled manually or by pumping up and down. Benson's senior bulletin describes two of her teachers "riding up and down in a small red express wagon," braving the danger of being "overturned by those frisky maidens who took a ride." See *The Horace Mann Record*, 14 December 1914, 2. Bill is most likely Bill Stayton, who dated Sally for some months and wrote to her for several years. As late as 1941, for example, he wrote specifically to congratulate her for the success of *Junior Miss* on Broadway.

23. Benson's last statement ironically foreshadows behavior that occurred in 1917 when many of her male friends were enlisting to fight in the First World War. She became engaged to everyone she was dating. See chapter 8.

24. Most likely, John is John Adams Moffitt, a senior. His *Mannikin* portrait is above Jack Molthan's and presents a serious bespectacled individual in contrast to the more debonair looking Molthan.

25. David Van Alstyne was president of the Horace Mann General Association in 1914.

26. Bill Stayton was also a friend of Babe's.

27. See the *Mannikin* 1912, 27. Bill continued his correspondence with Sally well into the 1940s.

28. Two prior restaurants had opened—one c. 1850 on South William Street (that only the very rich could afford) and a second at Fifth Avenue and 26th. This third business, where Sally most likely dined, had been opened in the 1890s on

the northeast corner of Fifth Avenue and 44th Street. Founded to compete with the ostentatious Waldorf Astoria, the new Delmonico's maintained an atmosphere of quiet elegance and its long-standing reputation for social exclusiveness. For more on Delmonico's, see Stern et al. 271–272, 293, and 785n15; see also Morris.

29. The next day, Babe arrived with Bill Stayton and together with Sally and Agnes "went up on the roof." A scrapbook Sally kept in senior year contains a postcard of buildings on Claremont Avenue. A penciled caption—"The Roof!"—tops a large circle inscribing 29 Claremont, site of Sally's many rooftop trysts.

Chapter 3. Summer of Discontent

1. A few days into his vacation, on June 20th for example, Sally wrote to him but didn't receive an answer until the 25th. Two days later, to her surprise, he wrote again, and, unable to "play hard to get," Sally replied that very day. As soon as he returned on Monday, July 1st, Babe called to ask if he could visit, but it was late so they just went for a walk around the block and argued about his whereabouts on Sunday. Finally, he admitted he had taken "L. Le C" for a drive. On Tuesday, they went to the field, sat on the rocks and talked. On Wednesday, Sally had a doctor's appointment, "went shopping all over town" afterward, and bought "some blouses, a belt, and a few other things" to look her best for the upcoming holiday picnic.

2. The identity of L. Le C. remains unknown.

3. The list included *The Circular Staircase*, *The Bolted Door*, A. K. Green's *The Woman in the Alcove*, *McClure's* magazine, *The Street Called Straight*, *Hearts and Charts*, *The Forsaken Inn*, and *The Window at the White Cat*.

4. Originally intended to "feed the average wage-earner and businessman in a hurry, Child's was a restaurant "with brightly lit, brasserie-like interiors." Its prewar décor of "austerely elegant white tile . . . mirrored walls . . . bentwood furniture and exposed ceiling fans," was subsequently adjusted to include "glittery, streamlining" for Times Square and "tasteful, period décor for Fifth Avenue." Its food and ambience provided a standard of "affordable excellence" for a "quite heterogeneous" clientele (Stern 275–276).

5. In 1912, a woman's bathing costume covered her from head to toe and included long, dark stockings.

6. In 1853, after keeping store alone for some time, Perry Peter Smith joined his brother-in-law, Benjamin, to open Jones and Co., a lumbering and mercantile business. Since forest land was increasingly needed for crops, the two shortly amassed a fortune clearing timber and selling construction logs. The Champlins and Smiths next invested their wealth in "lakers," large trading ships that plied the Great Lakes. Their sons (Sally's uncles) established trading offices in California,

Hiram in San Francisco and Ira P. in Stockton, but Alonzo Redway Smith (her father) moved to Missouri to join the mercantile firm of Dodd, Brown & Co.

7. Most likely this was Harriet Everett, though there were two other Harriets in Benson's class—Forbes and McConnell. I base this interpretation on the fact that Clyde Everett was among those who waved Sally off on September 22nd.

8. Though the nature of Sally's dental problems is not clear, the use of Novocain can be traced back to 1905. Sally may have been extremely sensitive to pain or psychologically magnifying it.

9. *The Smart Set* was a magazine begun as a journal for New York "society." It evolved into a "witty, literary 'Magazine of Cleverness'" (Wood 194) and "brought a measure of sophistication to the magazine world" (Yagoda 35).

10. A *pleurant* is a figure of a weeping monk often adorning a tomb; Gilby may be Gilbert Malcolm who was president of the Dramatic Society.

11. New in 1912, the Bender Hotel was fashionable for large dinner parties.

CHAPTER 4. HOUSTON

1. See *Houston, a History and Guide*, 108.

2. See *Houston, a History and Guide*, 258.

3. In 1896 Professor Chris W. Welch had opened the Houston Academy in a "large house at Polk and Jackson." It sent graduates to Yale, Harvard, University of Virginia, Washington and Lee, University of the South, and the University of Texas by 1900. "Many of Houston's most distinguished citizens of the mid-twentieth century got their start under Professor Welch" (Johnston 162).

4. The Waldo School had been established in 1904 by Miss Mary Waldo and her sisters, Virginia and Lula. "Daughters of Jedediah Waldo, vice-president of the Missouri, Kansas, and Texas Railroad, all three were college graduates," and Miss Mary had an "additional ten years of study in New York, Cleveland, and Paris" (Johnston 162).

5. Rice was celebrating its formal opening with gala activities. "On a prairie still cluttered with the rubble of construction, great scholars of the United States, Britain, Europe, and Japan" had arrived by steamship and train to "welcome this new institute into the academic world." Wearing their colorful academic regalia, men like Julian Huxley mingled with distinguished university colleagues who stayed on to give lectures, afterward sampling Houstonian luncheons, garden parties, concerts, and dinners (Johnston 159).

6. Located at 46th Street and Madison Avenue, Maillard's contained a tea room, an "Elizabethan Men's Café and Adam-style Women's Restaurant and candy shop [that] reflected the formality of prewar life more than the hurly-burly of the Jazz Age" (Stern et al. 275). Benson loved everything about it—the entrance with

its triple-arched arcade and finely detailed columns and pilasters; the elaborate crystal chandeliers suspended from high, paneled ceilings; the giant tapestry, softening and adding color to the marble panels; the arched mirrors, Louis XV walnut furnishings, and thick, richly colored carpets—all lending cachet to the atmosphere. See Albert J. MacDonald, ed., *The Architectural Forum* 40 (June 1924): 246–248.

7. The story, "Apartment Hotel," features Mrs. Morrison, a woman who tries to make her hotel apartment homelike. She visits "Maillard's new place" (built in 1923) at 385 Madison Avenue for lunch (*People Are Fascinating* 204).

CHAPTER 5. RISING SPIRITS

1. One of several attached buildings lining Fifth Avenue's west side between Ninth and Tenth Streets, it was a few blocks west of Bohemian Greenwich Village, once a quiet backwater of stately, pre–Civil War homes and now converted into flats. Sally's new home, like other buildings on Fifth Avenue, was limited to 125 feet in height, while in the adjoining cross streets, townhouses rose as high as 300 feet. Proportional to street width—ranging from one to two-and-a-half times the width—these buildings were designed to allow ample amounts of light and air thanks to city regulations that "discourage[d] the construction of large scale industrial lofts" and the encroachment of builders who might otherwise destroy neighborhoods thoughtlessly by disregarding their character and needs. More specifically, the Fifth Avenue Association had lobbied successfully to stem the tide of garment workers—largely "foreigners, primarily of Southern Italian and East European origin" (Stern et al. 31). Its goal was to preserve the character of prewar Fifth Avenue, heart of the "diamond and lobster and champagne world," as an "almost private preserve of the very affluent" (Stern et al. 293).

2. William Stayton, letter to Sara Smith, 30 June 1913. Bill Stayton had completed his freshman year at Harvard and was embarking on a year's leave of absence.

3. William Stayton, letter to Sally Benson, 16 June 1941.

4. Rector's, so well known internationally that its name was "never inscribed on the building," relied for identification on an "electrically illuminated griffin suspended from its façade." Spacious, "walled in mirrors from floor to ceiling, richly decorated in green and gold, lighted by sparkling crystal chandeliers," Rector's hosted "the aristocracy of the Gay White Way" (Morris 262, 327).

5. Lon, Jo, and their boys were spending a weekend at the Hotel Galveston enjoying the "finest surf bathing in the world" when their neighbors, the Joyces, telephoned to announce the new arrivals. "As soon as I came home tonight, I went to look for the Pussentaters," Lon wrote, adding, "the family is now safely locked in the barn and seemingly contented in their new home. I thought this would be

NOTES TO CHAPTER 5

of interest to you. 1. Abie Sidney Hyman Pussentater—a dirty yellowish that will look well in an alley and matches up with the average garbage can. Will probably be able to hold his own with a dawg. 2. Mandy Belle Purity Pussentater—jet black, image of Father, Waldo Pussentater. 3. Marcel Edouard St. Jean Montreal Quebec Marie Hank Pussentater—image of mother. Named in part, Hank, after Grandfather Hank Schrimpf of the well-known bone snatcher and all-round barrel snoucher. Write us whenever you can. Give our love to everyone." Alonzo Champlin Smith, letter to Sara R. Smith, 10 June 1913.

6. Sally Benson liked cats. Years later, she incorporated her love of cats in "Cat Ghost," a short story rejected by *The New Yorker* but published in *Emily*. In her last years in California she kept two cats in her Woodland Hills apartment.

7. As the student population increasingly mushroomed, the boys' division would separate in 1913–1914 and relocate to the school's present location on West 246th Street in Riverdale, New York. The new thirteen-acre Riverdale campus, formerly known as Alumni Field, had been providing students great sports facilities for the price of a long ride on the IRT. Now the boys would have access to the athletic field at Van Cortlandt Park. In 1915, a newly designed brochure and *Course of Study* for the Horace Mann School for Girls touted the advantages gained by the boys' departure: "ample space, superior equipment, and a healthful regimen" of indoor and outdoor activities, favoring "health of body and an intelligent appreciation of the demands of the home and social life" (7).

8. Sally wrote about her commuting experience and published an article in the *Record* when she became bulletin editor the following year. See *Horace Mann Record*, 19 March 1915, Vol. 1, No. 23, 1.

9. Newspaper articles daily reported activity "at the front" during the Great War in Europe.

10. Phil was editor-in-chief of the 1912 *Mannikin*, bulletin editor of the *Record*, and Dramatic Society treasurer.

11. Blaine Webb, letter to Sally Smith, 1 December 1913.

12. Bill Stayton remembered Sally's Horace Mann stories and reminded Benson of them in 1941. Writing to congratulate Benson on the success of *Junior Miss*, Stayton recalled how much fun he derived from reading her "stories of 'Useless Ennelbesser.'" Benson's actual character was "Eustace Ennelbesser."

13. One is a view of Horace Mann from Broadway and the southwest corner of 120th Street. Another is the school's entrance hall with its imposing statue of Athena and smaller Della Robbia Madonna on the stair wall. A third shows the auditorium where "chapel" occurred each morning. Long and rectangular, the room boasts a stained glass skylight, several other stained glass windows, a semi-circular stage, ascending rows of seats, and a balcony. Views of cooking and sewing classes are next, with two or three students at long, lab-like tables. Additional postcards display the swimming pool, the main gymnasium, and a gym class in session—the

girls attired in white middy blouses, short dark skirts, and dark stockings. Next is a picture of Alumni Field in Riverdale and some clippings of the 1913 senior play, *Trelawny of the 'Wells.'*

14. Long before their senior year, Sally and fellow Horace Mann students had grown accustomed to meeting rigorous academic challenges. The curriculum for first form included intensive theme writing, English grammar "essential for beginning Latin" (*Course of Study* 14), reading that "correlat[ed] with history, geography, and industrial arts; legends and myths; Swift's *Gulliver's Travels*; Stevenson's *Treasure Island*; Hawthorne's *Twice Told Tales*; and Dickens's *A Christmas Carol.* Second form added Southey's *Life of Nelson*; Malory's *Morte d'Arthur*; Cooper's *The Last of the Mohicans*; Macaulay's *The Lays of Ancient Rome*; and Scott's *Marmion.*

15. See *The Horace Mann Record*, 14 February 1912, 3. During Sally's tenure the requirements were modified slightly: write two editorials, the subject of one of these will be given. She also advanced the date for competing "so that the future Board may have a chance to work with and acquire a little information from this present Board." See *The Horace Mann Record*, 29 January 1915, 3.

16. *The Horace Mann Record*, Vol. 1, No. 1, 2 October 1914, 2.

17. *The Horace Mann Record*, Vol. 1, No. 1, 2 October 1914, 2.

18. *The Horace Mann Record*, Vol. 1, No. 2, 9 October 1914, 1.

19. *The Horace Mann Record*, Vol. 1, No. 2, 9 October 1914, 2.

20. *The Horace Mann Record*, Vol. 1, No. 3, 16 October 1914, 1.

21. Benson borrows the tile from Robert Herrick's poem:

> A sweet disorder in the dress
> Kindles in clothes a wantonness:—
> A lawn about the shoulders thrown
> Into a fine distraction,—
> An erring lace, which here and there   5
> Enthralls the crimson stomacher,—
> A cuff neglectful, and thereby
> Ribbands to flow confusedly,—
> A winning wave, deserving note,
> In the tempestuous petticoat,—   10
> A careless shoe-string, in whose tie
> I see a wild civility,—
> Do more bewitch me, than when art
> Is too precise in every part.

22. Sally refers also to the "many people starving in Belgium" but concludes, "Charity begins at home, to quote our old friend Robert W. Chambers." She is still

too involved in her own adolescent world to fully appreciate global needs or to imagine herself or her classmates responding to them. Similarly, the Christmas editorial focuses on traditional ways of celebrating the feast, making no mention of the poor.

23. See chapter 9, p. 91 (She even refused—for reasons more related to her growing antipathy toward her father—to send a Christmas gift to him in Santee, a small town east of San Diego, California.)

24. See "The Raffle," *The New Yorker*, 1 March 1941, 12–16.

25. See "The Paragon," *The New Yorker*, 9 March 1940, 20.

26. These were principles dear to Sally from her youth. See chapter 1, pp. 12–14, chapter 5, pp. 47–51, chapter 7, p. 68, chapter 8, p. 82. See also, the *Record*, Vol. 1, No. 16, 2.

27. Maxime Harrison-Berlitz was editor-in-chief of the *Record* while Sally was bulletin editor. Maxime would later marry Babe's brother Claus Doscher Benson.

28. See the 1915 *Mannikin*, 38.

29. The 1913 *Mannikin* devoted a full page to "The Silver Bay Conference." Eight Horace Mann delegates attended. Breakfast was at 7 a.m. on Saturday morning, followed by a meeting in the auditorium addressed by Miss Bertha Conde, head of the conference. Only one course, "Out-of-doors in the *Bible*, was open to secondary school delegates. This was followed by "Mission Study," and some Horace Mann students attended "The Emergency in China," while others went to "Country Life" or "Immigration." At 2 p.m. there was "Quiet Hour," a time for some to rest or write letters. Others who wished "to display their animal spirit" were relegated to the outdoors. At 4 p.m. there were parties followed by singing and stunts in front of the hotel. Evening provided a well-known speaker, a delegation meeting to review the day, and 10 p.m. was "bed, perhaps!" Other days included aquatic sports and rowing (see 1913 *Mannikin*, 37). A full-page picture of Horace Mann's delegation faces the write-up. Seven women in white blouses and long skirts posed behind a Horace Mann banner. A dock with pagodas, the water, and hills form the backdrop (36).

30. The friendship that began at Horace Mann continued for many years. Letters addressed to "Dear Nicolette" and signed by "Cuthbert"—Lawson's middle name—reveal the intimacy they shared and make plausible his being Benson's consort during her later sojourn in Paris. See chapter 10, p. 110.

31. Marsha McCreadie reports Golseth's observation that Benson was "considered a very good dialogue writer" and was paid $5,000 to write the dialogue for *Meet Me in St. Louis*. Yet, the film credits her only as author of the book on which the film was based (132). Benson's talent for writing dialogue also led Alfred Hitchcock to select her for the screenplay of *Shadow of a Doubt*.

32. Alonzo Redway Smith, letter to Sara Smith, 24 May 1915, part of Barbara Benson Golseth's memorabilia of Sally Benson, Tucson, Arizona.

CHAPTER 6. A WORLD AT WAR

1. She had "got[ten] to the vice-President and talked herself into a job." Later Benson claimed it was "shortly before her seventeenth birthday" that she obtained the bank position. She was either lying or suffering from a faulty memory, because she began work just before her eighteenth birthday in 1915.

2. These included Bill Stayton, Peter Milne, John "Jack" Johnston, Frank Brady, John Lawson, George Ely, and Jimmy (surname unknown).

3. Peter Milne, letter to Sally Smith, 18 November 1916.

4. Peter Milne, letter to Sally Smith, 19 December 1916.

5. See *The New Yorker*, 21 March 1931.

6. As William D. Miller notes, when the threat of the First World War first clouded America, "Allied supporters" made it seem that the "more ominous shadows came from Germany. From this initial tilting of the perspective, and through increasingly strident journalistic interpretations of the war as an apocalyptic crisis between Good and Evil," many young Americans "almost joyously" subscribed to a "pro-war sentiment that . . . amounted to a frenzy" (3).

7. Sally had confided to her 1912 diary the fervent hope that Wilson would be elected in November and her delight when he succeeded.

8. John was probably John Lawson, the playwright, whom Sally dated and corresponded with during 1917 into 1918. Peter was Peter Milne, whom Sally also dated.

9. For an excellent treatment of this phenomenon, see Rena Sanderson's essay, "Women in Fitzgerald's Fiction," in Prigozy (143–163).

10. The play enjoyed a short run on Broadway.

11. George William Ely II, letter to Sally Smith, 23 August 1917. A collection of Ely, Lawson, and Brady letters may be found among Barbara Benson Golseth's personal memorabilia of her mother.

12. Columbia University Archives and Columbiana Library.

13. In constructing a biographical note to accompany *Junior Miss*, Benson admits to becoming "engaged to nine different boys during the World War."

14. Barbara Benson Golseth, personal interview, 13 May 2001.

CHAPTER 7. WEDDING BELLS

1. A recent graduate of Vassar, Maxime Harrison-Berlitz had been Sally's classmate at Horace Mann and worked closely with her on *The Horace Mann Record*—Maxime, as editor-in-chief, and Sally, as bulletin editor. "Max," as her friends called her, appears gracious and competent in her *Mannikin* portrait. Her brunette hair is pulled back and parted in the middle to reveal a high forehead,

arched brows, a thoughtful, sweet expression and a slightly enigmatic smile, not unlike the *Mona Lisa*'s. Maxime's self-assuredness was supported by her blurb: " 'Tis not in mortals to command success. / But she'll do more, she will deserve it." Rather appropriately, since her family started the famous Berlitz language school, Maxime was secretary of the French Club and vice-president of the French Dramatic Society. She also belonged to the Dramatic Club, had a part in the Girls' League Play, and served on the *Mannikin* board. Sally had never mentioned Maxime in her 1912 diary because the two were not friends at the time, but in the 1915 *Mannikin* she alluded subtly to difficulties in working with Maxime. As sisters-in-law, however, Sally and Max began to socialize regularly, having outgrown their adolescent differences.

2. Writing on January 23, 1919, to offer regrets about not attending Sally's wedding, Leonard explains that she has recently moved to 1600 Rhode Island Avenue N.W. in Washington, D.C.—originally an Officers' Club—but newly opened to "a few lesser lights" like herself.

3. Though there were several classmates named Ruth, the letter writer/ friend is most likely Ruth Seggerman since she appears among the gift-givers on the occasion of Barbara Benson's birth.

4. The 1915 senior girls' *Mannikin*, probably as a sign of the class's affection, had named Miss MacAlarney "Biggest Bluffer" on its "Rumor of the School Room" (67). Sally's sister Agnes's class had dedicated their 1912 *Mannikin* to Miss "Mac," as they called her, devoting a full page to her portrait. Though seated, her captured presence is solid and majestic—imposing as the chair on which she rests her arms. Her face, however, is serene and her expression, kindly—hence, her title, "Biggest Bluffer." Other *Mannikin* issues demonstrate MacAlarney's devoted interest in educating her students and her generosity in guiding their Dramatic Society activities, even taking parts in their plays.

5. Several issues of *The Horace Mann Record* attest to Emma MacAlarney's active involvement in Horace Mann events as well as activities beyond the school. The May 15th issue in 1912, for example, reports her participation in the "Suffrage Parade" on May 4th, along with Miss Briggs and Miss Calhoun (3). She is credited with routing the boys from the corner of the gym during Sally's class party (1 May 1 1912, 1) and coaching the successful production of *Secret Service*, the senior play. The grateful seniors presented her with a set of Ibsen plays and a volume of George Bernard Shaw (17 April 1912, 3).

6. See, for example, William D. Miller's *Pretty Bubbles in the Air*, 198–199, for a description of the American Legion's protest of a planned performance of "German opera in the German language by German singers" as promoting "propaganda for German kultur."

7. See Barbara Benson's baby book. Benson exaggerated even in the pages of "Mother Stork's Baby Book," inscribed "To Barbara Clausine Benson from her

Grandma, Christmas 1919." The pink cover depicted a large stork, dangling from its beak a basket-with-baby-aboard, its face a photo-cutout framing Barbara's beautiful, cherubic face. Considering that Barbara was Sally's first child, one might expect that the baby book contained frequent and detailed entries, but that is not the case. For example, there is just one for February—"Valentines from Rose and Bobbin."

8. Writing about her grandson, Dusty, Benson recalled her feelings about her own daughter: "Yes, I kept staring at Barbara. I was pretty young and sort of felt she'd been left on my doorstep. I loved her, but I think it was Dusty who took the heart out of me. Bury this secret with me" (letter to William Maxwell, c. mid-April 1955).

9. Sally Benson, letter to Katharine S. White, c. September 1934. (Her words are eerily reminiscent of her doll-burying ritual.)

10. These were dolls that Benson recalled from childhood and incorporated in *Meet Me in St. Louis*.

11. Barbara Benson Golseth, personal interview, 13 May 2001.

12. Emily Many was a good friend and classmate of Sally's in their freshman year at Horace Mann. She may have moved away since she does not appear in the 1915 *Mannikin*. Sally and Babe lived near her after they moved to Creston Avenue in the Bronx.

13. Alonzo Redway Smith, letter to Sally Benson, 24 March 1921.

14. Sally's nickname for Anna Cora, "Wongus," appears occasionally in her correspondence. Like Edna St. Vincent Millay, Benson and her daughter Barbara after her, made up various nicknames for family members—a fetish of the time, perhaps?

15. An Aeolian Vocalion was a phonograph brand name.

16. In 1925, 10 percent of Village dwellers lived in newly built apartments ranging from the "white-collar type" to elaborate "liveried-doorman" types. The rent structure of the Village in 1930 showed a "conspicuous absence of middle range dwellings," with a greater proportion at the low end paying $20 to $30 per month and a smaller portion at the high end, $75 to $100 (Ware 22–23). The Bensons were among those paying the higher rents.

18. Best's was an upscale department store on Fifth Avenue at 51st Street.

19. See *The New Yorker*, 25 December 1943, 16–19.

20. See, for example, "You Can't Have a Career and Be a Good Wife," reprinted in Walker, 71–75.

21. John Wanamaker's department store was on 14th Street.

22. Barbara Benson Golseth, personal interview, 14 May 2002. The Knick-erbocker Ice Company was also the company for which Guy Thompson worked when he and Rose came to New York.

23. Sally Benson, letter to Anna Cora Smith, 21 July 1922.

24. However, Sally knew she would have to learn to contend with her cousin, Bobbin, a "dear little monkey—about six times more full of life than Barbara. He kept poking a finger in her eye in loving abandon—and she'd scream for him to stop—but when he did stop, she covered up her eye and said, 'Now you can't get it, Bobbin.' "

25. Barbara Benson Golseth, personal interview, 15 May 2002.

26. Ernest Vogt had been Benson's riding instructor in Los Angeles. He was also an old friend of Anna Cora.

CHAPTER 8. SECOND HONEYMOON

1. The cloud of anti-German sentiment inevitably hung on, intensified by Sally's witnessing firsthand the effects of Germany's bombs in France. Later, in writing *Meet Me in St. Louis*, Benson ironically describes her fictional Alonzo as exhibiting the same xenophobic attitude. See *Meet Me in St. Louis*, 228–229.

2. Sally Benson, letter to Anna Cora Smith, 29 August 1922.

3. Annual visitors to London, the three were traveling home via the United States for the first time. "Tell Agnes," Sally urged, "that their sister is married to Donald Macbeth, McCormick's violinist." Benson was pleased to offer these women her expert advice on what to do and see in New York.

4. Rachel Belt was Rose's maid.

CHAPTER 9. BACK TO REALITY

1. The original Washington Square Hotel was built as a residential or apartment hotel and named the Hotel Earle after its owner, Earl S. L'Amoureux. It extended from Sixth Avenue to the corner of McDougal Street.

2. Between 5:15 a.m. and midnight trains passed overhead every two to six minutes (McFarland 156).

3. The "little cinema" presented "European imports and the most sophisticated domestic products to an audience of 'discriminating intellectuals . . . who shrank from the ballyhoo, the impersonal and often ill-considered splendor of the big houses, as well as from the mediocrity of the films" (Stern et al. 264).

4. 4711 is a wine (and also a perfume).

5. Sally Benson, letter to Anna Cora Smith, December 1922.

6. Sally Benson, letter to Anna Cora Smith, 8 December 1922. In Bobsie's baby book, besides the details of the luncheon menu and table décor shared in the letter to Anna Cora, Sally had listed her daughter's luncheon guests: Norman,

Virginia Emmerman, Telka Ackley, Sonny White, Gregory, Richard Kuhne, Bobby Thompson, and Nolif. She saved the letters of acceptance the children's parents had sent and also made note of Barbara's presents: Doll carriage, ring, and handkerchief from Mother and Father; a xylophone from Aunt Ess; a fur hat from Aunt Ess; a book from aunt Rose; 4711, basket of pink and yellow flowers from Aunt Agnes, a horn and a duck from Annie. It is interesting that Sally could focus on such detail for special events but omit totally such things as "Signatures at Various Ages" or "Baby's First Book." She did, however, record "Baby's First Ride" at the Los Angeles Riding Academy on Caesar in May 1922, noting that "Mr. Hellman held her."

7. Sally's reasons for being angry with her father were several—causing the earlier disruption of the family's moving, first to New York and then to Texas; missing her graduation from Horace Mann; his drinking; his repeated disappearing from the family and leaving them financially insecure—to name a few. Sally was also angry because Alonzo had caused her mother so much suffering.

8. Anna Cora's letter continued:

> We had a very nice Christmas. The children were well remembered, but dear me, how different from my little ones! The children of today are so pampered all year Christmas means little more. Champlin loves his motion picture machine—never tires of it—and Richard likes his marble game best. I believe it came from you. I could not begin to tell you how many things Santa—friends, relatives sent. I gave Champlin cuff buttons—Richard brownie books—Sidney a little sweater for the house and some baby handkerchiefs—Lon ties—he wanted them most and needed them badly—Josephine some pretty green beads—earrings to match. Daddy and I did not exchange gifts. He had to have new shirts and ties before we left Los Angeles. Lon gave Jo a lovely dinner set and I think she gave him the usual well-assorted necessities such as shirts, gloves, smoker's table well-furnished, etc. to me a pretty purple dressing gown, a housedress, leather purse—Daddy sox and handkerchiefs, anyway. . . . Daddy and I got too much. I felt like a five-cent movie show, our gift offerings were so small, but by golly! There was a world of love went with them. Someday, Raggie, I may afford Whitby beads to go with your locket. I thought they'd look well on your red gown. I had planned everything so differently. I love everything more than I can tell you, you sweet lambs, how dear you are to me. Wasn't it fine, my box from Joe and yours came Saturday before we left. Allow me to compliment you, Reynolds, on the beautiful wrapping and printing on your package. . . . Daddy got your card, Rose, and wishes me to thank you. Thank you, Harry, for

attending to the insurance for me. . . . Thank you all, a Happy New
Year overflowing with prosperity and good luck.

Lovingly,
Mother

Anna Cora's enumeration of gifts and apology for not giving enough belie
the sentiment expressed in, "but by golly! There was a world of love went with
them." She seems conflicted regarding material expressions of wealth, an attitude
Benson inherited, it would seem.

9. *Judge* had peaked in popularity after the turn of the century, floundered
in the thirties, and expired on the eve of World War II (Douglas 43).

10. Barbara Benson Golseth, personal interview, 13 May 13 2001.

11. Barbara Benson Golseth, personal interview, 8 May 2002.

12. A good example is "Private Sale." Another is "The Overcoat." Neither
was accepted by *The New Yorker.*

13. Mrs. Doust, letter to Sally Benson, 5 August 1926.

14. Three days after receiving Doust's assuring letter, Benson received a note
from Bobsie:

Dear Mama,

We are going to have a play tonite and I am going to be a good fairy.
When are you going to come up and see me? I am having a good
time. How are you and Daddy? Is Tempy home yet? I wish I could
see him. Please write me soon.

Love,
Goofer

Barbara Benson, letter to Sally Benson, 9 August 1926. Perhaps Bobsie
had written the note in July but never mailed it. Perhaps Doust or her son saw
that the note was posted especially after Benson expressed dissatisfaction with her
daughter's appearance.

15. Letter written on July 17, 1926, by Sally Benson to her mother, Anna
Cora Smith.

16. The concept of the house and its hollow, echoing largeness is strikingly
reminiscent of Virginia Woolf's "Time Passes" section of *To the Lighthouse*, ironically published the same year as Benson's letter. Benson had read several of Woolf's
novels and reviewed *Between the Acts* for *The New Yorker.*

17. See "Homecoming," *The New Yorker*, 24 October 1942, 24–27.

18. Again, it is difficult to reconcile the spirit expressed by Benson in this reflective, affectionate letter with that so often seized upon by critics and reviewers who compare Benson to Dorothy Parker.

19. Because of Prohibition, these "dried drops" were the closest Anna Cora would get to a glass of ale for some time. "Ess" is Sally's sister Esther, and Toby is Esther's son and Sally's nephew. Sally Benson, letter to Anna Cora Smith, 17 July 1926.

CHAPTER 10. A WIDER WORLD BECKONS

1. Barbara Benson Golseth, personal interview, 9 May 2002.

2. "Quiet affairs" is Barbara Benson Golseth's appraisal of her mother's extramarital involvement with men. Undoubtedly, they were sexual, though in 1918, Theodore Dreiser used the term for nonsexual involvement.

3. Barbara Benson Golseth, telephone interview, 28 July 2000.

4. Barbara Benson Golseth, personal interview, 13 May 2001. Correspondence between Babe and Sally clearly demonstrates their strong attachment. Babe's affectionate and humorous letters were sometimes addressed "Dear Goofer," showing the playful nature of their relationship.

5. Babe, according to Dorothy Miller, Thurber's "closest friend in Columbus, Ohio," was the model for Thurber's character, Joe Ferguson, in *The Male Animal* (Kinney 187 and 610).

CHAPTER 11. CLIMBING THE CAREER LADDER

1. See Yagoda 54.

2. Here, again, there is a discrepancy between "public record" and actual fact, the former assigning 1930 as the year of this story's publication. It is likely that the 1930 date ascribed to Benson's first published *New Yorker* story derives from Benson herself, who gave that date in an oft-quoted interview with Robert van Gelder. Perhaps faulty memory led her to state: "In 1930 I got an idea for a short story and wrote it out. Someone told me to send it to *The New Yorker*. . . . Mrs. White . . . told me it was the best story of whatever its kind was that they'd had and asked me to write more" (Van Gelder 183).

3. Apartment hotels were "high class," as Caroline Ware notes (23). A ninth floor crowned the original buildings in 1912, and in 1917 a third structure, three stories high, joined the first two, bringing the entire hotel to the corner of

McDougal Street. In its present expanded version it stands in what is now a historic landmark district, but it is known as the Washington Square Hotel.

4. See chapter 9, p. 90.

5. As her diary of 1912 and subsequent correspondence show, Benson welcomed opportunities for fun and diversion.

6. See *The New Yorker*, 12 January 1929, 18, or *People Are Fascinating*, 208.

7. Van Gelder 183. In fact, though Benson's rejected stories were few, they did exist. *The New Yorker* turned down Benson's "The Realist" on July 27, 1934 and "The Comeback," on December 9, 1952, to cite two that marked the beginning and end of pieces Benson submitted to them. See *The New Yorker* Archives, Boxes 195 and 1648.

8. Katharine S. Angell, letter to Sally Benson, 24 December 1928.

9. Katharine S. Angell, letter to Sally Benson, 5 February 1929.

10. Like Sally, Rose was very attractive to men. Tall and statuesque, she was very outgoing and warm, loved to entertain, and kept her social calendar full. Guy preferred that she remain at home. "She was very social and charming, but he wanted her to stay at home. He once hit Sally and frightened me," explained Barbara Benson Golseth in a personal interview, 28 September 2001, at her home in Tucson, Arizona.

11. Benson's Washington Square address was not far from Esther's apartment at 116 Waverly Place, an area attractive to thieves. Crime was prevalent because bootleggers used their political connections to arrange the release of many thieves without trial. For more information on theft in Greenwich Village, see Morris 274 and 399–403, passim.

12. *Scaldinos* are hand-warmers but may also refer to hot water bottles to warm the feet.

13. The story appeared in the wake of the Depression, 15 March 1932, 23–24.

14. For other stories on this theme, see: "Hostess Gift," "Vive la France," and "War with Connecticut."

15. Sally Benson began freshman year at Horace Mann on equal financial footing with her peers, unlike Fitzgerald and his daughter. Scotty, he wrote, was "a poor girl in a rich girl's school. That was always my experience—a poor boy in a rich boy's school; a poor boy in a rich man's club at Princeton." *As Ever, Scott Fitz* (letters between Fitzgerald and his agent, Harold Ober), ed. Matt Bruccoli, 1972, 354, qtd. in Idema 188).

16. See her letters to Benson regarding Bobsie's needs.

17. See the obituary—"Lon Champlin Smith '07"—in the Princeton University Archives, 22 May 1929.

18. Barbara Benson Golseth, personal interview, 18 May 2002.

19. See Princeton University Archives, Class of 1907, Triennial, Quinquennial, and Quindecennial Records, 118, 100, and 194, respectively.

20. Barbara Benson Golseth, personal interview, 18 May 2002.

Chapter 12. Public Success and Private Sorrow

1. See "Echoes of the Jazz Age," in *The Crack-up*, 15.

2. See chapter 10, p. 109.

3. See Sally Benson, letter to Anna Cora Smith, 28 October 1920, and chapter 7, p. 71.

4. Barbara Benson Golseth, personal interview, May 2001

5. In fact, in 1942, when Benson recognized Dorothy Parker, Allan Campbell, Robert Benchley, and the Perelmans at the Players, she "did not go over and speak to them" because, as she explained later to Harold Ross, she really did not know Dorothy Parker.

6. See chapter 12, p. 123. Sally Benson, letter to Anna Cora Smith, undated, July 1926.

7. Barbara Benson Golseth repeatedly asserted that Benson would have been much happier if the Smiths had never left St. Louis. In Benson's "Carry Me Back," published in 1938, Benson's male protagonist is a Missouri native who achieved national fame through his radio show but longed to return to his rural roots. The piece is a powerful representation of nostalgia and reinforces Golseth's view of her mother. See *The New Yorker*, 27 August 27 1938, 13–15.

8. Wolcott Gibbs, letter to Sally Benson, 10 October 1930.

9. Formerly Katharine Angell, *The New Yorker*'s fiction editor had become Mrs. E. B. (Andy) White in 1929. Wolcott Gibbs, letter to Sally Benson, 16 October 1930.

10. See chapter 8, p. 85. As Sally noted in her letter to Anna Cora from the "Cedric," Babe loved stories about World War I aviation heroes.

11. For a detailed account of the partying indulged in by many Roundtablers, see Bernstein 211–217.

12. Helen, "tall and fearsomely thin, with a face that is at once delicate and firm, attracted several beaux, among them the artist Aristide Mian and Reynolds Benson, the husband of *New Yorker* writer Sally Benson. ("I was a good friend of Sally, too," Helen said. "That was how things were in the Village in those days" [Bernstein 215]).

13. Herbert Wright Shuttleworth was Jessie King Tolese's chauffeur in Cincinnati, Ohio. "Her children went into mourning" when she married him. Barbara Benson Golseth, personal interview, 28 September 2001.

14. Still standing, the large stone and white-clapboard house continues to be called "The Captain's House." It is located at the corner of Linden Lane and East Wharf Avenue, just off the Post Road (Route 1) in Madison.

15. For example, Rose Shuttleworth played "Mrs. Coade" in the Jitney Players' production of Sir James M. Barrie's *Dear Brutus* at the Wilcox Garden, 31 August and 1 September 1944. See the Archives of the Madison Historical Society.

In the forties Benson frequently drew on Rose's experiences in Madison. See, for example, "An Article of Faith" (*The New Yorker*, 29 July 1944, 23), "A Feeling of Space" (*The New Yorker*, 17 June 1944, 23), "Protect the Protestants" (*The New Yorker*, 15 October 1949, 66), and "Spirit of '76" (*The New Yorker*, 25 December 1954, 20).

16. Babe Benson, letter to Sally Benson, 30 July 1930. Earlier, Claus had retired as a partner with the firm of Pulleynt & Co. to spend more time at his Pleasantville, New York, home with Maxime and their adopted daughter, Rose Mary. When his tuberculosis worsened, he agreed to move to Saranac Lake, reputed for its clean air, in hope of a cure.

17. Barbara recalled the separation as occurring around the time of her eleventh birthday, which would have been in November of 1930. However, it would appear that there may have been several periods of separation before the Bensons divorced in 1946.

18. See *Current Biography* 1940 at http://webspirs3.silverplatter.com/cgi-bin/waldo.cgi

or *Current Biography* 1941, 70.

19. The decreased number for 1933 may be a result of Agnes Smith's suicide on June 17th. She had named Sally guardian of her three-year-old son, Tony.

20. The paucity of Benson's pieces in 1937 is explained by two factors: her long bout with flu early in the year and later, her negotiations with David Selznick for *Shadow of a Doubt*, a book destined to become a Hollywood film directed by Alfred Hitchcock with Benson among its screenwriters.

21. While a student at Horace Mann, Sally had accompanied Babe to the Polo Grounds where, though not much of a sports fan, she rooted for the St. Louis Cardinals when they played against the New York Giants. Her favorite sport, as it turned out, was horse racing, and she often indulged in betting on favorites.

CHAPTER 13. THE WRITER MAKES STRIDES

1. Sally's gloss for Maxime read: "Babe's brother's wife."

2. See undated broadside (c. 1931) found among Benson's memorabilia.

3. This incident is mentioned in Frank McShane's *The Life of John O'Hara*. However, McShane refers to O'Hara's puzzled complaint that "a lady had taken

away his coat and mandolin—God knows what he was doing with a mandolin—and given them to her janitor" (51–52). McShane does not seem to realize that his book contains a photograph of O'Hara playing the mandolin (see page 7 of photo signature following page 146). In fact, Benson's letters reveal that there were two separate parties. During one, she threw the "banjo" out the window and it caught in a tree. After another, O'Hara's overcoat had been left behind, and unaware of whose it was, she gave it to her janitor. When O'Hara came to reclaim it, the man refused to give it back. That O'Hara misremembered the events or that McShane did not know of O'Hara's presence at two Benson parties are possible explanations.

The banjo and its player are reflected—but with a twist—in Benson's "The Very Thing." See *The New Yorker*, 20 October 1934, 92.

4. Sally Benson, letter to Wolcott Gibbs, undated, c. 11 August 1934.

5. They married on June 25, 1935 (Kinney 597).

6. Agnes Smith, letter to Sally Benson, undated, c. 1931. Agnes refers to the infamous Madame du Barry, well-known prostitute and Louis XV's last mistress. She was killed during the Reign of Terror.

7. Had Barbara not requested Benson's diary, it would most likely have been lost, given the many times Benson moved.

8. Anna Cora Smith, letter to Sally Benson, 11 January 1932.

9. Barbara Benson Golseth, personal interview, 19 May 2002.

10. The "hutch" reference is to the house the Bensons planned to close on shortly in Madison.

11. Reynolds Benson, letter to Sally Benson, 18 August 1932.

12. Reynolds Benson, letter to Sally Benson, 24 September 1932. Babe's birthday was the 23rd.

13. Thayer Hobson, letter to Sally Benson, 10 December 1932.

14. Benson's office, like others at *The New Yorker*, was seemingly "designed to foster isolation." Like monks' tiny cells, these offices were "scattered over three floors, and interaction among the inhabitants was tacitly discouraged" (Yagoda 330).

15. Thayer Hobson, letter to Sally Benson, 22 December 1932.

16. Philo Vance was a fictional detective who appeared in mystery novels by S. S. van Dyne (pseudonym of Willard Huntington Wright) popular in the 1920s and influential on Ellery Queen, whose pseudonym was Barnaby Ross.

17. Ogden Nash, letter to Sally Benson, 19 January 1933.

18. Lou Little was the football coach.

19. Reynolds Benson, letter to Sally Benson, 9 February 1933.

20. Reynolds Benson, letter to Sally Benson, 21 February 1933.

21. See Death Records, 1931–1933, Town of Westport, CT.

22. Babe Benson, letter to Sally Benson, 20 June 1933.

23. Reynolds Benson, letter to Sally Benson, 22 June 1933.

24. As noted later, Benson had only four stories published in *The New Yorker* in 1933 whereas her average output in the thirties was eight per year.

25. Wolcott Gibbs had set his apartment on fire while smoking in bed. Benson subsequently rented the same apartment.

26. Ben Wasson was "Manager of the Literary Department" for the American Play Company, Inc., which represented American and foreign authors. Ben Wasson, letter to Sally Benson, 12 July 1933.

27. Harold W. Ross, letter to Sally Benson, 26 July 1933.

28. Rose's grandson, Joe Thompson, reports that Rose was miffed when Sally took all the credit for stories essentially hers. Personal interview, Tucson, Arizona, 15 May 2002.

29. Sally Benson, letter to Harold Ross, 27 July 1933.

30. Harold W. Ross, letter to Sally Benson, 28 July 1933.

31. Sally Benson, letter to Wolcott Gibbs, undated, c. 31 July 1933.

32. Sally Benson, letter to Harold Ross, c. 16 August 1933.

33. Wolcott Gibbs, letter to Sally Benson, c. 18 August 1933.

34. Babe Benson, letter to Sally Benson, 24 August 1933.

35. Katharine S. White, letter to Sally Benson, 26 September 1933.

36. Sally Benson, letter to Katharine White, 29 September 1933.

37. Katharine S. White, letter to Sally Benson, 5 October 1933. Curiously, two carbon copies of White's letter exist. On one, an annotation appears in ink after the word "standard." It reads: "either from the point of view of amusement." It is unclear which letter was sent to Benson.

38. Wolcott Gibbs, letter to Sally Benson, 24 October 1933.

39. See *The New Yorker*, 28 April 1934, 21–22.

40. Don Wharton, letters to Sally Benson, 7 and 15 December 1933.

41. Sally Benson, letter to Wolcott Gibbs, c. mid-December 1933.

CHAPTER 14. REFINING HER VISION

1. Lou Little was Columbia's football coach.

2. In her interview with Kinney, for example, Sally paints Babe as reserved and reticent, claiming "he didn't have anything to say to me" (513). See chapter 10, p. 111.

3. Tony's on 52nd Street was a speakeasy frequented by many celebrities for pre- or post-theater dining. The wren image may refer to Benson's condition after a time of rehabilitation. Sally Benson, letter to Wolcott Gibbs, May 1934.

4. Ben Yagoda's excellent study of *New Yorker* fiction identifies several criteria associated with published pieces. These include: continuity of character via "multipart reminiscences" or "linked stories"; "pegging"—identification of setting

and circumstances in the first paragraph; avoidance of low-life settings or characters; exposing "characters' lives and social settings in a harsher, more unforgiving light" than readers might expect; absence of plot; brevity, clarity, understatement; an "atmosphere of upper-class turn-of-the-century New York"; an intense awareness of human loneliness; cruelty—laying "traps of situation" for unwary, doomed characters (Yagoda 104, 154).

5. See *The New Yorker*, 18 August 1934, 17–20.

6. Anna Cora was one who practiced restraint at times of grief.

7. As further illustration, I refer to personal experience—a remembered conversation about my Irish-born mother's response to my grandfather's funeral. Exiting the church, my mother said to my aunt, "Oh, I think I am going to *caione*" (Celtic weeping-wailing mixture of loud sound produced to honor the loss of loved ones). My aunt, fearing embarrassment, strongly protested, "Oh, Mary, please don't!"

8. John Mosher, letter to Sally Benson, 26 July 1934.

9. Sally Benson, letter to John Mosher, 28 July 1934. If Benson had known that James Thurber regarded Mosher as "a human rejection machine," she might have taken some measure of comfort. See Bernstein 149.

10. Wolcott Gibbs, letter to Sally Benson, 10 August 1934.

11. Sally Benson, letter to Wolcott Gibbs, c. mid-August 1934.

12. Sally Benson, letter to Wolcott Gibbs, undated, c. August 1934.

13. E. F. Benson was an English writer known for short stories and Gothic tales.

14. Bernard Smith, letter to Sally Benson, 16 August 1934.

15. Bernard Smith, letter to Sally Benson, 5 September 1934.

16. Sally Benson, letter to Wolcott Gibbs, undated, c. 12 August 1934.

17. The term "jesus" was *The New Yorker*'s corruption of "genius," a term used in reference to the "current incumbent" (Yagoda 44 and 252).

18. James M. Cain, letter to Sally Benson, 25 August 1934.

19. Wolcott Gibbs, letter to Sally Benson, 7 September 1934.

20. James M. Cain was managing editor at *The New Yorker* and wrote to Sally on August 25th. See his letter on p. 161.

21. Katharine S. White, letter to Sally Benson, 12 September 1934.

22. Wolcott Gibbs, letter to Sally Benson, 7 September 1934.

23. A reader from St. Louis, Florence Hinchey, wrote to Benson on October 4th: " 'Mental Cruelty' . . . is a little masterpiece—worthy of Guy de Maupassant—so much in so few words! Most writers would make an entire book of it."

24. Benson's title was perhaps inspired by Gogol's story of the same title or by John O'Hara's "losing" his overcoat to Benson's janitor. See p. 132.

25. Charles Angoff, letter to Sally Benson, 11 September 1934.

26. Also included in this anthology were stories by William Faulkner, Zora Neale Hurston, James M. Cain, F. Scott Fitzgerald, Theodore Dreiser, Mary Austin, a play by Eugene O'Neill, and poems by Robert Frost and Carl Sandburg.

27. Edward O'Brien, letter to Sally Benson, 20 November 1934.

28. Martha Foley was O'Brien's replacement as editor of the annual anthology, *The Best Short Stories*.

CHAPTER 15. PERFECTING HER CRAFT

1. Most likely Benson refers to "Summer Is Lovely," published in *The New Yorker* on October 13, 1934. Since Benson's letters are for the most part undated, it is difficult to establish an exact story reference. Other possibilities might be "The Very Thing" (October 20) or "Something for Yourself" (November 3). Benson's statement: "Don't keep this story until Jack Frost sets in" dates Angoff's remark to sometime in October.

2. Sally Benson, letter to Wolcott Gibbs, c. October–November 1934.

3. Katharine S. White, in-house memo to Wolcott Gibbs, c. December 14, 1934.

4. Benson's proposed "Nutmeg series" was relegated to possible consideration as summer material. See p. 150.

5. Wolcott Gibbs, memo to Sally Benson, c. late January 1935.

6. Sally Benson, letter to Katharine S. White, c. January 1, 1935. Clearly, Benson is lying here. Recall that even as a Horace Mann student Benson had been both bulletin editor and yearbook coeditor. She had also published several short stories in *Quarterly*, the school's literary magazine. See pages 41 and 46.

7. Generally, authors or their agents negotiate a nonexclusive reprint permission for which they are paid.

8. On December 14, 1934, Babe had written to Barbara at St. Margaret's asking, "If you see or hear from Ma over the weekend, try to find out if she prefers a Royal or Pennington typewriter and let me know as soon as you can. Dad."

9. Sally Benson, letter to Wolcott Gibbs, 5 January 1935.

10. Barbara Benson Golseth, personal interview, 19 May 2002.

11. This would have been the annual anniversary party, no doubt, since the magazine's first issue appeared in February of 1925. Wolcott Gibbs, letter to Katharine S. White, c. mid-February 1935.

12. Wolcott Gibbs, letter to Sally Benson, 15 February 1935.

13. Wolcott Gibbs, letter to Sally Benson, 1 February 1935.

14. See *The American Mercury*, May 1935, 55.

15. Benson's collection—*People Are Fascinating*—is her sarcastic title for stories like Ruth's.

16. See chapter 10, p. 111.

17. See, for example, Benson's letter to Mary Baker on May 2nd further on, explaining how she made her connection with Selznick.

18. Herbert Block, letter to Sally Benson, 12 March 1935.

19. *Tortilla Flat* is one example. Clifford Odets was another of their clients.

20. The terms "collection" and "novel" were often used synonymously.

21. Sally Benson, letter to Wolcott Gibbs, c. March 1935.

22. Sally Benson, letter to Wolcott Gibbs, c. April 1935.

23. Wolcott Gibbs, letter to Sally Benson, 16 July 1935.

24. See p. 44.

25. Paul Palmer, letter to Sally Benson, 22 July 1935.

26. Wolcott Gibbs, letter to Sally Benson, 22 July 1935.

27. Sally Benson, letter to Wolcott Gibbs, 24 July 1935.

28. Wolcott Gibbs, letter to Sally Benson, 22 July 1935. Such natives would appear in "Woman's Place" (8 June 1935), "The Time Will Come" (11 July 1936), and "The Lilac Bush" (1 May 1943), to name a few.

29. Sally Benson, letter to Wolcott Gibbs, undated, c. early July 1935.

30. Henry Leech, letter to Sally Benson, 20 August 1935.

31. Robert A. Pines, letter to Sally Benson, 24 September 1935.

32. Pat Covici, letter to Sally Benson, 17 September 1935.

33. See chapter 10.

34. The piece was published December 25, 1937.

35. Pat Covici, letter to Sally Benson, 27 September 1935.

36. Wolcott Gibbs, letter to Sally Benson, 10 October, 1935.

CHAPTER 16. AFFAIRS, FINANCIAL AND OTHER

1. This policy had discouraged John O'Hara and led to his eventual breaking with the magazine in 1949. Despite his being a close friend and drinking companion of Gibbs, O'Hara subsequently submitted nothing for ten years.

2. Wolcott Gibbs, letter to Sally Benson, 6 March 1936.

3. Pat Covici, letter to Sally Benson, 11 February 1936.

4. Sally Benson, letter to Wolcott Gibbs, undated, c. April 1936.

5. Sally Benson, letter to Wolcott Gibbs, undated, c. May 1936.

6. Pat Covici, letter to Sally Benson, 25 June 1936.

7. See August 1, 1936, 143: 138.

8. Walton named "The Overcoat," "Suite 2049," "The Fur Piece," and "Something for Yourself."

Ogden Nash

LTC Donald G. Easton, USA-Ret.

FOUNDING SPONSOR

Sisters, Ester & Agnes
Rose - Gay thomp.

Bill Slayton - Boyd
Gilbye Summerville
Boy friends

Wishing Auguries
best of

Ben Wasson - her
agent.
Thayer Hobson - wanted
Gallup novel
Harold Ross-

Harold Ross. Publisher

fabliau "Fabliau" of sorts
of apathy"
Wilcott Gibbs - her editor
Katharine White - newyorker editor

Samovar- TALL Container with
Charcoal for heating water
for tea

9. See *Booklist*, September 1936, 33: 22.

10. Pat Covici, letter to Sally Benson, 9 July 1936.

11. Joseph Margolies, letter to Sally Benson, 20 July 1936.

12. Pat Covici, letter to Sally Benson, 23 July 1936.

13. Marian Ives, letter to Sally Benson, 3 June 1936.

14. Mary Hamman, letter to Sally Benson, 9 July 1936.

15. Harry E. Maule, letter to Sally Benson, 10 December 1936.

16. Sally Benson had plans to build her own house in Madison, Connecticut. She was still planning the project in 1941. See page 276.

17. Ernestine Taggard, letters to Sally Benson, 11 August and 10 September 1936.

18. Pat Covici, letter to Sally Benson, 13 August 1936.

19. Wolcott Gibbs, letter to Sally Benson, 21 September 1936.

20. Pat Covici, letter to Sally Benson, 14 October 1936.

21. Pat Covici, letter to Sally Benson, 28 October 1936.

22. Paul Palmer, letter to Sally Benson, 2 October 1936.

23. Marian Ives, letter to Sally Benson, 21 October 1936.

24. Paul Palmer, letter to Sally Benson, 19 November 1936.

25. It was not difficult to rent apartments in those days. Many were furnished and may have been located in "apartment hotels."

Chapter 17. Taking Charge and Branching Out

1. Katharine S. White, memo to Mr. Hoyt of *The New Yorker*, 19 January 1937.

2. Katharine S. White, letter to Sally Benson, 26 February 1937.

3. Katharine S. White, letter to Sally Benson, 23 March 1937.

4. Benson's story, "Suite 2049," won the O. Henry prize for 1936. It was reprinted in *O. Henry Memorial Award Prize Stories of 1936* by Doubleday, Doran & Co. in 1937.

5. Mary Baker, letter to Sally Benson, 16 February 1937. See p. 198.

6. James Hill, letter to Sally Benson, 19 January 1937.

7. "The Editors," letter to Sally Benson, 5 March 1937.

8. William James Fadiman, letter to Sally Benson, 13 April 1937.

9. St. Clair McKelway, letter to Sally Benson, 30 March 1938. By October, McKelway's view would change.

10. Sally Benson, letter to Katharine S. White, undated c. late May 1937.

11. Katharine S. White, letter to Sally Benson, 28 May 1938.

12. See p. 188.

13. Though Sally Benson preferred Nantucket, she knew that Babe loved Vermont and in one of their reconciliation periods, she agreed to spend the next summer with him in Dorset, Vermont.

14. Sally Benson, letter to Mary Baker, 2 May 1937.

15. Sally Benson, letter to Miss Baker, 2 May 1937.

16. William James Fadiman, letter to Sally Benson, 21 June 1937.

17. Max Wilkinson, letter to Sally Benson, 8 September 1937.

18. Oscar Graeve, letter to Sally Benson, 28 September 1937.

19. Katharine S. White, letter to Sally Benson, 20 September 1937.

20. Sally Benson, letter to Katharine S. White, c. 22 September 1937.

21. *Punch*, 17 February 1937, 195–196.

22. *Times Literary Supplement*, 20 March 1937, 214–215.

23. William James Fadiman, letter to Sally Benson, 20 September 1937.

24. Pat Covici, letter to Sally Benson, 24 September 1937.

25. Pat Covici, letter to Sally Benson, 30 September 1937.

26. Wolcott Gibbs, letter to Sally Benson, 18 October 1937.

27. Wolcott Gibbs, letter to Sally Benson, 5 November 1937.

28. Harold Ross, memo to Wolcott Gibbs, 26 October 1937.

29. Katharine S. White, letter to Sally Benson, 29 October 1937.

30. Ross was infamous for his "query sheets" with numbered questions corresponding to points in the story where an author had been ambiguous, illogical, or confusing. Ross would often read a writer's manuscript or galley proofs already edited and compile "a list of comments or questions keyed to specific points in the piece" (Yagoda 19 and 187).

31. Katharine S. White, letter to Sally Benson, 8 November 1937.

32. Sally Benson, letter to Katharine S. White, 11 November 1937.

33. Sally Benson, letter to Katharine S. White, 15 November 1937.

34. Katharine S. White, in-house *New Yorker* memo, 17 November 1937.

35. Katharine S. White, letter to Sally Benson, 1 December 1937.

36. Katharine S. White, letter to Sally Benson, 1 December 1937.

37. Weatherly is perhaps an analog for the Principessa Constance Wilcox who started the Jitney Players in Madison in the twenties, or for Benson's sister, Rose Shuttleworth, an active supporter of the Players.

38. Sally Benson, letter to Katharine S. White, c. 14 December 1937.

39. Sally Benson, letter to Katharine S. White, c. 18 December 1937.

40. Benson, in a moment of truth, admitted she hated hearing "cheap, lousy things like Eddie Cantor on the radio and having people comment, 'Well, you have to hand it to them. They get away with it.'"

41. Sally Benson, letter to Katharine S. White, c. 15 December 1937.

Chapter 18. Becoming an Entrepreneur

1. Katharine S. White, letter to Sally Benson, 6 January 1938.

2. Katharine S. White, letter to Sally Benson, 26 January 1938.

3. Katharine S. White, letter to Sally Benson, 3 February 1938.

4. William Maxwell, letter to Sally Benson, 27 May 1938.

5. Sally Benson, letter to William Maxwell, c. June 23 1938.

6. William Maxwell, letter to Sally Benson, 28 June 1938.

7. Sally Benson, letter to William Maxwell, 29 June 1938. (Maxwell similarly addressed her letters, "Dear Mrs. Benson.") Despite the familiar tone employed in such letters to Maxwell, Benson omitted the complimentary close, ending with a mere penciled signature. (Her letters to Gibbs, by contrast, had always ended: "Love, Sally.")

8. Sally Benson, letter to William Maxwell, 24 June 1938.

9. William Maxwell, letter to Sally Benson, c. late June 1938.

10. Sally Benson, letter to St. Clair McKelway, c. 27 June 1938.

11. St. Clair McKelway, letter to Sally Benson, 28 June 1938.

12. Sally Benson, letter to St. Clair McKelway, 30 June 1938.

13. Edward C. Aswell, letter to Sally Benson, 21 July 1938.

14. William Maxwell, letter to Ik Shuman, 19 July 1938.

15. See *Publishers' Weekly*, 6 August 1938.

16. Edward C. Aswell, letter to Sally Benson, 4 August 1938.

17. Sally Benson, letter to William Maxwell, 6 August 1938.

18. William Maxwell, letter to Sally Benson, 9 August 1938.

19. Donald S. Klopfer, letter to Sally Benson, 10 August 1938.

20. Charles A. Pearce, letter to Sally Benson, 9 August 1938.

21. Donald B. Elder, letter to Sally Benson, 15 August 1938.

22. See the *Democrat Chronicle*, Rochester, New York, 7 August 1938.

23. A further example of this need to prove herself occurred in her comments about her character, Tootie, in *Meet Me in St. Louis*. Benson told Harold Ross, for example, that she had made herself the "smartest" of all her siblings.

24. Frances Woodward, *Books*, 31 July 1938, 6.

25. R. C. Feld, *New York Times*, 31 July 1938, 6.

26. Katharine Simonds, *Saturday Review of Literature*, 6 August 1938, 18: 7.

27. Charles A. Pearce, letter to Sally Benson, 18 August 1938.

28. Bennett Cerf, letter to Sally Benson, 19 August 1938.

39. See, for example, Cerf's letter in chapter 21, p. 262.

30. George W. Joel, letter to Sally Benson, 29 August 1938.

31. George W. Joel, letter to Sally Benson, 7 September 1938.

32. Toby Wherry was the son of Esther Smith Probasco Wherry, Benson's sister.

33. Reviewer M. L. Becker of the *New York Times* praised the collection for maintaining the "flavor of the older book" and retaining the dialogue Bulfinch had so carefully translated from Homer and Virgil (*Books*, 7 December 1940, 7).

34. A. M. Jordon, *Horn Book Magazine*, January 1941, 17: 30.

35. *New York Times*, 10 November 1940, 22.

36. Pat Covici, letter to Sally Benson, 15 September 1938.

37. Laurence Pollinger, letter to Sally Benson, 28 September 1938.

38. Penciled vertically in the right margin, referring to Maxwell's wire praising "On a High Hill," Benson wrote: "except you, darling."

39. Sally Benson, letter to William Maxwell, c. 13 August 1938.

40. Sally Benson, letter to Katharine White, c. 17 August 1938.

41. Sally Benson, letter to William Maxwell, c. early October 1938.

42. William Maxwell, letter to Sally Benson, c. mid-October 1938. On November 17, Benson would sign her new contract with *The New Yorker*. A twelve-month contract, it would extend through November 16, 1939, and pay Benson ten cents a word for the first twelve thousand words and eight cents a word over that plus a bonus of 20 percent of her earnings provided the magazine accepted a minimum of ten stories during the year. Benson would, in turn, agree to give *The New Yorker* "firsts" (i.e., first-reading rights) on all her fictional pieces during the year. The latter proviso was initiated by Lobrano to retain the security of having a constant pool of fiction available and to dissuade writers from selling pieces to other publishers who paid better. For more, see Yagoda 161.

43. William Maxwell, letter to Sally Benson, 13 October 1938.

44. Bob Haas, letter to Sally Benson, 14 September 1938.

45. William Shawn, letter to Harold Ross, 12 October 1938.

46. Nancy Pearn, letter to Sally Benson, 21 October 1938.

47. Laurence Pollinger, letter to Sally Benson, 14 November 1938.

48. Laurence Pollinger, letter to Sally Benson, 2 December 1938.

49. Laurence Pollinger, letter to Sally Benson, 8 December 1938.

50. Laurence Pollinger, letter to Sally Benson, 13 December 1938.

51. Nancy Pearn, letter to Sally Benson, 15 December 1938.

52. *Times Literary Supplement*, April 1939.

Chapter 19. A World at War

1. Sally Benson, letter to William Maxwell, c. 7 February 1939. Note that by early 1939, the formal tone of Benson's salutation in letters to Maxwell

had changed to the more casual "Dear Maxwell" and her complimentary close to "With love from Sally."

2. Lawrence E. Spivak and Eugene Lyons, letters to Sally Benson, 25 and 30 January 1939, respectively.

3. George Waller, letter to Sally Benson, 28 February 1939.

4. Eugene Lyons, letter to Sally Benson, 6 March 1939.

5. Bennett Cerf, letter to Sally Benson, 1 February 1939. There seems to be no explanation for the swastika reference. In all my research I found no indication of anti-Jewish sentiment in Benson. Perhaps Cerf is referring to some private joke, but it is in bad taste.

6. Bennett Cerf, letter to Sally Benson, 7 February 1939.

7. Bennett Cerf, letter to Sally Benson, 28 February 1939. The reference to the swastika is puzzling, to say the least.

8. The piece was "Patron of Letters." It appeared in *The New Yorker* on June 10, 1939.

9. Sally Benson, letter to William Maxwell, c. 2 March 1939.

10. R. S. Hooper, letter to Sally Benson, 5 October 1939.

11. "The Farm" was a rehabilitation facility in the New Haven, Connecticut, area. Maria Elena Pignatelli remembers Benson with fondness. Possibly it was High Watch Farm, still operating today. See p. 247.

12. Gustave (Gus) Lobrano, letter to Sally Benson, 9 February 1940.

13. The back of the book was the place reserved for "sketches and reminiscences deemed as slighter or non-metropolitan." See Yagoda 72.

14. Ralph Paladino was a *New Yorker* staff member in charge of monitoring payments to writers, issuing their checks, and preparing monthly accounts of "how we stand with writers when we have special arrangements as to bonuses, etc." Paladino also kept records of expenses related to the maintenance and cleaning of typewriters as well as the upkeep of water coolers.

15. St. Clair McKelway had joined the *New Yorker* staff in 1933 and as Yagoda notes, was "drawn to low-life" and became an editor despite suffering from a "severe manic-depressive condition." See Yagoda 136–137.

16. Sally Benson, letter to Gus Lobrano, undated, c. February 1940.

CHAPTER 20. BEHIND THE SCENE

1. Benson's cats' names echo ones she and Lon gave their kittens in 1913. See chapter 5, p. 38.

2. Barbara Benson Golseth, personal interview, May 15, 2002.

3. Robert Hamilton Binkerd, letter to Sally Benson, 24 August 1939.

4. Sally Benson, letter to Ham Binkerd, 3 April 1940.

5. Sally Benson, letter to Gus Lobrano, undated, c. mid-April 1940.

6. Sally Benson, letter to Gus Lobrano, 20 April 1940.

7. Sally Benson, letter to Gus Lobrano, 20 April 1940.

8. The story, "Pilgrimage," appeared in *The New Yorker*, May 25, 1940.

9. Sally Benson, letter to Gus Lobrano, 20 April 1940.

10. Al Frueh was a caricaturist who illustrated Profiles pieces (Yagoda 261).

11. Sally Benson, letter to Gus Lobrano, undated, c. 26 April 1940.

12. Daise Terry was Katharine White's secretary.

13. Sally Benson, letter to Daise Terry, 30 April 1940. Terry was the administrator of the art department at *The New Yorker*. She "took notes, and later typed up a sort of minutes . . . later distributed to the participants" (Yagoda 119).

14. Wolcott Gibbs, memo to Sally Benson, undated c. August, 1940.

15. See chapter 1, pp. 12–13, where the young Sara Smith visited Jay's farm."

16. This detail of "careful wrapping" also occurs in one of Anna Cora's letters thanking the Bensons for their Christmas box. She makes special mention of how carefully Babe had wrapped the box so that it had arrived in mint condition.

17. Bob Haas, memo to Sally Benson, 25 October 1940.

18. Sally Benson, letter to Daise Terry, c. 4 May 1940.

19. Sally Benson, letter to Robert Hamilton Binkerd, c. early May 1940.

20. Sally Benson, letter to Harold Ross, 8 May 1940. Most likely, the Japanese figurine was one of Benson's projects at the Farm.

21. Sally Benson, letter to Gus Lobrano, c. early May 1940.

22. Sally Benson, letter to Gus Lobrano, early May 1940.

23. Gus Lobrano, letter to Sally Benson, 1 May 1940.

24. Sally Benson, letter to Gus Lobrano, c. mid-May 1940.

25. Sally Benson, letter to Gus Lobrano, undated, c. early May 1940.

26. William Shawn, letter to Sally Benson, 9 August 1940.

27. *The New Yorker* often paid writers by the length of their pieces.

28. Sally Benson, letter to Gus Lobrano, c. early June 1940.

29. Benson would write this experience into a piece she titled "Young Man." See chapter 24, p. 336.

30. Bertha Binkerd, letter to Sally Benson and Ham Binkerd, c. 28 June 1940.

31. Bertha Binkerd, letter to Sally Benson and Ham Binkerd, 1 July 1940.

32. Bertha Binkerd, letter to Sally Benson, 4 July 1940.

33. Bertha Binkerd, letter to Sally Benson and Ham Binkerd, c. early July 1940.

34. Harold Ross, letter to Sally Benson, 6 September 1940.

35. Constable and Co., Ltd., letter to Messrs. Pearn, Pollinger, & Higham Ltd., 25 October 1940.

36. Nancy Pearn, letter to Sally Benson, 19 November 1940.

Chapter 21. Affairs, Family and Other

1. Nancy Pearn, letter to Sally Benson, 27 February 1941.

2. Nancy Pearn, letter to Sally Benson, 17 January 1941.

3. William Webb, letter to Sally Benson, 26 February 1941.

4. Bennett Cerf, letter to Sally Benson, 8 January 1941.

5. Laurence Pollinger, letter to Sally Benson, 19 March 1941.

6. John Lawson, the playwright, had been Benson's friend from her senior year at Horace Mann.

7. Bennett Cerf, letter to Sally Benson, 11 March 1941.

8. Bennett Cerf, letter to Sally Benson, 2 April 1941.

9. Phyllis Cerf, note to Sally Benson, 3 June 1941.

10. Barbara Benson Golseth, personal interview 15 May 2002.

11. "Act 1, Scene 2" appeared in *The New Yorker*'s April 26th, 1941 issue.

12. Bob Haas, memo to Sally Benson, 17 March 1941.

13. For more on the relation of the Book-of-the-Month Club to sales and profitability, see Janice Radway's chapter "A Modern Selling Machine for Books" in Radway 154–186.

14. Some estimates run as high as 300,000 guaranteed sales.

15. M. Lincoln Schuster, letter to Sally Benson, 30 April 1941.

16. Iris Barry, *Books*, 25 May 1941, 5.

17. Gladys Graham Bates, *Saturday Review of Books*, 24 May 1941, 24: 11.

18. See chapter 18, p. 222.

19. Edith H. Walton, *New York Times*, 25 May 1941.

20. Parker claims she cried over the dying mouse in "Furtive Tear" and over older sister Lois's "I think it's perfectly charming" comment on the coat Judy so desperately wanted though "her wrists hung awkwardly from the sleeves, the bow caught her in the pit of the stomach." In dramatic fashion Parker advises readers that Benson's "*Junior Miss* is not a must but simply a delight . . . a complete pleasure [and] a luxury." See *PM's Weekly*, 25 May 1941, 47.

21. Warren Bower, letter to Sally Benson, 1 May 1941.

22. Warren Bower, letter to Sally Benson, 22 May 1941.

23. Dorothy Lobrano Guth, personal interview, 3 September 2001.

24. The story referred to is "A Furtive Tear."

25. In fact, a film of *Junior Miss* was produced in 1945 by Sun Dial in New York.

26. It is interesting that Benson moved from "tired of Judy" after the first two pieces, to proud, possessive "parent." She followed the radio scripts attentively, objecting frequently and ferociously when they misinterpreted Judy or Lois or their parents. Benson was particularly irritated when the wrong diction was assigned to their dialogue. See p. 315.

27. Yet, earlier she had read extensively novels that are classics. See p. 17.

28. Benson had written columns on Shearing and her *Laura Sarelle* that were published in *The New Yorker* in late April and early May of 1941. Benson was correct in figuring out that Joseph Shearing was a woman. Her actual name was Gabrielle Margaret Vere Campbell and she used several pseudonyms. For more information, see the Biography Resource Center online.

29. Bennett Cerf, letter to Sally Benson, 29 May 1941.

30. Ruth Gould, letter to Sally Benson, 27 May 1941.

31. Robin McKown, letter to Sally Benson, 14 May 1941. With a nod to women's position in media in the forties, Robin McKown sent directions with an apology: "I'm sorry about woman broadcasters being so inconsiderate as to have their programs so early in the morning. However, I do know her program is a very popular one."

32. Frank Cooper, letter to Sally Benson, 15 May 1941.

33. Frank Cooper, letter to Sally Benson, 20 May 1941. One wonders whether Benson had grown more astute in recognizing potential seduction in the guise of a publisher.

34. Parker Wheatley, letter to Sally Benson, 28 May 1941.

35. See Dr. Strang Lawson's program script for June 1, 1941.

36. Schuyler Crane, letter to Sally Benson, 24 April 1941.

37. Ken McCormick, letter to Sally Benson, 23 May 1941.

38. Mary Louise Aswell, letter to Sally Benson, 16 May 1941.

39. Eugene Lyons, letter to Sally Benson, 28 May 1941.

40. Kenneth Littauer, letter to Sally Benson, 30 June 1941.

41. The first story, at 5,240 words in length, brought her $515. The second piece, at 3,380 words, earned Benson $365.

42. They were: Carl Carmer, journalist and drama critic; Herbert J. Muller, critic and Purdue Professor of English; Kerker Quinn, editor and critic; Jeannette Covert Nolan, writer of children's and mystery stories; Nannine Joseph, New York literary agent; Stephenson Smith, critic; and Marguerite Vivian Young, poet.

43. Ham apparently trained as an accountant and had some expertise in writing business letters, both areas that were helpful to Benson. It is not clear whether she actually paid for these services, or whether Ham had a separate job.

44. Robert Hamilton Binkerd, letter to Sally Benson, 9 June 1941.

45. Robert Hamilton Binkerd, letter to Sally Benson, 15 June 1941. In the First World War, Babe could have benefited from similar influence but declined. See chapter 6, p. 59.

46. Robert Hamilton Binkerd, letter to Sally Benson, 16 June 1941.

47. Robert Hamilton Binkerd, letter to Sally Benson, 17 June 1941.

48. This would have been "5135 Kensington," the inspiration for *Meet Me in St. Louis*.

49. Benson's obituary in the *New York Times* states that she admired the work of Irwin Shaw. See *New York Times*, 22 July 1972, 30.

50. Joseph Brewer, letter to Sally Benson, 20 June 1941.

51. She continued to read and review mysteries even "on the road."

52. Sally Benson, letter to Gus Lobrano, 18 June 1941.

53. Gus Lobrano, letter to Sally Benson, 20 June 1941.

54. According to her obituary in the *New York Times*, Benson liked "going to races and playing the horses."

55. Sally Benson, letter to Gus Lobrano, 27 June 1941.

56. Harold Ross, telegram to Sally Benson, 10 June 1941.

57. Sally Benson, telegram to Harold W. Ross, 12 June 1941.

58. Harold Ross, telegram to Sally Benson, 13 June 1941.

59. Ralph Collins, letter to Sally Benson, 4 July 1941.

60. William Stayton, letter to Sally Benson, 16 June 1941.

61. Lena Gedin of Linnegatin 38, Stockholm wrote on June 6, 1941 seeking to publish a Swedish edition of *Junior Miss*, and Maria Constanza Huergo, a graduate of the Columbia School of Journalism, wrote on December 16, 1941, asking permission to translate and reprint "The Paragon," "New Leaf," and "Appreciation of Art," in the Sunday section of an Argentine newspaper. Huergo explained her reason: "Miss Benson writes about everyday life in New York in such an unaffected manner which I believe is eminently suitable to acquaint Argentine readers with 'real life' in the United States—not a Hollywood version."

62. Harold W. Ross, memo to Ralph Paladino, 16 September 1941.

63. H. D. Jolley of Ceco Steel in St. Louis, for example, thanked Benson for her July 7th letter and assured her he "would look forward with a great deal of interest to the remainder of your articles on 5135 Kensington Avenue." Jolley reminded Benson of the St. Louis custom of the summer "Trolley Party," a bit of information that may have inspired the leading song of the film version of Benson's "novel." Jolley explained, "The street railway company has several ornamental cars fitted up with easy chairs and a place for refreshments. These cars would be rented out for the evening by a group of young folks, and the entertainment consisted of riding about town on the Creve Coeur line to catch a few breezes on a hot summer evening." H. D. Jolley, letter to Sally Benson, 16 July 1941.

64. Vera L. Thompson, for example, wrote appreciatively on July 18th from Concord, New Hampshire to thank Benson for her "kindness in finding time from a very busy life to bother with a stranger's request. Your letter is something I intend to keep and try to live up to. I owe you a debt of gratitude which I hope to repay by following your advice and someday succeeding." Thompson offered to take Benson to lunch some time "between planes" on her way to her family home in South Carolina. "Your kindness to me is something I shall always remember and I would very much like to thank you again in person. I shall be in New York Sunday morning, August 2nd."

65. Charles B. Driscoll, McNaught Syndicate, 29 July 1941.

66. There was a Rogers Whitaker on staff at *The New Yorker* but Benson did not appear to have a personal friendship with him. For more on John Lawson, see pages 110, 180, 261.

67. Margit Nilsen, letter to Robey Lyle, 26 August 1941.

68. Edwin Seaver, letter to Sally Benson, 5 September 1941.

69. Henry La Cossitt, letter to Sally Benson, 15 September 1941.

70. Sally Benson, letter to the Dramatists' Guild, 7 October 1941.

71. Bennett Cerf, letter to Sally Benson, 10 October 1941.

72. Harry Maule was chief editor of Random House. See the *Boston Herald*, 23 October 1941.

73. Mabel Search, letter to Sally Benson, 10 November 1941.

74. Mabel Search, letter to Sally Benson, 18 November 1941.

75. Paul Streger was Benson's agent at Leland Heyward.

76. Wilella Waldorf in the *New York Post* sounded the one negative note. Benson was happy that reviewers at the *Journal-American*, *New York Times*, *Herald Tribune*, *New York Sun*, and *PM* had found the play variously "a harum-scarum antic and a darlin' play" (Brooks Atkinson), "a skittishly entertaining cold drama . . . for playgoers not afraid of the young" (John Anderson), "a thoroughly pleasant play" (Louis Kronenberger), "with a warm glow" (Richard Watts Jr.).

77. *New York World-Telegram*, 19 November 1941, reprinted in *Drama Index*.

78. Joseph Tiefenbrun was Benson's lawyer.

79. Sally Benson, letter to Bennett Cerf, c. late November 1941.

80. Bennett Cerf, letter to Sally Benson, 9 December 1941.

81. William James Fadiman, letter to Sally Benson, 21 November 1941.

Chapter 22. Becoming a Celebrity

1. Charles Laughton telegrammed Ham on the 27th: "I decided to open my mouth and say something: Happy Birthday. C. Laughton." Benson had interviewed Laughton in the twenties. Apparently, they remained friends.

2. The Garden of Allah was a residence where many Hollywood screenwriters lived. Living there at the time were Dorothy Parker and Alan Campbell, the latter working on a film with Helene Deutsch (Herrman 142).

3. Harold Ross, night letter to Sally Benson, 27 February 1942.

4. Barbara Benson Doster, letter to Sally Benson, 3 February 1942.

5. The coat reference is to Judy's new, ill-fitting coat in the first and title piece, "Junior Miss."

6. Sally Benson, letter to Gus Lobrano, 27 February 1942.

7. Parsons's syndicated column also appeared in the *New York World-Telegram* on Thursday, March 5, 1942. Anna Cora and Bird Binkerd must have been thrilled to read the column in their local papers.

8. Reynolds Benson, letter to Sally Benson, 1 March 1942.

9. Ross and Chasen, a former comedian, had "roomed together at 77 Park Avenue when Ross was between marriages," and when Chasen moved to Hollywood, Ross had "put up some of the money that enabled Chasen to open his first restaurant there" (Kinney 734).

10. Gus Lobrano, letter to Sally Benson, 6 March 1942.

11. Possibly the reference is to E. Phillips Oppenheim. More likely, it refers to George Oppenheimer, a Hollywood screenwriter.

12. William Shawn, letter to Sally Benson, 3 March 1942.

13. L. E. Pollinger, letter to Sally Benson, 27 February 1942.

14. Ken McCormick, letter to Sally Benson, 2 March 1942.

15. Ham Binkerd, letter to Ken McCormick, 23 March 1942.

16. Gus Lobrano, letter to Sally Benson, 22 April 1942.

17. Sally Benson, telegram to Gus Lobrano, 23 April 1942.

18. Sally Benson, telegram to Gus Lobrano, 24 April 1942.

19. Ham Binkerd, letter to Daise Terry, 3 March 1942.

20. Nancy Pearn, trans-Atlantic cable to Sally Benson, 26 February 1942.

21. N.T.G. stands for Nils Thor Granlund, a former New York City vaudevillian who booked high-class vaudeville acts for the Florentine Gardens, a nightclub in Los Angeles. He raised chorus girls' salaries to $50 a week (in New York City they were $100) and allowed soldiers in free. He brought at least one soldier up on stage and surrounded him with chorus girls, playing to audiences of cheering, whistling servicemen. He also donated $1,000 weekly to feed and entertain soldiers at a canteen. See the *Los Angeles Times*, 10 October 2004.

22. Utter-McKinley Mortuary in Mission Hills, California, continues to this day and currently offers a "Cemetery in Cyberspace."

23. Sally Benson, letter to Gus Lobrano, 8 March 1942. Doris Gilbert had been assigned to work with Sally on the radio scripts. She was later her partner in writing the treatment and first screenplay for *Meet Me in St. Louis.*

24. Harold W. Ross, letter to Sally Benson, c. 15 April 1942.

25. Sally Benson, letter to Harold Ross, 17 March 1942.

26. Barbara Benson Golseth, personal interview 14 May 2002.

CHAPTER 23. THE WAR ESCALATES AT HOME AND ABROAD

1. Bennet Cerf, letter to Sally Benson, 9 April 1942.

2. Wolf Associates, Inc. had the contracts for five *Junior Miss* radio scripts adapted by Marcella Burke.

3. Sally Benson, letter to Edward Wolf, 22 April 1942.

4. Gus Lobrano, letter to Sally Benson, 9 March, 1942.

5. Bennett Cerf, letter to Sally Benson, 30 March 1942.

6. Sally Benson, telegram to Daise Terry, 2 April 1942.

7. Crouse signed his letter, "As ever, Buck (Russell Crouse)." In 1930, he rented property of Benson's in Penn Yann, New York, and received a letter asking that he pay the rent as Benson needed the money. Crouse also worked at *The New Yorker* for a time on "Talk of the Town" (Yagoda 90).

8. As noted previously, within the year, Benson had become the legal guardian of twelve-year-old Frederick Anthony (Tony) Smith—Agnes's son—since his father, Fred Smith, had remarried and his new wife found the boy too difficult to manage.

9. See p. 320. To achieve that goal of its admittedly "war-mongering director" it had to break down American resistance to class. The film did so by illustrating the compassion and sympathy of purpose that existed between Britain's upper and middle classes.

10. Benson's only known experience of Bronx people goes back to her living on Creston Avenue in a professor's house that the Bensons rented for a few months in 1922. Clearly, she relies on hearsay and stereotype here.

11. Robey Lyle, letter to Sally Benson, undated c. spring 1942.

12. Harold Ross, letter to Sally Benson, 30 June 1942.

13. Alliene Valentine, letter to Sally Benson, 14 March, 1942.

14. In this connection, it should be noted that Benson, beside contributing to the British war effort by donating her royalties from "Love Letters," also received an award for her financial support of Boys' Town in Nebraska.

15. On April 15th, Bird Binkerd wrote to Sally and Ham, "there has not been a peep out of R.S.B. (Babe) since December." Bird feared that with Jud on the verge of being drafted and her daughter Barbara taking tests for a job and subsequently leaving Dorset, there would be little financial support. Ham would have to contact his father and urge him to provide "some support however meager." Nothing much was happening except that "we feel the war is very real." Bird could not afford tires for her car so had lost her independence. Putting in a vegetable

garden across the road would be her special project. She offered a few positive comments about the *Junior Miss* broadcasts and asked if there would be a movie as well. "God, I'll be glad to see and hear from you again. Bird."

16. It is no coincidence that the name "Buell" was also the name of the naval officer whom Ham relied on for a special appointment in the navy. See p. 277.

17. "Points" refers to the rationing stamps issued to all Americans to prevent hoarding and selling items on the "black market" during World War II. Buell's "Victory garden" was a patriotic concept adopted by most Americans who had access to even the smallest plot of land.

18. See "V Is for a Lot of Things," 5 June 1943, *The New Yorker*, 22–25. Other Benson fiction tackles similar class issues. See, for example, "Poor My Man," *The New Yorker*, 18 August 1934, 17–20, and "The Lilac Bush," *The New Yorker*, 1 May 1943, 20–22.

19. Robert Sachs, letter to Sally Benson, 31 March 1942.

20. Robert Sachs, letter to Sally Benson, 11 April 1942.

21. John H. H. Lyon, letter to Sally Benson, 15 April 1942.

22. Martha Foley, letter to Sally Benson, 27 April 1942.

23. Daise Terry, letter to Martha Foley, 22 May 1942.

24. The "Brownie" story is the "December 1903" piece. I have not identified the other.

25. Toby Wherry, letter to Sally Benson, 9 May 1942.

26. Leah Daniels, letter to Sally Benson, 2 June 1942.

27. Gilbert's "Free, White, and Twenty-one" and "Old Jonah Was Lost" appeared in *The New Yorker* on May 30, 1942 and August 8, 1942, respectively.

28. From the Screenwriter's Guild Inc. abstract, No. 22187, copy sent to Sally Benson by John T. Elliott of Leland Heyward, 24 July 1942. The movie premiered at New York's Palace Theater in October and was reviewed in the *New York Times*. Screenwriting credit was given to Sally Benson.

29. Bird Binkerd, letter to Sally Benson, 15 April 1942.

30. Edward E. Emerson, letter to Sally Benson, 28 September 1942.

31. Major Reynolds (Babe) Benson, letter to Sally Benson, 8 December 1942.

32. Reynolds Benson, letter to Sally Benson, 27 November 1942.

33. Joseph Thompson, personal interview, 17 May 2002.

Chapter 24. The World at War, Babe and Ham

1. Harold W. Ross, letter to Sally Benson, 25 February 1943.

2. When Benson revised her proposed "Shangri-La" series, she removed all reference to setting.

3. See chapter 6, p. 61.

4. See "Quite a Boy," *The New Yorker*, 8 February 1941, 44–46.

5. See http://www.geocities.com/Athens/Delphi/7086/010510f.htm, 12 February 2003.

6. See http://www.theotherpages.org/poems/kiplin11.html, 12 February 2003.

7. "A Toast to the Next Man Who Dies" may be found in the *New Yorker* Records, Box 29. The piece went to galleys on May 20, 1943, had its first revision on June 18, and was sent to Ross, who also had "queries." It was never published.

8. *The New Yorker*, 6 March 1943, 18.

9. Benson had directed Ham to purchase a ¾-mattress and box spring from Wanamaker's in 1940 for their apartment at 151 West 46th Street.

10. Babe's long list included, among others: *Twelve Months That Changed the World*; *Larry LeSueur* (about Russia); *Air Power* and *Total War* by Caldwell; *Variety of Weapons* by Rufus King; *The Body Fell on Berlin* by Richard Larkin (an RAF boy); *Without Lawful Authority*.

11. Captain Reynolds Benson, letter to Sally Benson, 31 July 1943.

12. Babe preferred to call his grandson "Butch."

13. Captain Reynolds Benson, letter to Sally Benson, 9 September 1943.

14. Captain Reynolds Benson, letter to Sally Benson, 19 August 1943.

15. Interestingly, Doster's hometown paper, *The Litchfield Enquirer*, reported the cause of death as "influenza."

16. Captain Reynolds Benson, letter to Sally Benson, 31 October 1943. Ironically, Babe's letter echoes one written by Granny Esther Smith regarding the suffering Anna Cora had experienced in the early years of her marriage to Alonzo Redway Smith. See p. 390.

17. Barbara Benson Golseth, personal interview, 15 May 2002.

18. Major Reynolds Benson, letter to Sally Benson, 12 February 1944.

CHAPTER 25. *MEET ME IN ST. LOUIS*

1. See pp. 324–325. Interest in Rose's diaries occurred when Rose moved from her Neptune Avenue address in Madison to the "Captain's House," an imposing structure on Linden Lane that is closer to the water.

2. "I'm the best thing in the picture, but then I should be. I wrote it and it's only natural that I made myself the smartest member of the family," said Benson in a 1944 *St. Louis Post-Dispatch* interview. See "Meet the Real Tootie: *Meet Me in St. Louis* is Autobiographical," 31 July 1994, 10.

3. Benson often used texts of poems or songs to convey a message indirectly.

4. The Pike was a mile-long stretch of the St. Louis World's Fair. It housed the concessions and amusements. It represented an investment of between seven and eight million dollars. See Stevens.

5. Both the first and last pieces end with Benson's distancing New York as though she may have wished she had never left St. Louis. Her daughter, Barbara Benson Golseth, claimed: "My mother would have been happier if she had remained in St. Louis. She always identified herself as being from St. Louis." Personal interview, 14 May 2002.

6. Before electric refrigeration was possible, a trained horse pulled the iceman's wagon through neighborhoods. Customers posted large signs signaling their need for twenty-five, fifty, seventy-five, or one hundred pounds of ice. The ice came in fifty pound blocks that were divided with an ice pick on the wagon's back step. Children like Tootie Smith often asked for the chips or a free ride on the step (Eisenkramer 18).

7. Barbara Benson Golseth specifically recalls her mother sharing this quirky behavior with her in childhood.

8. St. Louis, like many American cities in the southern, central section, was visited by epidemics of yellow fever, tuberculosis, and scarlet fever. The streets of St. Louis flooded regularly, and even during the World's Fair, many were mud-filled. Needless to say, the drinking water was not always pure.

9. Helen Yule, letter to Sara Smith, 28 April 1909. Charlie Swingley lived nearby.

10. Rose Smith died on September 20, 1886 and was buried three days later in Calvary Cemetery in St. Louis.

11. Alonzo Redway Smith, letter to Anna Cora Smith, 15 August 1886.

12. See *Meet Me in St. Louis*, 24.

13. Alonzo Redway Smith, letter to Anna Cora Smith, 9 July 1888.

14. In her "Additional Material" appended to the treatment she submitted to MGM, Benson described the rooms of 5135 Kensington as she remembered them. For the kitchen, she wrote there was an iron sink with a wooden drain board: "On the faucet (cold water) was a filter. The river water was so muddy that everything had to be filtered. St. Louis was full of malaria" (*Meet Me in St. Louis*, Sally Benson, Doris Gilbert, Script Department, Lowe's Incorporated, 24 April 1942, 2).

15. *Times and Places*, 4. Hahn adds that the rough alley was smoothly paved, becoming good for roller-skating. Young Tootie loved roller-skating down her alley as well.

16. Emily Hahn's *Times and Places* was initially published in *The New Yorker*.

17. As Davis suggests, her nostalgic portrait of childhood arose from "mild, neurotically displaced concern over, or denial of, the future . . . rather than a 'homing instinct' or . . . unsuccessful adaptation to . . . present surroundings" (9).

Chapter 26. The Making of
Meet Me in St. Louis

1. Sally Benson, letter to Frank Orsatti, 12 June 1944.
2. See the papers of Sally Benson.
3. The ashpits were concrete containers for ashes and other trash. They varied in size, the larger ones becoming something of a status symbol.
4. See the *Globe Democrat*, 23 November 1944.
5. Another source gives the Wickes Theater as the site.
6. Harold W. Ross, letter to Sally Benson, 24 November 1944.
7. Harold W. Ross, letter to Sally Benson, 27 November 1944.
8. *St. Louis Post-Dispatch*, 22 November 1944, 3 B.
9. Harold W. Ross, letter to Sally Benson, 2 November 1945. Benson's contract began on December 12th. She received a lump sum payment of $3,500.00 and had to submit eight pieces within the year.
10. "Lady with a Lamp," *The New Yorker*, 18 January 1947, 24–27.
11. For an excellent study of this phenomenon, see Donald W. Goodwin's *Alcohol and the Writer*. See also *The Thirsty Muse: Alcohol and the American Writer* by Tom Dardis.
12. Harold W. Ross, letter to Sally Benson, 27 March 1947.
13. Sally Benson, letter to William Maxwell, 20 May 1947.
14. Sally Benson, letter to Gus Lobrano, c. May 1947.
15. Harold W. Ross, letter to Sally Benson, 8 August 1947.
16. Harold W. Ross, letter to Sally Benson, 8 August 1947.
17. Harold W. Ross, letter to Sally Benson, 15 September 1947.

Chapter 27. Hollywood, Pinewood,
Broadway, and Beyond

1. "In All Due Respect," *The New Yorker*, 30 September 1947, 42–45.
2. "A Totally Different Person," *The New Yorker*, 15 November 1947, 34–36.
3. Katherine Pritchard is based on Rose Thompson Shuttleworth, Benson's older sister. Rose's grandson, Joseph Thompson, remembers that he and his college friends used to love to hang out with Rose at her home—"The Captain's House." She conversed with them and always made them feel welcome. One friend would even visit Rose independently of Joe.
4. "Seeing Eye," *The New Yorker*, 27 September 1947, 28–30.
5. "Just Depressed," *The New Yorker*, 7 May 1949, 69–72.
6. Gus Lobrano, letter to Sally Benson, 4 June 1948.
7. Sally Benson, letter to Gus Lobrano, undated, February 1949.

8. Sam Goldwyn, letter to Sally Benson, 7 November 1949.

9. William Maxwell, letter to Sally Benson, 21 February 1951.

10. Reviews are taken from the *Drama Index.*

11. William Maxwell, letter to Sally Benson, 3 October 1951.

12. Sally Benson, letter to Gus Lobrano, 7 December 1951.

13. Gus Lobrano, letter to Sally Benson, 17 December 1951.

14. Sally Benson, letter to William Maxwell, 21 December 1954.

15. Sally Benson, letter to William Maxwell, c. early January 1955.

16. Sally Benson, letter to William Maxwell, 7 February 1955.

17. Sally Benson, letter to William Maxwell, 17 April 1955.

18. William Maxwell, letter to Sally Benson, 25 April 1955. The piece Warner referred to was "Hospitality."

19. It should be noted that Benson's "Little Girl Doll" was published in *The New Yorker*'s October 21, 1944 issue. In it, Benson voiced similar concerns regarding a purchased doll.

20. Sally Benson, letter to William Maxwell, 4 April 1955.

21. "Rummage Sale," *The New Yorker*, 3 March 1956, 33–38.

22. Sally Benson, letter to William Maxwell, 9 July 1955.

23. Sally Benson, letter to William Maxwell, c. 4 July 1955.

24. Sally Benson, letter to William Maxwell, 20 July 1955.

25. Sally Benson, letter to William Maxwell, 12 August 1955.

26. From correspondence in spring of 2003 with Marshall Jamison via e-mail with David Boles, editor of *Go Inside*, an online magazine.

27. Brooks Atkinson, *New York Times*, 3 October 1955, reprinted in *Drama Index*, 267.

28. Richard Watts, *New York Post*, 3 October 1955, reprinted in *Drama Index*, 268.

29. Hawkins' appraisal of Josephine Perry—"In the end she realizes how cold a customer she is. Her only sympathy comes from a kindred soul, a boy as affected as she is"—seems an ironic reflection of Benson and Ham.

30. See *The New Yorker*, 3 October 1955, 92.

31. William Maxwell, letter to Sally Benson, 28 November 1955.

32. William Maxwell, letter to Sally Benson, 27 April 1956.

33. Sally Benson, letter to William Maxwell, 10 September 1956.

34. "The Artist," *The New Yorker*, 3 September 1955, 24–28; "The Other Side of the Island," *The New Yorker*, 28 May 1955, 33–37; "The Guest," *The New Yorker*, 30 July 1955, 53–55.

35. Sally Benson, letter to William Maxwell, 24 September 1956.

36. William Maxwell, letter to Sally Benson, 25 September 1956.

37. William Maxwell, letter to Sally Benson, 27 September 1956.

38. Sally Benson, letter to William Maxwell, c. December 1956.

39. William Maxwell, letter to Sally Benson, 17 January 1957.
40. Sally Benson, letter to William Maxwell, 21 August 1957.

APPENDIX B. THE SMITHS

1. St. Louis City Marriage Archives, Book 25, 505.
2. Solberg's letter provides an interesting peer's view of Alonzo:

My dear old friend,

Oh for a silver spoon! But your boy is sure to be fortunate . . . especially if he is as handsome as his father. You have my sincere congratulations and please carry them also to the proud "Mother hen." When next I go west, I will have to go via St. Louis to see that boy. Grandma Smith will be proud and happy. I am real pleased that you wrote me.

3. From the letters and memorabilia in Barbara Benson Golseth's collection one can locate Alonzo Redway Smith as employed variously at the following firms and locations: Dodd, Brown & Co., Importers and Wholesale Dealers in Staple and Fancy Dry Goods, St. Louis; Brown, Daughaday & Co. of St. Louis; Ferguson-McKinney Dry Goods Co. on 1201 Washington Avenue in St. Louis; Scotia, California; Field, Leiter, & Co., Dry Goods, Chicago, Illinois; Dallas, Texas.
4. Alonzo Redway Smith, letter to Anna Cora Smith, 8 July 1886.
5. Alonzo Redway Smith, letter to Anna Cora Smith, undated, c. 1886.
6. Alonzo Redway Smith, letter to Anna Cora Smith, 2 July 1888.
7. Poetry / This world is but a fleeting show, / And no wise man regrets it. / Man wants but little here below, /And generally he gets it. Alonzo Redway Smith, letter to Anna Cora Smith, 2 July 1888.
8. Rose also noted, "The baby [Agnes] is fifteen months and weighs twenty-two pounds."
9. In her *Junior Miss* collection, Benson later incorporated an episode where her Judy Graves character and friend bury a mouse they had tried to keep alive as a pet. The ritual no doubt echoes Benson's earlier doll-burial ceremony. See *Junior Miss*, 42–44.

While Benson's early life in St. Louis and Manitowoc held its share of joys, this first experience of death was a particularly significant one and marked Sally's personality. She had been the baby of the family for almost four years, and when Anna Cora told her about the expected new baby, Sara was just old enough to fear displacement. She resented losing attention because of the preparations and constant talk of the new baby's arrival. When John Perry suddenly died, Anna Cora tried to explain that he had gone home to heaven. Though her siblings grieved with their mother, Sara's feelings were, at best, mixed. She had never wanted a baby brother or sister and was delighted to resume center stage, with entitlement to spoiling by her mother and older siblings. She actually laughed when told of John Perry's death. On the other hand, that death awakened in her the feelings of guilt and self-loathing attendant upon surviving siblings. In addition, Anna Cora unwittingly contributed to Sara's survivor guilt an added component: her daughter's witnessing the effects of John Perry's death on her mother. Correspondingly, Anna Cora's loss of the child led her to baby Sally beyond the norm. The feelings Sally experienced—guilt, self-loathing, anxiety, low self-esteem—underlie the preoccupation with death and loss that surfaced later in her fiction.

A second experience of death—the passing of her grandfather on January 15, 1905 when she was just seven years old—deepened Sally's sense of loss and abandonment. Five years later, the move to New York City would introduce yet another set of losses: home, friends, and familiar surroundings. These early experiences of death and loss account for Benson's childhood custom of repeatedly burying her dolls. Whether or not she saw the connection is impossible to know. However, the memory was strong enough that she reflected it in the fictional Tootie Smith's repeatedly burying her dolls in a "doll cemetery" and digging them up when occasion required. While Agnes anticipated the fun of playing "all summer long with Bunchie Crocker on the beach or in the yard . . . walk[ing] in your bare feet," Tootie had other plans: "I'm going to have my cemetery . . . and a funeral every day. All my dolls are going to die, except Margaretha" (48).

10. See Betty Davies's "After a Child Dies: Helping the Siblings" in *Hospice Care for Children*, 144.

11. See Dorothy Judd's fine study of children's attitudes toward death in *Give Sorrow Words*, 17–28.

12. The first reference to Tootie occurred in a note Agnes penciled on December 12, 1900: "To Mr. J. Sidney Prophater, Cairo, Illinois, c/o Str. 'City of Memphis': Dear Grampa, Please bring the brownies. Sara wants you to come back. I hope that you will bring them. I will be glad if you do. I send my love to you. Yours lovingly, Agnes."

13. In *Meet Me in St. Louis*—both novel and film—Grandpa Prophater appears as a slightly eccentric character with a distinct fetish for hats.

14. Anna Cora's relaxed approach to her religious obligations was unusual for the time, and while it does not explain Sally's virtual withdrawal from the institutional church, it suggests at least a partial clue. A second example of her mother's laxity lies in the fact that Sally's baptism, like Agnes's, did not take place until almost five months after her birth. Agnes, born on April 1, 1894 was not baptized until September 16, 1894. Sally, born on September 3, 1897, was baptized "Sara Mahala" on January 23, 1898. At the time, Catholics felt obliged to attend

to infant baptism as soon as possible after birth, the norm being two weeks at most. Like John Perry, they were baptized in St. Mark the Evangelist parish church in St. Louis. Each of these children had godparents who were from Anna Cora's family, perhaps cousins: Marie Smith and Arthur Laughlin were Sally's; only one, Helena Laughlin, is listed for Agnes; John Perry's were Alphonsus and Rosa Smith. See Archival Records, Archdiocese of St. Louis.

15. Anna Cora Smith, letter to Sally Benson, 19 August 1929.

16. So claimed Golseth. Toward the end of her life, Sally Benson wrote the screenplay for *Domimique, the Singing Nun*. She also praised the Cabrini Sisters in California for their excellent tailoring of the costumes.

17. See, for example, "Midnight Mass," *The New Yorker*, 26 December 1931, 22–23.

18. See the entry for Sunday, December 15th in Benson's 1912 diary.

19. See *Meet Me in St. Louis*, 58 and 162.

BIBLIOGRAPHY

Primary Published Work of Sally Benson

Emily. New York: Covici-Friede, 1936, 1938.

"Eustace Ennelbesser, the Listless Usher." *The Horace Mann Literary Quarterly*, special edition, February 1915.

The Horace Mann Record; The Weekly Bulletin of the Horace Mann School for Girls. New York: Students of the Horace Mann School, 1914–1915 (Coeditor with Maxime Harrison).

The Horace Mannikin, Vol. 1. New York: The Senior Class of the Horace Mann School for Girls, 1915 (Editor).

Junior Miss. New York: Doubleday & Company, 1937.

Love Thy Neighbor. London: Constable and Co., Ltd., 1939.

Meet Me in St. Louis. New York: Random House, 1941 and 1942.

The New Yorker Records. Editorial correspondence with Sally Benson.

People Are Fascinating. New York: Covici-Friede Publishers, 1936. London: Constable, 1937.

Seventeen. New York: Samuel French, 1954.

Stories of the Gods and Heroes. New York: The Dial Press, 1940.

Women and Children First. New York: Random House, 1943.

The Young and the Beautiful. New York: Samuel French, Inc., 1955.

Unpublished Work of Sally Benson

"The Comeback." *The New Yorker* Records, c. 1948.

Eight Cousins. Play script of Louisa M. Alcott's *Little Women.* Unpublished papers of Sally Benson, Tucson, Arizona, 1944.

"Merrie Noel." Unpublished papers of Sally Benson, Tucson, Arizona, c. 1944.

Secrets. Undated screenplay. Unpublished papers of Sally Benson, Tucson, Arizona.

"Shangri-La." Unpublished papers of Sally Benson, Tucson, Arizona, c. 1944.

"A Toast to the Next Man Who Dies." *The New Yorker* Records, c. 1943.

SECONDARY WORKS CITED

Bauld, Harold J., and Jerome Kissinger. *Horace Mann-Barnard: The First Hundred Years*. 1987.

Beauman, Nicola. *A Very Great Profession: The Woman's Novel 1914–1939*. London: Virago Press, 1983.

Bell, Clare. *Hirschfeld's New York*. New York: Harry N. Abrams, published in association with the Museum of the City of New York, 2001.

Benson, Sally. Unpublished papers.

Bernstein, Burton. *Thurber: A Biography*. New York: Dodd, Meade, and Co., 1975.

Block, Maxine, ed. *Current Biography*. New York. H. W. Wilson, 1983.

Bruccoli, Matthew J. *As Ever, Scott Fitz: Letters between F. Scott Fitzgerald and His Literary Agent Harold Ober, 1919–1940*. Philadelphia: Lippincott, 1972.

———. *The O'Hara Concern*. New York: Random House, 1975.

———, ed. *Selected Letters of John O'Hara*. New York: Random House, 1978.

Chodorov, Jerome, and Joseph Fields. *Junior Miss*. New York: Random House, 1942.

Corey, Mary Frances. "The World through a Monocle: *The New Yorker* Magazine and Postwar American Culture, 1945–1953." Dissertation, University of California, Los Angeles, 1996.

———. *The World through a Monocle: The New Yorker at Mid-century*. Cambridge, MA: Harvard University Press, 1999.

Cuthbertson, Ken. *Nobody Said Not to Go: The Life, Loves, and Adventures of Emily Hahn*. Boston: Faber and Faber, 1998.

Daly, Maureen, Ed. *My Favorite Stories*. New York: Dodd, Meade & Co., 1948.

Dardis, Tom. *The Thirsty Muse: Alcohol and the American Writer*. New York: Ticknor and Fields, 1989.

Davies, Betty. "After a Child Dies: Helping the Siblings." In *Hospice Care for Children, ed. Ann Armstrong-Dailey and Sarah Zarbock*. New York: Oxford University Press, 1993.

Davis, Fred. *Yearning for Yesterday*. New York: The Free Press, 1979.

Dolkart, Andrew S. *Morningside Heights: A History of Its Architecture and Development*. New York: Columbia University Press, 1998.

Douglas, George H. *The Smart Magazines: 50 Years of Literary Revelry and High Jinks at Vanity Fair, The New Yorker, Life, Esquire, and The Smart Set*. Hamden, CT: Anchor Books, 1991.

Eisenkramer, Henry. *The Boy Next Door: Memories of Kensington*. St. Louis, MO: Maxamur, 1991.

Fordin, Hugh. *The Movies' Greatest Musicals*. New York: Frederick Ungar Publishing Co., 1984.

Goodwin, Donald W. *Alcohol and the Writer*. Kansas City: Andrews and McMeel, 1988.

Hahn, Emily. *Times and Places*. New York: Thomas Y. Crowell Co., 1937.

Herrman, Dorothy, S.J. *Perelman: A Life*. New York: G.P. Putnam's Sons, 1986.

Horace Mann School for Boys. *Course of Study*. 1914–1915.

Johnston, Marguerite. *Houston: The Unknown City*. College Station: Texas A&M University Press, 1987.

Judd, Dorothy. *Give Sorrow Words*. New York: Haworth Press, 1995.

Kinney, Harrison. *James Thurber: His Life and Times*. New York: Henry Holt, 1997.

MacDonald, James A., ed. *The Architectural Forum*, Volume 40, No. 6, June. Boston: Rogers and Manson, 1924.

McComb, David. *Houston, a History and a Guide*. Austin: University of Texas Press, 1987.

McCreadie, Marsha. *The Women Who Write the Movies: From Frances Marion to Nora Ephron*. New York: Carol Publishing Group, 1994.

McFarland, Gerald W. *Inside Greenwich Village, 1898–1918*. Amherst: University of Massachusetts Press, 2001.

McShane, Frank. *The Life of John O'Hara*. New York: E. P. Dutton, 1980.

Meade, Marion. *Dorothy Parker: What Fresh Hell Is This?* New York: Villard Books, 1988.

Miller, William D. *Pretty Bubbles in the Air: America in 1919*. Chicago: University of Illinois Press, 1991.

Morris, Lloyd. *Incredible New York: High Life and Low Life from 1850 to 1950*. Syracuse: Syracuse University Press, 1951.

Nourie, Alan, and Barbara Nourie, eds. *American Mass-Market Magazines*. Westport, CT: Greenwood Press, 1990.

Ostrander, Gilman. "The Revolution in American Morals." In *Change and Continuity in Twentieth-Century America: The 1920s*, ed. John Braemer, Robert Braemer, and David Brody, 332–338. Columbus: Ohio State University Press, 1968.

Peterson, Theodore. *Magazines in the Twentieth Century*. Urbana: University of Illinois Press, 1964.

Prigozy, Ruth. *The Cambridge Companion to F. Scott Fitzgerald*. Cambridge: Cambridge University Press, 2002.

Radway, Janice. *A Feeling for Books: The Book of the Month Club, Literary Taste, and Middle-Class Desire*. Chapel Hill: University of North Carolina Press, 1997.

Remnick, David, and Henry Finder, eds. *Fierce Pajamas: An Anthology of Humor Writing from "The New Yorker."* New York: Random House, 2001.

Roberts, David. *Jean Stafford: A Biography*. Boston: Little, Brown and Company, 1988.

Stern, Robert A. M., Gregory Gilmartin, and Thomas Mellins, eds. *New York 1930: Architecture and Urbanism between the Two World Wars*. New York: Rizzoli International Publications, 1987.

Stevens, Walter Barlow. *The Forest City: Views of the Universal Exposition, St. Louis, 1904*. St. Louis, MO: N.D. Thompson Publishing Co., 1903–1904.

Thurber, Helen, and Edward Weeks, eds. *Selected Letters of James Thurber*. Boston: Little Brown and Co., 1980.

Van Gelder, Robert. *Writers and Writing*. New York: Scribner's, 1946.

Walker, Nancy A., ed. *Women's Magazines 1940–1960: Gender Roles and the Popular Press*. New York: St. Martin's Press, 1998.

Ware, Caroline F. *Greenwich Village, 1920–1930*. Boston: Houghton-Mifflin, 1935.

Wilson, Malcolm, ed. *The Crack-up*. New York: New Directions, 1945.

Yagoda, Ben. *About Town: The New Yorker and the World It Made*. New York: Scribner, 2000.

INDEX